What's the Use
of Lectures?

Donald Bligh

Fifth Edition published in Great Britain in 1998 by
Intellect, School of Art and Design, Earl Richards Road North, Exeter EX2 6AS

Consulting Editor:	Masoud Yazdani
Copy Editor:	Jennifer Proverbs
Illustrator:	Wolfram Donat
Cover Design:	Amanda Brown
Cover Illustration:	Sarah Yolland
Production:	Ele Fountain
	Lucy Kind
	Julie Strudwick

British Library Cataloguing in Publication data available

ISBN 1-871516-79-X

Printed and bound in Great Britain by Cromwell Press, Wiltshire

Contents

Part 4
Alternatives when Lecturing is Inadequate

Part 5
Preparation for the Use of Lectures

Preface to the Fifth Edition

When I first published this book more than 25 years ago I was astonished at its success. The first edition sold out in 10 weeks and demand has been steady ever since. Seemingly it satisfies a need.

Like musical composition and performance, lecturing is an art. Skill is acquired by practice rather than by reading books. Yet just as the budding composer may wish to study forms of composition known to have been successful, but later disregard them, so new lecturers may think it worth while to consider the findings of research into lecturing before developing their own style.

Using a different analogy, Nisbet has suggested three levels of proficiency: the learner driver, the ordinary road user and the rally driver. The first is learning the rules; the second has everyday skills, and some bad habits; the third can break many of the elementary rules - 'a dangerous style, but a delight to the connoisseur'.

Unfortunately there can be no book of rules for lecturers. Except for obvious points, such as the need to face the class and to be audible, there are few rules in lecturing. There is no more agreement about what is a good lecture than there is about good music. Indeed, enquiries show that different individuals want not only different, but conflicting, things from a lecture (e.g. Falk, 1967). Consequently, as most lectures will be assessed at both extremes of a general rating scale, lecturers will do well if they please more than half their audience. Therefore it is not the purpose of this book to lay down rules. Some suggestions are offered for consideration, but its chief purpose is to present information that will help lecturers in taking their own decisions. It cannot say what those decisions should be. The treatment is necessarily general. Inevitably readers are left with the task of selecting what is relevant to their needs.

Many new, and not so new, lecturers seek advice. Anyone who has the temerity to offer it lays himself open to be shot at when ever he goes into a lecture room, or if he never does so, since it is often assumed that he should be the embodiment of perfection. I cannot claim to be anything but an ordinary road user who frequently makes errors of judgement, and I am certainly not a virtuoso performer. However this may be an advantage. When concerned with training teachers in higher education, I was more able to help with difficulties with which I myself had struggled as a new lecturer. In skills that came more easily to me, I was less able to appreciate the difficulties of others. Thus I doubt the premise that consultants should be perfect; indeed I suspect this book is something of a personal confession.

It is the policy of most people engaged in staff development to cooperate with colleagues in the discussion of common problems and to publicize solutions of wider interest. This book may be viewed as a wider part of that discussion. The information it contains is as much to raise, as to settle, issues.

Because of its developmental character it can be skimmed, but not so easily skipped. It is hoped that readers will be able to get a good idea of its coverage by reading the summaries at the beginning of each Part and Chapter, before reading the text. They may then jump to any section that interests them with relative ease.

Because there is no consistent vocabulary in Education, some explanations may be required on my use of terms. A 'lecturer' is one who 'lectures', while a 'teacher' is one who teaches by any method. I use 'lessons' as a general term to cover any complete period of teaching and 'lecture' as a period of more or less uninterrupted talk from a teacher. This definition has psychological implications. I am using 'lecture' as a period of 'output' by the teacher; but a period of 'input', 'reception' or 'perception' by the audience. A 'period' is a lesson or part of a lesson. Words such as 'seminar' and 'tutorial' mean different things in different institutions. The use of these and some other general terms is given in Figure 15.1.

The lecture method may be used in many circumstances both within and outside educational institutions. Readers will appreciate, however, that available evidence may show a bias towards universities where most of the research has been carried out.

Although I have revised the book extensively for this edition, readers will notice I have retained much of the earlier research because it continues to be relevant. The development of meta-analyzes has not changed my broad conclusions in Part 1. There has been a lot of research on memory since the first edition, but much that is relevant to this book was already published then. The same is true of work on attention. The amount of research evaluating teachers is prodigious. Yet much of it is surprisingly uninformative about lecturing. Indeed I sometimes think the selection of criteria tells us more about the evaluators than the lecturers. The chapters that have expanded most are those on making a point, note-taking and handouts. The chapters on explanation and lecturing styles are new, but there is still a lot we do not know about these topics. There has been a considerable increase in the number of publications presenting alternatives to lectures, particularly innovations using recent developments in technology. Unfortunately relatively few use objective comparisons of effectiveness and those that do, largely confirm my conclusion in Chapter 2 that there is not much difference in the effectiveness of methods that present information. The students' task to perceive, understand, think and remember is much the same what ever way the information arrives. The most important innovations in future will be in task design, not in the presentation of information. In a way, much of this book is about what lecturers should prepare, but there is almost no research on how they should do so. Consequently I have made few changes to Part 5.

It has been argued in this book that the lack of effective feedback from the audience is a major defect of the lecture method, but the same defect is even more true of books. Feedback from previous editions has been flattering, Parts 2 and 4 being most favorably received.

These anonymous respondents are amongst those who should be thanked for their advice on this volume. I am particularly grateful to John Richardson for attempting meta-analyzes and drawing attention to some errors. Others include the late Ruth Beard, Richard Ellis, Anthony Fothergill, Jim Hartley, Masoud Yazdani and most of all, Barbara, but of course the responsibility remains mine.

Summary of the book

The purpose of this book is to provide information on the lecture method for lecturers, particularly new lecturers. It also has a broad theme running through it based on questions lecturers may ask.

How much is scientifically known about lecturing?

Although some questions have now been well researched, the truth is we still know very little of scientific value on many aspects of lecturing, and what is known as a result of controlled empirical investigations is not known sufficiently widely.

When there is a situation in which a large number of people have personal experience of lectures and lecturing but few have much knowledge based on independent measures, the strength with which opinions are held is frequently greater than the strength of their grounds. Because the opinions of students and lecturers do not always correlate with independent measures, I wish to urge some caution in accepting opinions in preference to the results of systematic investigations.

Is the lecture metahod any use?

The answer to this question depends on what it is to be used for. In spite of the opinions commonly expressed, comparisons of the effectiveness of the lecture method with other teaching methods (Part 1) suggest that it may be used appropriately to convey information; but it cannot be used effectively on its own to promote thought or to change and develop attitudes, without variations in the usual lecture techniques. Research also suggests that there are consistent differences in the effectiveness of individual lecturers. These two points imply that lecturers' techniques are as important as their selection of an appropriate method. This raises the question of choosing techniques to make a lecture effective.

What techniques make a lecture effective?

If we suppose that the objective is to convey information, this question can only be answered by looking at the psychological factors which influence the way information is acquired in lectures (Part 2).

These factors are then used in Part 3 to answer such questions as:
'How can information best be organized?'
'How do you teach one item of that information?'
'How do you find out how well you have taught it?'
'What's the use of taking notes? Or giving duplicated notes?'
'What sort of difficulties are likely to be met and how can they be overcome?'
'If I do have to lecture to stimulate thought or change attitudes, what evidence is there on how to do it?'

How can other methods be combined with lecturing?

The psychological factors mentioned, the limitations of the lecture method and the fact that teachers have a variety of objectives which cannot all be achieved by lecturing, make it desirable that lectures are combined with other methods. Some suggestions of ways to do this are made in Part 4.

What is needed in preparation?

The use of specific lecture techniques and planning particular combinations of teaching methods require a series of decisions. Although the manner of preparation is a matter of taste, there is likely to be some similarity in the order in which the decisions need to be taken (Part 5).

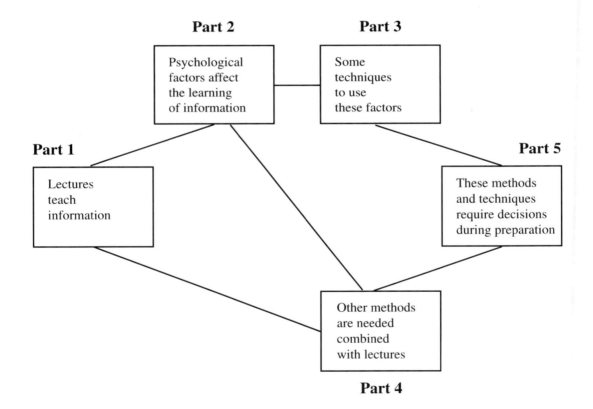

Diagram to show the book's main lines of development

Part 1
What Objectives Can Lectures Achieve?

1. Opinions of what Lectures Achieve

The acquisition of information

The promotion of thought

Changes in attitudes

Behavioral skills

Conclusion

Lecturing is still the most common method when teaching adults. In spite of educational research and changing technology, surveys over decades show remarkably little change (Marris, 1964; Hale, 1964; Saunders *et al.*, 1969; Costin, 1972; Bowles, 1982; Karp, 1983; Nance and Nance, 1990; Gunzburger, 1993; and Lesniak, 1996). Nor is the dominance of lecturing confined to educational establishments. In commerce and industry the same is true (Glogovsky, 1970). In politics they call them 'speeches'. In the churches they are called 'sermons'. Call them what you like; what they are in fact are more or less continuous periods of exposition by a speaker who wants the audience to learn something. That learning may be of different kinds.

There are four logically distinct kinds of objective: 1. The acquisition of information, 2. The promotion of thought, 3. Changes in attitudes, and 4. Behavioral skills.

Universities and colleges are dedicated to the disinterested search for the truth by research. Faculty spend much of their time teaching students the canons of criticism in their discipline and discouraging expression of opinion not based upon careful study of publicly verifiable facts. So we should expect faculty to apply the same rigor to the question 'Which, if any, of these four kinds of objective can be achieved by lectures?'.

Not a bit of it! On educational matters, it is not uncommon for faculty to sound off their opinions before consideration of wider evidence. Even amongst educationalists, it has become quite fashionable to trust personal experience alone, not just in areas where only personal experience can testify, but on answers to questions that are publicly verifiable. (See for example Ramsden, 1992.) Personal experience has a role, but any method of enquiry should be matched with the kind of question being asked. Where the question seeks a generalization, personal experience is less reliable.

Claims have been made to support the use of lectures for all four kinds of objective.

The acquisition of information

The acquisition of information includes knowledge of principles and simple comprehension, in addition to knowledge of facts, terminology and concepts. In a study subtitled 'a personal experience', Kowalski (1987) reports that 73% of students saw the main function of lectures as 'the transfer of facts'. Faculty talked about the transmission of concepts, principles, facts, information and terminology, and providing a framework. Over half of an equal probability sample of faculty (Isaacs 1994) believed lectures could give important facts (74%), explain difficult points (72%), discuss interesting points (72%), provide a framework for private study (63%), provide information not available elsewhere (63%) and give 'enrichment material' (50%). Their information can be more topical than textbooks and provide a synthesis or the latest research.

An authoritative government report (Hale, 1964) sought the opinions of faculty on the function of lectures. These included 'introducing and opening up a subject' and the 'provision of a framework for reading'. Especially in science subjects it was claimed that an oral method is clearer and less wasteful of time when dealing with complex material. The gradual build-up of complex diagrams and the presentation of three-dimensional information in models or by demonstrations, were not possible from reading. Lectures could be coordinated with laboratory work. They may provide necessary information when satisfactory textbooks are lacking, and they could give a selective emphasis when there are too many books. Hale also claimed that 'the lecture has an essential place and cannot be replaced by reading combined with discussion'. It was 'economic of staff time' and 'can cover more ground than a tutorial or seminar'.

But assuming it is possible to assess student achievement, and examiners frequently do make this assumption, whether it could be so replaced is a question that can be answered by observation and experiment. The lecture's indispensability is not obvious from present evidence. Similarly, the lecture method is not economic in terms of time or anything else, if it cannot achieve its required objectives, and this achievement is open to investigation. In the same way I am suspicious of lecturers who see virtue in 'covering more ground'. What is important is what the students learn, not how much the lecturer covers.

There are some common elements in these opinions, but it remains to be shown whether lectures can fulfil these functions. If they can, whether they do depends on the effectiveness of lecturers, and that in turn depends on their technique. These objectives imply that a careful relationship of lecture material to required reading is an important aspect of a lecturer's preparation. Phrases such as 'introducing and opening up', 'framework', 'gradual build-up' and 'selective emphasis' suggest that the organization of subject matter is also crucial. Accordingly, both these are topics that must be dealt with later.

The promotion of thought

Faculty also seem to believe that lectures can promote thought. According to Hale, faculty also regarded the lecture as a means of awakening critical skills in the student.

The emphasis here should be on 'awakening'. It doesn't claim that critical thinking can be taught by lecturing, nor that lectures are the best way of developing it.

Incredibly, the report considered lectures less authoritative because of 'the variety of minds and points of view with which a student makes contact (whilst) attending lectures, compared with tutorials'. But it seems unlikely that most lecture courses provide more than one lecturer on a given subject, let alone on a specific issue within that subject. Furthermore, lecturers are usually chosen as 'authorities' on their subject; and the lecture method is regarded as instructor-centred and providing an authoritarian social situation compared with student-centred discussion methods which are described as more 'democratic' (W. J. McKeachie in N. L. Gage, 1963).

The report said that 'A lecture should be . . . more profound than what is said in discussion', but since it had previously used the 'immaturity of students' to justify lecturing, one wonders how many profound thoughts can be got across in a lecture. Presumably, lectures to promote thought will be more common with more mature students, and the organization of such lectures will be quite different from those which 'provide a framework' or 'dovetail with prescribed reading'.

McLeish (1976) claims the lecture 'is undoubtedly the most economical method by which the individual can present in a personalized and continuous argument the general framework for understanding the fundamentals of a particular subject, and involving the audience in reflective thought that moves in time with the on-going performance'. But I do doubt it. Furthermore, more than any other function, faculty in Isaacs's survey thought lectures 'make students think critically' and 'demonstrate the way professionals reason'. But we shall see in the next chapter, that these subjective opinions have scant supporting evidence.

Changes in attitude

Objectives classified as 'changes in attitudes' include: (a) the acquisition of values that are part of the discipline, such as professional ethics and scientific integrity, and (b) interest and enthusiasm for a subject. It may also include (c) changes in personality, such as personal adjustment to a professional role, self-awareness, sociability and interpersonal skills; but few people would claim these as common objectives of lectures.

However (a) and (b) are frequently assumed and proclaimed. The idea that lecturers inspire their students any more than very rarely, is part of the folklore of academe. In general students do not report that they are inspired with timetable regularity. That such opinions should conflict, is one of the weaknesses of substituting opinions for more objective evidence.

Behavioral skills

There is virtually no published evidence on faculty's opinions on the place of lectures when teaching behavioral skills. They may well believe it has no place at all. They clearly believe in the need to practice the skills and that the practice takes a long time. Whole afternoons are allocated to laboratory work in science, and to studios in art.

Weeks are spent in schools by student teachers. Months are spent by paramedics on clinical placements. Years are spent overseas to learn a foreign language and culture.

What is not clear are faculty's opinions on how lectures should be combined with practical work.

Conclusion

Since the achievement of attitudinal objectives usually depends on the interaction of the teacher's personality with those of students it will be difficult to make useful generalizations about the techniques required, but some are attempted in Part 3.

Thus, in claiming that the acquisition of information, the promotion of thought, changes in attitude and behavioral skills are four kinds of objective for which the lecture may be used, it is assumed that the lecture is a suitable tool for achieving these. To use the lecture method for these objectives is to act on the assumption that it is the most suitable method available. But that is something that can only be judged more objectively by comparisons with other methods. Chapter 2 aims to do this, though I shall be the first to admit that objective comparisons are fraught with difficulties. Chapter 3 outlines some of these.

2. Evidence of what Lectures Achieve

The lecture is as effective as other methods to transmit information.

Most lectures are not as effective as discussion to promote thought.

Changing students' attitudes should not normally be the major objective of a lecture.

1. Lectures are relatively ineffective to teach values associated with subject matter.
2. Lectures are relatively ineffective to inspire interest in a subject.
3. Lectures are relatively ineffective for personal and social adjustment.

Lectures are relatively ineffective to teach behavioral skills

I shall argue with reservations that on the available evidence:
* with the possible exception of programmed learning and PSI (Personalized System of Instruction or 'Keller Plan'), the lecture is as effective as any other method for transmitting information, but not more effective;
* most lectures are not as effective as discussion methods to promote thought;
* changing student attitudes should not normally be the major objective of a lecture; and
* lectures are ineffective to teach behavioral skills.
Therefore the main objective of lectures should be the acquisition of information by the students. Administrative, economic or other considerations may force their use for the promotion of thought, attitudes or behavioral skills, but lectures should not be accepted as the normal vehicle to achieve these objectives.

The lecture is as effective as other methods to transmit information

When comparing the effectiveness of lectures with another method there are three possible conclusions: they are more effective, less effective, or there is no significant difference.

Table 2.1. summarizes experimental comparisons of lectures with other teaching methods where acquisition of information is the criterion. In the Appendix to Table 2.1 at the end of this chapter there are details of each of the experimental comparisons: the name(s) of the author(s), the methods compared, and the criterion used. Appendix 2.1 also explains the classification of teaching methods used in this and subsequent tables in this chapter.

With the exception of comparisons with PSI, the majority of comparisons show no significant difference. Those that do show a difference are fairly evenly balanced either way. It is hard to avoid the conclusion that, with the exception of PSI, lectures are as effective as other methods to teach facts, but not more effective.

Indeed Table 2.1. probably under represents insignificant results. This issue has been the subject of more experimental observation in the United States than any other issue in the field of teaching methods in Higher Education. As long ago as 1963, McKeachie (who is probably better acquainted with the field than anyone else) said that a host of comparisons remain unpublished because there are no significant differences to report. The same is true today. A review of doctoral and masters theses in Dissertation Abstracts shows that postgraduate students continue to make similar comparisons (each no doubt with some previously untried variables), but the broad conclusion remains the same: when it comes to acquiring information, there's not much difference between lectures and other methods, except for PSI. I return to my reservation about PSI in Chapter 3.

I maintain this broad conclusion; but I recognize it is broad. Inevitably there are reservations within that breadth. But rather than cloud my message at this stage, I will discuss them in the next chapter.

Table 2.1. The number of experimental comparisons of lectures with other methods where acquisition of information is the main criterion

Teaching Method	Lectures less effective	No significant Difference	Lectures more effective
PL and PSI related ˙	20	17	8
Discussion (various)	18	54	22
Reading & Independent study	10	21	9
Enquiry (eg projects)	6	6	3
Other (mostly audio TV CAL)	27	57	20

˙(See Appendix 2.1)

Dubin and Taveggia (1968) reviewed ninety-one studies comparing two or more teaching methods on one or more 'measures' of course content. Most of these assessments used 'objective tests' of the multiple-choice, true/false, or sentence completion type also used for course examinations. Most of these were tests of factual information, but not every report makes this clear. By using more than one criterion, one study may produce more than one comparison between methods. Thus the figures in the central column in Table 2.2 may exceed ninety-one. But since the learning of students assessed by more than one measure may be duplicated in these figures, Dubin and Taveggia eliminated this overlap by using only one figure per study. The figures in brackets give this comparison.

However, it may rightly be objected to both Tables 2.1 and 2.2 that figures giving the total number of studies or comparisons do not prove anything if those favoring one method are highly significant and those favoring the other not statistically significant at all. Accordingly, where possible, Dubin and Taveggia computed standardized scores from the standard deviations and the numbers of students reported to be involved. In all cases they found no significant difference in effectiveness between any of the methods listed in Table 2.2. I shall consider this objection again in Chapter 3 when discussing meta analysis.

There were a very large number of studies comparing lectures with television when video cameras first became widely available in the 1960s. I have not included them in Table 2.1 and Dubin and Taveggia did not consider them. Reference can be made to two reviews. Chu and Schramm (1967) summarized 202 comparisons at the college level; 22 favored TV, 152 showed no significant difference and 28 favored the lecture. With adults the figures were 7, 24 and 2 respectively. Dubin and Hedley (1969) reviewed 191 comparisons of television with traditional teaching, and although most of the differences were insignificant at the 5% level, they thought, over all, there was a slight balance in favor of traditional teaching. Table 2.1. includes comparisons published since these early reviews. They broadly confirm previous comparisons: there is not much difference in the effectiveness of lectures and other methods to teach information.

If there is no difference between the effectiveness of the lecture and other methods on tests of information, it seems reasonable to infer that the lecture is as effective as these methods in transmitting information.

Table 2.2 Summary of ninety-one studies comparing teaching methods

Method 1	% favoring Method 1*	Number of comparisons	% favoring Method 2*	Method
Lecture	54.7 (51.1)	201 (88)	44.8 (48.9)	Discussion
Lecture	45.8 (37.5)	59 (8)	51.5 (50)	Lecture and discussion
Lecture and discussion	31.2 (41.7)	16 (12)	50 (41.7)	Discussion
Lecture	52.8 (52)	72 (50)	47.2 (48)	Supervised reading
Lecture and discussion	50 (52.2)	34 (23)	50 (47.8)	Supervised reading
Lecture	40 (40)	20 (20)	60 (60)	Unsupervised reading
Face-to-face Instruction**	50 (49.4)	116 (81)	50 (50.6)	Supervised reading
Face-to-face Instruction**	41.9 (40)	31 (25)	58.1 (60)	Unsupervised reading

* Both significantly and insignificantly.   ** Lectures, discussion and laboratory teaching
The figures in brackets give only one comparison from each experimental group.

However, if you are a thorough skeptic, you may retort that there is no difference between them because none of them teach anything at all! But there's an answer to that. By comparing results of tests before and after teaching, the experiments provide evidence that lectures and other methods do transmit information. Furthermore, the study by Fodor and two by Gulo (See the Appendix to Table 2.1) where lectures were compared with irrelevant activity or no teaching at all, each found lectures to be superior. Moreover in some comparative studies a control group with no teaching is also tested, and it is clear that lectures result in greater gains. Consequently available evidence suggests that lectures do teach, at least some, information.

Therefore, the lecture is one method of achieving the first kind of objective and its use for this purpose is at least sometimes justifiable. But since the other methods are equally effective, this conclusion does not necessarily justify the frequent heavy reliance on the lecture method.

However, it is not recommended that discussion methods should be used primarily to teach information. They are expensive in staff time, and the one significant comparison Dubin and Taveggia did obtain was that unsupervised reading is superior to discussion for the acquisition of information.

Most lectures are not as effective as discussion methods for the promotion of thought

Although there is not the same quantity of experimental evidence, I shall argue that the studies that have been made, common sense, and present psychological knowledge give a consistent picture in favor of this proposition; and that if lectures are to be used to promote thought, the technique to be used should be different from the descriptive style traditionally used to 'survey an area of knowledge'. For example, Corman (1957) found that a knowledge of the principles used in solving problems made no difference to the number of problems students could actually solve, and information on how to approach problems could only be applied by the most intelligent group. Knowledge is not enough. Students need practice in solving problems and applying principles.

It is probably because the construction of questions is relatively difficult that there have been many fewer experimental studies comparing the effectiveness of teaching methods for the promotion of thought. Nevertheless reference to Table 2.3 gives a very clear impression. Dubin and Taveggia did not compute standardized scores to answer the objection that mere quantity of studies does not prove a case if the minority group display highly significant results. They didn't need to. I have only found two studies to suggest that lectures stimulate thought better than discussion methods.

Table 2.3 also shows that lectures are ineffective compared with 'other methods' to promote thought. This is a surprise. However, reference to the Appendix to 2.3 on page 277 will show that most of those other methods involved more student activity than listening to lectures. PSI involves discussion, and it is hard to imagine that teachers using role plays, modelling, simulations, case presentations and so on do not follow up with discussion of what has been observed by these methods.

I should be the first to accept that this is a broad generalisation. There are many kinds of thinking. Cabral-Pini (1995) evaluated flexibility and and creativity. Tillman was intereted in students seeing issues from many points of view and reserving their judgement. That might be called open-mindedness, whilst Fielding et al (1983) wanted students to form their own opinions. Gist was interested in the quantity and diversity of ideas; Lam in the depth of questions asked. All these and many more are worth while educational objectives that lectures have been comparatively ineffective to teach. (See the Appendix to Table 2.3.)

Secondly there are many kinds and contexts of discussion amongst these comparisons. For example, apart from methods simply described as discussion, Mohr (1996), Cabral-Pini (1995) and Smith (1995) used cooperative discussion; Hingorani (1996), Tillman (1993), Self (1989) and others used case discussion in different contexts. Khoiny (1995) and Jensen (1996) are amongst those using problem based discussion; and Sawyer (1981) used microcounseling.

Yet in spite of the variety, with few exceptions, discussion is consistently more effective than lectures in getting students to think.

Why is this? Compared with discussion methods the students' role in lectures is relatively passive. They sit listening; their activity usually consists of selecting information from what is said, possibly translating it into their own words or 'shorthand', and then writing it down. Bloom (1953) re-played tape-recordings of lectures and discussions to students and asked them at intervals to recall the thoughts they had in the original situation. Admittedly the stimulated student recall was subjective, but the sample was large. It is difficult to suggest a better way of obtaining such data and Siegel *et al.* (1963) have since found the method 'reasonably valid' when compared against independent measures of students' learning. During lectures 36.8% of the time was spent in 'passive thoughts about the subject' and 'thoughts evidencing simple comprehension', compared with 20.3% during discussion. 31% of lectures were spent with irrelevant thoughts, compared with 14.5% during discussion. During discussions the students spent 8.3% of the time attempting to solve problems and to synthesize (interrelate) information, compared with 1.0% during lectures. All these comparisons were statistically significant and suggest that during discussion students are more attentive, active and thoughtful than during lectures.

This has been known for a long time, but too many teachers seem to ignore it. When Hovland and Mandell (1952) demonstrated that students are more likely to accept a conclusion if the lecturer states it at the end of an argument, than if all the same evidence is presented with the conclusion left unstated, they showed the inability of students to draw an inference during a lecture. Barnard (1942) and Dawson (1956) found that while a lecture-demonstration was superior for teaching specific information, problem-solving discussions were better on tests of problem solving and scientific attitude. When Asch (1951) and James, Johnson and Venning (1956) used a non-directive form of discussion, usually known as free-group discussion, students displayed wider thinking and considered more solutions to problems than those who received traditional teaching. This may reflect flexibility and open-mindedness.

Table 2.3. The number of experimental comparisons of lectures with other methods where promotion of thought is the criterion

Teaching Method	Lectures less effective	No significant Difference	Lectures more effective
Discussion	29	1	2
Reading & Independent study	1	3	1
Enquiry	5	1	1
Other methods	12	17	0

In effect what is being said here is that if students are to learn to think, they must be placed in situations where they have to do so. The situations in which they are obliged to think are those in which they have to answer questions because questions demand an active mental response. Although it could be modified to do so, the traditional expository lecture does not demand this. (Taplin, 1969, Dunn, 1969, Elton, 1970 - see Parts 3 and 4). The best way to learn to solve problems is to be given problems that have to be solved. The best way to 'awaken critical skills' is to practice using the canons of criticism. The best way to develop powers of analysis is to keep analyzing situations and data. If this thesis seems obvious common sense, it should be remembered that some people place faith in their lectures to stimulate thought and expect thinking skills to be absorbed, like some mystical vapours, from an academic atmosphere. Psychologists are likely to wince at the imprecision of such a notion; and learning to think is not an absorption process.

The common-sense view finds support from psychologists. Harlow (1949) described 'learning to think' as the acquisition of learning sets. Monkeys and children were rewarded for selecting the odd one out of three objects. They were trained to make progressively finer and more abstract discriminations and, more importantly, were able to apply the 'odd one out' principle to problems they had never seen before. Similarly, as problems became more complex, they seemed able to apply principles from previously experienced problem situations. Practice with basic simple problems improved, and made possible, the solutions to more complex ones. Gagne (1965) points out that when students are given a problem to solve, they may not only apply principles, but combine them to form new higher order principles. This ability is essential to the development of a student's powers of thought. (Indeed Gagne implies that the combination and application of principles is what 'thinking' is.)

The important point here is that the essence of learning to think involves practice and that lectures do not normally provide opportunity for this, still less do they provide an opportunity for the active expression and testing of thoughts.

The Gestalt School described problem solving as a process of achieving 'insight':
(i)   by recognizing the problem;
(ii)   by gaining familiarity with its elements, such as the concepts involved;
(iii)   by constant reorganization of the elements;

(iv)   possibly incorporating a considerable period of irrelevant activity or overt inac-
        tivity; and
(v)   culminating in a flash of insight displayed by the sudden demonstration of the
        solution.

For example, children taught to find the area of a rectangle by multiplying its height by its length, may try various ways to rearranging a parallelogram before suddenly hitting on the idea of cutting off a right angled triangle and replacing it on the other end to make a rectangle, so that they may use the rule they already know (Wertheimer, 1945). The first two stages may be achieved in lectures if the lecturer raises problems and discusses them from a variety of perspectives, but in the uninterrupted lecture the remaining stages are neither encouraged nor usually possible. There is little pressure on students to tackle the problems raised themselves (they depend on the lecturer to do this, and they are rarely disappointed.) Nor are they given time to reorganize the sometimes unfamiliar concepts presented by the lecturer. Furthermore, the whole of a student's experience and expectations of the lecture method favor it as a period of 'information input' rather than 'information processing'. The lecturer who wishes to promote thought by lecturing must overcome the conservatism arising from student experience!

I am not denying that thought may take place during lectures - although Bloom's study suggests that not much does (1953). Obviously it may. Those students who become lecturers probably think more than most. I am suggesting that the traditional style of continuous exposition does not promote it in such a way as to justify lecturing to achieve this objective. Similarly I am not denying that lectures can provide the necessary information for students to think about when they get home; but the teacher must do something to make sure that they do think about it, and this requires something more than the traditional lecture.

Similarly students will think during lectures, insofar as they have time, if they already have a disposition to do so. The lecturer provides information to think about. But that is different from the lecture method promoting thought. Marton and his disciples (Marton *et al.*, 1984) have contrasted students who have 'deep' and 'surface approaches' to learning. No doubt the former think more in lectures. Others have emphasised the personal context of learning (Ramsden, 1992). Alison King has shown

How children calculated the area of a parallelogram (Wertheimer)

the benefits of instructing students to generate their own questions during a lecture. Ausubel (1968) has argued that having a concept in mind in advance of a presentation (an 'advance organizer') can help students to reorganize the material. But saying that some students are predisposed to think in lectures is quite different from saying that lectures teach them to do so.

Changing attitudes should not normally be the major objective of a lecture

The personal nature of attitudes makes this argument more difficult to assert with the same confidence as used regarding information and thought. The assertions are necessarily generalizations. The general argument is that lectures are not as effective as more active methods for changing attitudes and the method should only be used when effective.

The three kinds of attitude objectives specified earlier were:
1.   the acquisition of values and attitudes associated with subject matter,
2.   interest in the subject as a discipline, and
3.   changes in personality and social adjustment. These need to be considered separately because in some subjects there is a much stronger case for using the lecture method to achieve 1. than 2. and 3.

1. Lectures are relatively ineffective to teach values associated with subject matter

Party political speeches and broadcasts are not effective in changing people's voting habits, but they do help to confirm the preferences already held. Sermons rarely convince agnostics, but they give solidarity to the faithful. Similarly lectures are ineffective in changing people's values, but they may reinforce those that are already accepted.

Elections dominated by television and other media presentations sometimes lead to disenchantment with politicians generally. There is a good reason for this. Presentations can produce doubt by giving negative information that is inconsistent with the values of the audience; but arousing positive enthusiasm requires something quite different. Enthusiasm, and motivation generally, cannot be *given* in presentations such as broadcasts and lectures. Motivation is an inner flame that has to be there already. Passive reception of information will not fan the flame (unless there is an emotionally prepared mind). That requires energy and activity in the mind of the receiver. For example, Dresner (1990) showed that students who already thought politicians can change things, were more likely to change their behavior after a lesson on environmental issues.

The greater effectiveness of discussion in changing attitudes and values has been known by psychologists for a long time and no one now spends much time trying to prove it. In a now classic experiment Lewin and his colleagues (1943) gave exactly the same information on the merits of eating whale meat to groups of housewives in lectures and discussions. The discussion groups were asked to indicate by a show of hands whether they would try the meat. When questioned some time later 32% of the discussion groups had served it compared with 3% of the lecture groups. In a similar study Lewin (1943) found that group discussion and decision was more effective in persuading mothers to feed orange juice and cod liver oil to their babies, than giving the same information individually. The relative importance of discussion upon individual decisions has been disputed in the case of students (Bennett, 1955); but Pennington, Haravey and Bass, (1958) and Mitnick and McGinnies (1958) have found that when discussion shows some consensus, it has a greater long-term effect upon attitudes than lectures. Judging from an experiment by Hovland, Janis and Kelley (1953) with students as subjects, lecturers' effectiveness in achieving their objectives is more strongly influenced by their personalities than by their academic expertise. Assuming their influence is for the good, it seems reasonable to think that their personalities would be more effective in a teaching method using two-way interaction.

Table 2.4. The number of experimental comparisons of lectures with other methods where change in attitudes and values associated with the subject matter is the criterion

Teaching Method	Lectures less effective	No significant Difference	Lectures more effective
Discussion	19	11	4
Other	9	13	3

Other experiments are summarized in Table 2.4 and detailed in the Appendix to Table 2.4. Apart from the report by Gerberich and Warner (1936) there appears to be a strong case that discussion methods are more effective than lectures in changing attitudes. If we look at the exceptions in the Appendix to Table 2.4, it is hardly surprising that lectures influence attitudes more than no teaching at all (Kipper and Ben-Ely, 1979). And in debates (Pederson, 1983) there is often pressure to persuade others, and not be persuaded oneself. In the study by Benson (1996) the effect of discussion is diluted. The power of social conformity to influence attitudes in group situations (Asch S.E., 1951; Sherif and Sherif, 1956; Cohen, 1964) is well known and I shall not enlarge on it here. Zimbardo (1960) has shown that 'a good group spirit' is an important variable affecting changes in students' attitudes, but in a lecture with minimal student interaction, there is hardly a group at all in the accepted sense of the word (Abercrombie, 1978).

Both discussion and decision making also involve the activity principle in learning. This may be taken further in simulations and role play teaching methods. LeBlanc (1996) found that nurses who experienced simulations showed better attitudes to the elderly in clinical practice 8 weeks later, though they did not show significantly better on a questionnaire immediately after teaching. Dresner (1989-90) found students changed their home heating habits after a simulation, but not after a lecture. Culbertson (1957) has demonstrated that subjects with unfavorable attitudes to Blacks changed most if forced to act the Black role. Observer attitudes changed less, and controls changed least.

Similarly King and Janis (1956) have shown a greater attitude change in students required to present the speech of another student who held the opposite view, than those who only heard the speech. These, and other experiments summarized in Table 2.4. show that active methods are more effective in producing changes in student attitudes than passive listening. The activity principle is important in many forms of professional training such as teaching, medicine and social work where attitudes are important.

2. Lectures are relatively ineffective to inspire interest in a subject

The inspirational function of lectures is asserted more often than it merits. Admittedly most of us can remember a few lectures that stood out and influenced us as students, but they are usually few compared with the total number of lectures received. Also, the same lectures do not inspire everyone because not everyone has a mind prepared in the same way. Furthermore in many cases the inspiration is short-lived and leads to little further action. For example Hartley and Cameron (1967) found that only three out of twenty-two students who stated their intention to do further reading after a lecture had in fact done so one month later.

This is not to say that student motivation is not one objective of a lecture. It can and should be. My argument is that, as a generalization, lectures are not effective in generating enthusiasm in a subject and that therefore student motivation should not normally be the major objective and purpose of using the method. Admittedly, there are exceptional lecturers who may enthuse their audience with great regularity late on a Friday afternoon, but ordinary mortals who do not have a distinctive personality cannot achieve this excellence and should not try to copy them. There is another reason why I think this is normally impossible. The excellence of one lecturer often depends on a contrast with others. The student's intellectual diet requires a variety of foods for well rounded development.

Table 2.5. The number of experimental comparisons of lectures with other methods where increased interest in subject matter is the criterion

Teaching Method	Lectures less effective	No significant Difference	Lectures more effective
Discussion	5	4	1
Other	11	7	3

Reference to the Table 2.5 shows that there have been very few studies comparing lectures with other teaching methods, if we take students' attitudes towards their academic discipline as the criterion. While the majority suggest that lecturing is less effective than other methods, the Appendix to Table 2.5 shows that the alternatives are not consistently of one type. Although half involve some interpersonal responsiveness and elicitation of thoughts or feelings from the students, compared with Table 2.4, a greater proportion are, like lectures, some kind of presentation method.

Consequently, whilst Table 2.5. supports my contention that the inspirational role of lectures is often grossly overstated, on its own, it does not strongly suggest an explanation for this fact. Effective teaching to change attitudes and values is usually best achieved by their elicitation in discussion, followed by their rational consideration. A possible explanation is that the alternative presentation methods (listed in the Appendix to Table 2.5) had some novelty value compared with lectures; but that assumes that attitudes to the teaching method influence attitudes to the subject.

This raises another criterion relevant to the inspirational role of lectures - their popularity (see Table 2.6). It seems unlikely that students will feel inspired and enthusiastic about their subject as a result of the lectures they hear, and at the same time, either wish to have fewer lectures or disapprove of the method. 'Lectures are interesting; we wish we had fewer of them', seem to be inconsistent remarks. (I admit there could be circumstances in which students might reasonably assert both propositions. They could be so inspired that they want more private study time to follow the enthusiasm of the moment; but I see little evidence of such all-consuming enthusiasm.)

Table 2.6. The number of experimental comparisons of lectures with other methods where students' preference for the method is the criterion

Teaching Method	Lectures less preferred	No significant Difference	Lectures more preferred
PSI (See Appendix 2.1)	12	5	3
Discussion	17	3	1
Other	18	11	10

There can be little doubt about the unpopularity of the lecture system amongst students. Remembering that PSI includes discussion with student proctors, Table 2.6 shows students' preference for discussion methods. In a survey of eight colleges and universities by students (Saunders *et al.*, 1969) there was a consistent desire for more seminars and fewer lectures (except in art colleges where students spent thirty hours per week in studio work). In another survey of 1052 students in twelve teachers' colleges, over half preferred seminars to lectures and rated them superior for 'inspiring ideas' and 'developing standards of judgement', while lectures were rated highest for obtaining information (Stones, 1970). McLeish (1970) obtained ratings of teaching methods from ten teachers' colleges and several universities. There was a marked preference for seminars and tutorials, and relative distaste for lectures, in all groups. Interestingly, the students' distaste for lectures was exceeded by all five groups of lecturers who were questioned, and one wonders how much enthusiasm for their subject the lecturers engendered in these circumstances. The Hale Report also shows the students' disenchantment with the lecture method, but a more favorable attitude from university teachers. Similarly when considering seven teaching methods, students of English, education and dentistry ranked lectures seventh for efficiency, fifth for enjoyment, but easily first for their frequency (Flood Page, 1970).

However, it is to be expected that there are differences between groups of students. Observations in Adult Education together with reports by Reid-Smith (1969) and Gauvain (1968) suggest that this unpopularity may not be true with older students. In an enquiry by Woolford (1969), although in general students were more satisfied the more they were able to participate, those who were more able, less emotionally stable or less extroverted preferred participation to be restricted. There were no differences between those from different social backgrounds.

Most students in the inquiry by students themselves (Saunders *et al.*, 1969), thought 'the acquisition of information' to be the most important kind of objective of lectures, although 41% thought lectures should stimulate independent work. (The four most popular objectives were, 'to impart information' (76%); 'to provide a framework' (75%); 'to indicate methods of approaching the subject' (64%); and 'indicate sources of reference (47%).)

In particular, arts and humanities students seek stimulating ideas. Since lectures are criticized for poor preparation and presentation, or as repetition of standard textbooks, perhaps the lack of stimulation is the fault of the lecturers who commit these errors rather than the lecture method itself. Students desire stimulation, but they do not get it. If that is the case lecturers must attend to this aspect of their technique, for unless they can surpass their average colleague my conclusion will remain the same: whilst stimulating student interest in a subject might be one objective of a lecture, it should not normally be the major objective, because the method is relatively ineffective for this purpose.

3. Lectures are relatively ineffective for personal and social adjustment

An individual's personality consists of relatively permanent characteristics. Therefore, almost by definition, we should not expect any teaching method to have immediate effects. In particular lectures are situations in which students are expected to be relatively passive. They are not situations in which students are expected to 'socialize' or in which we might expect their personalities to develop by being expressed. The focus of attention is on lecturers and what they say, not on the students. Consequently to use the lecture method to develop students' personalities, their social responsiveness or their self awareness, is to make the same kind of mistake as to expect prisoners to adjust to society by putting them in solitary confinement.

With this in mind, the balance of studies in Table 2.7 might at first seem surprising.

Table 2.7. The number of experimental comparisons of lectures with other methods where personal and social adjustment is the criterion

Teaching Method	Lectures less effective	No significant Difference	Lectures more effective
All methods	14	8	4

We might expect many non-significant findings and none at all in which lectures were more effective than other methods. However, on closer inspection in Appendix 2.7, Erlich's finding is the only real surprise. Non-significant findings are often not reported. A few constructive words from a lecturer (Tuohimaa *et al.*), before medical students have to dissect their first human corpse, are more likely to reduce anxiety than nothing at all. And not only was the lecture in the Yorde and Witmer study coupled with discussion, but the relationship between psychological stress and muscular tension in the face, as measured by electromyographs (EMGs), is far from established.

More pertinent is the fact that all the methods more effective than the lecture are relatively active and expressive with immediate feedback, usually from peers. Accordingly I am confident in my conclusion that changes in personality and social adjustment should not normally be the major objective of a lecture. Teachers of clinical medicine, management, social work, education, and other fields where these things are important, will need to use other more active and expressive methods.

Lectures are relatively ineffective to teach behavioral skills

If you want to teach a behavioral skill, at some stage the student should practice it. If you are training an athlete to run 100 metres, at some point in that training they should practice running 100 metres. If you want to teach carpentry, by all means talk about safety in using chisels and demonstrate how to use them; but at some stage it will be necessary to let the students practice using a saw, plane, chisel and all the other tools. If I am to undergo surgery, I want the surgeons to have practiced the operation before; their being told about it is not enough.

You might think this principle is obvious. And so it is to ordinary people. But it is quite beyond some of the most intelligent people our educational system has produced. They want their students to do well in examinations, but they never give practice in doing them. They want their students to use the library effectively and they lecture them as they show them around, but they don't design practical exercises in using it. A professor, who wanted to teach me surveying, gave us a lecture; but we never handled the equipment or tried to survey a field. Verbal presentations present words; and words are what students get from them. If you want them to be able to do something, put them in a situation where they practice doing it.

Table 2.8. and its Appendix show the operation of this principle. Studies only show lectures to be more effective when the other methods compared are presentation methods or no teaching at all. The fact that two studies show lectures and no teaching at all to be equally effective, does not inspire confidence in lectures for this purpose. Most of the comparitors showing no significant difference from lectures are discussion or presentation methods. They don't give relevant skills practice. Most of the comparitors more effective than lectures, do.

The truth, it seems, is that the principle is not obvious when the consequences of the behavioral skills are not so physically observable. The criteria in the Appendix to Table 2.8 are nearly all interpersonal skills. The effects of a chisel, a saw and a plane are obviously different. Perhaps that is why no one has done experiments to test the effects of lectures on carpentry skills. The effects of lectures, discussions and role plays are not so obvious - at least not immediately.

However, before we condemn lectures completely for this purpose, it is worth reflecting that most physical skills have an information component. 'Knowing how' often includes some 'knowing that', and lectures are as effective as other methods for teaching that information. Thus we should expect a presentation, such as a lecture, before behavioral practice to be an effective combination. Most students get lectures before dissecting a cadaver or filling a tooth; but such instruction is not so extensive before learning to swim or drive.

Table 2.8. The number of experimental comparisons of lectures with other methods where the development of behavioral skills is the criterion

Teaching Method	Lectures less effective	No significant Difference	Lectures more effective
Practice of the skill	13	8	0
Observation (eg Demos)	5	12	2
Other methods	9	10	5

Conclusion

I hold that a great deal of evidence supports the four generalizations stated at the beginning of this chapter, provided they are taken for what they are – generalizations. However I must admit to several reservations, but I don't think they are sufficient to damage these four broad conclusions.

It is those reservations that I must now declare in Chapter 3. If they are perceived as niceties I appreciate that some readers will want to skip that chapter. They can do so with impunity. It is not essential to understand the rest of the book.

3. Summary of, and Reservations with, the Argument so far

Summary and implications of the argument so far.

Reservations.

1. The breadth of criterial categories.
2. The problem of mixed criteria.
3. Imprecise definitions of teaching methods.
4. The problem of uncontrolled variables.
5. Partial resolution with the Picture building paradigm.
6. The need for meta-analysis.
7. PSI a possible exception.
8. The problem of different enthusiasms.
9. Constraints force the use of lectures for inapproapriate objectives.

Summary and implications of the argument so far

Although it is sometimes believed that the lecture method can fulfil four kinds of function, the available evidence suggests that it can only effectively achieve one - the students' acquisition of information. Lecturers should only use methods that can achieve their objectives. It is therefore suggested that teachers should use the lecture method primarily for this purpose. If they wish to achieve other objectives they should use other methods wherever possible.

The available evidence suggests that discussion methods are superior to promote thought and attitudes. Practical activities are best to teach practical skills.

My argument, as so far presented, says nothing about what teachers' objectives ought to be. Where teachers have academic freedom, that is their decision. Where the curriculum is decided by others, that is theirs.

That does not prevent me from expressing my opinion that the major objectives of education are to do with affect - emotions, attitudes, motives and feelings, particularly feelings for others. A knowledgeable person with evil intent is a menace; an ignorant person who is well intentioned can make a valuable contribution. When the chips are down, it is more important to be happy than wealthy or knowledgeable. Happiness is an emotion.

Similarly the promotion of thought is more important than knowing facts and principles. It is a truism that facts and principles are useless if they cannot be used. But any use of facts or principles implies their application and their application necessarily entails thought, even if sometimes at a fairly simple level.

It follows that discussion is more important than lecturing; but it does not follow that teachers should never lecture or even that the time allocated to lecturing on a timetable should not exceed that allocated to discussion. That is a matter of judgement in particular cases. Possibly the size of the knowledge base required for profitable discussion may justify time devoted to the acquisition of facts. (Laying the foundations of a house often takes longer than constructing the rooms.) But the acquisition of knowledge from lectures or any other method, is not an end in itself.

It follows that lecturing should always be pursued as a means to some other end. Those ends must always be kept in mind by lecturers and students alike. Otherwise lectures become useless - necessarily useless.

This conclusion has far reaching implications for lecturers' attitudes, techniques and preparation. In particular almost every lecture must be prepared and given with a clear idea of how it is to be combined with discussion or some other method. That is why this book makes constant reference to buzz groups and similar methods. Planning a series of lectures, even by visiting speakers, without planning their follow up, is a useless activity - unless you have touching faith in the subsequent initiative of the audience to do that job for you.

Reservations

Although I believe the conclusions stated at the beginning of Chapter 2 are broadly justified, such arguments are never as tight as one wishes them to be.

1. The breadth of criterial categories

First I must admit that, whilst the categories of criteria I have used may be justified as logically distinct and that is my reason for using them, they are very gross. There are many different kinds of information, thought, attitudes and physical behavior. The comparisons cited do not consider whether lectures or other methods may be suitable to teach particular types of information, forms of thought, and so on.

The criteria of teaching effectiveness are very difficult to specify with precision for experimental purposes and this is particularly true where the objectives are concerned with thought and attitudes. Ideally the criteria should match the teacher's objectives, but where measures are precisely specified they tend to be too restricted educationally.

2. The problem of mixed criteria

Furthermore, many of the experiments use course grades or end of course examinations which purport to test more than information. But, contrary to examiners' common beliefs, when they are asked to explain the grades they award, research repeatedly shows that over 70% of the marks are given for memory of facts. (McGuire, 1963; Beard and Pole, 1971; and Black, 1968.) I have therefore put experiments with these mixed unspecified criteria in Table 2.1. (Admittedly, I could have omitted them from consideration; but I certainly could not have included them elsewhere.) I therefore accept that there is an unspecified impurity in the criterion called 'information' in Table 2.1.

Yet I could retort that, insofar as those impurities are to do with thought and attitudes, they should bias comparisons with discussion in Table 2.1. against lectures. If anything, that consideration should strengthen the claim that lectures can teach information.

However, I don't claim that the conclusions based upon the tables in Chapter 2 are anything more than broad generalizations to guide decisions on the use of lectures. They are modest claims, not detailed ones. Nonetheless their implications are important for everyday teaching.

3. Imprecise definitions of teaching methods

Thirdly the boundary definitions of teaching methods are not precise. There is no general agreement how far the details of lecture or discussion technique may differ before the teaching is described as a different method. For example after what length of time does a tutor's contribution to a discussion become classified as a lecture? Many research reports talk about 'the traditional lecture method'. Closer scrutiny reveals that in practice this may include questions or short periods of teacher controlled discussion. We shall see that a short well placed period of discussion can make quite a difference. I have therefore regarded them as Lecture-Discussions.

There is a particular difficulty in interpreting researchers' use of the word 'teacher-centered'. It is reasonable to regard all lectures as teacher-centred, but not all teacher-centered methods are lectures. Where do you draw the line? I have simply had to use my judgement as to how far the teaching consisted of 'a period of more or less continuous exposition by the teacher', based upon researchers' descriptions (which are all too often inadequate).

Consequently, even though, as a generalization, discussion methods promote more thought than lectures, the spectrum of events and styles classified as a lecture or discussion may be extremely wide. Therefore, at the margins, some lecture styles may stimulate more student involvement, and promote more thought, than some discussions.

4. The problem of uncontrollable variables

Of no teaching method is the mix of component techniques uniform. Few details of teaching technique appear in the experimental reports, but these may be as important as the choice of overall method. There are so many interacting variables in any period of teaching that any specified teaching method covers a wide range of activities. Each period contains thousands of micro variables which may or may not be important. For example, on one occasion a micro variable, such as a facial expression, could have long lasting effects; on a thousand other occasions, it might have no effect at all.

It is not hard to see that these variables and their interactions are experimentally uncontrollable, both because there are so many of them, and because pertinent events in any classroom are intrinsically unpredictable.

At this point there is a twist in the argument. The reservation that there are so many uncontrolled variables may effectively destroy a conclusion based on one or two experiments. For example if we only knew of two experiments showing that discussion promotes thought better than lectures, the generalization would be relatively unsafe.

But when there is a large number of experiments pointing in the same direction, it is stretching credulity to object that extraneous variables always distort in the same direction. We should expect them to distort sometimes one way, sometimes the other. We should expect a clouding of the picture. Hence we should expect an even balance with most studies in the non-significant group. This is what we have got where acquisition of information is the criterion, but it is not what we have got with the promotion of thought, changing attitudes and the acquisition of behavioral skills. The lecture is shown to be unsuitable for the latter objectives in spite of uncontrolled variables clouding the picture. Hence the existence of uncontrolled variables does not vitiate my conclusions with regard to the latter objectives; it strengthens them.

There are other factors that cloud the picture and which, when taken into account, make my interpretation more certain. For example, if in the tests used, there are some questions that all students get right and some that none get right regardless of the teaching method they experienced, these questions cloud the discriminatory power of the test. (For example, Cannon, 1985, found that every question was correctly answered by every student.) Since it is extremely rare for published reports to mention discarding test items with low discriminatory power, I can only conclude that most studies suffer from this clouding effect. The smaller the differences between the methods or techniques being compared, the more sensitive the tests need to be.

However, it may be retorted, with regard to the acquisition of information, that clouding is precisely what Tables 2.1 and 2.2 show. In other words, my proposition, 'Lectures are as effective as other methods for teaching information, but not more so' is simply the result of clouding by uncontrolled variables and poorly discriminating tests. It may be so. If there are as yet undiscovered differences in effectiveness, let us hope better research will discover them. But if the differences are so difficult to detect, in terms of practical decisions, the implications for teachers remain unchanged: 'The lecture is as effective as other methods to transmit information'.

It seems, therefore, that the problem of uncontrolled variables weakens the first proposition of Chapter 2 based upon Tables 2.1 and 2.2, namely that 'the lecture is as effective as any other method for transmitting information'; but it strengthens propositions 2, 3 and 4, based upon Tables 2.3 to 2.8, namely that most lectures are not as effective as more active methods to promote thought, affect and behavioral skills.

5. Partial resolution with the Picture building paradigm
To compensate for the problem of uncontrolled variables I have tried to gather and present as much relevant evidence as possible so that random variables may even out. As in other professions, teachers often have to take action on limited evidence, and within those limits I think the arguments are reasonable.

The traditional scientific paradigm breaks down under the weight of uncontrollable variables. The paradigm I am using in Chapter 2 is not the scientific paradigm. Many critics of experiments in teaching methods have not understood this. The paradigm in Chapter 2 is not the paradigm of experimental psychologists. It is not a matter of failing to disconfirm a hypothesis. There is no acid test.

I am using a picture building paradigm such as is used in management. Education is a management discipline - the management of learning. There are no certainties. As managers, teachers face a succession of decisions based upon comparisons. (Shall I do this; or shall I do that?) They have the form 'If you want to achieve X, in circumstances Y, it is generally best to do Z. The generalization that it is best to do Z is reached by comparing the options.

What evidence can contribute to the comparison? Anything relevant the manager can get hold of; but it is also important to recognize what would be relevant, but is unavailable. The best evidence consists of objective comparisons where the variables have been controlled as far as possible. Case studies and impressionistic opinions may contribute; but case studies may not be generalizable and impressions may lack objectivity.

All such pieces of evidence contribute in the same way that dots can make up a general picture. Step away and look at the dots from a distance, and you will be able to see the general picture. But look closely and you will not be able to make a valid interpretation until more dots are added at that point.

Tables 2.1 to 2.8 give general comparative pictures. If I had distinguished teaching methods and the criteria of their success more finely, that would be like looking more closely at part of the general picture. But then there would be fewer comparisons in each category and to generalize would be more risky. How closely you need to look depends upon how narrowly a particular decision needs to be focused.

6. The need for meta-analysis

Now there is an objection I have failed to meet. In the picture building analogy one dot represents one experimental comparison. But supposing one experiment involves a very large number of students and a result that is statistically highly significant, whilst another with small sample gave a different, but not very significant result. Should they be given equal weight? Surely not, but in Tables 2.1. and 2.3. to 2.8. they are. Simply counting votes in what is sometimes called the 'box score method' is open to this criticism.

For the past 20 years (Glass, 1976) there have been techniques of meta-analysis which can attach weights to different experiments according to their level of statistical significance and their power based on the number of students involved. (See Hedges, 1982 and Rosenthal, 1984 for two different approaches.) An attempt was made[1]. Unfortunately getting the data has been impossible in too many cases. Many reports don't give the relevant statistics. Most are unpublished and only appear as abstracts in Dissertation Abstracts International or the Educational Resources Information Center. Obtaining all the originals was too expensive and many are not now available.

So for my failure to use meta-analysis I must plead guilty. Hopefully someone else will take up the challenge. Meta-analysis might detect more subtle differences. For example, Szczurek (1982) found that simulation and games were more effective than lecture-discussion for low ability students, but not for students as a whole. However in Chapter 2, I have only tried to draw a very general picture. Later in the book I shall need to draw more specific conclusions and I should be the first to admit that many of them are based on too little evidence, bearing in mind the large number of relevant variables. But managers cannot wait for academic purity or proof. They must take their decisions as best they can on the evidence currently available. Teachers must do the same.

7. PSI is a possible exception

I have to recognize another major reservation to the proposition that 'Lectures are as effective as other methods for teaching information, but not more so'. On the basis of available evidence the use of PSI is more effective than the use of lectures.

Briefly, PSI is a system of instruction in which a course is divided into units of roughly a week's work. Students are presented with written materials (which might instruct them to carry out experiments or other activities). They can work at their own pace. Before they proceed to another unit students must pass a short test on the previous one. The test is administered by a more senior student called a 'proctor' who will tutor his/her peers on their test responses. Attendance at lectures is only allowed as a reward for progress.

There were a large number of comparative studies of lectures and PSI in the early 1970s and the majority favored PSI. Reviewing published reports Kulik *et al.* (1976) found 38 of 39 comparisons with lectures favored PSI, 34 of them significantly, when end of course performance was the criterion. Of those specifically comparing retention of information, all 9 significantly favored PSI. Where some thought was required all 5 favored PSI, 4 significantly. Ruskin and Hess (1974) reviewed 239 studies of PSI and in most it compared favorably with traditional methods. I have only included later comparisons in Table 2.1 and its Appendix, and the same superiority of PSI is clear.

Furthermore there is some reason to think that, compared with lectures, PSI students subsequently set themselves higher standards. Hedges (1975) compared lecture-discussion with PSI on three physics courses. PSI students not only performed better on these courses but on subsequent traditional courses in chemistry and biology in spite of controls for Scholastic Aptitude Tests (SAT) and first year grade point averages. However this is not confirmed by Taber (1974).

That said, the position is not so simple. PSI is not a single teaching method; it is a total course design. It includes tests and peer tutorial discussions which practice thinking skills. The tests in most of the experiments included elements testing thought. So it could be that the PSI experiments only tell us what we already know - that lectures do not promote thought as effectively as problem solving exercises and follow up discussions.

The validity of the comparisons has also been challenged where the questions that form part of PSI were the same, or very similar to those used in the experiments. Students in traditional lectures did not practice answering questions.

In practice, there is a further doubt about the wholesale adoption of PSI instead of lectures. We can imagine that PSI puts students under pressure. The need to pass a test in order to progress, coupled with some exposure to peers if you fail, is a threat. There is no pressure like peer pressure. It is therefore to be expected that students will work harder at PSI courses than others and this could also help to explain the better results from PSI than lectures. But if this pressure was applied to all courses, it would be too much for many students to handle. Indeed there is already some evidence that dropout is higher from PSI courses. Nevertheless the weight of comparisons favoring PSI is impressive.

8. The problem of different enthusiasms

There is another reservation that is not well answered by the picture building paradigm. The people who carry out comparative experiments are often enthusiasts for one of the methods. Enthusiasm encourages learning and may differentially influence the results. Their enthusiasm is usually for an innovation compared with traditional teaching, the lecture method, for which there is less, if not little, enthusiasm. If this is the case, there would be a consistent bias against the lecture method in Tables 2.1. to 2.8. in Chapter 2. It would favor PSI. Of course, this reservation is mere surmise. We cannot know what enthusiasms existed in the hundreds of experiments reported; and even if we had been an observer at all of them, enthusiasm is very difficult to measure and allow for its effects.

9. Constraints force use of lectures for inappropriate objectives

Whether or not my arguments for restricting the use of the lecture method to teaching information are correct, there are constraints upon teachers which may prevent them from following my suggestions. Teachers are frequently placed in situations where administrative and educational considerations conflict so that they are forced to use lectures for inappropriate objectives. For example, a lecturer may be allocated to a magnificent new lecture theatre with steeply banked terraces which may be suitable for an illustrious occasion, but for everyday use is very inconvenient for anything but the formal lecture method. In these cases faculty have tough assignments. But since I have shown only that the traditional form of lecture, with continuous exposition from the teacher, is not conducive to student thought, it is possible that a mixture of methods with lectures could be more successful. This possibility must be explored in Part 4. Similarly I have argued only that changing students' attitudes should not normally be the major objective of a lecture; but lectures can change people's attitudes and therefore we must also consider evidence that throws light on the achievement of these aims (Chapter 17).

Conclusion

It will be clear that, although I have several reservations about the four propositions at the beginning of Chapter 2, I believe them to be generally true. They imply an important role for lectures, but a much more limited one than they are often given.

Lectures are not indispensable. Other methods can teach information just as well. Some of their advantages expressed in Chapter 1 have not been considered. Opportunities to use other media are now so available that the claims for lectures as more up to date and cheaper to present are not so viable as they once were. Yet, insofar as those media also present information, the teaching principles in the rest of this book may well apply.

1. For this I am greatly indebted to Professor John Richardson of Brunel University.

Part 2
What Factors Affect the Acquisition of Information?

4. Factors Influencing Memory

Structures and processes.
1.   Memory as a sequence of processes.
2.   Evidence for two kinds of memory.
3.   It's not that simple.
4.   What happens when students listen to a lecture?

Factors causing forgetting.
1.   Retroactive and proactive interference.
2.   'Trace decay'.
3.   Amount of information.
4.   Repression.

Factors aiding memory.
1.   Meaningfulness.
2.   Whole or part.
3.   Organization.
4.   Rehearsal.
5.   Repetition.
6.   Feedback.
7.   Arousal.
8.   Transfer of learning.

Conclusion.

It takes at least two to communicate: a communicator and a receiver. People sometimes talk as if communication is a process of injection by the communicator. It isn't. They talk as if information can be transferred directly from one person's mind to another's. It can't. It requires activity by the receiver.

Whatever our objectives in lecturing, they can only be achieved subject to the physiological and psychological limitations of the students. Lecturers have to work within these limitations. If the acquisition of information is accepted as one of these objectives, it will be useful for lecturers to be able to apply a knowledge of the factors limiting the acquisition of information in lecture situations.

Since the brain has a coordinating function, these factors could include the whole of human psychology. However, Part 2 will be limited to a consideration of memory, attention and motivation with reference to teaching skills.

Structures and processes

1. Memory as a sequence of processes

The brain can be thought of as a physical structure within which various processes may take place. It is primarily a structure of nerve fibers (neurons) and the processes are the stimulation and transmission of impulses along the neurons. Eventually some impulses could be transmitted along these neural pathways to muscles resulting in observable behavior.

If we think of the stimulation and transmission of impulses as information, we can say that previously established pathways *'encode'*, that is interpret and organize, incoming information. Interpretations are *constructed* from *selected* information as part of encoding. If *'stored'* ' by establishing new pathways, they will influence later interpretations when they are reactivated or *'retrieved'*. Thus memory entails three processes: encoding, storage and retrieval.

2. Evidence for two kinds of memory

Although psychologists now also talk about a sensory memory, it used to be thought that there are only two kinds of memory, a short-term (STM) and a long-term memory (LTM). There are six kinds of evidence for this:

(a) Structural changes in the brain

First, there was physical evidence. For example, there were experiments in which an animal's brain was frozen and yet it retained skills it had learned before the period of freezing. These suggested that there were some kind of structural changes which were preserved in spite of the freezing.

There was also anatomical evidence. For example structural changes occur at the synapses - the gaps between neurons in the brain - so that subsequent nerve impulses pass more easily from certain neurons to certain others.

(b) A logical distinction

Secondly, there is a logical distinction between a process and a structure. The content of memories grouped as STMs are all processes, which is why they are temporary. The retrieval of LTMs may be a process, but their content is determined by neural structures.

(c) Electrical activity and chemical stimulation of the brain

There is physiological evidence for the temporary nature of sensory and short-term memory processes. Electrical activity in the brain seems to die away in a matter of seconds.

Physiological studies using electro-convulsive therapy and chemical stimulation of the brain suggested that the physical consolidation of these memory processes into LTMs may go on for anything up to half an hour (Broadbent, 1970). If Broadbent was correct in emphasizing the importance of retrieving information in the first half hour in order to consolidate memory of it, this may be the maximum time that a lecturer should speak without giving students a task that involves retrieving it.

(d) Common experience

It does not require elaborate physiological evidence to show that there are at least two kinds of memory. It seems to be common sense, as well as common experience, that there is some kind of temporary holding mechanism in the mind as well as a long term store. For example if we want to think, we have to hold certain ideas in our mind before we can work on them. That is why Baddeley calls STM a *'working memory'*. Since thinking is important for students, the factors which influence it are educationally important.

How are thoughts held longer than three or four seconds? One answer is that, with extra motivational energy, some active neural pathways go round in circles or loops, their impulses activating other areas of the brain as they go. This *spreading activation* is the very essence of creativity, thought and higher education. In this way new concepts are associated and distinguished.

(e) A limit to the number of items memorized
It has long been evident that there is a limit to the number of items one can hold in the mind at once. This is clearly not the case in long term memories.

(f) The methods of association
There is also some evidence that in short-term memory one associates acoustically, while in long-term memory one associates according to the meanings of words. Thus, there seems to be a difference in the methods of association - the levels of processing.

3. It's not that simple
However more recent research shows that it is not that simple. If impulses are transmitted along neural pathways, it is clear that there is a sequence of processes over periods of time. The impulses could be initiated by any of the senses, or by the brain itself. Since the brain has a network of neurons, many pathways are possible. So many different processes could be involved in memory. (Figure 4.2.) Let's consider some of them:

(a) Sensory memories
Firstly, there is a logical difference between a *STM* working with concepts that have previously been stored in *LTM*, and a *sensory memory*; that is the temporary holding of stimulation or sensations that have just been received through the senses before much encoding takes place. In practice there is more of a continuum than this logic might suggest.

A well known experiment by Sperling is now interpreted in terms of visual sensory memory (iconic memory) and may tell us why students need so many glances

J	F	8	M
3	Q	W	D
Y	B	K	2
H	5	V	G

Figure 4.1 The type of stimulus grid used by Sperling (1960)

to copy a diagram. Sperling (1960) presented sixteen letters and numbers in a 4 x 4 grid for a short period of time, and only then told the subjects whether they had to remember all sixteen, or just the four in a particular column or row.

The proportion that subjects remembered was twice as great when they only had to remember four than when they had to remember sixteen. This suggested that the subjects possessed more information in the brief moment after exposure than they could give. The memory of some of the items faded while they were remembering others.

(b) Temporal differences

The length of sensory and short term memories also vary with how much encoding there has been. Sperling's visual images (icons) seemed to be available for only half a second, although this could be extended to nearly 5 seconds if subsequent visual interference was minimised. There is some evidence that if a lecturer's words reach stage 2 in Figure 4.2. (that is a string of words not yet identified as having any meaning) students can remember a sequence up to 2 seconds long regardless of whether the words are long or short. By use of a kind of mental echo chamber known as an echoic store, the material can typically be held for up to 5 seconds.

Yet if I ask you to divide 147 by 19 in your head, you may well hold the numbers longer than that. So the length of these memories differs with how deeply the information has to be processed.

(c) Sense modalities

Thirdly, since there are distinguishable pathways for each of the senses, it makes sense to talk about separate sensory, short-term and long-term memories for each. For example a brain damaged patient might have an impaired *auditory* STM whilst their *visual* STM is unaffected. Our auditory and visual memories can be distinct.

(d) Other distinctive abilities

Furthermore there is evidence for several components of STM, each with its own capacity. For example the *verbal auditory* STM used by students in lectures is distinct from other auditory STMs.

(e) Contrasting LTMs

You might also think there are important differences in LTMs between remembering the way to the station, how to swim, the date of Pearl Harbour and that 3 x 5 = 15.

(f) Baddeley's working memory

This diversity poses a problem. How are these memories coordinated? It is clear that human beings act in a coordinated way most of the time. There has to be some kind of central processor. Baddeley calls it a 'central executive'. It sounds a bit like a ghost in the machine that does everything wonderful that cannot yet be explained. But Baddeley (1996) believes it is supported by two slave systems, the three together making what he calls 'working memory' rather than STM.

One of the slave systems is an articulatory loop and phonological store (12-10-26-2 in Figure 4.2). Using sub-vocal speech this can extend the length of verbal auditory STM from 2 to 3 or 4 seconds. There is some vagueness in Baddeley's conception regarding the level(s) at which it operates. The loop can receive information from LTM as well as directly through stimulation. It is also a holding mechanism that permits thinking. But I have no doubt there are many such feedback systems in the way the brain is wired.

The other slave system is a comparable system for visual information which he calls a 'sketch pad'. Clearly a lecture with any visual display uses both systems.

(g) Other complexities

There are other problems about memory. For example, what pathways tell us that we don't know something? Conversely it can be shown that we often know things we did not know that we knew. This is called implicit memory. It is demonstrable when students solve problems, take decisions or make judgements using information they could not explicitly recall. Lecturers depend upon it when this week's lecture builds upon last week's, yet students are not sufficiently familiar with last week's to articulate their understanding.

We shall see throughout the book that each of the complexities listed above is relevant to lecturing in different ways.

4. What happens when students listen to a lecture?

What happens when students listen to a lecture and take notes? The schema presented in Figure 4.2, perhaps controversially, adapts and modifies a model proposed by Ellis and Young (1988). Their work is based upon pathways of stimulation (or lack of them) demonstrated amongst stroke and other brain damaged patients. It should be noticed that the boxes are not objects. They do not necessarily correspond to identified locations in the brain. They are processes - activities - no doubt *connecting* different parts of the brain. Figure 4.2. represents students' brains as essentially dynamic - in spite of what their teachers might believe. Their brains are information processors. One process stimulates another, or at least may do so. Although there are probably more feedback loops than are depicted here, the arrows indicate which processes may stimulate which others. Thus they also depict chronological sequences.

(a) Auditory analysis of sense data

First, students must hear the noise the lecturer makes, hold it in sensory memory long enough to distinguish it from other noises in the environment, analyze it into individual speech sounds (phonemes), and group the phonemes together to make syllables whilst ignoring variations in pitch, speed and accent. See (1) in Figure 4.2.

(b) Word recognition

After auditory analysis, the syllables, either singly or in groups, need to be recognized by (that is, matched with) an auditory store of words (2). A particular feature of a lecture context is that some words cannot be recognized. They are unfamiliar, new, possibly technical terms. If students want to spell them, they may have to pay attention to the individual phonemes (3) and associate them with graphic shapes such as upper and lower case letters, numbers or other symbols (4).

(c) Contextual factors

Some syllables will be identified because of their context in the lecture. This suggests there is some kind of selective facilitation by part of the brain concerned with concepts (5).

What is significant for note-takers and lecturers teaching them, is the short and temporary nature of this auditory STM. Though meaningfulness might extend it, we saw that auditory verbal STM for a string of words normally only lasts up to 2 seconds before the impulses decay. (This might explain why President Reagan's one-liners were

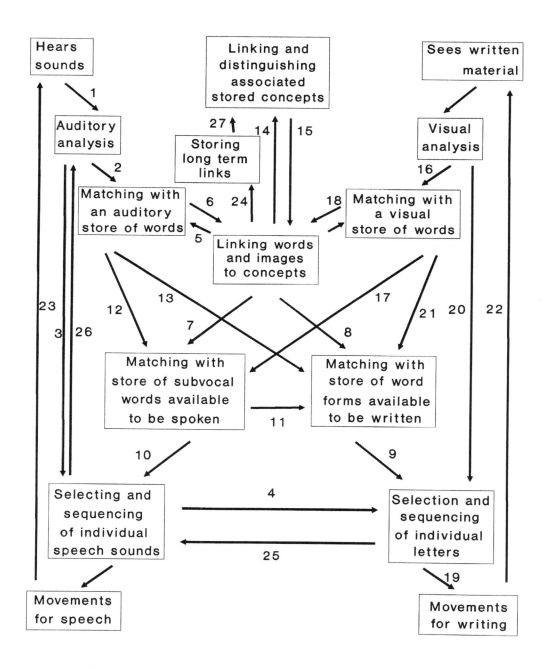

Figure 4.2 Processes when listening and note-taking in lectures. Schema adapted and modified from Ellis and Young (1988)

memorable.) It challenges lecturers to make their key points in no more than two seconds each. If they use long words, students can remember fewer at a time.

(d) Articulatory loop
However we saw that auditory verbal memory can be extended using sub-vocal speech, what Baddeley (1996) calls an 'articulatory loop'. He also says articulatory processes can take written material and convert it into sub-vocal speech so as to become part of the phonological store (16-17-10-26). This suggests students can copy small chunks from the chalkboard with scant knowledge of their meaning.

(e) The construction of meaning by encoding
The capacity of sounds and written symbols to arouse concepts is their meaning (6). Thus the meaning of words is a causal relationship between stimulation of an auditory store of words and a conceptual network (6).

This requires a process of encoding in order to understand. It is a function of short term memory (STM). Encoding has been described as processes whereby information is transformed by associating, discriminating, chunking or coding it. Di Vesta (1972) argues that these processes are necessary when note-taking involves extracting, summarizing and organizing information.

To encode students must segment the sounds from the lecturer into words; match them with an auditory store; get a preliminary recognition of their meaning possibly using probabilities in the context; decipher their syntax; incorporate gestures and other visual information; construct a possible meaning for the whole sentence; test it against context and other long term knowledge; and try other meanings if it fails the test. All this must happen, much of it unconsciously, before the processes lecturers really want can begin, namely, the use of long term memory and attitudes to apply, analyze, relate and evaluate what has been said.

(f) Thinking
The recognition and thought about what the lecturer is saying could result in a repeated cycle of stimulation, (6-14-15-5-6), which interferes with matching the next group of words uttered by the lecturer. In other words what we all know: there is a problem of divided attention if the student spends too long thinking about what the lecturer has just said. Students are under pressure not to think during lectures!

(g) Expression or recording?
Once students know the meaning of what a lecturer has said, they may search their minds for ways to express it either in sub-vocal speech (7) or in writing (8). If the latter (8), they must then select and sequence letters, numbers or other symbols to write (9). If the former (7), they may subvocally select and sequence speech sounds (10). These may directly stimulate the selection and sequencing of individual letters and other graphic shapes (4). Alternatively when concepts have stimulated a memory for spoken words (7), they may be directly associated with their written form (11).

In practice we all know that, as students, we tend to write down the same words that the lecturer used. In short, there is some direct stimulation from hearing the words to sub-vocal expression of them (12) without much understanding of their meaning (6-5-6).

(h) Visual counterparts
It might be reasonable to suppose that there is a corresponding set of processes when students copy written material (16 - 22).
(i) Levels of processing
In summary, there is reason to think that in lectures there is a succession of processes students must undertake. They are sometimes described as levels of processing. The deepest levels employ the cycle 14-15-14-15 etc in a variety of ways, whilst students with a disposition or intention to memorize will emphasize 24. In European research these two levels are contrasted as deep and surface learning, but most researchers and teachers would agree with Craik and Lockhart (1972) that deep processors remember more.

Factors causing forgetting

1. Retroactive and pro-active interference
Interference has long been regarded as the most important cause of forgetting. For example, students may learn certain facts in one lecture and then go away to a second lecture which tends to interfere with their memory of the first one. This is called retroactive interference. The interference occurs afterwards. Pro-active interference is the other way round. What the students learned in the first lecture may interfere with what they learned in the second. Pro-active interference occurs when the first lecture interferes; retroactive, when the second lecture interferes. Of the two, retroactive interference is the more powerful, though it is difficult to distinguish it from the effect of recency.

It is well known that facts learned just before going to bed at night are better remembered than those learned at other times. Similarly it is to be expected that if there is a pause in the middle of a lecture, the facts presented just before the pause will be better remembered than those elsewhere, provided that the pause is not filled by distracting, or interfering stimulation. This brings out a point which is frequently overlooked. Silence in between teachers' remarks is a very important part of a lecture. Silences provide time for consolidation and thought. Their timing requires the skill of an actor. They are useful after rhetorical questions or when a problem has been posed, and provided attention is maintained they may need to be longer in the third quarter of a lecture where interference is greatest. Interference is probably the chief cause of forgetting in lectures, particularly when the lecture is too fast.

The more similar their subject matter, the greater the interference. This is because, when many of the same nerve pathways are involved, there is ambiguity over which should be inhibited. In this instance spreading activation is a nuisance. One pattern of pathways is not sufficiently distinguished from another.

Interference is particularly potent over short periods, such as a few seconds. That is why many teachers, when they say something important, leave a moment for it to sink in before they go on. When experimental psychologists give subjects a long list of words to learn, it is often found that the memory of the first and last few words is better than those in the middle. This is known as 'the bowing effect' (Figure 4.3). One reason why words in the middle of the list are not remembered so well is that they suffer from both pro-active and retroactive interference.

Glanzer and Cunitz have shown that with a slower presentation the effect of trace decay, (see next section) or a longer period of retroactive interference, produces poorer recall of the first items (see Figure 4.3) while the end of the list is sufficiently recent to remain unaffected. This recency factor is illustrated by the fact that, if the time of recall is delayed, recall of items at the end of the list is further impaired, but not those at the beginning, which Glanzer and Cunitz thought had entered the subjects' long term memories. If, during the delay, the subjects can repeat the words to themselves, they can counteract the impairment. In effect this 'rehearsal' keeps the words recent.

Contrary to what many students may believe, most lectures do not consist entirely of nonsense words. Therefore some caution is needed in applying these findings; but if we suppose that a lecturer gives a definition, law or principle that he expects the students to take down, most of the above points may be illustrated. If the students start to write before the lecturer has finished enunciating the definition, this act may interfere

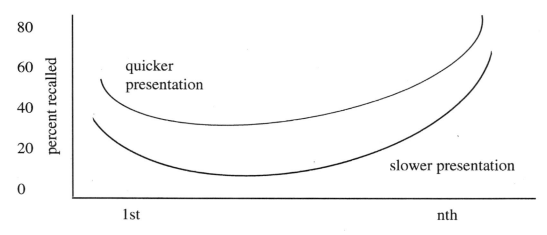

Figure 4.3. Diagrammatic representation of the bowing effect (after Glanzer and Cunitz, 1966)

with their memory of words they have just heard. If they wait until the enunciation is complete, the middle will probably be lost, especially if the definition is long. If the enunciation is slow, repetition will compensate for the consequent impairment of the memory of the opening words, but retention of the middle section will still be poor. Further repetition or slowing of pace may be necessary if a handout or other written source is not available (which, if the information is important, perhaps it should be).

Johnston and Calhoun (1969) have shown that the same thing occurs in short lectures. Facts were not remembered so well when they were presented in the middle of an 8 minute talk. Tannenbaum (1954) found the same with 10 minute presentations. He played 12 tape-recorded news broadcasts each with the same 12 items with their positions rotated and found that items at the beginning and end were remembered better than those in the middle, 10 minutes after the newscast. After rearranging the order of a 20 minute tape recorded lecture, Holen and Oaster (1976) obtained a bowing effect, but unlike Johnston and Calhoun, students showed better mastery of the beginning of the lecture than the end. All these experiments used presentations less than 25 to 30 minutes - a period related to the consolidation of STMs. I obtained a different result using lectures composed of four rotated 10 minute sections. I found a powerful recency effect. Scores for the last 20 minutes were best. Scores for the first 10 minutes were worst, presumably because they relied on long term memories suffering from interference during consolidation (Bligh, 1974). We shall see in the next Chapter that there are other reasons for regarding lectures over 25 minutes as making extra psychological demands.

It seems likely that the bowing effect can be neutralized by structuring lectures with contrasting approaches, novel points or surprising facts in the middle. I said the interference by one fact with the memory of another is strongest where the two facts are similar. Statements that are different stand out and are well remembered even when they are in the middle. In a simulated TV news broadcast, Gunter et al (1981) compared memory of three similar news items followed by a contrasting topic with four that were all the same. The contrasting item was better recalled both immediately and in a delayed test. Gunter *et al.* interpreted this as release from pro-active interference but, as we shall see in the next chapter, it could be interpreted in terms of arousal and raised levels of attention. Others have called the item 'isolated'. Kintisch and Bates (1977) found that extraneous remarks in the middle of a lecture, such as jokes and announcements, were better remembered than key points and details 2 days and 5 days later. Holen and Oaster isolated a point by first remarking, 'This seems to be an especially significant point'. Not surprisingly it was better remembered than those immediately around it in the lecture sequence. Suffice to say, effective lecturing is a much more subtle business than many new lecturers may suppose.

2. Trace decay
'Associative interference is (also) generally agreed to be the most potent cause of forgetting in long-term memory' (Broadbent, 1970). It is for this reason that students are advised to vary their subject of study.

To avoid distortions from using meaningful material, Peterson (1966) presented three-letter nonsense syllables to subjects and found there was very rapid forgetting in the first six seconds after the presentation. He suggests that any trace in the perceptual mechanism quickly fades after presentation. This is consistent with what is known about sensory memory, the early stages of STM and electro-chemical brain processes. The rapid forgetting is sometimes called 'trace-decay'. The amount of forgetting has been shown to increase with the number of items to be remembered (Murdock, 1961). More recent research suggests that interference is probably more responsible than trace decay for forgetting after 5 seconds (Baddeley 1996).

Similarly, it is to be expected that a student's memory when taking notes of what a lecturer has said will also quickly fade, particularly if points are not crystallized by a short key phrase. It is partly for this reason that important points in a lecture should be presented in a brief and semi-permanent form on the blackboard, overhead projector, screen, or a handout. We shall see that these provide supplementary holding mechanisms when the lecturer wants students to think about presented information.

3. Amount of information

A very common cause of forgetting is trying to learn too much. Katz (1950) has shown that adding to the number of elements in an intellectual task causes confusion and inefficiency after a certain number has been reached. It is a common fault of lecturers with good intentions to try to teach too much. Russell *et al.* (1984) have shown that students learn more when information density is not too high. When high, retroactive interference is severe (recency effect); and if very high, the middle of the lecture suffers

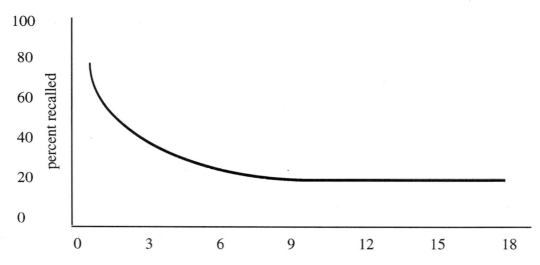

Figure 4.4. Recall of three unrelated letters in relation to the interval since presentation. (Peterson, 1966).To eliminate 'rehearsal', subjects were required to count backwards in threes during the interval.

(a bowing effect). Short-term memory has a limited capacity. Miller (1967) says that the average number of items of knowledge that a person can hold in short-term memory is 7 plus or minus 2. It may be said that, when playing Kim's Game, one can usually remember more than 9 of the small articles on the tray, but this is probably achieved by grouping them in some way, and this, of course, is a way of aiding one's memory.

It is for this reason that I have grouped these twelve factors affecting memory into four concerned with forgetting and eight with aiding the student's memory. You will see that some of the factors could have been classified in either sub-heading. I have found, when presenting these twelve points in a lecture, that student-teachers remember them better if grouped in this way.

Since the capacity of short-term memory is a factor in intelligence, one might expect students to be able to hold more items in their mind at once than the average member of the population; but this is only one factor in intelligence and students are selected on a wider range of abilities.

There are some students who do not take notes in lectures and some lecturers who prefer students not to. While note-taking may interfere with students' memories and inhibit their organization of information, it is usually advisable where the lecturer makes more than seven points worth remembering. (See tabulated evidence in Chapter 9).

4. Repression

People forget what they do not want to remember. In other words, motivation is an important cause of forgetting. Freud called this 'repression'. Repression is sometimes thought of as being unhealthy. It may be if it leads us to be dominated by irrational motives, but in most people it is a very important defence mechanism which prevents us from being mentally disturbed by unpleasant memories. It is important in an academic context to be aware of the temptation to ignore facts that do not fit our interpretations and feelings. One of the functions of discussion both in teaching and research, is to force us to face facts which we prefer to ignore. Of course, motivation can also aid memorization, but this will be dealt with in a separate section.

Factors aiding memory

1. Meaningfulness

One of the most important factors affecting memory is the meaningfulness of what is to be remembered. By this I mean how far it fits in with the ideas the person already has. This can be demonstrated quite forcibly by looking at the following three lists of words for about ten seconds each and then writing down those that can be remembered.

It will probably be found that there are considerable differences in the memory of the three lists, yet each consists of the same thirty letters. But they do not each consist of thirty different items to be learned. In one there are ten words to be learned, and in another, two or three phrases. Thus the meaning of what has to be learned makes a drastic difference to the quantity. This is why the meaningfulness of what is taught is so important in teaching. By using established pathways it enables information to be grouped into chunks - what is called the 'chunking' of information.

In a lecture containing terms that students do not understand, they are faced with grammatically correct sentences which have no meaning for them. They may take notes with the hope of making sense of them later or they may refuse to write down what appears to lack meaning. Because, as we have seen, meaning is an important factor affecting long-term memory, the latter strategy is unlikely to produce effective learning. The former relies on the accuracy of short-term memory. But how accurate are students' short-term memories for sentences they do not understand? By taking five 'normal

yma	try	the
uyo	can	lid
ont	but	may
teh	you	not
dil	yet	fit
ryt	not	yet
ubt	the	you
nac	may	can
tey	fit	but
tif	lid	try

'Chunking' information

sentences' each with five words and the same syntactic form, and systematically exchanging words with the same syntactic functions, Marks and Miller (1964) obtained grammatically correct but meaningless sentences (e.g. 'Soapy wildcats give smoky damsels'). By scrambling the word order of the 'normal' sentences they obtained 'anagram strings', and 'word lists' were formed by scrambling the word order of the 'meaningless sentences'. Figure 4.5 shows the ability of students to write down the five-word strings in the correct order for each of the four types. The results show an improvement with practice on successive trials but the important point for us is that short-term recall of 'normal sentences' is two to five times that of meaningless sentences. This difference is likely to be increased with longer sentences.

Although it is difficult to talk about the intelligibility of lectures in quantitative terms, observations such as these suggest that the effect of lecturing in simple language is sufficiently important to justify very careful preparation.

An important function of active methods of learning, such as writing essays and discussion, is to force students to relate the subject to their own conceptual frameworks. Students can only say what the subject means to them, personally. Because the conceptual frameworks of the lecturer and the students are not the same (see Abercrombie, 1960), and the lecture method is largely a one-way process, maximum intelligibility is unlikely to be achieved by the lecture method alone.

Educationalists frequently suggest the need to 'get down to the students' level and start where they are'; it may be trite, but it is none the less true. What the lecturer says only has meaning for the students if they can relate it to ideas they already possess.

Consequently, when I am asked 'Should a lecturer cover the ground laid down in the syllabus, even when some students don't understand, or go at a slower pace and get behind?' the answer must be the latter. In either case some students will not know as much as one would like, but in the latter the lecturer knows what they know and what they do not, while the students have a firm framework round which they may build by reading. In the latter case students may catch up by systematic study; in the former neither the lecturer nor the students know the size or place of the gaps in knowledge. Consequently no systematic, planned build-up is possible and no lecture based on previous parts of the course can be assuredly intelligible to the students. These points apply not only to knowledge, but to the 'thinking skills' or 'patterns of thought' that are normally learned early in a course and which new lecturers can easily overlook as needing to be taught. If lecturers considered their courses in terms of the learning achieved by students rather than a succession of performances by lecturers, this question would seldom be asked.

2. Whole versus part learning

There is a very debatable question whether students learn better by trying to take in everything at once or by splitting a subject into small parts. Psychologists disagree whether learning the whole of something, or only part of it at a time is better. It is probably better to learn a poem by heart in large sections, because if it is broken into small sections the student also has to learn how to put them together again. This is an extra task. On the other hand, with complicated tasks which must be understood, this is a small price to pay for the greater simplicity that results from dealing with small units. Rote learning and some experimental skills are sequential tasks like learning the poem; but understanding, for example in the social sciences, can frequently be acquired only by appreciating the component parts of the total social situation first.

3. Organization

Organization is involved in both the previous two factors. If subject matter is arranged in a logical way, it is easier to understand as a whole. Organization of subject matter is particularly important with adults and in academic subjects. This is why the clear

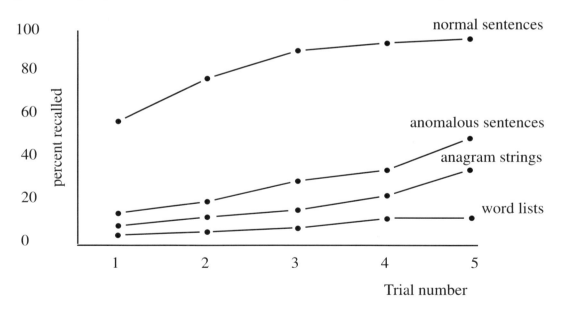

Figure 4.5. Average per cent of five-word strings which were correctly recalled for each of four types of strings over five trials.

statement of the organization of a lecture, the writing of essays, and the tidy summary of a rambling discussion are important for student learning. Chapter 7 gives ways to organize lectures.

4. Rehearsal

Many psychologists believe that rehearsal is a very important factor in aiding memory. Rehearsal consists of saying the subject matter to oneself, or in some way going over it after the initial presentation. If Broadbent (1970) is correct that rehearsal, or 'retrieval', within half an hour of the initial presentation, is very important for the consolidation of learning, the provision of buzz-groups, silent revision, or even short tests within the lecture situation are important teaching techniques. Chapters 19 and 20 give further ideas.

Similarly, it is important that the practice of skills by students should closely follow the theoretical discussion. Indeed, the immediate provision of situations in which the student must apply information, after hearing it in a lecture, is an important and under-used teaching strategy. Neurologically, it encourages spreading activation so that connections are made between concepts. It contextualizes the subject matter, gives it meaning and makes it relevant. McLeish (1968) found that students who averaged 39 per cent on a test of factual material immediately following a lecture, scored only 3 per cent less a month later when, in the meantime, they had received and discussed the lecture script.

The importance of rehearsal is most strikingly displayed in data reworked by Bassey (1968) from a series of experiments by Jones (1923). Five groups of students (A-E) were given a lecture. Group A was tested immediately, B after one day, C after one week, D after two weeks, and E after three weeks. The results, and those of subsequent tests, are shown in Figure 4.6. It will be seen that even after sixty-three days Group A retained more than B retained after one day. It is inferred that this is the result of A's immediate rehearsal. Thus the immediacy of rehearsal is an important factor in long-term retention. Bassey is probably justified in assuming the comparability of the content and groups across Jones's experiments; and whilst Jones's data does not justify quite such a smooth graph as Bassey draws, the general argument is valid.

One of the functions of note-taking in lectures is to arrest the decay of memory traces by rehearsal of what is written. Reading notes immediately after the lecture will be more effective than 'vision' for the first time (hardly 'revision'!) two weeks before the examinations; but rehearsal during the lecture itself would be even more effective. It practices retrieval and the activation of particular neural pathways and loops, thereby making recall and thought more probable. McQueen *et al.* (1994) have demonstrated the same point using weekly lecture quizzes. Practice strengthens responses.

It is the responsibility of the lecturer to provide opportunity for this by arranging short buzz-discussions between neighbours on issues raised, the provision of questions or even short periods of silence specifically to recall notes. (In each case the purpose of these activities must be explained to the students to ensure their cooperation).

5. Repetition

Every teacher knows that repetition consolidates learning, provided there is some initial learning to consolidate. Most teachers have to say a thing a number of times before an acceptable proportion of the class remembers what has been said. Repetition differs from rehearsal in that it is repetition by the teacher. Rehearsal requires an activity by the student.

Following an experiment on learning to associate pairs of stimuli, Rock (1957) concluded that repetition strengthened, or consolidated, associations once they were formed, but played no role in their formation. Although Rock's experiment has since

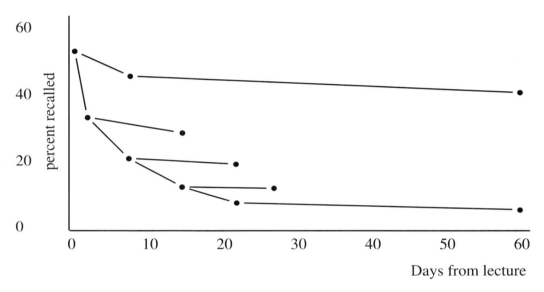

Figure 4.6. The value of rehearsal following a lecture (after Bassey, 1968)

been the subject of controversy in the psychology of verbal learning, it makes good sense if applied to a lecture situation. Kiewra *et al.* (1991) presented the same lecture three times. On the first, students noted the most important points. The second and third presentations gave an opportunity to add less important information and build higher level concepts.

If there is no learning from the first presentation, repetition does not help. Beard (1970) describes an occasion when a lecturer, having been told by the class after half an hour that they had not understood a word, proceeded to repeat the performance in a quarter of an hour. Such a repetition is unlikely to be any more effective than the first performance. To take an extreme case, imagine a lecture in a foreign language you don't understand. Your understanding will not be improved however many times you hear it, because no encoding is possible. But if there had been some learning on the first occasion, the repetition could have had some interactive or consolidating effect; in this case the learning of the first occasion could have provided a conceptual framework, a set of neural pathways, to give some meaning to the second. (Barnes *et al.*, 1983).

6. Feedback

Students' learning of cognitive and motor skills is normally better if they know how well they are doing. Such knowledge of results, or feedback, can be either rewarding or punishing. The terms 'reward' and 'punishment' have a wide meaning in this context. A smile, or a tick on a student's work, may be rewarding. A sigh or even silence can be punishing in some circumstances. In both cases such knowledge is more effective the sooner it is acquired after testing. Persistent punishment leads to discouragement and a decline in performance at memory tasks, while persistent reward normally gives encouragement and leads to a gradual improvement. Both are equally effective at first, because students can learn from their mistakes and their successes. It will be seen from this that knowledge of results may be effective in two ways. It can provide information on which the student may act. It may be a regulator of student motivation. Information is most important at first; motivation is more important later.

These principles are important in all contact with students but particularly when handing back written work. The most effective teaching probably consists of selective reward and punishment according to the teacher's objectives and the personalities of the students. Teachers, too, need to have knowledge of their results.

It is important to notice that teachers and students require this knowledge of results as soon as possible if they are to make use of the information it contains. Habits and expectations form quickly. Feedback received after three weeks of a one-year course will have more effect on a teacher's, or a student's, motivation and amount of energy, than on how that energy is directed. The most effective feedback is given before that time. (N.B. Three weeks is about 10% of a year long course, 20% of a semester.) Results of examinations are too late.

7. Arousal

It is fairly obvious that people remember things better when they are alert than when they are tired. (Sherwood, 1965). But since this is dealt with in the section on 'arousal' in the next chapter, no more will be said about it here.

8. Transfer of learning

Finally, something may be easier to learn because it is similar to a previous experience. This is called positive transfer of learning. The greater the similarity, the stronger the transfer. If memory of the first thing hinders memory of the second, it is called negative transfer of learning. Thus, practice at one skill affects the performance of similar skills. As we cannot hope to teach students everything, positive transfer of learning is a very important principle. Education is impossible without it. To take an elementary example, if a child is taught how to multiply two numbers together, the teacher relies on the fact that he will be able to transfer this skill to other numbers. We rely on the same principle of transfer in tertiary education with skills such as analytical and critical thinking. It is for this reason that training in study skills is essential for all students.

Level of performance

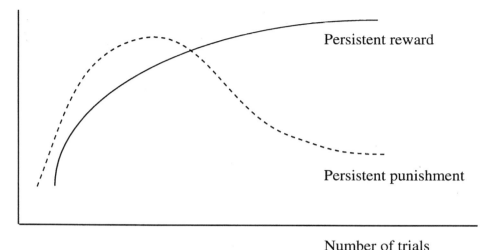

Persistent reward

Persistent punishment

Number of trials

Figure 4.7. The relative effects of persistent reward and punishment.

Conclusion

In this chapter we have seen that information can be brought to mind either when it is being actively transmitted or by activating such transmissions along pathways determined by neural structures. The transmissions are temporary; the structures are long term. The job of teachers and students working together is to develop the structures. Factors preventing and aiding this are then considered in turn.

That may not be the usual way teachers think about their job. At one level it confirms what the reader knows already: what the lecturer says should be stimulating, well organized, meaningful to all students, and delivered at a speed that all can follow. At another level it makes possible an analysis of what we do, and what we ought to do, when we lecture. Part 3 applies that analysis. But the analysis is not complete. In the rest of Part 2 we need to look at students' attention and motivation and what lecturers can do to maintain and intensify them.

5. Factors Affecting Students' Attention

The effects of arousal.

Factors affecting student arousal.
1. Variations in stimulation in the learning situation.
2. The students' arousal regimes during periods of teaching.
3. The students' daily work/rest regime.
4. The students' physical environment and bodily condition.

Although there are many different meanings of 'attention' (Treisman, 1966), in this context we are concerned with the students' ability to concentrate. The problems for teachers are, firstly, what factors affect student concentration, and secondly, how can we use our knowledge of these factors to help them?

There are two broad factors: arousal and motivation. Both of these refer to the amount of energy a student has. 'Arousal' refers to a general level of activity: it is a measure of non-specific stimulation of a student's cerebral cortex which facilitates the transmission of nerve impulses from one part of the brain to another. 'Motivation' is the energy directed towards a specific kind of activity or goal. (These are intended as non-technical explanations of the terms, not definitions.)

The effects of arousal

At what level of arousal should a teacher aim to keep students? The graph in Figure 5.1 (sometimes known as the 'inverted U curve') shows a typical level of performance in relation to arousal. Students (in lectures?) can be conceived as varying from a state of deep coma to berserk anxiety!

It will be seen that at the extremes of relaxation and over-activity, the level of performance at, for example, a learning or manual task, is poor. But between these extremes there is an optimum level. We live most of our lives on the left-hand side of the optimum level. If people are stimulated their level of arousal increases. They can be overstimulated but the more common fault of lecturers is to be insufficiently stimulating. Arousal varies with personality factors. Extroverts require more stimulation than introverts to reach their optimum level. Using Cattell's 16 Personality Factor test, a professor called Boreham reports that inattention in lectures is related to self reports of 'untroubled adequacy' (Boreham, 1984; Boreham and Lilley, 1978).

As long as they are not too relaxed students generally perform better at difficult tasks if they start at a lower level of arousal. This is because the effort required raises the level of arousal to the optimum. Conversely, with simple tasks there is a temptation for students 'to take it too easy', and make silly mistakes. Consequently a higher initial

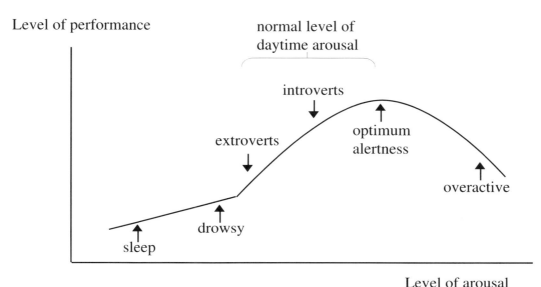

Figure 5.1. The 'inverted U curve'

level of arousal favors good performance at easy tasks. This generalization, depicted in Figure 5.2, that lower initial arousal produces better performance at difficult tasks, is known as the 'Yerkes-Dodson Law'. It probably applies within the normal range of wakefulness. It aids understanding of experiments such as Thorson and Lang's (1992). Using televised 'talking head' lectures, the insertion of videographics produced an orienting response with increased arousal (measured physiologically). In other words, arousal shifted from left to right in Figure 5.2. Learning of difficult and unfamiliar material suffered, whilst retention of easier and more familiar material presented at these times, was enhanced.

It may be concluded that a teacher must aim to keep students at the level of arousal appropriate to the task and this usually means finding ways to increase or maintain it.

Factors affecting student arousal

We shall consider these four factors:
1.   Variations in stimulation in the learning situation
2.   The students' arousal regime during periods of teaching
3.   The students' daily work/rest regime
4.   The students' physical environment and bodily condition

1. Variations in stimulation in the learning situation

Broadly speaking, variations in stimulation increase arousal and hence increase the students' attention. It seems reasonable to expect from this that lectures and audio-tapes

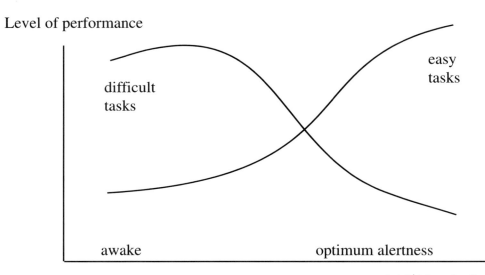

Level of performance

difficult
tasks

easy
tasks

awake   optimum alertness

initial level of arousal

Figure 5.2. Diagrammatic representation of the Yerkes-Dodson Law

will be particularly poor teaching methods for maintaining students' attention unless a special effort is made to prevent their minds from wandering. In the lecture situation the students maintain roughly the same postural position, listen to the same human voice, and look at the same visual field.

(a) Auditory stimulation

Lecturers should always ask themselves, 'How can I vary my presentation?'. One of the unwritten world wide assumptions about lecturing is that lectures are solo performances. But why should they be? Betts and Walton (1970) provided auditory variation in university physics lectures to nearly four hundred students by alternately presenting differing points of view as a dialogue in which one gave the logical organization of the subject, while the other interposed questions and gave illustrations or demonstrations. Comedians have long known that they can hold their audience far longer when there are two of them. Television companies know viewers will switch channels if they don't keep changing the speaker, even in news programs. The same has been shown in psychological experiments. For example, Gruber (1964) demonstrated that alternation between auditory and visual presentations will raise levels of attention to a vigilance task. The same goes for lecturing - without varied stimulation, students mentally switch off.

Variations in auditory stimulation can also be introduced in lectures if there are frequent opportunities for questions and discussion. Therefore buzz-groups and controlled discussion are important techniques for the teacher, especially in large classes where loss of student attention is frequent and easily unnoticed. The provision of occasional silence for the rapid revision of notes gives students an opportunity to frame questions in addition to a change in stimulation.

(b) Visual stimulation

Visual illustrations have an arousing effect whether or not they provide necessary information. I have found that students' heart rates will rise 10 beats per minute in the 6 seconds after switching an overhead projector on or off. Human vision has an orientating reflex towards movement so that some lecturers find they can draw attention to important points by using hand movements. Others overuse such gestures. At secondary school level Wyckoff (1973) found that increases in stimulus variation as measured by teacher mobility, gesturing and pausing, increased students' recall of factual information from lectures. The opposite was the case at elementary school level where, perhaps, the pupils were already near optimum arousal.

College decor should also not be ignored. The fact that it is usually financed from a different source has easily lent support to the mistaken assumption that it is irrelevant to student learning. Drab buildings will produce a lower standing level of arousal and the use of color in slides or overhead projector transparencies will be particularly alerting.

(c) Postural position

An audience will be more alert if their spines are upright. It is difficult for the lecturer to provide variations in postural position for the student, but opportunities to gather round the lecturer's bench for a demonstration, or to move to a short discussion group, should not be rejected as too much trouble if they can also achieve course objectives.

(d) Novel stimulation

The essential requirement is for the teacher to provide novel stimulation at intervals, if not continuously, throughout a lecture.

This point cannot be emphasized too strongly. The idea that lecturers should use the lecture method and no other for 50 minutes on end is absurd; yet it is quite a common practice. The remarkable tolerance of students for this diet is all the more surprising when one considers that the effect of monotonous stimulation is common knowledge without its verification by psychological experiment. MacManaway (1970) reports that 84 per cent of his students said 20-30 minutes was the maximum length of lecturing to which they could attend.

Television is thought to be a medium which holds attention, but Mills (1966) and Wood and Hedley (1968) found long ago that 15-20 minutes was the optimum viewing time when the material had to be learned. Barrington (1965) reports an optimum of about 25 minutes. Smith and Wyllie (1965) found that over half the students benefited when TV and conventional methods were mixed.

Discussion is less prone to lack of concentration partly because of the variety of voices that the student hears, and partly because there is self stimulation if the students themselves are actively involved, and this is more effective than external stimulation.

Many students always occupy the same seat in the library for private study.

Superficially it would seem that if the book to be studied is the only novel item in the environment, the students are likely to concentrate on it. In practice the monotony of the rest of the environment has a more powerful de-arousing effect. Thus it is better for students to vary their place of work.

(e) Intensity of stimulation

Variations in the intensity of stimulation are also arousing. A sudden loud noise will make a person jump; but a continuous loud noise has a deadening effect. Buck (1963) has shown that a railway accident may be caused by habituation to the loud sound of an alarm bell two feet from the driver's ear if this stimulation is persistent. Similarly, it is a well-known trick that the sudden lowering of a lecturer's voice can emphasize a point because it attracts attention.

2. The students' arousal regimes during periods of teaching

(a) The attention decrement

Figure 5.3. shows the typical decrement curve for a person's attention to a single task over a period of time. With more difficult tasks extroverts show a greater decline after the first half-hour than introverts (Bakan, 1959). This pattern is normally displayed in the level of performance of both students and their teachers in their respective work situations. In addition it has been suggested (McLeish, 1968; Lloyd; 1968) that student attention takes 5 minutes to settle down at first, and rises and falls during the last five or ten minutes of a fifty-five minute lecture. Lloyd hypothesizes that the lecturer's level of performance conforms to Figure 5.3.; and since the effectiveness of a lecture depends on both the lecturer and the students, it will conform to the lower of the two levels (Figure 5.4.). The lecturer's level is normally higher owing to greater self-stimulation. Lloyd confirmed his hypothesis with reference to the number of notes students took. It may be objected that subject matter is not equally noteworthy throughout a lecture. Perhaps the rise at the end of the lecture would occur if the lecturer said, 'To sum up, ...' and all hitherto somnolent students immediately grabbed their pens to make amends for their earlier indolence.

What is needed is either a measure of arousal independent of the subject matter, or measures of learning in experiments that control for it. Both have been attempted.

Heart rate is one indication of arousal, but it is not a definitive measure of it, nor is the relation to learning a direct one. I took students' heart rates every 6 seconds throughout lectures and at first found the pattern confirmed Lloyd's hypothesis including the rise at the end. Indeed on one occasion when, at the end of normal time, the lecturer asked to continue for an extra 10 minutes, there was a double rise in heart rate at the end! There is no obvious explanation for this rise. Even disregarding the student intervention, Figure 5.5. seems to show it in both lecture and discussion (see also Figure 18.1.); but it does not always appear (Figure 5.6.). Figure 5.6. shows separate regression lines for the first half hour and the second part of four lectures. They suggest that these two periods in lectures are quite distinct.

Confirming Lloyd's observation using other measures, Scerbo *et al.* (1992) report that students note less and less as the lecture proceeds; but immediate recall does not show the same decrement. I have also been unable to confirm the decrement in attention using objective measures of students' learning during periods of lecturing lasting forty minutes. The four quarters of each of four lectures given in four different orders to four groups, failed to show a decrement in learning according to their position in the order of presentation. On the contrary using an immediate test, learning in the last 20 minutes seemed superior, suggesting the importance of recency when the test is immediately after the lecture. We have already seen that arousal is by no means the only factor influencing learning. In any case, the threat of a test immediately after the lectures may have 'concentrated the mind most wonderfully'. So this experiment is not sufficient grounds to say that psychological conditions affecting attention are fundamentally different in lecture situations from those studied by psychologists. Furthermore, Giles *et al.* (1982) did find that learning was greatest in the second 15 minutes of a 60 minute lecture.

Following Lloyd, Maddox and Hoole (1975) monitored the 'information units' noted by students at 5 minute intervals through a 50 minute lecture as a proportion of what the lecturer considered ideal; but the number spoken by the lecturer confirmed Lloyd's pattern. He slowed down. Consequently the proportion noted by students was relatively constant, whilst the number decreased. In short, the efficiency of lecturer and students decreased together much as Lloyd describes.

What can we conclude about the attention decrement? To generalize is difficult. On a subjective level, it is a common experience that concentration for a full hour is not

Level of attention

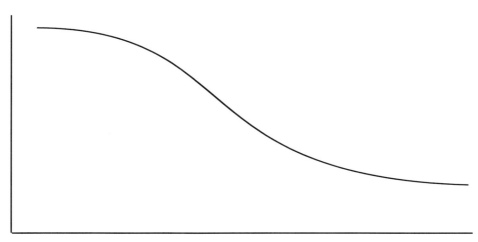

time

Figure 5.3. The decrement in attention

Level of performance

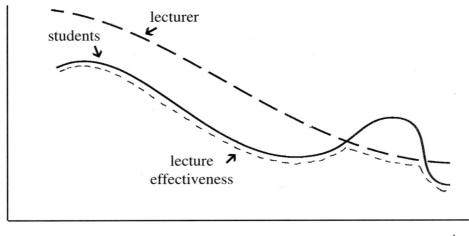

Figure 5.4. *Level of performance during a lecture (after Lloyd, 1968)*

easy. There is reason to think that a lecture of 20-30 minutes is long enough unless there is varied stimulation. Note-taking does decrease during a lecture, but evidence on the temporal pattern of learning during lectures is equivocal as judged by immediate tests. However the results of immediate tests have a strong short-term memory component. Neither life nor examinations are immediate tests using short-term memory. They use long-term memories. We shall see in Chapter 9, that the opportunity to review notes strongly improves scores on delayed tests. Hence the decrement in note-taking will reduce knowledge in the long term; and it is the long term that matters.

(b) The effect of a short break

A short break will allow the level of attention to recover, though later decrements will be quicker than the first. Mackworth (1950) has shown that performance on a vigilance task, requiring attention to a dial, will return nearly to its starting level after a short rest period. Adams (1955) found a marked improvement in attention to a manual skill after a brief rest; but improvement was not so great when the rest was spent watching others do the same thing as when it was a complete change. A change is nearly as good as a rest. Wilkinson has reported an improvement for up to 30 minutes following a break of 25 seconds. If these experimental findings are applicable to teaching, there is a strong case for short breaks and changes in teaching method in each period of teaching (see Figure 5.5).

If Mackworth's, Adams's and Wilkinson's findings are relevant and are applied to McLeish's and Lloyd's model (Figure 5.4) we may obtain Figure 5.7, which implies a gain as a result of rest. A three-minute buzz group could have a similar effect because it

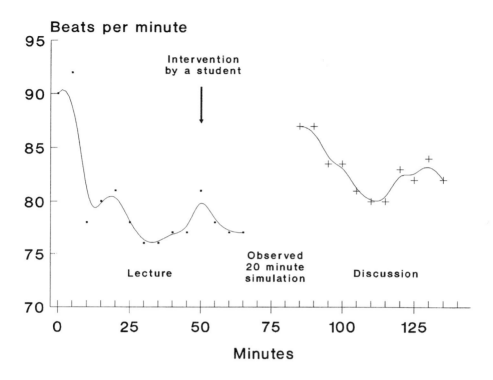

Figure 5.5. Students' heart rates in class.
Four students in a class of 14 listened to a 70 minute lecture, passively observed a simulation for 20 minutes and then took part in a discussion for 1 hour. Their heart rates were recorded every 5 seconds. Thus each mark is the mean of 240 observations in a 5 minute period. Though the sample is small, the Figure illustrates several features: the decrement in the first 25-30 minutes, the effect of one student intervention on others, the partial restoration of arousal at the start of a new activity (discussion).

would provide a variation in stimulation. The rate of decrement shown is arbitrary and is steeper with more boring subject matter. Students may be bored because the subject matter is too easy, incomprehensibly difficult or not personally interesting. The more bored the students, the more frequent the variations in teaching methods should be. Consequently it is not suggested that the number of rest or buzz periods should always be limited to one.

These ideas are an extrapolation from psychological evidence from specific vigilance situations. They are confirmed by common teaching experience and by controlled experiments in teaching. Notice, the pauses may be quite brief. Weaver and Cotrell (1985) reported more student involvement, understanding, thought and feedback as a result of specific mental exercises in the middle of a lecture (eg 'Tear out half a sheet of paper and write your reactions to the lecture so far'). In an important experiment Ruhl and Suritsky (1995) compared the effectiveness of lectures with three two-minute pauses, the provision of a lecture outline and a combination of these two procedures. The pause procedure alone resulted in better free recall of lecture ideas and more complete lecture notes. This result could reflect the opportunity to fill in gaps in notes and to revise and rehearse what had been said rather than, or in addition to, superior levels of attention. Whatever your psychological interpretation, the educational advantages of short breaks remain. Johnstone and Percival (1976) observed students' non-attention in ninety 50-minute chemistry lectures given by 12 lecturers. After initial non-attention when settling down, the next lapse typically occurred between 10 and 18 minutes and lapses became more frequent reaching a point before the end when students could not attend for more than 3 or 4 minutes at a time. Attention was very much worse in a TV overflow room. Attention varied with the difficulty of the subject, the rate of delivery, the legibility of blackboard writing and the

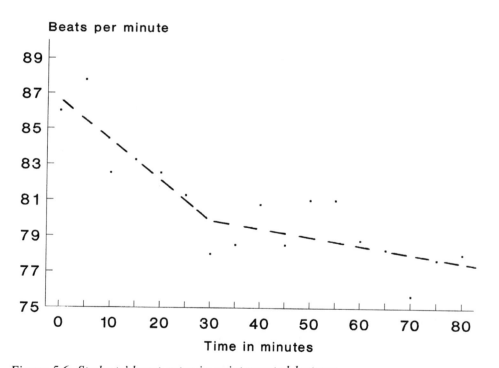

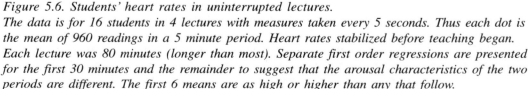

Figure 5.6. Students' heart rates in uninterrupted lectures.
The data is for 16 students in 4 lectures with measures taken every 5 seconds. Thus each dot is the mean of 960 readings in a 5 minute period. Heart rates stabilized before teaching began. Each lecture was 80 minutes (longer than most). Separate first order regressions are presented for the first 30 minutes and the remainder to suggest that the arousal characteristics of the two periods are different. The first 6 means are as high or higher than any that follow.

lecturers' personalities. Yet, a most powerful point, non-attention could be postponed, or even eliminated altogether, by short buzz group discussions.

3. The students' daily work/rest regime.

The same decrement in attention, with consequent need of variation in teaching methods, occurs through the day as within a lecture. Some people reach their optimum level of performance during the morning, others at mid-day, but very few people indeed are at their best in the afternoon. In a series of experiments using identical lectures, I found that students scored better on immediate tests at eight cognitive levels after lectures starting at 9.30am than 11.15am, and better at 11.15am than 2.00pm (Bligh, 1975). Likewise comparing students with themselves on different occasions, or with each other on the same test items, Holloway (1966) found scores better at 9.00am than 4.30pm.

Similarly most people are more alert on Monday and Tuesday than Friday! Yet these facts are commonly ignored by both teachers and those who organize their timetables. Since attention to lectures is more difficult in the afternoon and evening, they should be shorter, more varied, more stimulating or give way completely to small group teaching or other active methods of learning at that time.

Jane Mackworth (1970), after reviewing studies of drivers and others after some hours of activity, concludes that 'prolonged performance in a monotonous task may interfere with the ability to make decisions at a fairly high cortical level, but not with automatic activity'. This is consistent with the remark that 'lectures are periods of time

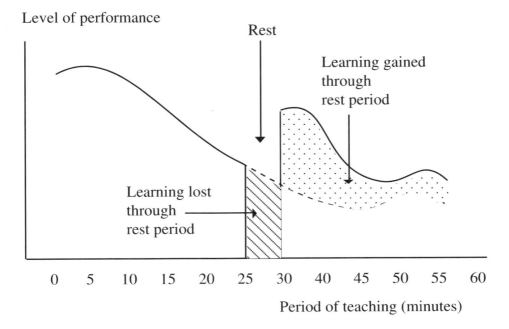

Figure 5.7. Hypothesized pattern of performance during a lecture with a break

during which the notes of the lecturer are transferred to the notebook of the students without going through the brains of either'.

When the level of arousal is lowered either by the time of day or by loss of sleep, knowledge of results of the performance arouses the cortex, with consequent improvement (Wilkinson, 1961; Mackworth, 1970). Discussion of problems in small groups provides the student with this knowledge of results in a way that lectures or other presentation methods never can. Therefore, lecturers facing a class on 'the morning after the students' night before' or the day after the 'Rag Ball', will be well advised to use discussion methods. Apart from some Russian work, there is little evidence in favor of sleep learning: practice of the art during lectures is not recommended!

Readers of advertisements for a well-known bedtime drink will know that 'research has shown that there are many different levels of sleep'. The inverted U curve shows that the same might be said of wakefulness.

The important point is that the level of arousal is continuously fluctuating and even during apparent wakefulness there will be brief moments of sleep known as 'microsleeps' (Oswald, 1966). Contrary to what one might at first expect, students' heart rates fluctuate more towards the end of lectures when students seem more tired. Microsleeps are more frequent amongst sleep deprived or tired students, but in between microsleeps normal mental capacity is not greatly impaired. Thus, a student will work more slowly, but not necessarily less profoundly, when tired. The 'microsleeps' are frequently characterized by the 'dream state' of sleep. Thus, we might say that a person's mind wandered for the moment. The over-conscientious or anxious student may often be detected by wary observation of frequent 'microsleeps' during lectures or tutorials. This could be a useful advanced warning that gentle student-counseling may be necessary.

From the point of view of the student, a lecture is a paced situation and Wilkinson (1963b) has shown that those suffering sleep deprivation work slower, but not less accurately at mental tasks. In this case, the lecturers must either lecture at a slower speed and risk being dreary, or place the students in self-paced situations such as discussions or practical work. If they lecture at their normal speed students may miss vital information during 'microsleeps'. The work of Pepler (1959) and Wilkinson (1963a and b) suggests that the marked decrease in the speed of work over twenty to thirty minutes can be averted by short breaks every five minutes. While their subjects were more sleep deprived than most students, the principle of short breaks should not be ignored when the need arises.

Some students claim that they work better against a background of noise. There is some evidence (Wilkinson, 1963b) that sleep-deprived subjects work better where noise has an arousing effect, but this effect wears off after half an hour. Those who have slept normally work better under quiet conditions, but their work will not greatly deteriorate in noisy conditions during the first thirty minutes. These two findings suggest that twenty to thirty minutes noise is enough. If students have a lower level of arousal later in the day, these findings may be relevant to teaching at that time.

It must be frankly admitted that in this discussion I have taken big steps in reasoning from the precisely specified conditions used by experimental psychologists, to the variable and uncontrolled conditions in which teachers work. Only further investigation can show whether the inferences are correct. There is a great deal we simply do not know about the normal teaching situations. To some extent the onus is on my critics to say why teachers and students should be different. The evidence available suggests that when students are tired, when teaching later in the day, or when subject matter is difficult, varied teaching methods, including the use of discussion techniques, are most likely to be effective.

4. The students, physical environment and bodily condition

The effect upon attention of variations in blood chemistry, especially following the use of drugs, has received much recent publicity and study; but for our purposes concerned with effective teaching, the important physical factors are common knowledge and will therefore be mentioned summarily. A modern, centrally overheated and humid lecture room induces student drowsiness. The fact is well known, but it is easily overlooked when lecturers are more concerned with their subject than their students, or when, being in an active role themselves, the room condition has little effect on them personally. The sharp contrast with the air outside may result in objections if a window is opened more than a little. One solution is to open the door, for moving air may have an arousing effect without lowering the temperature.

The need for a varied postural position has been mentioned. The distracting effect of uncomfortable chairs in lectures is well known, but it is rare for lecturers to take countermeasures. If the effect is made clear to the students, a break of two minutes during which they are expected to 'stretch their legs', may be unconventional, but pays dividends. The best position is probably an erect but relaxed spine. The effect of deep armchairs in small group teaching is less obvious. The students may contribute as frequently as usual, but owing to their posture they may not note points or references that they otherwise would, and their lower intermittent arousal would not favor their memory of them.

A large lunch and a small quantity of alcohol will increase the somnolent effect, while tea or coffee may overcome it. Hunger may be arousing at first, but then a distraction. For those who are over studious, the lack of physical exercise, which was enforced at school, may result in a monotonous environment and an increase in weight with a consequent decline in arousal.

Conclusion

In Chapter 4 we saw that consolidation of memories may take up to half an hour. Lectures longer than that are therefore likely to interfere with that consolidation process. In this chapter we again see evidence to suppose that lectures should not be longer than 20-30 minutes - at least without techniques to vary stimulation.

Admittedly the evidence is mostly indirect and more research could be done. But a combination of psychological and physiological studies using a range of criteria, together with common experience, are beginning to form a composite picture that the first 20 - 30 minutes of a lecture are different from the remainder. The remainder is probably less effective and less efficient.

Part 4 of this book describes and recommends some ways to vary student activity and maintain attention.

6. Motivating Students

The importance of motivation.

How can we motivate students?
1. Enthusiasm from the lecturer.
2. Cultivate existing motives.

Common motives of students.
1. 'Deep' and 'surface' approaches.
2. The desire for relevance.
3. Curiosity.
4. Achievement and fear.
5. The need for social interaction.
6. Activity and esteem.

Conclusion.

The importance of motivation

There is little doubt that student motivation is an important factor affecting the performance of students in their courses. Indeed, there is some evidence that it is more important than intelligence; but when saying this it must be remembered that the range of intelligence of students is small compared with the range in the population as a whole. In one department of engineering, Beard, Levy and Maddox (1964) found a predominantly negative correlation between measures of intellectual ability and first year examination results, but in another, ostensibly similar department, this was not the case. They considered the effects of teaching upon motivation as a possible explanation of the difference. From a long-term study Himmelweit and Swift (1971) have reported that measures of motivation correlated more highly with achievement in Higher Education than measures of intelligence or social background. High-drive introverts usually perform better in examinations than low-drive extroverts (Furneaux, 1962; Malleson, 1967; Walton and Drewery, 1967; Entwistle and Entwistle, 1970; Entwistle and Wilson, 1970). The two studies by Entwistle suggest that the success of high-drive introverts is related to their 'good study methods' in that they 'work carefully, think ahead, are conscientious and recognize the importance of working conditions'.

An alternative or additional explanation is that motivated students work longer, rather than more intensively. This view receives support from Evans (1967) who found that students highly motivated to achieve spent more time on a learning task and were better at it. Thoday (1957) found that students work shorter hours when examinations or other assessments are in the relatively distant future.

If longer study time is the only explanation, we might expect that students with higher intelligence would perform better over a fixed period such as a lecture. There is some evidence for this, particularly when thought is possible or required; but it is by no means always the case (Guetzkow, Kelly and McKeachie, 1954; Hudelson, 1928; Jamieson, James and Leytham, 1969), and Guilford (1959) has pointed out that the mental processes required of students are often quite different from those used to do intelligence tests. After experiments in programmed learning Stolurow (1960) observed that achievement is only related to intelligence when the teaching is bad! Corey (1934) has shown that intelligence has less influence on the effectiveness of lectures than on that of reading. In general, previous performance at college and university, rather than school, has better predictive power than standardized tests (Warburton, Butcher and Forrest, 1963; Halpin, 1968; Nisbet and Welsh, 1966).

We may conclude that the importance of stimulating motivation in lectures lies as much in its long-term effects, as in attention during the lecture itself.

How can we motivate students?

If, therefore, motivation is at least as important as intelligence in influencing students' achievements in learning, the practical problem is how to motivate students.

1. Enthusiasm from the lecturer

There's only one thing more contagious than enthusiasm, and that's the lack of it. The way to interest a class is to display interest oneself. This has the support of several experiments. Mastin (1963) instructed lecturers to teach one topic with an 'indifferent' attitude and another the following week 'enthusiastically'. The characteristics of 'indifference' and 'enthusiasm' were vetted by a board of 'experts'. Nineteen out of twenty classes did better on multiple-choice tests after the 'enthusiastic' lesson. There was no interaction between intelligence and the degree to which students were affected by enthusiasm. Teachers who were apparently enthusiastic influenced the attitudes of their students more strongly and were rated more highly by them. In a similar experiment Coats and Smidchens (1966) found that 36 per cent of the variance in tests of audience recall were attributable to the 'dynamism' of the speaker. Dynamism was measured using behaviors such as gestures, eye contact, vocal inflections and speaking without reading a script. Students take more notes, and taking notes results in more learning, when the lecturer is enthusiastic (Stewart, 1989).

However there are also some experiments with rather ambiguous results for the effectiveness of enthusiasm. In the Stanford experiments, mentions by observers of enthusiasm, energy and vitality were positively related to learning for some lectures but not others (Unruh, 1968). In 8 out of 10 comparisons by McCord (1944) ratings of speech characteristics of enthusiasm correlated more highly with achievement scores than with objective measures of the characteristics themselves. Marsh (1984) reported that lecturer expressiveness had a large effect on test performance when other sources of motivation were low; but when incentives to learn or to do well in a test were added, the effect of expressiveness was insignificant. At school level, Wallen found that ratings of 'stimulating' correlated with teachers asking questions, praise and encouragement, and hostility and reprimands; but were unrelated to learning (cited in Rosenshine, 1970).

It is possible that personality characteristics explain these ambiguities. Low conceptual level students are better motivated to learn course content by direct instruction; with students capable of higher conceptual levels, motivation is enhanced by indirect methods which allow them to think for themselves (Hancock, 1994). Magnusson and Perry (1989) argue that expressive, enthusiastic teaching can be measured by features such as the amount of a *teacher's movement, eye contact* and *varied voice intonation*. These increase arousal. Students (with an inner 'locus of control') who can inwardly channel their aroused energy towards their desire to learn, will increase their learning. But those (with an external locus of control) who cannot control their inner anxieties or intruding thoughts, need feedback or some other external stimulus before or during the lecture if the lecturer's enthusiasm is to be infectious.

We may conclude that it pays to be enthusiastic and to act as if you are, even when you are not. But don't be too disappointed if you don't enthuse everyone all the time. Interaction with the class will increase the motivation of those whose temperament is not so conducive to enthusiasm.

2. Cultivate existing motives

Personally I have found no other reliable answer to the question, 'How can we motivate students?' Part of the reason for this is that not all students are motivated by the same thing. In this respect the factors affecting motivation are a little different from those affecting memory or arousal. Secondly, unlike information, motives cannot be presented by a lecturer to students. The lecturer's task is to cultivate motives the students already possess. They are cultivated by practice in being expressed. That is why lectures are relatively ineffective for this purpose.

Once teachers know what their students' latent motives are, they may first stimulate a need for the motives to be satisfied, and then present their subject as a means of obtaining satisfaction. For example, if a student has chosen to study medicine because of a genuine human sympathy, the teacher in anatomy would be wise to show, on some occasions, how the subject could be applied. A caution should be observed that the motive stimulated should be relevant and not over-used. When teaching in a college with a large number of unwilling students, a teacher in a non-vocational subject attempted to discuss social relations in the context of sexual motives. It was not long before it became known that students thought him 'a little queer'.

Thus, in spite of the differences between students, the lecturer's task will involve using the motives they already have. This raises the question, 'What motives do they commonly have?'

Common motives of students

1. 'Deep' and 'surface' approaches

In the past 20 years there have been extensive researches into students' approaches to learning. Typically students have been interviewed about how they studied a written text, but there is every reason to believe that the dispositions revealed apply equally well when listening to lectures. Students are motivated differently according to their approach.

In 'surface' approaches, students' intentions are to store information - in other words to memorize facts and principles without much thought. They conceive of the learning process as increasing their knowledge, and knowing facts, principles and procedures to be used. They think of the teacher's role as presenting information and the students' role as reproducing it in examinations in order to demonstrate that they know it.

In contrast, 'deep' approaches emphasize thought rather than memory. They integrate new ideas to those already possessed. New knowledge is organized and rearranged in the context of the students' previous knowledge, not the lecturer's. Thus its meaning is different and personal to each individual. Students using a deep approach look for fundamentals. They exercise imagination. They distinguish principles from examples. They look for the overall structure of ideas and relate new ideas widely and to their personal experience.

We may infer from Table 2.3, that a deep approach is not normally achieved in lectures. But the situation is more serious than that. There is reason to believe (Gibbs, 1992) that the lecture system positively encourages a surface approach and discourages the very intellectual skills that higher education claims to foster. The supposition is that students will think about the lectures afterwards, but over timetabling and excessive course material too often leave little time for that. Methods of assessment using factual objective tests or encouraging regurgitation in examinations, make matters worse.

It behoves lecturers to lecture less, to convince students of the intellectual aims of their courses, and to create opportunities, in lessons and outside, in which thinking can flourish.

2. The desire for relevance

Marris (1964) has reported that most of the students he interviewed at four institutions wanted their studies to be at least indirectly relevant to their careers, but they saw that a narrowly specialized course was not likely to be the most useful. In the light of the recent difficulties of even doctoral students in obtaining employment, this judgement appears to be valid. However, only about two-fifths of the students in Marris's survey thought that their studies would be relevant to their later careers.

There is also a connection between vocational relevance and student motivation during specific teaching periods. When I asked student-teachers to assess my lectures, there was a statistically significant correlation between their ratings of 'interest' and 'relevance to teaching', (but the assumption that students will work harder at things which they claim to find interesting, requires empirical confirmation).

3. Curiosity

In recent years there has been less emphasis on developing motivation through manipulating rewards and punishments, and more on how to use students' 'natural curiosity'. In schools there has been an increase in project work. Universities, too, have increased the role of theses, projects, long essays and small scale investigations in undergraduate work. But Table 2.5 shows that lectures are relatively ineffective to stimulate interest in a subject.

So the problem here is how to use lectures to generate curiosity. Berlyne (1960) has found that students' learning and interest were improved if students were asked questions rather that told facts. The most successful questions were those that were least expected, particularly if the subject was already familiar. Katona (1940), after numerous experiments, implies that lectures should begin with stimulating questions. Not any question will do. In an experiment using televised lectures Cresswell and Lin (1989) found that eye contact and inserted questions correlated with student interest and satisfaction, but did not seem to impact directly upon students' short term memories. The questions seemed to arouse attention rather than aid memory. McKeachie (1965) has suggested that effective questions are likely to contain a conflict or a paradox which may be resolved during the rest of the lecture, and has concluded that the interplay between the familiar and the novel may be a very important factor in the development of curiosity.

However, the sensitive lecturer will be aware of strong individual differences in response to paradoxes and uncertainty. For example, in one study (Feather, 1969) students who were judged as rigid or 'dogmatic' were less interested in novelty and unfamiliar information.

4. Achievement and fear

Examinations are powerful motivators either through fear of failure or through the desire to achieve personal success. Fear of failure evokes the minimum effort to pass. The drive to achieve demands maximum effort for personal satisfaction.

(a) Fear of failure

Fear of failure becomes greater as the examinations, or assignment deadlines, become closer; while if any inspiration is obtained from a lecture, its power diminishes as the occasion recedes into the past. The deadlines for course assignments create undulating pressures. Correa (1994) claims that as student interest in a subject increases, the optimum number of lectures increases and the number of exams necessary to motivate, decreases. When the length of courses increases, to motivate students it will be necessary to increase the number of exams, but not the number of lectures.

But fear is not normally conducive to high student motivation. Janis and Feshbach (1953) gave presentations on dental health to three groups of students and varied the emphasis on the frightening consequences of dental neglect. The use of minimum fear was most effective both in the extent to which they changed their dental habits and in the degree to which they resisted counter arguments. McKeachie (1965) claims that the threat of a test makes students concentrate harder, but an experiment by Coats and Smidchens (1966) to test this hypothesis proved inconclusive. Kuz'mina (1976) found that average students learned more from lectures when they knew they would be tested on it; but knowing that did not affect the performance of good and poor students.

(b) The desire for personal achievement

Rather than threats, positive encouragement is better. There are enough suicides on campus already. Particularly with students listening to their second language, an empathic lecturer is more effective (Barnes *et al.*, 1983). Marsh (1984) showed that financial incentives improved concentration and test performance, particularly when the information content was dense.

The desire to achieve depends on knowing what to achieve. You might think that if you want students to achieve, or strive towards, something, they are more likely to do so if they know what it is. That is the usual finding. Yet it is remarkably rare for lecturers to tell their students what they should be able to do by the end of the lecture, that they could not do at the beginning. Royer (1977) confirmed that students given instructional objectives before a lecture displayed more intentional learning than others; but in her particular experiment, students given the objectives only at the end of a lecture displayed incidental learning when they were able to retrieve sufficient information and relate it to the objectives.

5. The need for social interaction

There is considerable psychological evidence that the desire for interaction with other people is a very strong motive, and this may be particularly true with young people. Yet the lecture method notoriously neglects it, and attention would probably be improved if another method was used to satisfy it during a lecture period.

How far should a teacher bear this motive in mind when selecting a teaching method? Deutsch (1949) showed that students were more attentive, displayed better comprehension, produced more work and were more favorable to the teaching method when they worked cooperatively in groups than when they competed as individuals. The relative popularity of seminars and tutorials demonstrated in Table 2.6 could also be partly explained by their satisfaction of this motive. Batson and Johnson (1976) designed a course to maximize student motivation by providing a supportive context, challenging students' conceptions of themselves and society, and ensuring they had a sufficient background to raise pertinent questions. Students' ratings compared favorably against other courses when there was no final examination; and they preferred discussions led by their peers to those led by graduates. All this suggests that learning should be considered it its social context.

Burke (1955) takes this wider. After a controlled experiment on teaching methods using measures of college marks, social activities, leadership, athletic participation, personal problems, academic adjustment, reading ability, IQ, attendance, age, opinions of courses and teachers, and social and emotional adjustment, Burke concluded that not only teaching methods, but the total college environment, may be important for how well first year students adjust to college life. Loomis and Green (1947) concluded from a study of mental conflicts in a typical state university that 'unhappiness in college is chiefly caused by lack of social acceptance, not sex or poor grades'. Yet it is clear that social interaction and acceptance could be adequately achieved outside the teaching situation.

Therefore the importance of using teaching methods that may satisfy the desire for social interaction will probably depend on how well it is satisfied by other means at other times.

6. Activity and esteem

Achievement and social interaction are associated with students' needs to feel involved and to have the respect of others. All are motives of which the lecture method makes poor use. Patton (1955) found that students were better motivated when asked to share decisions on the running of a course and when teaching methods required greater participation. Those who were more active were also prepared to accept more responsibility. With mature students, Collier (1966) has reported that the involvement required in syndicate method (see Table 15.1 on pages 192ff) stimulated higher motivation than teaching by traditional methods.

One of the most important things for a teacher to learn is to give praise. Because faculty often prefer cautious understatement to enthusiasm, giving praise sometimes requires a conscious effort. Students may learn what they should not do by making mistakes; they learn what they *should* do by the rewards of success. 'Nothing breeds success like success' is a more pertinent dictum than 'We learn by trial and error'. To develop the drive to achieve, students need to believe that achievement is possible. This may be fostered if they can taste the fruits of success.

In short, positive feedback is a powerful motivator. Therefore to motivate students in this way requires the lecturer to provide the opportunity for feedback that lecturing itself does not give (for ways of doing this see Part 4 and Chapter 13 in Part 3).

Conclusion

No doubt the readers can think of relevant motives that I have not considered, particularly those that are appropriate to their subject; but there is little objective evidence on the way to motivate students even though motivation is generally recognized as important. It is clear that the teacher has to build on motives that the students already possess, but in some cases these are inappropriate to the lecture method. Therefore alternative methods may sometimes be needed. Consequently the techniques for the development of student motivation require a conscious decision at the time when teaching is prepared, and some spontaneity in abandoning a prepared procedure when motivation appears to flag during a lecture.

Part 3
What Lecture Techniques Apply
These Factors Most Effectively?

7. Lecture Organization

Common forms of lecture organization.

1. Hierarchic forms.
2. Chaining.
3. Variations and more complex forms.

Making the organization clear.

1. Introductions.
2. For each new point.
3. For conclusions.

Conclusion: The importance of organization.

There are two common forms of organization used by lecturers to structure information they have to teach, but each has variations and may be used in conjunction with the other so that, in practice, lectures do not conform to a few simple patterns. Nevertheless, a knowledge of the basic forms may help the new lecturer to organize information when preparing lectures, and if the organization is made clear to the students they may find the lectures easier to follow.

Common forms of lecture organization

1. Hierarchic forms

Although the 'classification hierarchy' and the 'problem-centered lecture form' are both hierarchic, in many respects the latter is so distinct that it is not regarded as hierarchic and the former is therefore referred to as 'the hierarchic form'.

(a) The classification hierarchy

The classification hierarchy is the most common basic form. Essentially it consists of a classification, with its criterion as the heading. In other words, different points of information are grouped together with a unifying feature as a heading (Figures 7.1 and 7.2).

Assuming that the organization of information requires grouping in some way, this is about the simplest form there can be. Each item of information is linked with only one other idea, so that the grouping aids the memory, while there is a minimum of links to be remembered. Since, for most people, there is a limit to the number of items they can remember under one heading, it is advisable to sub-divide them when there are over nine, and preferably when there are over five (G. A. Miller, 1967, in Chapter 4, page 43).

Being simple, the classification hierarchy is ideal for the clear presentation of facts. In other words it is ideally suited to the main functions of regular lectures, teaching information and surveying an area of knowledge before its study in further detail. For the same reason it is particularly suitable when first dealing with a difficult topic. When the objective is to give a 'framework', it provides a few 'pegs' on which students may hang further ideas. Thus at first it is useful where it is intended that students should undertake further reading.

If the subject matter is difficult and sub-headings are required, it is advisable to remind the students of the major headings, (I and II in the diagram) and the second order points 1., 2. and 3. before going on to introduce a new level in the hierarchy (a), (b) and (c). This reminder will be called 'taking stock'. It is a technique used in programmed learning where the linear form of the program may obscure the overall structure of the information being presented, or where the students need to be reminded of what they should have learned. A new level in the hierarchy means that a student must keep two kinds of link in mind at once. This, in addition to the facts to be remembered and noted, is an extra load on memory. For this reason, 'taking stock' is a very important technique where the lecture organization is not written in front of the student or for some other reason the student's memory must take the load normally borne by a blackboard or projected summary.

The sequence of presentation is different from the form in which the topic is organized. The order in which points are made requires jumps from one level of the hierarchy to another. It is at these 'jumps' that students easily become 'lost'.

Lectures with a hierarchic organization are the easiest for a new lecturer to give. They require attention to one thing at a time. They do not require much dramatic ability.

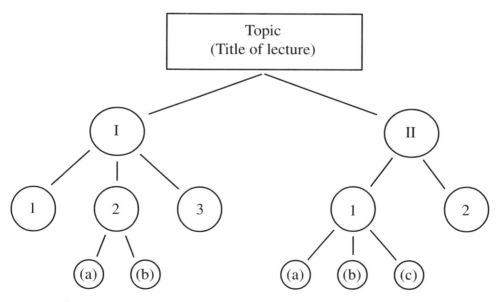

Figure 7.1. An example of the classification hierarchy form to show 'links'

It is relatively easy to see when the timing of a hierarchic lecture is going wrong, and to accelerate or slow down without clouding the major points.

The main disadvantages of the hierarchic lecture form are derived from the very simplicity which in some contexts is its virtue. A simple classification of information can produce a rigid way of thinking if students only think of a given fact in one context. For this reason it is necessary to couple hierarchic lectures with discussion problems or essay topics that require more flexible thinking. Flexibility in thinking may be stimulated by suggesting reading with a variety of sources and points of view.

I   _____

     1.   --

     2.   --

           (a) ....

           (b) ....

     3.   --

II   _____

     1.   --

           (a) ....

           (b) ....

           (c)...

     2.   --

Figure 7.2. Sequence, and probable blackboard organization, of a hierarchic lecture.

The second major disadvantage is possible boredom. Lectures are stimulating and interesting when they link ideas that had not been linked before in students' minds; but, as we have seen, part of the simplicity of the hierarchic lecture is obtained by minimizing links between facts.

We may conclude that the hierarchic lecture form is very useful when introducing complex and difficult subject matter, and for the major function of most lectures, the presentation of facts. Like the lecture method itself it is less suitable for stimulating interest and thought. Consequently it is more likely to be used with younger and less able students.

(b) The problem-centered lecture

When using the problem-centered form the lecturer asks a question or presents a problem, and thereafter gives information, arguments and hypotheses as possible solutions, so that everything said focuses on the initial problem. For example, the approach may be a telescoped presentation of a scientific investigation.

It is hierarchic in that possible solutions are subsumed under the major problem, while factual evidence and simple inferences are taught with reference to each of these hypotheses (Figure 7.3.).

It is distinct in that the relationships between the evidence and the possible solutions, and between the solutions and the problem, are not relationships of classification, but involve a process of reasoning. This difference is important when considering the kind of objectives that may be achieved by this form of lecture.

Although they only demand limited patterns of thought, problem-centered lectures will be appropriate for promoting thought in those circumstances in which it is not possible to give the problem to the students directly in discussion. It is also suitable for stimulating students' interest if the problem can be made to arouse their curiosity.

Arousing students' motivation in this way involves creating a certain kind of tension, which is not at all easy for the new lecturer. It involves some dramatic skill to convey puzzlement, the use of rhetorical questions, and considerable skill in timing the presentation of the next piece of evidence or when raising objections to the latest hypothesis. Because of the thought demanded from the student, the problem-centered form requires variations in pace which are more subtle than those in a lecture using a classification hierarchy.

When giving a problem-centered lecture it is essential to get the problem clear at the beginning. If students do not understand what the problem is, the rest of the lecture, consisting of attempts to solve it, will be completely lost on them. We have seen the importance of 'meaning' in teaching information, and that it depends on the ability of the student to relate items together. In the same way the evidence presented in the body of a problem-centered lecture has little meaning if it cannot be related to the central problem.

For this reason it is advisable to keep referring back to the central problem in much the same way that 'taking stock' has been recommended. This may be done each time a possible solution is presented by explaining in an almost elementary way how it solves the problem. It is necessary to explain why each hypothesis is a possible solution, because experiments have shown (Hovland and Mandell, 1952; Bligh, 1974) that students do not make even the most important and simple inferences when in lecture situations. Furthermore it is a very common mistake for lecturers to fail to make allowances for their own assumptions, expertise, intelligence and familiarity with the problems, and to think that inferences are easier for the students than they are.

The choice of problem requires considerable thought and is best made at the time when the course is planned, not when the lecture is prepared. I find that choosing an appropriate problem, and the precise way of posing it, are creative tasks, and the steps in achieving them follow the stages described by the Gestalt school of psychologists (see page 15) culminating in a new insight into the subject of lecture. Artists and creative scientists have described a similar process (Poincaré, 1908; Stephen Spender, 1952). The stages are often spread over several weeks and if I have a number of courses to prepare, I may be concerned with choosing more than one problem at the same time.

We have seen that the problem should arouse motivation, suit the students' level of attainment, and, if the objectives include the provision of a framework of information, it should synthesize what is to be taught.

More than other forms of lecture, the problem-centered approach makes assumptions about students' previous knowledge and their ability to handle new concepts.

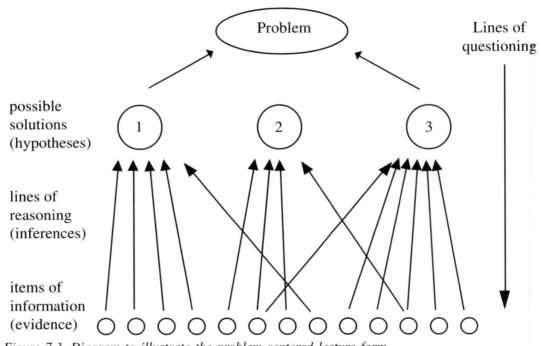

Figure 7.3. Diagram to illustrate the problem-centered lecture form.
Items of information are used as evidence to support hypotheses by use of reasoning. The hypotheses are directed towards solving a problem. Students are required to follow lines of reasoning by relating ideas together. They are also required to understand how the hypotheses are possible solutions. (Although Chapter 2 of this book is obviously not a lecture, the reader may find some similarities between its organization and this simplified diagram).

For all these reasons the problem-centered lecture is the most difficult to give and to follow, but if given satisfactorily it is also the most rewarding for both the lecturer and the student.

2. Chaining
This form of organization simply consists of a sequence. A story consists of a chain of events and perhaps it is because both our experience and our speech are in sequential

form that chaining seems a natural form of exposition. Indeed Oaks (1996) reports greater recall of instructional content immediately, 3 weeks and 5 weeks after instruction in a story telling fashion, than after the traditional lecture method.

Not all chains are a simple series in terms of time. As with the hierarchy, the links may involve a reasoning process so that there is a chain of argument. A chain of cause and effect may be in the time dimension but not be at all simple. Reference to Chapter 21, and indeed Part 5 as a whole, will show that it has an overall chaining structure (although in detail it is obviously more complex). Introductory textbooks usually show a hierarchic form. Some of the most difficult lectures to follow consist of a chain of ideas each associated with the last, but with no overall dimension. When the Cambridge philosopher, Wittgenstein, lectured he is said to have talked out loud about a problem that concerned him at the time, in between periods of silent thought. Therefore ostensibly his lectures had a problem-centered form, but in practice the leaps of his creative mind, when considering the chain of argument in one possible solution, were such that the students' main task was to keep track of his thoughts. (This kind is not recommended unless the lecturer has the audience in the 'palm of his hand', because they require the students' minds to wander with the lecturer's.)

Assuming the links between one stage and the next are easy to follow, chaining is a form of organization that maintains attention very well, as may be evident from the use of stories with children; but if attention is lost, it is difficult for the student to pick up the thread again. Since all students will have 'microsleeps', in addition to which their minds may either wander or be stimulated to explore some relevant issue, the lecturer who adopts the chaining form must employ tracking devices so that students may mentally return to where they left off.

Firstly, it is particularly important to make clear when moving from one stage to the next. This may be done by writing the stages on the blackboard or some other continuous display, as one goes along, giving each a number. It is not enough for the lecturer to say 'Next....' and pass on with scarcely a break. Secondly, lecturers should 'take stock' of the chain. This should be done with increasing frequency as the lecture progresses, because, as we have seen, the students' memories have limited short-term capacities, and consolidation by rehearsal or repetition becomes increasingly necessary as the limits are approached (Figure 7.4). A third device with some kinds of subject matter is to state the final stage or goal clearly at the beginning so that students can see where they are being led or what is finally being explained. For example, it can be helpful in a chain of causes and effects in history, or a series of reactions in chemistry, to know the final consequence or product.

In these forms of chaining, once the stages have been written on the board, much of the lecturer's energies may be devoted to explaining why each stage follows from the previous one.

3. Variations and more complex forms
Because of their clarity these basic forms are probably the easiest patterns of organization from which to take notes. For this reason they are suitable for first-year or

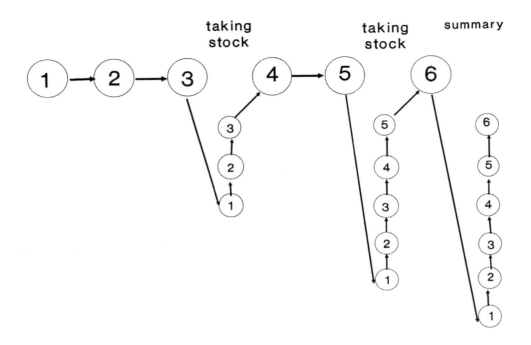

Figure 7.4. Diagram to illustrate the organization of a six-point chaining lecture with a

other students who have yet to learn how to take notes skillfully. The selection and organization of notes requires more skill than many lecturers appreciate, and since, as far as their own lectures are concerned, lecturers have the responsibility to provide training in these skills, although some do not recognize it, more complex patterns should be introduced gradually.

(a) **The comparison**

A common variant of the hierarchic form is the comparison. It is a form of paired classification. The style of blackboard or overhead projector summary shown in Figure 7.5 prevents a load being placed on the students' short-term memories, because they do not have to recall the two items labeled with the same number simultaneously, before making the comparison. (Admittedly there may still be short term 'recognition' involved, but this is easier than 'recall'.)

The style may become a little more complex if similarities and differences are distinguished (perhaps when teaching to achieve the same objectives as are assessed by 'Compare and contrast....' examination questions). See Figure 7.6.

A variation with three sections is shown in Chapter 2 and its appendices, when comparing lectures and other teaching methods, with reference to one dimension (their relative effectiveness).

Criterion	Upper Limb	Lower Limb
1 Size	1	1
2 Strength	2	2
3 Dexterity	3	3
4 Structure	4	4
5 Functions	5	5
6 etc	6	6

Figure 7.5. Diagram to illustrate the style of blackboard summary for an anatomical comparison.

Criterion of	Upper Limb	Lower Limb
Contrasts		
1 Size	1	1
2 Strength	2	2
3 Dexterity	3	3
4 etc	4	4
Similarities		
1 No. of digits	1	
2 Joints	2	
3 etc	3	

Figure 7.6. Compare and contrast.....

(b) The thesis

If one regards a complex argument as the answer to a problem supported by a chain of reasoning, a lecture presenting a thesis is likely to be a combination of the chaining and problem-centered forms (Figure 7.7).

The thesis and comparison forms may be combined if both sides of an argument are considered. It should be noticed that arguments against a thesis may either consist of a counter thesis, or objections to statements made in favor of it (Figure 7.8).

When giving a thesis lecture one may move from one point to another along the links in either direction. If the thesis is an explanatory one, and this is quite usual, then movement is progressively from the raw data towards the thesis proposition that is claimed to explain it. If, on the other hand, one states the thesis proposition and then persistently questions the evidence for it, the broad movement of the lecture will be from the general to the particular.

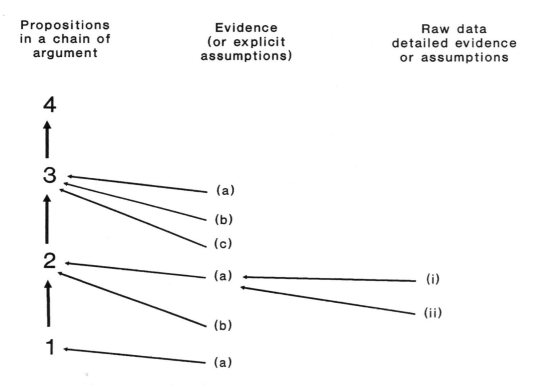

Figure 7.7. The form of a thesis lecture.
Proposition 4 represents the hypothesis, or solution to the lecture's central issue. If the thesis is being argued for, it is likely to be presented in the order 1, 2, 3, 4. If it is being questioned it is more likely to be presented in the order 4, 3, 2, 1.

In the first method one presents data that need to be explained; in the second one considers a hypothesis by progressively testing it in more detail with observed facts. In practice thesis lectures do not usually conform to either of these pure styles. The most common style is to select some of the observed data, present the thesis proposition as an explanation, and then fill in the intermediate steps of the argument with reference to raw data when appropriate. In effect the lecturer says 'These are the facts to be explained, this is the explanation, now how does that explanation fit the facts?'

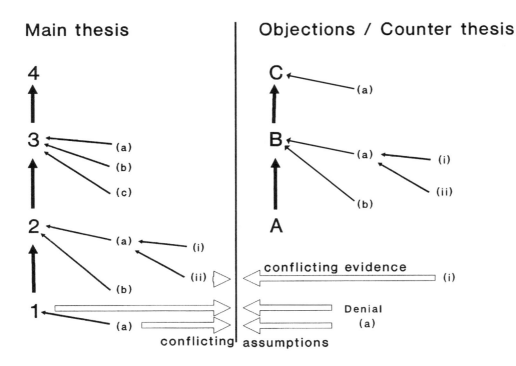

Figure 7.8. Diagram to illustrate the relationships between points in a thesis lecture including both sides of an argument.

Each number or letter represents a point made by the lecturer. As in Figure 7.7., the arrows represent lines of reasoning (inferences) towards the conclusion. Opposed arrows represent opposing points.

Each of these three approaches has its place but they are each appropriate for different objectives. Suppose a lecture is to be given on Darwin's theory of evolution. The first approach is suitable to arouse students' curiosity and motivation. The lecturer may ask rhetorically: 'How can we explain the fact that the birds on the Galapagos Islands show such extraordinary forms not found elsewhere in the world?' This is a question that Darwin himself must have asked. As the lecturer gives the observations and answers that Darwin made, he attempts to take the students through the same adventure of ideas that excited the scientific investigator. It seems probable that by helping the students to identify with the scientist they may become more appreciative of his difficulties, his methods of investigation and the historical perspective of the subject; but to my knowledge there are no studies to confirm or deny these possibilities. Nevertheless, if these objectives can be achieved by this approach, it is important.

If one asks different questions about the same subject matter, different patterns of thought will be required to answer them. Therefore it seems reasonable to suppose that the second approach will be appropriate to stimulate critical thinking in large lecture classes or in other situations where critical seminar discussion is not possible. If the lecturer presents Darwin's general conclusion, the principle of natural selection, asks 'Why should Darwin have thought that?', and then proceeds to criticize the theory with reference to observations, he may use precisely the same information, but achieve a very different result in his students. But again, I know of no controlled experimental evidence either way to verify that lecture organization affects the patterns of students' thought. One advantage of this approach is that widely scattered information may be related to the central thesis and in this way produce stimulating, original and broadening lectures. For example, a criticism of Darwin's theory could lead to a consideration of Mendelian laws of inheritance and modern genetics, so long as the overall organization is not unbalanced.

The third approach may be used to survey a theory without taking students through the rigor of its reasoning. It is used to present information about a point of view. The students are told what Darwin noticed and are given his explanation, but they are not led to appreciate the thoroughness of his observations, the scientific context of the theory, or subsequent modifications of it. There is no pressure on the lecturer or the students to consider the detail between Darwin's initial observations and the final production of his theory. Consequently, this approach is used by those with a crammed syllabus, but if the intermediate detail and reasoning are neglected, there comes a point when it ceases to be a thesis lecture. If the observations that produced a problem for Darwin are presented alongside his answer as a pair of facts, there is no challenge to the students' curiosity and no demand for them to follow a line of thought. Thus, although the third approach can be clearer than the other two because the students can see where the chain of reasoning is leading, there is a temptation to skip important links in the argument. If this is taken too far there ceases to be a thesis, and objectives involving students' thought and motivation are not achieved.

(c) The logical dichotomy

A particularly useful variation of the hierarchic form is the logical dichotomy. Its merit is that is may break down a complex subject without omissions. A social scientist may wish to discuss the 'advantages' and 'disadvantages' for 'men' and 'women' of recent legislation on welfare. In this case the 2 x 2 grid may make the subject clearer to permit students to concentrate on the subtleties of the law.

The complex increases and decreases in imports and exports during a period of economic change could be broken down in a similar way. In fact, it is a useful tip when teaching something that is inevitably difficult, to lighten the load by making the easy parts very easy.

The presentation of dichotomies as simple grids is obviously not possible when there are more than two of them, but they may be elaborated in other ways. Figure 7.10 shows an attempt to analyze some of the relations between body and mind for medical students with no previous background in philosophy. The visual presentation of this schema with an accompanying explanation produced better comprehension than the same information given only orally. It could have been represented diagrammatically in other ways as in Figure 7.11.

(d) The network
Some subject matter does not lend itself to tidy organization for lecture presentation. Each facet is linked with many others to produce a complex network of

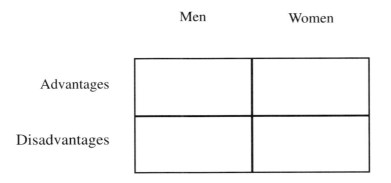

Figure 7.9. Visual display for the logical dichotomy

interrelationships. But because a lecture necessarily takes place in time, it has a linear form. Lecturers are therefore faced with a double task. First, in their preparation they must break their subject down into one of the simpler forms by selecting some links and neglecting others. Then, if it is important that all the links should be made, those that are at first neglected will need time to be established by going over the subject a second time with a different emphasis and possibly a different interpretation. For example, the complex network of interacting factors leading to the location of an industry could be classified by a geographer to form a hierarchic lecture in different ways emphasizing economic, historical or physical aspects. This is a fairly gross example, but the network problem arises within more specialized fields (Figure 7.12). As we have seen, the linear form of lectures and books was too great a restriction on what Wittgenstein wanted to say. This was partly why his lectures had an unusual form and why his book *Philosophical Investigations* consists of separate numbered sections which, each being connected with many others, do not fit into an ordered sequence without distortion of the overall network.

A lecturer in group dynamics was concerned with the question 'What is it that makes a number of people a 'group'?' He wished to consider factors which were so interrelated that they formed a network. You are invited to construct the pattern of relationships by completing the dashed lines (to form solid ones) where you consider that one factor will affect another. You are then invited to decide the order in which the factors should be introduced to a class of students. (It is appreciated that not all readers are experts in group dynamics, but most will have some knowledge - perhaps more than they realize!)

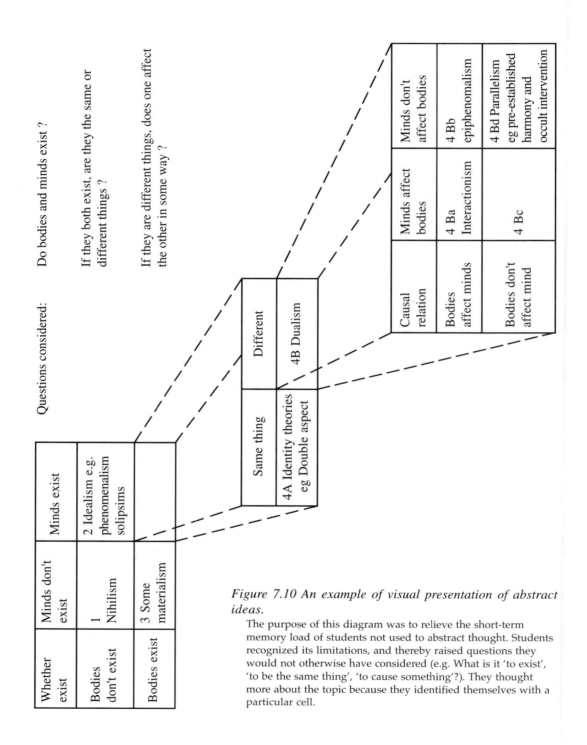

Questions considered:

Do bodies and minds exist ?

If they both exist, are they the same or different things ?

If they are different things, does one affect the other in some way ?

Whether exist	Minds don't exist	Minds exist
Bodies don't exist	1 Nihilism	2 Idealism e.g. phenomenalism solipsims
Bodies exist	3 Some materialism	

	Same thing	Different
	4A Identity theories eg Double aspect	4B Dualism

Causal relation	Minds affect bodies	Minds don't affect bodies
Bodies affect minds	4 Ba Interactionism	4 Bb epiphenomalism
Bodies don't affect mind	4 Bc	4 Bd Parallelism eg pre-established harmony and occult intervention

Figure 7.10 An example of visual presentation of abstract ideas.

The purpose of this diagram was to relieve the short-term memory load of students not used to abstract thought. Students recognized its limitations, and thereby raised questions they would not otherwise have considered (e.g. What is it 'to exist', 'to be the same thing', 'to cause something'?). They thought more about the topic because they identified themselves with a particular cell.

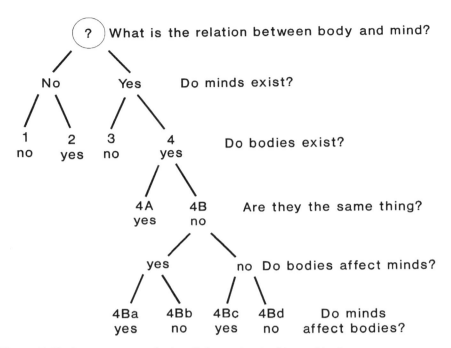

Figure 7.11. An attempt to depict dichotomies in hierarchic form.
Some students prefer this diagram to Figure 7.10, some the other way round, and others
prefer no visual representation at all.

Making the organization clear

It is not my purpose here to assert dogmatically that lecture organization must be made clear in particular ways. What follow are suggestions.

The importance of lecture organization and its connection with the understanding and overall view of the lecture topic has been mentioned in Chapter 4. Yet when Beighley (1954) changed the order of certain paragraphs in a lecture he found no significant difference in the students' retention of the information. Does this imply that the role of organization is over-stated? I think not. It is not simply a question of whether a lecture is organized in a certain way, but whether it is seen by the students to be organized. Beighley does not give this point sufficient weight. A lecture may seem to be well organized in the lecturer's notes, but have no apparent pattern when delivered. Ideally students should be able to state the intended organization, and how one fact is broadly related to the rest, at any time during the lecture. Firstly, because they need to take notes if the amount of information to be retained exceeds the amount they can remember, and secondly because Gage's study (1968) shows that these links are essential to understanding (see page 110).

Making the organization clear involves giving macro signals about it (sometimes called 'macro markers'). Chaudron and Richards (1986) found they result in better learning. Macro signals are of three kinds: those introducing the lecture; those indicating a move to the next key point; and those signaling the conclusion. Some of these are listed in Table 7.13.

In order to test the importance of organization, I once conducted an experiment comparing a lecture which made the organization clear, with a lecture using the

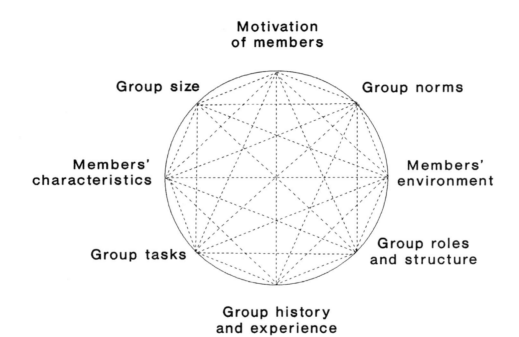

Figure 7.12. An example of a network

identical words except that certain signals were removed. There wasn't much difference in students' learning. But when I removed all indications of organization a glaze came over the students' eyes half way through and note taking ceased. Instinctively I used more non-verbals to maintain attention (thereby destroying experimental control). I then abandoned the experiment on moral grounds. Without links, the lecture simply fell apart. Morally I could not justify treating students in that way. However, what is pertinent is something I should have realized from the beginning.

Learning from lectures has a tendency towards being all or nothing. To a considerable extent, the key points either hang together or they don't. There are not so many positions in between points being organized and being randomly arranged.

Table 7.13. Common macro signals of lecture organization

Signal function	Signal words commonly used
Introductions	What I'm going to talk about is... OK... Right... All right... Last time... to begin with... Let us begin
New key point	The next thing is... another development was... as you may have heard... firstly... you can imagine what happened... the problem is... the surprising thing is... display on blackboard or screen.
Conclusions	To sum up... in conclusion... in this lecture... Where does this take us?... How does all this answer the question with which we began? Well... x, y and z in this lecture will lead us to consider the question Q next time.

Although we talk about degrees of understanding (and examination grades often assume a continuum) understanding is not like that. Understanding consists of relating ideas. That necessitates knowing something of both ends of the relation. The Gestalt psychologists got it right. Understanding involves grasping how the whole thing fits together (Chapter 4). As I said in Chapter 4, for the sentences in a lecture to have meaning, they have to relate to ideas the students already have. Organization of a lecture is all about relating. My students could compensate when I removed some relationships; but when I removed the lot, the whole lecture fell apart as a heap of random utterances.

1. Introductions - State the organization at the beginning
Therefore a lecture is likely to be more effective if its organization is given at the beginning. There are several ways of doing this. It can usually be done very naturally as an explanation of how the lecture's objectives are to be achieved. Most lecturers give the main headings of their lecture, rather like the sub-headings in a chapter of a book. Others outline its content.

Susan Thompson (1994) analyzed lecture introductions and concluded they usually have two functions: giving the framework of the lecture and setting its context.

Function:	Giving Framework	Setting context
	1. announce lecture topic,	5. show importance and relevance of topic
	2. outline the structure,	6. refer to earlier lectures
	3. indicate its scope and,	7. relate new topic to given material
	4. present lecturer's aims.	

Thompson made two pertinent observations: first that lecturers mix and muddle these functions. For example mentioning 1, 4, 6, 7, 4, 3, 5 in that order was typical. It might be better to follow the order in Table 7.14.

Second, although the majority of students in her survey thought introductions should include background information, they needed to learn how to link ideas using information about a lecture's structure and context. This deficiency needs to be tackled more by faculty as a whole at the beginning of a course, than by individual lectures within it.

Aims

1.   announce lecture topic
2.   present educational aims
3.   show importance of educational aims

Context

4.   show relevance of topic to aims
5.   refer to earlier lectures
6.   relate new topic to intellectual context and resources

Framework

7.   outline lecture structure
8.   indicate scope

Table 7.14. *A recommended sequence for lecture introductions.*

Some lecturers may feel that by summarizing all they intend to say at the beginning, they will have 'shot their bolt' and have nothing left with which to arouse interest when attention flags. In this case the overview needs to be given in a way that whets the appetite. The elaboration of points will require interesting details, visual illustration, humor and an occasional anecdote. Another technique, which is not exactly describing the lecture organization, is to outline the main ideas in the lecture.

A related technique is to give, what Ausubel (1968) calls, an 'advance organizer'. Advance organizers are maximally clear concepts at a higher level of abstraction, generality and inclusiveness than the material in the lecture they precede. They are concepts the audience already possesses which will link and integrate the material that follows. Their function is to bridge the gap between what the students know already and what they need to know. They provide a scaffolding. The difficulty with this technique is to find a concept that satisfies all these criteria. Evans (1996) found that the use of an advance organizer at the beginning of a short lecture improved students' recall strongly, but did not facilitate inferences.

2(a) For each new point - Itemize

Itemization has several advantages:

(i)   First, in the absence of an advance organizer, each item provides a peg on which detail may be hung. Detail is best remembered by association and the item provides this.

(ii)   Secondly, while it may be obvious to lecturers that they are going on to a fresh point, this is not so obvious to listeners, least of all students who are not already familiar with the topic.

(iii) Thirdly, if students day-dream, or have microsleeps, they may easily lose the thread of an argument. If points are itemized they will know they have lost a point, they may pick it up again more easily and they may fill it in with the help of another student later. Much as most people are unaware that they dream three or four times each night (Oswald, 1966) most students are probably unaware how much their minds wander during lectures (Bloom, 1953).

(iv)   Fourthly, itemization is an aid to memory. Revision from notes is more thorough if the students knows 'there are five points to be remembered on this topic and seven on the other.'

2(b) For each new point - use a visual build-up

The organization of itemized points will be clearer if they are displayed on a blackboard or screen immediately after being mentioned. This has a number of functions:

(i)   With most lecture forms numbering, insetting and underlining assist clarity by differentiating points and indicating their relative importance.

(ii)   Students are more likely to note what is written on the board partly because they believe it must be important if the lecturer has taken the trouble, and partly because they have time to write it when the lecturer stops his steady flow of words to do the same (Hartley and Cameron, 1967).

(iii) For these two reasons, the display is a valuable technique of emphasis.

Lecturers who are not confident of their ability on the blackboard are tempted to neglect it. One way over this difficulty is to use an overhead projector which may show either normal handwriting done at the time, or prepared acetate sheets which may be progressively displayed as the lecture develops. Alternatively, a handout containing the main headings well spaced, with blanks in between for the students to add supplementary detail, is useful; and since handouts may be passed on to absentees, they are particularly valuable at the beginning of a course or at other times when it is important to convey the organization of subject matter. Such displays of lecture organization (using the blackboard, overhead projector, handouts, or possibly other methods such as flannel graphs and charts) play a particularly important part in aiding comprehension when a 'network' or other complex form is used because the relations between possibly abstract ideas can be pointed out visually.

If using a blackboard, it is a useful convention to use one side for progressively building up the lecture organization as the lecture proceeds, and use the other side for more spontaneous and temporary illustration such as the spelling of new terms or names. The latter side may be rubbed out several times in a lecture, whilst the organization is permanently displayed and developed. A similar approach can be used with overhead projector transparencies where a lecture theater has two screens. If you only have one overhead projector, and are replacing the organization transparency to show others, make sure you place it separately, not in the pile of those you have finished with otherwise you will have to go hunting through that pile when you move to the next key point.

Using an overhead projector has some advantages over the traditional blackboard for presenting lecture organization. The organization can be progressively revealed or shown all at once. Not only is black on white perceived 15% quicker and copied with fewer errors (Seymour, 1937), but color is more pleasing against a white background and color coding can be used to contrast levels in a hierarchy. Transparencies provide a permanent record and continuity between one lecture and the next. The overlay facility allows both build-up and break down of complex diagrams (e.g. of anatomy or engine parts).

3. For conclusions, take stock and summarize

It has already been suggested that summaries of a whole lecture both at its beginning and end are often recommended (Clark and Clark, 1957; Henderson, 1970). The technique of 'taking stock' which consists of reviewing what has been said up to that time, is valuable for setting the next point in its context. It aids learning by showing how the parts are related to the whole.

New lecturers sometimes think that constant repetition is unnecessary and boring if students have already understood; but we have seen that it is for these students that repetition has value because it reduces the amount of later forgetting. Certainly the dictum "First tell 'em what you're gonna tell 'em. Then tell 'em, and then tell 'em what you've told 'em." can usefully be applied to lectures and is particularly appropriate to those who teach a difficult subject or who cannot easily get down to the students' level of understanding.

Conclusion: The importance of organization

I argued in Part 1 that the major objective of lectures should normally be the teaching of information and in Part 2 that students' memory of information is strongly affected by its organization. It follows that the organization of lecture information normally strongly affects the achievement of their major objective. Although there is obviously an infinite number of possible lecture forms, I have tried in this chapter to suggest suitable forms of organization for this objective, and I have tried to show that, even when the major objective is the promotion of thought or the arousal of interest, the appropriate form of organization must be chosen if lectures are to be effective. This in turn suggests the importance of thoughtful lecture preparation in which the organization is carefully related to the lecturer's objectives. Furthermore, in most cases it is not enough that information should be organized; it must be seen by the students to be organized.

8. Making a Point

Introduction.

'The general form'.
1. Concise statement.
2. Display.
3 Re-expression.
4. Elaboration.
5. Feedback.
6. Recapitulation and restatement.

Examples of other forms.
1. Explaining difficult points.
2. Proceeding at the pace of the class.
3. Motivators.
4. Definitions.

Aids to comprehend a point.
1. Chalkboard.
2. Overhead projector.
3. A warning about other visual images.
4. Verbal signals.
5. Non-verbal signals.
6. Other factors influencing comprehension of a point.

Conclusion.

Introduction

It is easy to think that there is no difficulty in making a point in a lecture, that the lecturer simply states it and then proceeds to the next. Such a lecturing style is unlikely to be effective. It would be too concentrated, too fast and few students would remember or note much of what was said, because important factors influencing memory, such as the roles of rehearsal, repetition and retroactive interference, would be ignored.

A 'point' here means a fact, generalization, principle or concept that is to be taught. It is an item of information. Because there is no uniformity between subjects, lecturers or their objectives, the term is necessarily vague. By saying the point is to be taught, it is assumed that the lecturer intends the student to remember it. It excludes asides and detail used for arousing interest. Knowledge of the point is assumed to be one of the objectives of the lecture. A list of the information objectives of a lecture will be a list of the points to be made.

Teaching a point in a lecture is quite different from making it on paper. Readers may go at their own pace and re-read if they do not understand. The lecture audience can do neither of these. They are committed to the speed of the lecturer and cannot return to a point unless the lecturer does. Thus the presentation of both the lecture as a whole, and each major point within it, requires organization to ease the students' understanding.

However, as with lecture organization, there is obviously no one way to teach a point. It will depend a great deal on its psychological nature (for example, whether it is easy or difficult, abstract or concrete, verbal or aural), the kind of students (for example, their ability, motivation, cooperation and familiarity with the subject) and many other variables. In an interesting experiment in the teaching of secondary school mathematics Trown (1970) found that extroverts learned better when an example was presented before a general rule was adduced (the 'inductive method'), while introverts preferred to be given the rule first and then an example of its application (the deductive method). At university level Horak and Horak (1982) found a similar difference between internal and external students respectively.

The technique known as the 'rule-e.g.-rule' procedure caters for both styles of thinking. As its name suggests, the teacher first states a key point, or 'rule'; elaborates it; and then repeats the 'rule' before moving on to the next point. This technique is known to be effective in programmed learning.

Contrary to common opinion the best way to teach a point will not greatly depend on whether the point is classified under chemistry, history, fine art or any other subject, except insofar as each subject tends to contain points of a particular psychological nature. The differences in teaching methods for chemistry and history are derived from their different psychological requirements, not from the philosophical considerations that define the subject. However, since some subjects have a predominance of one kind of psychological objective, the emphasis in teaching methods may be qualitatively different. Consequently the suggestions that follow are inevitably generalizations which readers may apply to their own particular circumstances.

The following procedure for making a point I shall call 'the general form' because it is based on the 'rule-e.g.-rule' pattern yet includes the most common techniques in the order in which they are most likely to be used; but it is not, of course, being suggested that every point a lecturer makes should conform to this pattern.

'The general form'

1. Concise statement

Usually the first requirement is to state the point in as concise a way as possible. This may be a simple sentence of seven or eight words with one key word or phrase in it, particularly if the point to be taught is a concept. If it is possible to avoid sentences with strings of modifying clauses, the point will be simpler and more easily remembered because it will have more meaning (Friedman and Johnson, 1968). As we saw from research on 'echoic memory', the key point should take less than 5 seconds to state, and preferably not more than two.

The preparation of a lecture with these simple sentences is not always easy. This is hardly surprising as some subjects cannot be made simple. The choice of key phrases is best made during preparation. It may be that the person who knows his subject but cannot teach it neglects this aspect of preparation.

Table 8.1. The general form is based on the 'rule-e.g.-rule' technique

Rule	1.	Concise statement
	2.	Display
	3.	Re-expression
E.g.	4.	Elaboration
		(a) Detail
		(b) Illustration
		(c) Reasons and explanations
		(d) Analogies
		(e) Asides
		(f) Relating
		(g) Examples
	5.	Feedback
Rule	6.	Recapitulation
	7.	Restatement

2. Display

The lecturer should then display the key word or phrase on the blackboard or screen as part of the progressive build-up of the lecture, (which is not to say that the blackboard should not be used at other times). The reasons for this in terms of reducing the load on short-term memory, the ease of students' note taking, the use of rehearsal, the clarity of organization, a method of selective emphasis, and its effect on timing and retroactive interference have already been mentioned. The display of points also facilitates visual memory which is preferred by some students and permits easy back reference by the teacher later in the same lecture.

If the lecturer then moves away, perhaps in the direction of his notes, without saying anything, students taking notes will be able to write it down without their view being blocked and their attention being divided. The lecturer will know when to go on, by looking at the class to see when they are ready. Hence, looking at the class is important at this stage.

3. Re-expression

If the point is then re-expressed another way the alternative words may have more meaning for those who have not understood, and repetition will aid the memory of those who have.

It is tempting to imagine that when students have understood a point, they understand it in the same way as the lecturer; but the lecturer has a wealth of background knowledge and experience to which the point is related. Understanding is a matter of degree, consequently re-expression frequently provides students with an opportunity to broaden it by relating the point to their background (Abercrombie, 1960).

4. Elaboration

When the point has been re-expressed - usually in an expanded, and less pithy form - some elaboration is usually necessary. This may take many forms.

(a) Detail

Able students may welcome more detail if they have a framework of concepts, or an advance organizer, to make it cohere and coherent. Less able students are less likely to have the framework and are less skilled at relating detail to it. When giving detail the lecturer must therefore observe the non-verbal reactions of less gifted students.

(b) Illustration

Others may want visual illustration. It is not always appreciated that, just as it is necessary to state a point in a number of different ways, it is sometimes necessary to illustrate it in different ways. These may be different ways of representing information such as statistical data, different pictures of the same object from various angles including various cross-sections, or different kinds of visual aid. Ideally two or three simple illustrations are better than one that is complex, but supposing the latter is necessary the lecturer should proceed from simple to complex aids and then back to the same simple ones again so that each can be related to every other. The role of visual teaching is sometimes undervalued by university lecturers who are selected on the basis of their verbal, rather than spatial, abilities in examinations or publications.

(c) Reasons and explanations

A third feature of the elaboration stage is giving reasons for, and explanations of, the point being made. This is so important that the next chapter is devoted to it; but logically that chapter fits in here. In most subjects reasons and explanations are an essential part of 'understanding'. They are vital if a college education is to consist of anything more than learning isolated facts.

Reasons require thought; therefore it is important to slow down one's speed of delivery. Because thought requires rehearsal without interference, this should be done, not by speaking each sentence slower, but by providing silent pauses at the end of each sentence. These pauses are important 'thinking times' for the student. Because reasoning and explaining require relating facts together and the student must therefore hold a number of ideas in mind at once, thinking is a more difficult task than holding one fact at a time in order to write it down as notes, particularly when the points being related are new. Morgan and Puglisi (1982) confirm that pauses at the end of sentences help to overcome this difficulty. Whilst at first they produced no improvement in recognizing verbatim sentences from a lecture, in a second experiment there were small but significant benefits from students' deep and elaborative thought about sentences with pauses, compared with sentences without such pauses.

It is important to look at the class to see if they have followed after each stage in a reasoning process. If lecturers wait until the end of a chain of reasoning before seeking feedback, and students have not been able to follow, they then have to find out which link in the chain is broken. They can only do this by going through the whole argument again, one link at a time, as they should have done in the first place. Sometimes students can prevent this repetition by saying what link in the chain they cannot follow and even why they cannot follow it. But this is less common than one is led to think, because students who can say this are usually among the more articulate. They have understood enough to know what they do not understand. Most students who do not understand an explanation cannot say why, and many, not wishing to reveal their ignorance, would not do so if they could. Indeed, in a survey of over a thousand college of education students, 60% said that the presence of a large number of people in the room would deter them from asking questions, even when invited (Stones, 1970).

(d) Analogies

Because Jesus taught using parables, for some people, teaching by analogy has good credentials. The first problem with analogies is that they usually impose an enormous mental load. Any student with a critical mind (and developing critical minds is the central aim of higher education) will want to check their validity by distinguishing similarities and differences between every element of the analogy and the target subject matter, and to check how far the elements relate together in the same way. The number of items of information manipulated in this process depends on how many elements there are; but it is not difficult to see that the number could be far larger than could be dealt with before the lecturer goes on to his next sentence. Thus analogies can leave students more confused than enlightened if the lecturer does not give time to check their validity.

The second limitation of analogies is that whilst they may explain, they do not justify. They attempt to match a structure of concepts, but they do not give reasons for believing the structure is what the lecturer claims it to be. Notwithstanding that they may help to *explain the reasons* for something, they nonetheless offer explanations, not reasons.

To overcome these limitations, Brown and Clement (1989) at the University of Massachusetts Scientific Reasoning Research Institute specify three explanatory factors: choosing a familiar concept for the analogy, explicit description of the analogical connections with what is to be explained, and engaging students actively in the process of analogical reasoning. They warn that presentation methods, such as texts or lectures, are less suitable than interactive methods for the last of these.

When analogies are successful they teach the structure of concepts precisely because it is those relations that the students have to check out. There is empirical evidence for this. Evans and Evans (1989) used post-tests to probe whether metaphors helped to assimilate, make concrete or structure concepts and found that students made general inferences that they could only have made by seeing how concepts relate. Using the analogy of a factory in a lecture on parts of a biological cell, Bean *et al*. (1990) found that students lectured with an accompanying pictorial study guide using the analogy, did better than those with the same study guide without the pictures. The advantage of pictures is that they can show multiple relationships. By relating distant concepts, one might think that frequent analogies over a long period would foster lateral thinking and creativity; but I know of no evidence for this.

Experimental support for using analogies is weak. For example, Bell (1983) combined lectures and role play using metaphors in one, both and neither. Although there was temporary evidence that metaphors improved retention of information, they had no effect upon its acquisition or wider application.

I conclude that the use of analogies in lectures is a risky technique. (I must leave the reader to judge how far the parables were valid and whether they purported to justify or to explain.)

(e) Asides

The use of asides is sometimes associated with a vague amorphous lecturing style. Indeed it might be thought that asides are, by definition, irrelevant and should not occur in a well organized lecture. Strodt-Lopez (1991) has shown this is not so.

Asides have many functions. They are not incidental, even though the lecturer might introduce them with, 'Incidentally...'! They can clarify, consolidate and evaluate. Asides can explain by linking ideas. A thorough understanding of a topic requires links between all its aspects. Owing to the sequential nature of a lecture, systematic lecture organizations inevitably break some of these links. Asides can reinstate them. In this way asides have an important role in creating the coherence of a topic. Asides in different parts of a lecture should often be explicitly linked. They can anticipate and refer back. All this is consistent with McAleese's finding that asides do not increase vagueness, even though the density of information (points and examples) in a lecture may be reduced.

Asides can also develop diverse perspectives on a subject and thereby bring it alive. They allow development of thoughts parallel to the main line of development. They can develop a personal view commenting on the basic information. Strodt-Lopez believes that when another person's theory is being expounded, this can maintain a professor's credibility. Clearly asides have a place in a well organized lecture.

However, whilst there is no reason why minor comments and asides should not be added into any part of the elaboration stage, if they are pertinent criticisms they will embed, or 'nest', as critical key points within other key points. Embedding of this kind is confusing to students. It is a particular danger in the thesis form (see page 77). It is clearer to deal with key points positively and then return to critical points and major qualifiers. In this way criticisms and reservations are presented at the same level as the points they criticize.

Similarly asides will confuse if they are not signaled both at their beginning and end. The entry signal is often a slight lowering of the voice or a straying from the lecturer's notes, rather than verbal. Indeed the words might not be very different from words that would occur in the main exposition. This can create problems for students if the lecturer does not take special care to give a clear signal. The exit signals (Table 8.5.) are often accompanied by a short increase in volume and pace, and the lecturer may re-enter the main line of the lecture by repeating the key point, or a key word or phrase from it.

(f) Relating

To put a point in its context, it is useful to relate it to general knowledge, other subjects, other parts of the same subject or what was said two weeks ago. Relating points encourages re-deployment of concepts and discernment in their use. Not only is relating ideas often what makes a lecture interesting, but some teachers claim that this is what they expect students to do in their final examinations. If it is one of the objectives of teaching a topic that students should be able to relate it to other branches of the discipline, it seems reasonable to expect the lecturer to demonstrate these relationships sometimes.

There are a number of ways of doing this. For example:
(i)   applying lecture information, preferably in interesting ways
(ii)   specifying the main issues and showing where opinions on one are likely to result in particular opinions on another
(iii)   posing questions
(iv)   making comparisons
(v)   formulating expectations
(vi)   evaluating
(vii)   drawing conclusions and
(viii) confronting failure.

(g) Examples

Where possible examples should be brief, familiar and in concrete terms. When an example is given the students have to match it with the major point that has previously been made. Consequently, they must hold the point in mind while the lecturer gives examples. This is not easy if they do not already understand it clearly, because, as short-term memory fades, increasing call is made on long-term memory. But we have seen that long-term memory depends much more upon meaning and therefore assumes the understanding that the example is intended to give. Thus, long examples can defeat their own purpose.

If the reader as a student has ever remembered examples from a lecture, but forgotten what they were examples of, it will be clear that holding the general point in one's mind is what proved to be too difficult. The lecturer must therefore employ strategies to avoid this forgetfulness in students. These strategies may consist of a visual aid to memory, writing more than key words on the board, or repeating the general point at the appropriate moment. Lecturers may need to analyze examples so that each element in it is matched explicitly. To take a simple example, if the general point involves 'levers', a 'fulcrum' and 'weights', and the example is a see-saw with two children on it, the lecturer would need to make it explicit that 'The children are the weights.....etc.' If the example is simple and brief, forgetting is less likely.

Let humor be natural, not forced. *Humorous examples* have an obvious merit, but the general point is sometimes lost in the laughter. Bryant *et al.* (1980) report that humor enhanced students' approval of male lecturers, but had the opposite effect with female lecturers except when their humor was at someone's expense! According to Vogel (1996) non-tendentious humor can relieve tension, increase interest, enhance memory, mask embarrassment and foster group cohesion when giving sex education to adolescents. Humor appears to make no difference to recall immediately after the lecture, but if it is relevant and related to the point being explained, it improves recall later (Javidi and Long, 1989; Downs *et al.*, 1988; Kaplan and Pascoe, 1977). Consequently, a pause to give time for the matching to take place, explicitly relating the example to the major point, or the provision of a further example, is usually advisable.

There is some merit in examples disclosing *personal experience*. Nelson (1989, 1992) found that, compared with hypothetical examples, personal examples improved students' attitude towards the teacher, increased their confidence and increased their recall of lecture material. She interprets these findings in terms of the dictum that increased personal certainty increases personal liking. There may be sex differences:- when a male professor used self disclosing examples on 15 minute tape-recorded lectures, McCarthy and Schmeck (1982) found men showed better recall and women rated the professor more attractive and trustworthy.

I find I can never think of good examples at the time of lecturing. They therefore have to be prepared in advance. In fact, it is quite a good idea to carry a small notebook and collect ideas and examples at all times.

5. Feedback

Feedback should be an important and continuous process throughout a lecture, and for this reason a special section is devoted to its techniques later; but it has a particularly important place after the elaboration. Lecturers need to know whether they have got their point across before going on to the next; firstly, because later points may depend upon it, and secondly, because the opportunities feedback provides for consolidation of relatively short-term memories by rehearsal cannot be taken later. Furthermore, if ascertaining whether an objective is achieved is so unimportant that one need not bother, one may ask whether the objective was worthwhile in the first place. If it is worthwhile but the lecturer fails, he must either make another attempt to achieve it, or assume that the students are capable of achieving on their own what they could not achieve with the lecturer's help. In the first instance, at least, the fresh attempt will be easier before the first explanation is forgotten.

6. Recapitulation and restatement

The recapitulation and restatement are not the same. They are placed together here because they occur in rapid succession as a kind of summing up and either may precede the other. The recapitulation is a reminder of examples, explanation and evidence. The restatement consists of repeating the same words that formed the key statement. It is often helpful at this stage if the same concise statement is used, not simply because the repetition consolidates its learning, but because, if a further re-expression is used, it has to be related in the students' minds to everything else that has been said on the point. A restatement of the same words requires recognition, rather than recall, by the student; and the former is easier. Furthermore, if the lecturer is too fast for the key statement to be fully noted when it is first uttered, and if it is not written on the board, many students wait for its precise restatement.

Examples of other forms

There are many variations on the General Form, some of which are appropriate for particular objectives.

1. Explaining difficult points

For example a lecturer may have to teach difficult concepts, or principles that are so unfamiliar to the class that the initial concise statement would be unintelligible. The use of the concise statement straight away assumes that the point can be made in language the students understand.

Table 8.2. Making a difficult point

Example	1.	Examples or illustrations
	2.	Observation of students
	3.	Careful analysis and reasoned interpretation of examples
Rule	4.	Concise statement of key point
	5.	Display (on blackboard or OHP screen)
	6.	Re-expression
Rule	7.	Recapitulation
Example	8.	Another example or application showing relevance
Rule	9.	Recapitulation
	10.	Restatement of key point

If this is not so, it may be appropriate to start with examples or illustrations, followed by observation of students. Then a slowly reasoned interpretation of the examples is given, before arriving at the concise statement, use of the board and the re-expression. Because students will not remember essential details of the examples and reasoning before they know what the lecturer is driving at, a recapitulation may be helpful. Another example or relation to other aspects of the subject is usually advisable when the topic is difficult, culminating in a recapitulation and restatement.

In effect these ten stages amount to an, e.g.-rule-rule-e.g.-rule, pattern in which the initial examples are an attempt to make the unfamiliar familiar before giving the concise point.

2. Proceeding at the pace of the class

In topics which require thought by the students as the lecturer proceeds, or where, as in a chaining lecture, it is important for the class to follow every stage namely, question, feedback, reasoning, concise statement, display, re-expression, recapitulation and restatement, it is useful to keep the class and lecturer together.

Table 8.3. Pacing a point

Example	1.	Question
	2.	Answer - Feedback
	3.	Reasoning
Rule	4.	Concise statement of key point
	5.	Display and observe gaze
	6.	Re-expression - observe note-taking
Rule	7.	Recapitulation and
	8.	Restatement of key point

This is achieved by using feedback so that the class appreciate the point just before it is concisely expressed. Without this prior understanding an 'eg-rule-rule' pattern of this kind in which there is no elaboration after the initial statement of the point would be unsatisfactory because factors affecting memory, such as rehearsal, meaningfulness and relation to the whole, are neglected. Repetition is used, but this, as we saw, depends on some prior learning.

3. Motivators.

To motivate is to change attitudes; and we have already seen that the lecture method is not very suitable for that. To motivate is a bit like selling. Every competent salesman knows that to get a sale, the product must satisfy a personal need. To do that, he must first ascertain what the customers perceive their needs to be. That requires consultation rather than speeches. (If feasible, to spend 5 minutes with every student individually at the beginning of a course, is a worth while investment if it can be used to find out what motivates them.) However, in the context of 'making a point', I shall assume that this is not possible.

Initial questions can arouse interest. For the reasons just mentioned, immediate feedback is desirable; but even rhetorical questions have some arousing effect. They need to be asked with enthusiasm.

The pattern thus produced may be questioning to arouse curiosity, reasoning or feedback to answer it, display of the key phrase, making a concise statement, re-expression, application or relation to other points to provide relevance, recapitulation, feedback to give personal contact and a sense of achievement, and finally restatement of the key point.

In the 'general form' the features which arouse motivation are found in the elaboration. These are here distributed to prevent the motivation level from falling and to eliminate longer periods in which the key phrase is dryly presented. Similarly, to present the display before the concise statement attracts attention if it is not always done that way.

Table 8.4 Motivation from a point

Example	1.	Arouse interest - questions for curiosity and personal relevance
	2.	Reasoning or feedback to answer
Rule	3.	Display
	4.	Concise statement of key point
	5.	Re-expression
Example	6.	Interrelate and apply the point to satisfy motives
Rule	7.	Recapitulation
Example	8.	Personal interaction - involvement, questions and feedback
Rule	9.	Restatement

4. Definitions.

Definitions are a specific kind of key point. You might think that because definitions need to be precisely worded, they cannot be reformulated using different words. Flowerdew (1991) has shown this is not so. Representative speech acts can be modified using pragmatic strategies, such as politeness and indirectness. Definitions can even be taught by what he calls 'external' modification using asides, rhetorical questions and eliciting questions.

Flowerdew (1992) found that, whilst there were big variations between topics and lecturers, definitions were given, on average, once every 1 minute 55 seconds in chemistry and biology lectures when English was students' second language. Definitions often cluster, but he found no evidence that they occur more at the beginning (though Bramki and Williams, 1984, say that they do).

Definitions have a number of specific forms. Using 'definition' a little loosely, Flowerdew says there are four kinds of definition: formal, semi-formal, substitution and ostension. Formal definitions commonly take the form: $A = B + C$, where B is a class and C is a characteristic or quality of some members of that class; eg A puppy is a dog that is young (Trimble 1985). This could be elaborated using the 'General form', but that is not always necessary. Semi formal definitions often consist of examples followed by 'these are called X'. That is a simple example-rule format. A combination of semi formal followed by formal, is quite effective. Substitutions are typically synonyms, paraphrases or derivations. Ostensive definitions consist of pointing, either physically with the use of visual aids, or by showing how a word is used.

Jackson and Bilton (1994) coded 921 definitions in 20 science lectures. Although 52% finished with a lecture signal and 12% with a comprehension check, 64% were introduced without a signal. (See Table 8.5.) Jackson and Bilton observed that 44% had the $A = B + C$ form. 8% had one or more reformulations of C in which D and E were substituted for it one after the other. And in 56% of the first formulations both B and C included technical terms. Reformulations, D and E, were less technical.

More worrying, 24% of the definitions observed involved embedded definitions within the definition. For example the definition of a geological 'conglomerate' included explanations of 'bonded' and 'finer sediments'. A definition is a relation of at least three concepts $(A = B + C)$. To hold two definitions in mind and substitute one in the other, is too big a load on most students' short term memories. Consequently the fall off in comprehension scores is dramatic (Bligh 1974).

As with all teaching, the art is to keep it as simple as possible.

Aids to comprehend a point.

From the students' point of view, one of the disadvantages of the lecture method is that words fleetingly come and go unless they are captured either in notes or in their long term memory. Chalkboards and overhead projectors reduce this difficulty by allowing a more extended presentation of what the lecturer chooses to display.

1. Chalkboard
(a) Advantages
The advantage of chalkboards is that they are widely available; they are cheap to maintain; and they are relatively easy to use. A lecturer can progressively build up a summary of a lecture by displaying its organization of key points on the left, whilst using the right side for temporarily illustrating aspects of their elaboration. In this way the lecturer's behavior signals for each key point the elements of rule-eg-rule, or what ever form is adopted. The temporary displays typically include simple diagrams and the spellings of unfamiliar words.
(b) Disadvantages
Unfortunately chalkboards are messy to use; once erased work cannot be easily re-presented, as for example a reminder of the organization of the previous lecture. Boards involve turning away from the audience, so that audience reactions are not so easily gauged. Compared with prepared transparencies on an overhead projector, writing is an extra task which can detract from thinking time and attention to the finer points of lecturing technique. On a blackboard the use of color is limited to white, yellow and the lightest shades of other colors. Dark blues, reds and browns are less visible, particularly in a large room.

For this reason a white board with felt pens, rather than chalk, is preferable. Furthermore perception against a white background is both quicker and more accurate (Seymour, 1937 and Snowberg, 1973). White boards can also have magnetic properties so that overhead transparencies, or other thin plastics, can be made to stick with static electricity by placing them on the board and simply rubbing briefly. Alternatively magnetic bars can be used to pin newsprint or other large sheets of paper for display. Magnetic rubber shapes are also available in several colors and can be slid around on the board to illustrate, for example, the journey taken by blood cells in the heart and lungs.

However, there is a danger. Dazzling presentations do not necessarily result in learning. The more technologies allow lecturers to illustrate concepts, or large amounts of information, in ways that students cannot record in their notes or immediately commit to long term memory, the less efficient lecturing becomes. It may be entertaining for the big occasion; but entertainment is a different objective from learning and educational development.

(c) Technique

Some tips may be useful for the new lecturer who has previously only written on paper. Writing on paper uses the wrist and fingers. When writing on a board the movement is more in the elbow and shoulder. To become accustomed to this and the vertical surface of a board, visit the lecture room when it is empty a day or two before your first lecture and practice making large sweeping lines. Notice where your feet need to be and how horizontals require you to move them. Do this before you attempt to write.

Writing gets worse with age; so set yourself high standards at the beginning. Use script, not cursive (joined) writing. Have in mind three horizontal lines: one under letters that do not have tails, another above lower case letters, and a third at the top of capitals and tall lower case letters such as 'l', 'h' and 'k'. Practice making letters o, e and c circular. What position do you need to take to write at the top of the board, and how well do you bend your knees when writing at the bottom?

Practice writing at the top of the board and at the bottom. Shoulder movements are difficult at the top. Writing with bent knees and back at the bottom can be tiring. If your line of writing goes up or down, you probably need to move your feet to a more comfortable position. If it goes up, you are probably too close to the board; if it goes down you are probably writing too far to one side of your body.

When you come to lecture, start with a clean board. Clean it systematically with downward strokes so that dust does not go everywhere; and do the next lecturer the courtesy of leaving your board clean when you finish.

If you are right handed, when you move away from the board, move to one side as if pivoting on your left foot, so that you obstruct no one's view. It is quite a good idea to step right away and look at what you have written from the students' point of view. Check your spelling! Just as when first learning to type, the keyboard can't spell; so beginners embarrassingly misspell words on the chalkboard that they would never misspell on paper.

2. Overhead projector

(a) Advantages

Overhead projectors (OHPs) are now widely available, if not standard equipment, in most lecture rooms. They have the advantage that transparencies (OHTs) can be prepared in advance. They can be written in color or smartly produced in black and white using wordprocessors. Heat copiers can produce OHTs of complex pictures or diagrams most lecturers would have neither time nor skill to draw. Although pens can be used for color shading, thin colored translucent film can be cut to shape and will adhere to an OHT by static electricity if smoothed into place. Similarly silhouettes can be obtained by superimposing paper shapes.

Overlaying OHTs allows a progressive build up of writing or images and can show spatial relationships of images that are best first shown separately (eg OHTs of mountain ranges and rainfall distribution; or blood supply and the nervous system).

Diagrams and other visual material can be more detailed and more accurate than most chalkboard work. OHTs can remind students what was said in the previous lecture when explaining a detail or reviewing the whole. In this way they can be important linking devices.

Unlike the chalkboard, they let the lecturer present written material and observe audience reaction. For this reason it is sometimes said that they permit eye contact to be maintained. For a sensitive lecturer this is not strictly true. The students' eye gaze goes past the lecturer to the screen behind.

(b) Disadvantages

Even experienced lecturers who rely on overhead projectors find it difficult to adapt what they have prepared when bulbs blow or there is a sudden malfunction. Some makes of OHP have a spare bulb inside and it is worth getting to know how they work.

Where the screen in not perpendicular to the projected light, rectangular images are portrayed as trapezia. This is known as keystoning. It may not matter much when writing is displayed (indeed, by moving the OHT, a line of small writing can usefully be magnified at the top of the screen) but obviously diagrams are distorted. The distortion can be corrected where the top of the screen can be moved closer to the projector. Some screens have this facility.

The facility to produce OHTs by photocopying tempts lecturers to display far too much written material, often with a print size that is too small and too indistinct. When projected on a screen, 32 characters per line is generally regarded as a maximum.

(c) Techniques

OHP pens are either water or spirit based. Water based pens have the advantage that errors can be quickly erased by a damp cloth or a lick on a paper handkerchief; but they may blotch when you put your sweaty hand on them during the lecture, and they don't survive well in hot and humid climates. To avoid blotching when writing with either type of pen, it is advisable to rest your hand on a piece of paper, not directly on the OHT. Spirit based writing is not easy to correct unless wiped clean at once.

To prevent errors it is a good idea to write what you want on paper at the desired size, and then place the paper under the OHT when you write. I use lined computer paper because the lines can guide lower case letters like 'e', 'a', 'u' etc; the height of 'l', 'h', 'k' etc; and the tails of 'y', 'g', 'p' and so on. Practice making the round parts of letters c, e, p, q, b, d etc as truly circular. It is worth practicing a letter 'e' so that the hole in the middle is not filled in. It should not be less than a quarter of an inch high. Not writing large enough is a very common error. Typing and book print are normally far too small.

Use black, blue, red or green. Yellows and orange do not project well. If you use browns and purple make sure the lines are thick or else they, too, will not be visible.

Check the equipment and focus before the lecture begins. When in focus most OHPs project fine concentric circles, but most people check with a transparency. Check that the size of the image just fits the screen. If the OHP has a fan blowing hot air, make sure it is not blowing at you, or else your mouth will quickly dry with uninspiring consequences. The fan can be a problem. Make sure there is a place where you put OHTs once you have used them. It is sometimes a good idea to have a different place for those you know you will show again later in the lecture. I usually manage to put them where the fan blows them out of sequence all over the floor so that I can never find the one I need to use again!

A very lucid technique (the progressive revelation technique) is to have one OHT showing the structure of the lecture with its headings, subheadings or key points. A sheet of paper is placed over the OHT and progressively withdrawn to display each heading or key point in turn as the lecturer reaches the 'display' stage in making a point.

I call the OHT showing the lecture structure, 'the continuo'. The lecturer returns to it over and over again as successive points are reached, interspersed with others dealing with aspects of the Elaboration. (Table 8.1).

In the same way that good chalkboard board technique involves using one side of the board to build up the structure of the lecture and the other side for ad hoc illustration, so there is a lot to commend using two OHPs with a screen in each of the corners behind the lecturer. One is for the continuo; the other for elaboration. This enables everything the lecturer says to be contextualized within the lecture's organization. Understanding the context is an important aspect of understanding the meaning of what is said.

3. A warning about other visual images

Notice that films, television, demonstrations and other moving images are as fleeting as the lecturer's spoken words. Unless an image is held still for two or more seconds there is likely to be an information overload (cp Baddeley's visuospatial sketch pad, see Chapter 4.) Slides or other still images illustrating the crucial steps are more memorable. For example, when demonstrating massage students will copy more accurately if the demonstrator stops still at several positions in the movement so that they register in the students' minds. Students can then move from one position to the next when they massage. Conceiving, remembering and copying a movement is much more difficult because, in effect, it is a very large number of images. The capacity of short term memory becomes overloaded.

Similarly, although the amount of information that can be conveyed visually in a short space of time is astonishing, visual overload by lecturers who show one colored slide after another in darkened rooms is extremely common. Carousels holding dozens of slides encourage this vice. A few well chosen slides, with an opportunity to take notes after each, is better. Ten slides an hour is, in most cases, enough. It may be a truism that visual aids are aids to making a point; but too often lecturers confuse them with the points themselves.

Furthermore, as Abercrombie (1960) showed in her classic work, students' interpretations of what they are shown are often varied and inaccurate. The presentation of slides and moving images need to be followed by perceptual checks in discussion. Lecturers cannot safely assume that their audience have seen what they see.

4. Verbal signals

It is no use giving a structured account of a point if the structure is not clear to the students. This clarity is achieved by lecture signals, or what are sometimes called

Table 8.5. Common verbal signals in lectures

Signal function	Signal words commonly used
Topic shifters	
	Today I'm going to talk about ... I will tackle this issue from three main perspectives ... Four main arguments have been proposed. I shall consider each in turn ... I'm now going to consider ...
Rule - Key point markers	
Emphasis	and most important ... a major development was... a compelling argument is... a significant factor was... considerable... maximum... great... very... unbelievably... in fact... naturally...
Itemizing	First,... firstly,... A...B...etc... next... the following... after that... in addition... lastly... and finally... turning now to my second main point ... that brings me to my second point ...
Re-expression	By this I mean... To put that another way... What I'm saying is... in effect this means...
e.g. - Elaborations - Relaters	
Detail	Let's consider this. If you think about that... Let's look at that. You see... Enlarging upon that...
Logical reasons	Therefore... we may conclude that... from this we see... it follows that... it can be seen that... the import of this... a corollary is... the significance of this is... logically... in principle... so... the reason why... this means that... if x then y.

Causal reasons	Consequently... as a result... the upshot was... the outcome was... it influenced... a factor was... because... then... that was how...
Temporal sequence	At the time... after that... eventually... in due course... for the moment... what happened was...
The same	Furthermore... also... similarly... in the same way... in addition... like... akin to... the equivalent... is tantamount to... comparable... by analogy... this amounts to...
Different	However, ... on the other hand... but... compared with... in contrast... unlike... as distinct from... the opposite of that... alternatively...
Examples	For example... as an illustration of this... for instance... applying that principle... in particular...
Entry to asides	By the way... Personally I think... This is connected with... I might add that... As I remarked earlier... As I shall mention in a minute... to digress for a moment...
Exit from asides	Any way... as I was saying... to continue... to get back to the main point... in any event... it's interesting that...
Feedback or 'Comprehension check'	OK? Is that clear? Is everybody with me?

Rule - Restatement

Recapitulation	To sum up... In conclusion... The point I'm making is... What this amounts to is...

Summarizers

	What I've been arguing in this lecture ... In this lecture I have ... Let me summarize what I've been saying. ...

'discourse markers'. These signals reduce ambiguity. For example, the reason for something could be a key point or it could be part of an explanation. Similarly a lecturer may itemize key points in the introduction, and may also itemize facts, reasons or causes in the detailed elaboration. Lecture signals can distinguish these contexts. The student who cannot distinguish a lecturer's key point from its detail, its context, the reasons for it, or particular examples of it, will have a poor understanding of the lecture and will be poorly equipped to exercise the powers of criticism and judgement that I hold to be the fundamental objectives of a higher education. It is customary to blame the student for such shortcomings, but the fault all too often lies with the lecturer who fails to adapt to the abilities of students.

This lays an obligation upon the lecturer to give lecture signals. Lecture signals are all those words phrases or sentences which mark out parts of a lecture as key points, restatements, definitions, examples, comparisons, lists, asides, corrections, reminders, cause/effects repetitions, summaries, inter-sentence links and so on (Wijasuriya 1971; Young and Fitzgerald 1982).

There are three levels of signals, (though some signals could be regarded as at different levels in different contexts). There are what DeCarrico and Nattinger (1988) call 'global' signals. In particular there are topic shifters used when changing from one topic to another and summarizers typically used at the end of a lecture, though they could be used at other times.

Secondly there are 'key point' signals indicating that a key point is being made. These occur at the beginning and end of the forms described earlier in this chapter. Typically they consist of itemization at the beginning of a point and a restatement at the end.

Thirdly there are 'micro' signals, or what DeCarrico and Nattinger call 'local signals'. They indicate different elements within the Rule-e.g.-Rule of the General Form or other forms.

DeCarrico and Nattinger list five 'local' signals occurring during the elaboration of a point: exemplifiers, relaters, evaluators, qualifiers and aside markers, but I think they underestimate the variety and subtlety of micro signals. However their classification (which was written for newly arrived foreign students) draws attention to a possible weakness in the way I have presented the 'General form'. It could be said that I underplay the role of criticisms, reservations, qualifiers and other evaluations of key points, reasons and explanations. Arguably minor qualifiers and asides can be introduced into elaborations at any stage, not just one, provided they do not become so lengthy as to distort the clarity of the key point being made.

Table 8.5 lists common signal words and phrases. There could be many more. Obviously signals are very much a matter of personal style. Signals under the headings Rule, e.g. and Rule can be related to Tables 8.1 to 8.4. For many lecturers the re-expression glides naturally into giving further details and renders signals unnatural. Most feedback is non-verbal. The important point is that signals must be recognized and understood by the students, particularly when they are trying to take notes.

DeCarrico and Nattinger (1988) recommend that foreign students should learn not only to recognize common lecture signals, but also learn expressions which commonly cause them confusion (eg 'as it were' and 'as X would have us believe'). They also remark that some expressions, such as 'Right', 'Now' and 'Well', confuse foreign students because they serve as pause fillers as well as signaling a new point or topic.

It is worth mentioning that there can be negative verbal signals, though their effect is more often on the listener's attitude to the speaker than reduced effectiveness in making a point. In the experiments by Sazar and Kassinove (1991a, 1991b) it was both. Profanities had a negative effect on the acquisition of content and on cooperation during the lecture. Cooperation after the lecture was not affected. The religiosity of the students made no difference.

So far in describing ways to make a point I have described different structures of explanations and the signals that indicate the elements structured. But there is far more to making a point than its structure.

5. Non-Verbal signals

I am concerned here with non-verbal influences upon the effectiveness of students' learning when a lecturer makes a point. I am not concerned with the lecturer's appearance, dress, posture, body type or other factors that might affect students' perceptions of him as a person.

It is clear that non-verbal communications affect verbal learning in a lecture, but it is not every movement that has an effect. When a lecturer (Hood, 1987) used whole-body movements either in or out of synchrony with what he was saying, it had no effect upon students' learning except some loss of credibility! On the other hand Coats and Smidchens (1966) compared two 10 minute lectures, one with no gestures, no direct eye contact, minimal vocal inflection and a lecturer who read his script albeit with good volume and diction; the other was a lecture delivered from memory with dynamic gestures, eye contact and vocal inflection. Scores on 10 multiple choice questions were significantly higher after the dynamic lecture.

What is not clear is how non-verbals influence verbal learning. Normal conversation takes place within a range of 2 to 15 feet. The tendency for audiences not to sit in the front few rows almost seems like a deliberate attempt to reject non-verbal signals. The difference in angle subtended on a student's retina in the middle of a lecture theater to communicate eye contact with him rather than a neighbor, must be so minute that one wonders that it is ever discernible.

Furthermore (i) some non-verbals, such scratching, rubbing eyes and other forms of self grooming ('adaptors'), have nothing to do with lecture content;

(ii) others which might 'regulate' conversation, such as eye signals that one has finished talking and expects a reply, are less appropriate in a lecture;

(iii) there are few gestures that directly substitute for words ('emblems') and those that do are more likely to be obscene than academic! and

(iv) the most informative are 'illustrators' in which behavior describes the lecture content in some way, for example a spiral motion when describing the double helix in biology. (Ekman and Friesen, 1969.)

In an attempt to study non-verbal signals Susan English (1985) analyzed video-recordings without using the audio track and listed changes in body position, gesture, facial expression and eye gaze. The audio track was then analyzed for verbal signals and the transcripts were used to identify the functions of the non-verbal cues. They reflect elements of the 'General Form'. When starting a new point, lecturers turned their body, looked down at their notes and changed their physical position. When comparing and contrasting they turned their heads and shifted their eye gaze with hand movements indicating first one and then the other. Emphasis was made by nodding the head, pointing a finger or a striking motion with the hand. Curiously, gestures when exemplifying included leaning on the lectern and turning palms upwards. Counting on the fingers indicated listing or sequencing, whilst standing behind the lectern to read notes was common when giving a restatement or summary.

(v) Probably the most important function of non-verbals is to communicate feelings ('Affect displays'). They are more powerful than words. If a lecturer says something pleasant in an unpleasant way, or says something unpleasant in a pleasant way, the way it is said is more influential on how it is perceived.

For ordinary conversation Argyle and Henderson (1985) have posited rules of intimacy, friendship and relationships at work. For example if one person moves closer, the other might compensate with less eye contact. Compared with conversations, what is unusual about lectures is the emotional distance between the lecturer and the audience. This is reinforced by the lecturer's status, the formal language used, age differences, expertise, the physical distance from the audience and a defensive position behind a lectern or other furniture. Yet students appreciate lecturers who can break down these emotional barriers. Moving in front of the lectern, using conversational language, engaging eye contact with individuals longer than a glance, and giving opportunities for audience participation are all ways to decrease emotional distance.

It is possible that gestures not only have emotional impact upon the audience directly, but indirectly through self stimulation of the lecturer. Using a 2 x 2 experimental design, Gauger (1951) compared lectures with and without gestures, and lectures in which the audience could both see and hear the lecturer with those in which he could only be heard. Learning was best from the lectures where gestures could be seen; but even when the gestures could not be seen, students' achievement scores were better than when the lecturer did not use them. Presumably gestures affected the speaker's dynamism - emphasis, inflection and pacing.

Although the study of non-verbals in lectures is in its infancy, it is clear that they have very varied effects. Gestures notoriously become mannerisms. Used naturally not self consciously, yet used and developed with discretion, they can increase a lecturer's impact.

6. Other factors affecting comprehension of a point

Comprehension is affected by linguistic factors such as sentence length, ambiguity, the amount of information in a sentence, the extent of redundancy, its predictability, and paralinguistic factors such as gesture and facial expression. Foreign students in particular have difficulty with non-linguistic factors such as speed, manner of delivery, interpretation of rhythm and stress, background noise and the lecturer's reliance upon non-verbal signals when students have their heads down writing notes. It is quite common for lecturers to speak slowly and simply to non-native speakers at first, but then to forget and speed up or use ungrammatical idioms. Such pressures upon foreign students prevent the construction of meaning and therefore prevent them building links between ideas - what is sometimes called 'deep', as opposed to 'surface', learning.

Comprehension is not a simple 1:1 correspondence between words and meanings. Lecturers seldom contextualize what they say, so students must impose their own context. This is difficult for students from cultural backgrounds different from that of the lecturer. Foreign students, for example, will be baffled by words like 'Dickensian' if they have no knowledge of Dickens, his characters and the nineteenth century cultures he described.

Ovaiza (1985) has drawn attention to the difficulties foreign students have with humor, figures of speech, idioms of a discipline, prepositional phrases (eg 'put up' for 'constructed') and the differences between written and spoken language. Conversely, Tiffin (1974) has shown that English people understand only 65% of the English spoken by Yoruba students from Nigeria.

Conclusion

The purpose of describing these forms and signals is to show:
(i)   that making a point in a lecture involves a number of elements that may need consideration during preparation;
(ii)   that the effectiveness of lectures may depend upon the way these elements are combined; and
(iii)   that the skills in combining them can be learned.

It is not intended to stultify all lecturing into a few forms or to inhibit those who have more natural gifts for exposition. The ways of making a point are not formulae to be rigidly applied. Lecturing requires interaction with the audience rather than a predetermined formula. Furthermore, the scientific study of teaching skills (as distinct from teaching methods) has scarcely begun. Yet, while a pragmatic approach may therefore be the best, it should nevertheless be well informed.

9. Reasons and Explanations

The importance of making links.

Reasons are explanations.
1.   Regulative explanations.
2.   Analytical explanations.
3.   Spatial explanations.
4.   Temporal explanations.
5.   Kinematic explanations.
6.   Causal explanations.
7.   Functional explanations.
8.   Mental - cognitive, value, moral and purposive explanations.

Conclusion.

Logically this chapter fits under the heading 'Reasons and Explanations' (Section 4(c) of the General Form) in Chapter 8. But I think its ideas will be clearer presented separately.

In attempting to explain explanations, it moves to a meta-level. Consequently it is the most difficult chapter to understand, and it is the most speculative and forward looking. It is also difficult to write in that the truth of my assertions are most likely to vary with the reader's academic discipline where a more prudent author would fear to tread.

In experimental studies of learning in lectures the factors associated with the greatest variations in students' scores are differences in subject matter. In other words differences in the information students need to know to answer the experimenter's tests, has more effect on the scores than anything else. It follows that the greatest gains in lecturing effectiveness will eventually be obtained from analysis of processes entailed when learning specific items of information.

We might think of information as difficult to learn when it involves a large number of brain cells and relatively few pathways to activate them. When information is familiar, there are well established pathways. Complex ideas are partly acquired by establishing linking pathways between more simple ones. Learning is a process of linking information. The analysis of the best ways to learn information will be a matter of identifying the links.

The importance of making links

It must be frankly admitted that there have been relatively few experimental studies of the most effective way to explain individual points. It has been assumed, no doubt rightly, that it will vary with the point in question, the students' background and variables previously mentioned. But firstly, even these are assumptions that have not been well tested, and secondly, if they are correct, this fact need not preclude experiment to establish principles of lecturing technique any more than in other disciplines which study interacting variables.

The most thorough experimental studies of micro-teaching techniques in lectures are those conducted by Gage (1968) and his associates at Stanford University, but the students used were sixteen-year-old pupils in high schools and the degree to which the results of such findings can be transferred is always a matter of opinion until further studies are conducted. In their first experiment Fortune, Gage and Shutes (1968) used forty lectures, sixty pupils and twenty topics, each based on a 'Report' from the journal 'Atlantic'. The lecturettes lasted 15 minutes and were tested by a ten-item comprehension test. When the test scores were adjusted for the ability of the pupils and the relative difficulty of the topics it was found that the lecturers were individually consistent in their ability to explain the same topic to different groups on different occasions, but they were not consistent in their ability to teach different topics. Pupils' ratings of the 'clarity of presentation' correlated with the lecturers' effectiveness as measured by the test scores. Rosenshine (1968) confirmed that there are consistent and detectable differences in the explaining ability of lecturers. The fact that some lecturers are better than others renders it likely that there are at least some lecturing skills that can be learned. (I concede that inheritance and early experience can have a powerful influence on later intellectual, particularly verbal, abilities.)

The task remained to find out what these skills are. Since Gage and Unruh (1967) had demonstrated a high correlation between the estimates of lecture effectiveness by visiting judges and their objective effectiveness as measured by multiple-choice comprehension tests, Gage (1968) concluded that these important lecture skills are at least observable.

Rosenshine (1968) then set to work to find 'the cognitive and stylistic correlates of lecture effectiveness'. From the forty lectures on 'Yugoslavia', he selected at random five of the ten most effective and five of the ten least effective and subjected the transcripts to content analysis by groups of independent judges who scored them on a host of variables. These included the average length of a sentence, the use of sentence fragments, the number of prepositional phrases per sentence, self references, aspects of syntax, instructional set, techniques of familiarizing the class with new concepts, the use of previous knowledge, the use of learning sets, devices for focusing attention, organization, emphasis, repetition, redundancy of language, the speed of talking and so on. The factors that discriminated between the five effective and five ineffective lectures were then cross validated on the remaining effective and ineffective lectures. The factors that survived this cross validation were then tried out on the best and worst lectures on 'Thailand'.

The two factors that survived this double screening process were what Rosenshine calls 'explaining links' and the degree to which lecturers used the rule-eg-rule technique. The latter was dealt with in the last chapter. It should not, of course, be thought that the other factors mentioned above are not important. The fact that they did not survive the double screening procedure shows only that they are not important for all lecturers, in all subjects and for all students.

By observing 'explaining links' Kozoil (1986) analyzed what he called the 'Kinetic Structure' of communications by assessing its continuity and progression of ideas. He said the structure of a lecture can be measure by coefficients of conceptual commonality, progression, new activity and related activity. The mathemetics lectures he observed scored lower on all these coefficients than biology lectures. The more example problems a mathematics lecturer presented, the lower were the commonality and related activity coefficients.

The importance of 'explaining links' is confirmed by Johnson P. E. (1967) who has shown that the ease with which students associate concepts in Newtonian mechanics is proportional to the frequency with which the words are mentioned, multiplied by the number of ways they are linked together when presented.

It is also confirmed by the fact that experts represent more, and different, links in their minds than novices (Van Patten et al, 1986). This is most easily demonstrated in chess, but it also applies to academic disciplines. Expert chess players conceive of sequences and abstract patterns of moves, whilst novices consider only one or two moves at a time.

Reasons as explanations

We have already seen that understanding is enhanced by 'explaining links'. Indeed understanding consists of relating ideas to ideas we already possess.

The question now is 'how should lecturers build up explaining links?' In most cases there will be no problem. The points lecturers want to teach are in a certain context in their minds. They know what that context is. The course, or the organization of the particular lecture, can usually be prepared so that students know that context. If so, when lecturers make a point, students will see the connection. They will make the links for themselves. The art of teaching is to help students make links.

Difficulties arise either when students don't know the context, or when they don't make the connection, because the context is not uppermost in their minds, even though they know it.

In either case the lecturer's strategy will be to try to sketch in the context and to show the links he makes. Lecturers cannot make links for the students. That is something that has to go on in their heads. All lecturers can do is to show what is in common between the context that explains and the point to be understood. It is a bit like the prosecution's case in a criminal court. When explaining the guilt of the accused, the prosecution must present the context of an offense and try to link it to the defendant. The job of the defense (and of negative academic criticism) is to show that the links are not made.

At this point it looks as if this book cannot help much further. Lecturers' problems lie in their subject matter of which I have no knowledge. But it is worth drawing attention to different types of explanation. There are at least eleven different kinds. They tend to have different contexts. Knowledge of these types may help lecturers in their hunt for gaps in students' knowledge and their failure to make links.

To explain a fact or some other proposition, it normally needs to be linked to at least two other facts or propositions. Only one, and possibly none, will be of the same kind as the fact being explained. Figure 9.1 shows what the other kinds frequently are for each kind of explanation.

In practice we often only give one fact or proposition as a reason. We assume the listener knows the other; to give it seems like insulting the listener's intelligence. It may be; but too often when lecturing we commit the opposite crime. We assume that everyone knows things that some don't. It is usually better to remind an audience of what you think they know than to try to link new ideas to ignorance. Links with ignorance are not links at all. Most people don't mind being told a few things they know already. It's encouraging; and lectures would be far too intensive if they weren't.

1. Regulative explanations

Regulative explanations implicitly, if not explicitly, involve a general rule, an instance of that rule, and the application of the rule to that instance. For example:

	Most employees pay tax	(A general rule)
	Smith is an employee	(An instance/example of an employee)
Therefore	Smith probably pays tax	(Application of the general rule)

To show that an instance is indeed an example of a general rule involves showing the elements or patterns of concepts in common between the instance and the rule. In this example it would involve showing that Smith has the defining characteristics of an employee.

When lecturers get feedback that students have not understood the conclusion, there are four possible causes, and they must check out all four: Students may not
(i)   accept or understand the general rule;
(ii)   accept or understand that Smith is an employee;
(iii)   accept or understand that Smith being an employee is an instance of the general rule; or
(iv)   be able to reason applying the rule to the instance in order to draw the conclusion.

It is a common error to assume that the students' difficulty lies in one of these four when it lies in another. In that case lecturers' further attempts at explaining will be ineffective and may create feelings of frustration in both the lecturer and the students. Repeated frustration leads to anger and despair.

It could be argued that every explanation is regulative in one sense, because explaining links are made according to rules - normally some kind of logic. There are some disciplines, notably mathematics, linguistics, law and logic itself, which study logical and stipulative rules as well as applying them. Most disciplines try to establish empirical generalizations which may then be applied in further study.

Explanatory types
and their supporting premises

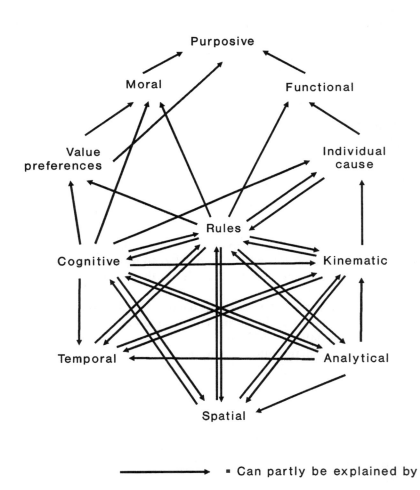

Purposive

Moral

Functional

Value
preferences

Individual
cause

Rules

Cognitive

Kinematic

Temporal

Analytical

Spatial

⟶ ▪ Can partly be explained by

Figure 9.1. The arrows point in the direction of the kind of statement that is frequently explained by statements of the kind whence the arrows came. For example, to explain my purpose in going to a drugstore, I may say I want (value) what I'm going to buy; and it is the function of the store to sell it. (See Bligh 1997)

Generalizations are often best explained by saying how they were established - the facts and the reasoning that related them to form a generalization. Stipulative rules are best explained by saying who stipulated them, their context and why. For example new laws are usually stipulated in a social context.

Another strategy when students have difficulty in understanding regulative explanations is to break down the reasoning into small steps. Each of these steps will also be the application of a rule. This is particularly relevant to mathematical subjects including physics and engineering. When students cannot see how one line of a calculation is derived from another it is not only necessary to set out the intermediate steps, but to write words such as, 'Substituting x-y, in equation E we get:- ... ', which explain those steps in more detail.

2. Analytical explanations

An analytical explanation explains something in terms of its constituent parts. By drawing attention to the constituent parts of something, it shows how they fit together. Indeed, in the last paragraph where I advised breaking reasoning into smaller steps, I was recommending using an analytical explanation to explain a reasoning process. The use of one explanatory type to elucidate another is quite common. Regulative and analytical explanations are fundamental. So they often seem to be elements in other kinds of explanation.

Analytical explanations say that X, Y and Z are different, and together they make W. The emphasis appears to be on the differences between X, Y and Z. What is not so obvious, but which can be important when clarifying analytical explanations, is that X, Y and Z are normally distinguished upon one or more dimensions they have in common and which makes them part of W. For example, if the human skeleton is analyzed into its constituent bones, despite the differences that distinguish them, the bones have characteristics in common. For example, they are made of similar material, have physical similarities, occupy space and normally have certain spatial relationships to each other. They may be regarded as having in common that they occupy a spatial dimension; and if so, it is upon that dimension that they are distinguished. Likewise the blood may be analyzed into red and white cells, plasma, etc. according to their different functions. In doing so, the analysis recognizes that they each have functions. They have a functional dimension.

Subject matter can often be analyzed various ways using different dimensions. Compared with its spatial analysis, the skeleton might be analyzed, and its parts classified, quite differently according to the functions of the bones (e.g. protection, support, mobility, etc). In this case they will be classified on a functional dimension (most bones being in several categories). We saw something similar with 'compare and contrast' lecture forms in Chapter 7. That's not surprising. To compare and contrast requires an analytical method. See Figures 7.5 and 7.6.

Figure 9.2 The role of dimensions in analysis.

Dimension	Civil cases	Criminal cases
Who brings the case Aiming to establish The court "imposes" Redress is called	An individual "sues" Loss "Awards" Compensation	The state prosecutes[*] Blame not consequences "Sentences" Punishment

* Private prosecutions are rare.

A common difficulty with analytical explanations occurs when students either cannot see that the whole is made of the constituents, or cannot see how the constituent parts fit together to make the whole. Both these difficulties can be overcome if the lecturer recognizes and can represent the dimension on which the parts are distinguished. For example, when analyzing the differences between civil and criminal law, it is not enough to present the two right hand columns in Figure 9.2. Give also, the first column, the dimensions in common upon which they are distinguished. State the dimension first; then distinguish the parts. It is a matter of asking oneself, 'What do X, Y and Z have in common?' and 'What is the conceptual knife that is used to distinguish them as constituent parts of the whole?'. In the example in Figure 9.2 the law is divided into Civil and Criminal cases. Each case is brought by someone, aiming to prove something, hoping the court will impose some redress.

3. Spatial explanations

Obviously visual aids can be used to explain spatial concepts. Leave some silence immediately after displaying them; otherwise you divide the students' attention. Spatial explanations give understanding by relating distances or by fitting certain shapes, patterns or structures together. They are common in chemistry, geography, astronomy, biology, architecture and many other disciplines. How do you apprehend that, of all possible shapes, a sphere has the maximum volume for the minimum surface area? No doubt you might prove it using mathematical rules, but originally you probably realized it intuitively when seeing a bubble or some other spatial image. Your understanding initially, and probably even now, was spatial. Lecturers in biology rely on intuitions about shape to explain optimum exchanges of heat, liquids or gases through membranes. Chemists not only imagine molecular and crystal forms, they represent the periodic table spatially, with regard to the number of electrons in an atom, for ease of understanding.

Figures in Chapter 7 illustrate how spatial representations can be used to explain relationships that are not, themselves, spatial. This is a significant point for lecturers. Most faculty partly owe their success to their verbal fluency. Students, too, are commonly selected on the basis of their verbal performance in examinations, but some may be more talented spatially; so it is worth lecturers thinking how they could represent their material spatially.

4. Temporal explanations

Temporal explanations are a good example of explanations that can be represented spatially. Use visuals to describe temporal relations. They give understanding by temporal comparison of states of affairs or events on a time dimension. Because time is linear, when temporal explanations are difficult, they can be represented visually. For example it is difficult for students to appreciate the enormity of the relative lengths of geological periods without some kind of visual aid.

Temporal explanations also have a logic that can benefit from visual representation. It is not always so simple as A precedes B, and B precedes C, therefore A precedes C. The anthropologist or historian reporting research using radio carbon dating, documentary evidence, and so on, each with margins of error, may need to take the audience through quite complex arguments about probabilities.

5. Kinematic explanations

When perceptions best fit together by assuming that an object or objects have moved from one place to another over time, the explanation is kinematic. No cause of the movement is given. For example Wegener's Theory of Continental Drift said that continents had drifted apart, but it was 40 years before Tectonic Plate Theory suggested possible forces to cause the movement.
Paradoxically, if you want to teach someone how something moves, use two or more still images, not moving ones. For example, use slides, not film or TV. If you teach massage or some other manual skill, show where the hands start, where they should finish, and one or two positions in between before demonstrating the movement in full. Moving images are usually too quick and present too much information to remember or copy.

Kinematic explanations require the lecturer to describe and match the circumstances before and after the move. In Wegener's case this meant matching the shapes of the continents and their geological formations. Similarly astronomers make intermittent observations of comets and other stellar objects. Some comets are said to come, go and return many years later. But the only justification for explaining the later appearances as being the same comet that appeared many years before, is to match its characteristics on the two (or more) occasions.

If students don't understand or accept that an object has moved, all the lecturer can do to show that the object, before and after, is the same object, is to match its characteristics on the two occasions ever more closely. Ultimately it is the student's mind that must make the link one way or the other.

6. Causal explanations

Speaking loosely, a cause is a distribution of forces or objects at one point in time, such that it is followed by another distribution. The first distribution and its attendant forces is the cause; the second is its effect.

As with kinematic explanations, the lecturers need to describe the before and after circumstances, but with causal explanations, the forces at work must also be given. These may be psychological (motivations) or physical.

In practice, forces are quite difficult to specify. Consequently causal explanations are much rarer than many people suppose. For example, when explaining the content of a blood sample someone may say, 'The liver purifies the blood'; but that doesn't explain how it does it. Even explanations in scientific journals purporting to be causal, are often functional.

7. Functional explanations

Most functional explanations describe what something or somebody regularly does in certain circumstances with certain effects. They are usually generalizations about the circumstances, the something (an agent) and the effects. Being generalizations they are often supported by statistics.

Functional explanations are very common, particularly in the social and biological sciences. 'The liver purifies the blood' describes its function. The Theory of Evolution largely deals with the functions of organs and organisms. An economist might describe functional relationships between prices and demand. There is an implied cause; but functional explanations give generalizations about effects, not causes. In fact the precise causes of functional relationships are usually unknown. Furthermore not all functional relationships are based upon causes. Most philosophers argue that the functions of language, including expressions in mathematics, operate according to rules rather than causes. The relations described are more like correlations than causes; more like correspondences than consequences.

A common error in subjects like economics and engineering, is to present the functions only in mathematical form and not in words. Try as many ways as possible.

The lecturer's job is to describe the circumstances, agent and effects selecting what is pertinent. Where they are generalizations from repeated observations, selection is necessary; but of course a selective presentation of facts permits bias and distortion.

The fact that the causes of functional relationships are often unknown might make some lecturers feel vulnerable to students' questions; but students accept that not everything is known and that their lecturers don't know everything even in their own subject. There is no harm in admitting it.

8. Mental - Cognitive, Value, Moral and Purposive explanations

Mental explanation is a general name for explanations where what is explained are phenomena obtained by awareness of one's own mind. The method is very common in the study of literature, history, social work and other applied studies of human behavior. The method is self awareness - introspection. They are subjective explanations. Phenomena include cognitions, value preferences, morals and purposes. Mental explanations include each of these explanatory types.

Cognitive explanations show the compatibility of information from awareness of one's own memories, knowledge/beliefs, sensations, perceptions, reasons, thoughts, or other cognitive experiences.

Values, moral and intentions have an emotive component. They are normally explained and justified by a fact of another kind plus a more general value, moral principle or purpose. When giving these explanations lecturers need to give both. It is extremely common, particularly in debate, to give only facts and to assume that the values, moral principles or general intentions are agreed. Both need to be explicit.

Because of their introspective nature, mental explanations require some empathy from the lecturer's audience. Empathy is an attitude. It cannot be injected or presented by the lecturer. The lecturer can only appeal to the better nature of the audience.

Conclusion

The study of explanations is in its infancy though it may grow rapidly with development in artificial intelligence. Effective explanations link what is to be explained to two or more ideas already in the students' minds. If these two ideas are not already in the students' minds, they too will need to be explained. If so, at least one of them will need an explanation of a different type. Figure 9.1 shows what the different type is likely to be.

When students don't understand there are two strategies worth adopting. One is to ask, 'What does my audience already know about this topic and how can I use that as a starting point?' The other is to anticipate likely points of difficulty and to work out the premises (explaining links) in greater detail for these trouble spots.

If, when giving the lecture, you notice that some points seem difficult to understand, mark them on your notes. Afterwards work out how they could be better explained by analyzing links and assumptions in your own understanding. If possible try to remember how and why you understood the point when you first met it or thought of it. Then expand your lecture notes accordingly so that your explanation will be more lucid next time. Don't wait until then. Work out how the explanation could have been better while the topic and lecturing experience are fresh in your mind. That is quicker in the long run. Furthermore, if this is done straight away, it may be possible to correct misunderstandings at the beginning of the next lecture.

10. Note-taking in Lectures

The reasons for taking notes.
1. To aid memory during the lecture.
2. To aid revision.
3. To see the developing structures of a topic.
4. To relate and organize during further study.
5. To select what is important.
6. To know what has to be learned.
7. To maintain attention.
8. To provide evidence of attendance.

Helping students to take notes
1. Advice to lecturers
2. Advice to give students
3. Teaching note-taking skills

Conclusion

The reasons for taking notes

As I said in Chapter 4, Figure 4.2 represents students' brains as essentially dynamic - in spite of what teachers might believe. They are information processors. One process stimulates another, or at least may do so. Although there are probably more feedback loops than are depicted here, the arrows represent which processes may stimulate which others. Thus they also depict chronological sequences.

In view of the complexity of these brain processes, lecturers might ask 'Should students take notes in my lectures and if so, how can I help them do so?' The answer to the first question depends on what they are taking notes for. There could be many reasons, as considered in Figure 10.1

Students could take notes (A) to help them during the lecture or (B) for later use. These are sometimes described as (A) encoding and (B) storage. In either case note-taking might be helpful (i) to aid memory, (ii) to understand the organization and structure of the topic, (iii) to identify what information is important, or (iv) to ensure that attention has been paid to what has been said. On this analysis there are eight possible reasons as shown in Figure 10.1. The overwhelming majority of students rightly believe that lecturers expect them to take notes (Hartley and Davies, 1978; Davy and Dunkel, 1989). Lecturers who don't, cite alternative sources of information as their reason (Isaacs, 1994).

The question now is what evidence is there to recommend note-taking for each of these purposes?

Figure 10.1 Why take notes?

	A.	To help encoding during the lecture	B.	Storage for later use
(i) **Memory**	1.	Aids to memory	2	Revision
(ii) **Understanding a topic** **and its structure**	3.	See the development of a topic	4.	Reorganize, relate and study topics
(iii) **Content**	5.	Select what is important	6.	Know the syllabus covered
(iv) **Attention**	7.	Concentrate	8.	Evidence of attendance

1. To aid memory during the lecture

Note-taking aids memory. It fosters encoding, articulation and rehearsal. There have been a very large number of studies to investigate whether note-taking assists memory of lecture content during the lecture itself. In a typical experiment of this kind half a class takes notes, whilst the other half is instructed not to do so. To control for individual differences, on another occasion note-takers and non-note-takers are reversed. Tests on memory of the lecture content are given immediately after both lectures, or after a specified delay, and results for note-taking and non-note-taking are compared. These experiments have been criticized on the grounds that their circumstances are unnatural, the lectures are often unusually short, students are sometimes told of the tests in advance, the quantity, efficiency and style of notes varies with the type of test anticipated, the topics are not always relevant to their courses and individual differences are seldom considered (Trueman and Hartley, 1978; Carrier and Titus, 1981).

Nevertheless the evidence is overwhelming that note-taking during a lecture does aid memory of the lecture. Indeed Ladas (1980) has cogently argued that experiments, and tabular summaries of them, such as in Table 10.2, underestimate the significance of findings. Furthermore several studies using correlations report that the probability of remembering facts noted is significantly higher than those not noted (Howe, 1970b; Aiken, 1975; Thomas *et al.*, 1975; Fisher and Harris, 1973 and 1974a; Crawford, 1925; and Einstein *et al.*, 1985).

Some personality factors interact with these results. For example students with high capacity short-term memories are better able to take notes and consequently perform better on follow up tests (Berliner, 1969), but it does not follow from this that less able students should only listen (Catts, 1987). Dogmatism and intolerance of ambiguity hamper performance on recall tests, perhaps because students with these traits are less able to link facts. These students do better when lectures are explicitly thematic (Di Vesta and Gray, 1972 and 1973) or when ideas are explicitly associated in other ways. Surprisingly, on the other hand Lacroix (1987) found no connection between students' cognitive style (environmental dependence/independence) and the number of words or information units noted, the efficiency of their notes, their use of chalkboard information or their scores on immediate and delayed tests of learning.

Table 10.2. Does Note-taking aid memory?

Twenty-nine studies favoring note-taking as an aid to memory.

Aiken et al 1975	N-t in interval between 4 minute lecture segments vs. no n-t.
Baker et al 1974	One study, test of concepts.
Baker & Lombardi 1985	Information in notes related to test performance.
Bentley and Blount 1980	Immediate recall of information.
Berliner 1969, 1971, 1972	Immediate and one week delayed matched tests.
Brobst 1996	Free recall
Crawford 1925	Two studies . Immediate and a few days delayed recall in essays and quiz.
Di Vesta and Gray 1972	Free recall and MCQ.
Di Vesta and Gray 1973	Two studies. Free recall and True-False tests.
Einstein et al 1985	N-t remember more important facts. Non-n-t less discriminating.
Fisher and Harris 1973	Objective test and free recall. They also correlate with note quality.
Hult et al 1984	Immediate test of encoding related to information units noted.
Jones 1923	Immediate and delayed recall up to 8 weeks.
Locke 1977	N-t of lecture information not on blackboard correlates with grades.
Maqsud 1980	Immediate and long term free recall.
McHenry 1969	Four studies. True-false and MCQ comprehension tests.
Peper and Mayer 1978	N-t increases attention
Peper and Mayer 1986	Two studies. N-t increases deeper learning.
	N-t better for applying principles; non-n-t for reproduction.

Peters and Harris 1970	MCQ after a tape-recorded presentation.
Poppleton and Austwick 1964	Higher test scores for students with lengthy notes
Stewart 1989	Simple immediate recall.
Thomas 1972	Serial position of recalled material.
Trueman & Hartley 1978	Correlation between n-t and men's exams. Women inconsistent.
Weiland and Kingsbury 1979	Immediate and 10 day delayed quizzes.

Nineteen studies showing No Significant Difference.

Aiken *et al.* 1975	No n-t vs parallel n-t.
Baker *et al.* 1974	One study test of concepts.
Carter and Van Matre 1975	Free recall and sentence completion tests.
Catts 1987	Immediate and delayed recall and application; immediate comprehension.
Crawford 1925	Three studies free recall in essays, true-false tests & quizzes.
Eisner and Rohde 1959	N-t vs n-t after 30 minute lecture. 50 T/F item test after 2 and 21 days.
Fisher and Harris 1974a & b	Free recall and MCQ correlated with no. information units.
Freyberg 1956	Immediate test.
Henk & Stahl 1985	N-t v. Non-n-t. Recall little enhanced.
Howe 1970a	Test delayed 14 days.
Jones 1923	Two studies with 3 and 12 day delayed tests of recall.
Macmanaway 1968	Unforeseen test after one week.
McClendon 1958	No n-t vs normal n-t, detailed n-t immediate & 5 week delay.
Milton 1962	Freshers' exam results.
Pauk 1963	Comprehension.

Seven studies favoring no note-taking.

Catts 1987	Comprehension on 1 week delayed test
Freyberg 1956	Unexpected test after 14 days.
Maqsud 1980	Students taking fewer notes better on immediate and long term free recall.
Peper and Mayer 1986	Problem solving involving some transfer of learning.
Peters 1972	Recall of definitions and MCQ test when presentation is fast.
Thomas et al 1975	Correlation between n-t and recall.
Van Matre et al 1975	Free recall and sentence completion tests.

KEY

| N-t | = | Note-taking | | T/F | = | True/False |
| MCQ | = | Multiple Choice Questions | | | | |

The reason why note-taking aids memory could have something to do with other purposes, namely, maintaining students' attention and the activity of selecting what facts are important. There is no evidence on how these purposes interact. Equally the reasons might be that the act of noting requires rehearsal and repetition of what has been said; or that in order to select and summarize, note-taking forces students to seek the meaning of what has been said (e.g. 'encoding'). And we have already seen that attention, retrieval, repetition and meaningfulness are all factors aiding memory. Indeed there has been quite a debate about whether rehearsal or encoding is the more important. Whatever the cause, the effect upon memory is clear and justifies note-taking in lectures.

2. To aid revision

It seems fairly obvious that students who have notes to revise from, will do better in examinations than students who don't. Available evidence confirms this. See Table 10.3. Furthermore nearly all students use notes for this purpose. Surveys by Hartley and Davies (1978), Davy and Dunkel (1989), Razzell and Weinman (1977), and Isaacs (1994) all attest the importance of note-taking for revision purposes by over 90% of students. Indeed, up to a point the more notes students take, the better they do in examinations (Walbaum 1989).

Some researchers have asked which is more important: to aid memory during the lecture (by encoding) or to aid revision (by rehearsal)? The question is part of the wider debate about the importance of encoding perceptions and rehearsing stored memories.

Kiewra *et al.* (1989, 1991) have shown that for lecturers they are both important. Not surprisingly students who took notes and reviewed them did better on tests of recall and recognition of information than those who only took notes and those who were only able to review another student's notes.

Table 10.3. Does Note-taking for Revision improve performance?

Twenty studies favoring note-taking for revision

Annis and Davis 1977	Essay and Multiple Choice tests.
Bentley and Blount 1980	Delayed recall.
Benton et al 1993	Length and organization of essays
Carter and Van Matre 1975	Free recall and sentence completion tests.
Crawford 1925a	Two studies using free recall in essays and true/false tests.
Di Vesta and Gray 1972	Free recall and MCQ.
Fisher and Harris 1973	Two studies, free recall and True-false tests.
Freyberg 1956	Expected test after 8 weeks.
Hartley and Marshall 1974	Test following review.
Howe 1970a	14 day delayed test.
Howe and Godfrey 1977	Four studies with free recall or objective tests.
Kiewra et al 1989	Recall and recognition of facts.

Kiewra et al 1991	Recall and synthesis of facts.
Maqsud 1980	Delayed free recall of information.
Palkovitz and Lore 1980	Test after opportunities to review notes.
Razzell and Weinman 1977	Factual test.
Walbaum 1989	MCQ and Short answer examinations.

Five studies showing No Significant Difference

Barrett et al 1981	Cued recall in immediate and delayed tests.
Fisher and Harris 1974a 1974b	Free recall and MCQ.
Kiewra et al 1989	Higher order thinking.
Peters and Harris 1970.	MCQ

No studies against note-taking for revision.

However there are significant individual differences in habits of note-taking and review. Several studies (eg Trueman and Hartley, 1978; Razzell and Weinman, 1977; Giles *et al.*, 1982) show women writing more notes than men; and Nye (1978) found that freshers take more notes than more experienced students; but Howe (1977) says that the most effective notes are those with the largest amount of information in the smallest number of words and it is possible that men are more efficient in this respect. He reports wide variations between students regarding the number of words written, the use of abbreviations and the omission of words like 'the' and 'a' (Howe and Godfrey, 1977). Wilding and Hayes (1992) have shown that these measures of efficiency also vary with students' age, study strategies and surface learning. Nye found that students who took rough notes intending to write them up, wrote less, and scored less well on final course grades.

The studies reported in Table 10.3 mostly gave an opportunity for revision by using a delayed test. (Significantly, in the study by Palkovitz and Lore 1980, students who did not take this opportunity performed badly.) But in two studies students wrote notes and revised during pauses of a couple of minutes between lecture segments; and this technique proved very effective (Carter and Van Matre, 1975 and Bentley and Blount, 1980). NB. Once again there is evidence for the advantages of breaking the continuous exposition of lectures.

What perhaps is not so obvious is that students who review lecture notes in pairs, employ better strategies for extracting and structuring the information, than individuals revising on their own (O'Donnell and Dansereau, 1993; Kelly and O'Donnell, 1994). Putting these two findings together, we may surmise that pairs of students revising and restructuring their notes for two minutes between lecture segments, would be very effective. In essence, that's a buzz group. I recommend them.

3. To see the developing structure of a topic

Whether note-taking enables students to see the structure and development of a topic during the lecture itself depends on how they take notes. Peper and Mayer (1986) have argued that insofar as note-taking involves encoding, it generates conceptual links in students' minds.

On the other hand, if they simply take a sequential record, maybe under headings and sub-headings given by the lecturer, the links may be restricted and students will only perceive the organization and development if they take time out to look over what they have written as a whole; or if the lecturer takes time to describe and display the lecture's organization. Both these take time, albeit a very short time. If lecturers proceed at such a pace that students can hardly keep up with what is being said, students will be under too much pressure to see the topic as a whole.

However there is a non-sequential method of note-taking in which the students build up their own conceptions of the structure of the topic as the lecture proceeds. These are usually called networking, patterned notes, tree diagrams or concept maps. Anita McClain (1986) calls them 'mind maps' and the technique was much publicized by Tony Busan (1974). This method results in a branching or network structure of concepts as shown in Figure 10.4, rather than a traditional sequential record of specific facts using those concepts and reflecting the organisation of the lecture.

Tree diagrams can depict the organization of key points in a lecture, but it is difficult to note details by this method. Research comparing the effectiveness of concept maps and traditional linear notes reflects this fact. Comparisons by Dansereau *et al.* (1979) using prose material suggest that concept maps result in better memory of key ideas, but are not so good for remembering detail. Both methods were considerably better than taking no notes at all, but the degree of difference may reflect the fact that Dansereau gave his students five and a half hours training in taking notes as part of a 15 week course in study methods. Concept maps use fewer words and there is evidence that, when the test is immediate and presentation is short, noting only key words is as effective as recording everything (Howe, Ormond and Singer, 1974). With lectures of normal length, detail is lost.

Ideally both methods are necessary; but to use both at the pace of a lecture is quite difficult. McClain claims that concept maps liberate students to think, use both sides of the brain, increase comprehension, set up clear graphic structures that allow easy recall, and encourage creative thinking by their open-ended nature. These claims have yet to be justified.

One problem with concept maps is that the lines could have any of several possible meanings. Lambiotte *et al.* (1993) taught their students to label arrows with the following letters according to their meaning. Arrows tend to point away from the central concepts of the lecture.

←t←	is a type of	→d→	definition
←p←	is part of	→a→	is analogous to
←c←	is a characteristic of	←e←	is evidence for
→l→	leads to	→eg→	for example
→i→	influences	→n→	next

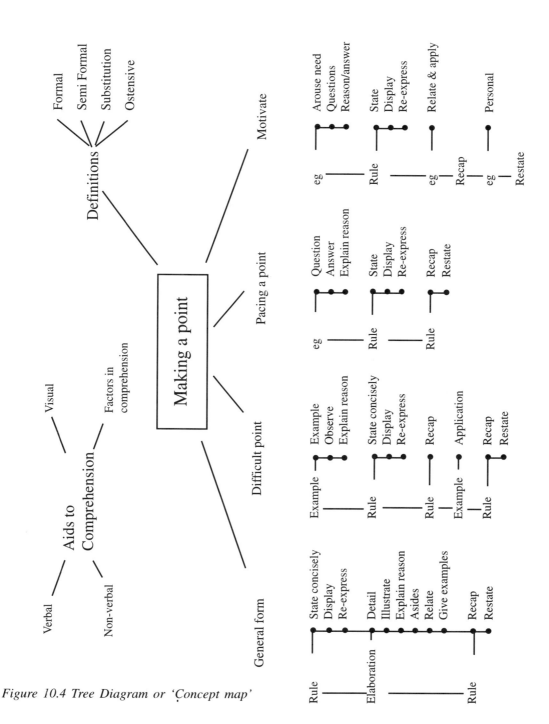

Figure 10.4 Tree Diagram or 'Concept map'

Unfortunately students given concept maps to review a lecture demonstrated less accurate comprehension of concepts than those given word lists. But the idea that relationships between concepts are mostly confined to these ten is interesting and could provide a useful 'shorthand' for taking notes in lectures.

A further difficulty is that students cannot anticipate or plan the shape and direction of the map on the page when first putting pen to paper. An effective solution to these difficulties is to give a concept map as a handout showing the lecture organization as an advance organizer (see page 86), and let students note details in their own way (Baggett, 1994). It is also easier to search for information amongst concept maps than amongst text (O'Donnell, 1993).

I conclude that if students are to make their own concept maps in lectures instead of traditional note-taking methods, they will need more guidance in how to make them than they usually get; and even then, their effectiveness is uncertain. They may, however, have a role as lecture guides.

4. To relate and reorganize during further study
Arguably to take facts and principles and to reorganize them by interrelating and applying them in order to answer questions and solve problems is an essential part of any academic discipline and virtually any profession students may enter. If so, to permit further study by interrelating and reorganizing lecture material must be a very important aim in taking lecture notes. Indeed a vital and much neglected part of private study is to interrelate as many different parts of a discipline as possible, not just the facts that are mentioned in the same lecture. Many essay and examination questions test students' abilities to interrelate in this way.

In the past 20 years there has been a great deal of research into student note-taking in lectures and into students' study methods; but there has been very little on how note-taking influences study methods. Nearly all the research assumes that the purpose of note-taking is to aid memory rather than the promotion of thought, further enquiry, or future enthusiasm for the subject.

An important exception is the work of Entwistle and Marton (1994) and their colleagues. They interviewed a small sample of students immediately after their final examinations and asked about their revision procedures. They suggest there are five 'forms of understanding'. Implicitly they are stages of development with some students progressing no further at each stage:

(i)   Absorbing facts, details and procedures related to exams without considering or changing their organization. In effect they revised from a precis of the lecture and scarcely related or reorganized the material at all;

(ii)   Accepting and using only the knowledge and explaining links provided in the lecture notes to form logical organizations of subject matter, such as arguments 'for' and 'against';

(iii)   Relying mainly on notes to develop summary organizations solely to control exam answers;

(iv)   Developing their own organizations of subject matter from theories and strategic reading to represent personal understanding, but also to control exam answers; and
(v)   Developing organizations of subject matter from wide reading which relate personal understanding and involvement to the nature of the discipline.'

Interestingly, students used what I call 'visually derived' relationships to reorganize material. Former visual relations of ideas including notes, were now linked more abstractly. This could strengthen the case for using tree diagrams and for lecturers making more effort to represent relationships between ideas visually. For example, a matrix like Figure 10.1 cross relates concepts. These are important processes of thought. Kiewra *et al.* (1988) gave notes in the form of a matrix and found that students could transfer the knowledge better than those who had a complete lecture text or summary and reviewed them. In a number of experiments mentioned earlier, Kiewra and his colleagues compared the performance of students who took notes but did not review them (encoding only), students who took notes and reviewed them (encoding + review), and students who did not attend the lecture who were given another person's notes (review only). Those who took notes and reviewed them wrote longer and better organized essays (Benton, 1993), and in one case (1991), but not in another (1989) were better able to synthesise the information given. On one occasion 'review only' also produced more synthesis than 'encoding only'.

All this suggests that the cycle of processes 14 and 15 in Figure 4.2 are more likely during review than during a lecture. Little thought can take place in a lecture. The cycle 6 and 5 is not much better when there is a continuing flow of words from the lecturer to be processed. The truth is, despite the labels given by Kiewra, a lot of encoding goes on in the 'review only' condition, and encoding is actually distracted and inhibited by yet more words arriving to be processed in the so-called 'encoding only' condition. That's why thinking in lectures is so difficult.

One powerful note-taking technique to encourage thought is to generate questions that require students to relate and reorganize information. Students should be taught to use it. Alison King (1992) found that students trained to generate questions at the end of a lecture retained more information after a week than students trained to summarize the lecture and those who reviewed their notes, though the summarizers did better on an immediate test. In another study (King, 1991) questions generated during a lecture and answered individually or by partners resulted in better learning than reviewing notes, either individually or in pairs both immediately and after 10 days. Similarly, Rickards and McCormick (1988) have found that pre-lecture questions enhance the intellectual quality of students' notes.

Why are self-generated questions so effective? Answers to self-generated questions and the questions themselves, relate to stored concepts that already have meaning for the student (processes 14 and 15 in Figure 4.2). In other words self-generated questions and their answers ensure that new information is accommodated within a preconceived organization of ideas. They reorganize the information presented in the lecture.

Reorganizing lecture material is often frustrated because students do not spread out their notes. Consequently further information obtained by independent study is noted separately, not visually incorporated into a single organized body of notes. With this learning strategy students are left with sets of notes separated according to their source rather than the relevance of their content. The integration of ideas on the one hand, or their discernment on the other, is thereby made more difficult.

5. To select what is important
There have been several studies investigating how far students are able to select and note what the lecturers themselves deem to be noteworthy in their lectures. Since research shows that students don't remember what they don't note, and it is not possible to note everything, skills in noting what is important become critical.

Several studies show that students lack these skills. It is not so much that their notes contain inaccuracies or errors, though Maddox and Hoole (1975) comment that nearly every senior student in their study made some, and Howe and Godfrey (1977) found that some students omitted negatives! It is that the proportion of important points noted is very variable. For example McDonald and Taylor (1980) report that only half their fourth year students recorded two-thirds of the noteworthy points; and Baker and Lombardi (1985) found that students noted only 50% of a lecture's main ideas. Crawford (1925) reported that students failed to note 47% of the important points; Locke (1977) gave a figure of 40%, and Hartley and Cameron (1967) 76%; while Hartley and Marshall (1974) reported that freshers noted only 56 information units out of a possible 520.

Jackson and Bilton (1990) showed that students were unaware of lecture signals and had difficulty in extracting key concepts from a lecture exposition, particularly when one explanation or definition was embedded in another. Notes by students who could extract important points showed no standard abbreviations or form of shorthand, and displayed poor layout and insufficient relationship between items of information. Hughes and Suritsky (1993) also observed that students with learning disabilities have poor note-taking skills such as paraphrasing, abbreviating and recognizing lecture signals. Where students have difficulty in following a lecture, they rely almost exclusively on copying from overhead transparencies or the blackboard. Davies (1976) says that oversupply of information leads to confusion when students cannot select appropriately; they cannot cope with individual elements of an argument unless it fits into a wider framework; and these inadequacies can lead to lack of confidence and despondency.

Einstein *et al.* (1985) reported that both note-takers and successful students remembered points of high importance, while non-note-takers and less successful students remembered points of greater and lesser importance equally. Since recall was related to what was noted, these results were interpreted as a failure by non-note-takers and less successful students to select what was important during the lecture.

All these criticisms of students' competence, plus the fact that more senior students take more complete notes, suggest that freshers need help to learn note-taking skills, particularly the skills in selecting what is important. Note-taking can become habitual and indiscriminate. There is a legend that if you have a mixed class of freshers and postgraduates and you want to know which is which, say 'Good morning'. The freshers will reply 'Good morning'; postgraduates write it down. To select what is noteworthy requires thought and judgement. Consequently this is where students need most assistance. I will consider this in the next section.

6. To know what has to be learned

Every discipline is so wide that no one, least of all a student, could be competent in all aspects of it. The content of lectures often indicates which aspects students should select for further study. In this sense, note-taking records the syllabus.

This is particularly the case in subjects such as the mathematical sciences and philosophy, which can only be studied by working out problems for oneself. Memory of factual information has a relatively minor role. In these subjects the function of lectures is often to guide students to the problems they should work on in private study, rather than dispense factual information. In effect the syllabus consists of a number of problems. Students do not learn how to solve them by taking lecture notes. They note the syllabus of problems and possible directions to explore them.

7. To maintain attention

It is common experience that if one does not take notes in lectures, the mind tends to wander. Peper and Mayer (1978) claim that note-taking increases attention and results in greater concentration on the material to be learned. Note-taking is an activity which maintains a slightly higher level of arousal because the activity is self stimulating. Neurologically, there is a feedback mechanism to the brain stem which arouses the brain in general. There is some evidence from tests of immediate recall (Crawford, 1925b; Howe and Godfrey, 1977) that the benefit of note-taking is greater when lectures are over 30 minutes. Howe and Godfrey interpret this in terms of note-taking maintaining attention after that length of time.

The converse is also true. Enthusiastic, stimulating lectures result in more note-taking.

On the other hand over half the students in the surveys by Davy and Dunkel (1989) and Hartley and Davies (1978) reported that note-taking sometimes interfered with their understanding of lectures, presumably because their attention was divided. Peper and Mayer (1986) reasoned that, since the whole brain should be aroused by note-taking, memory and thought should benefit equally. However, contrary to their earlier claim, they found problem solving benefited more than factual memory. The attention hypothesis was thus weakened. Furthermore, the extent to which note-taking maintains attention might also be disputed insofar as students take fewer notes as lectures proceed (Lloyd, 1968; Locke, 1977; Scerbo et al., 1992). The intensity of divided attention could well cause fatigue, particularly when noteworthy points are dense or the lecturer's delivery is fast.

It seems likely that note-taking maintains, and even improves, attention for a while; but thereafter the benefits may be small or even negative.

8. To provide evidence of attendance

Although in some laboratory subjects students submit reports of practical work as evidence that they have taken the course, to require students to hand in lecture notes as evidence that they have attended lectures is extremely rare. Indeed Hyde and Flournay (1986) report that some students with poor attendance achieved outstanding academic results. (However their conclusion that mandatory attendance can harm performance, does not follow.)

Helping students to take notes

'How to study' books and records of unpublished educational conference papers abound with advice for students on how to take notes, but little of it is supported by solid research. Two exceptions are the work of Hartley and Davies (1978) and Howe (1977). There is even less research on lecturing techniques to assist easy note-taking.

1. Advice to lecturers

This advice can be listed summarily:

(a)   Organization.
Organize your lectures with key points as described in Chapter 7. Use visual techniques to display the structure of lectures on a blackboard, screen or handout. Then stick to it. Students complain that some lecturers don't (Van Metre *et al.*, 1994)

(b)   Making a point.
Make those points in the ways described in Chapter 8. In particular use lecture signals described in that chapter. Display the key points on the blackboard or screen and pause briefly for emphasis after making them.

(c)   Handouts.
Use handouts to give, not only the structure of key points, but bibliographic references, information that needs to be accurate, diagrams, concepts that are complex or difficult, and spellings of technical terms.

(d)   Feedback.
Observe students noting a point and wait until nearly all have finished before going on to the next. In practice it is not too difficult to observe what students in the front few rows are writing even though, to the lecturer, it is upside down. Occasionally, when getting formal feedback using questionnaires or interviews, include a question about the ease or difficulty of note-taking.

(e)   Separate listening and note-taking.
Create opportunities to separate students' listening and note-taking. Aiken *et al.* (1975) obtained a better performance from students when they only took notes between 4 minute segments of a lecture than when they either took notes in the normal way ('in parallel') or didn't take them at all. However this benefit seems to diminish with longer segments, presumably because longer segments give too much to remember and then note. Eisner and Rohde (1959) found no advantage with 20 minute segments.

In some circumstances it pays to instruct students not to take notes to begin with, and then go over the material a second time with suitable pauses for students to note what they wish. Obviously this double presentation takes extra time. It is justified when a topic is conceptually difficult or when the first explanation is so visual, perhaps in a semi-darkened room, that students will not understand if they take their eyes away to write.

(f)   Pauses for review.

Have occasional pauses during lectures when students are instructed to review what they have written. This is particularly advisable when successive concepts and explanations in a lecture build upon each other in what I call a steep conceptual gradient. These pauses also provide opportunities for students to fill in details and personal thoughts that they couldn't note at the time.

(g)   Question generation.

Having introduced the topic of your lecture, try asking the students in groups of two or three, to write down what they think are the most pertinent questions to answer when studying that topic. Get feedback of five or six questions. The best questions may well be the ones you never thought of. Give time during, or at the end of the lecture, for students to answer their own questions.

(h)   Don't go too fast.

Lecturers can have a feeling of satisfaction that they have done their duty once they have presented information, regardless of whether students could receive it. The lecturer who gets behind and then rushes the last part of his lecture in order to cover the ground, panders to this feeling. Lecturer speed is students' major complaint so far as note-taking is concerned, particularly when the concepts are unfamiliar (Van Metre *et al.*, 1994). Peters (1972) presented definitions at 130 words per minute and 192wpm, and text at 146wpm and 202wpm. The lower speeds are fairly normal. The higher speeds resulted in significantly lower MCQ scores and fewer notes.

2. Advice to give to students

(a)   Organization.

Familiarize yourself with the way lectures are organized. See Chapter 7.

(b)   Abbreviations.

Develop your own set of abbreviations or short-hand for words and concepts that occur frequently in your subject.

(c)   Layout.

Use layout techniques and space out your notes so that you can add later detail, personal thoughts, and information and ideas from further study. Use the left hand page in your notebook for 'tree diagrams' or 'concept maps'. Notes from further study can also go on that page. In this way notes on the same topic are kept together and are more likely to be connected in your mind. It doesn't pay to save paper. Use broad lined paper so that you can write in a hurry and still be able to read it in several months' time.

(d)   Note questions and problems.

In spite of the emphasis upon memory of facts in this chapter, think of note-taking as noting questions and problems rather than facts. The facts are merely ammunition to answer the questions and solve the problems. Note questions and issues that occur to you as soon as you can. If you don't, they have often gone for ever. The same applies to criticisms and other thoughts about a topic. Where they are your questions, criticisms and thoughts, initial them as yours. Otherwise you might think they are the lecturer's if you only return to your notes after several months.

It is particularly important to note what you don't understand even though - through lack of understanding - these questions are difficult to pose. If you don't note them, you won't know where you are ignorant and that can be fatal in examinations.

(e)   Keep an ideas notebook.
Have a special small personal notebook you carry with you all the time, to note questions and passing thoughts about your discipline and the world in general. This is particularly important when you have essays, projects or dissertations to write. Let your ideas notebook include ideas about your private life. It's good to get them down, not to bottle them up. Where appropriate, relate them to your studies.

(f)   Immediate review.
Review your notes as soon as possible after the end of a lecture before memory of associated detail is lost. In fact look them over before you leave the lecture room. Add in any details, thoughts, questions and criticisms that come to mind. Add in cross references (perhaps opposite on the blank left hand page) to other courses or parts of the same course.

(g)   Have a prepared mind.
Read an elementary text (e.g. articles from Scientific American) on a topic before going to a lecture on it. Familiarize yourself with names and technical terms. The purpose of this is to allow your brain to process information quickly during the lecture. With extra speed you will get much more from the lecture, instead of spending time trying to work out what was meant. Devise suitable abbreviations that can be written quickly during the lecture. If possible - and it's not always possible in advance of the lecture - identify contrasting schools of thought so that you can quickly relate them to what the lecturer says. A prepared mind is a matter of having what Ausubel (1968) called 'advance organizers'. It is what makes a lecture have meaning.

3. Teaching note-taking skills
Courses on note-taking mostly consist of a mixture of precepts and exercises practicing specific skills. They are valuable for second language students at pre-enrollment. Whilst some use live lecturettes, others are packages with audiotapes (Hamp-Lyons, 1982). Videotapes would be better to teach the interpretation of body language, gestures and visual signals. Carrier and Titus (1981) used behavioral modification techniques.

Most courses concentrate upon listening skills - focusing attention, responding to 'cues' or signals, comprehension, using abbreviations, identifying what is important, paraphrasing, analyzing lecture structures and summarizing. (Hughes and Suritsky, 1993.) Relatively few go on to practice critical listening (McKibben, 1982).

Pollio (1990) has demonstrated that instruction in note-taking increases the completeness of notes and enhances learning. It is less clear which skills are most important, but noting questions is certainly one of them. We have already seen that students who are questioning perform better than those who review notes and those who summarize them (King, 1992). This finding has been repeated in a whole series of reports by King herself and others. No doubt these results depend upon the test used, but they are striking because reviewing (see Table 10.3) and summarizing are known to be very effective. In another experiment (King, 1989) students using self-questioning techniques significantly improved their lecture comprehension over time. Students using a reciprocal peer-questioning procedure in small cooperative groups achieved higher levels of critical thought (King, 1990). Spires (1993) also reports that instruction in how to take notes combined with self-questioning improved the quality of notes and immediate comprehension amongst low achieving college freshmen.

Self-generated questions at the beginning of lectures are very effective because they provide advance organizers related to ideas the student already has. In this way they give the content of the lecture meaning to which they can relate. They help students to inter-relate ideas and thereby overcome a basic weakness of the lecture method - that lectures are linear whilst knowledge and thought require multiple connections

How can students learn to generate questions for themselves? The process must be in their minds. It cannot be presented by teachers. Alison King (1994, 1995) gave students a list of generic question stems (see figure 16.1 page 210) and the thinking process that each was expected to induce. Each student was then expected to bring three questions to class.

Conclusion

We have seen that students' notes are important yet often inadequate, not least because taking notes is a complex activity often required at speed. To overcome these limitations, lecturers increasingly provide summary notes or 'handouts'. It is these we must now consider.

11. The Purpose, Preparation and Use of Handouts

Purpose.
1. Teaching objectives.
2. Information: as a leveler, to release time, and to reduce pressure.
3. A lecture guide.
4. To save note-taking.
5. To stimulate thought.
6. To guide and stimulate reading.

Preparation and use.
1. Stages in preparation.
2. Paper.
3. Layout.
4. Timing.
5. Availability.
6. Insuring their use.

Training in reading.

Conclusion.

Purpose

Judging from the frequency of their questions, this is a subject that worries some new lecturers. How handouts should be used depends on what they are to be used for.

The function of handouts is probably infinitely varied. I shall limit myself, here, to the ways they are commonly used in conjunction with lectures.

1. Teaching objectives

If the students have not already received it as part of a syllabus, a very important handout before the first lecture is a list of objectives that the course is intended to achieve, for students usually learn better if they know what they have to learn. Without common aims, students and lecturers will work at cross purposes. A major exception to this rule is the learning of attitudes. If students are told that an objective of a course is to change their attitudes, adverse reactions are likely.

2. Information: as a leveler, to release time, and to reduce pressure
(a) Leveler.
Handouts may be used to give factual information before a lecture. They may be used

in this way as a "leveler" where their objective is to ensure a common basic background before a topic is further elaborated or developed. Thus, they are a means of teaching more detail than could normally be absorbed in a lecture, and of building complex concepts upon more simple ones which would have been unfamiliar without the handout.

(b)   To release time.

The presentation of information before a lecture period can release time for discussion and other activity (MacManaway, 1968, 1970) or relieve the pressure of a crammed syllabus. Testing students' analysis, application and memory of information, Hohn *et al.* (1990) could find no difference between giving complete and skeletal notes. In both cases students did better when the lectures contained more facts, and it seemed possible that the handouts enabled students to handle more information. However, Russell *et al.* (1984) obtained contrary results. They varied the information density in lectures and gave the same handout to guide note-taking in all cases. When the information density was high, students forgot basic facts given at the beginning. Russell *et al* . believed later information caused retroactive interference and it seems the handout did not reduce it.

(c)   To reduce pressure.

Similarly, as described later, handouts may be used to prepare students for a problem-centered lecture. In this case their function is to relieve students of the psychological pressure of absorbing new information and free them to think about its application, validity or relation to other topics.

Since in these cases it is important that the students have acquired the information before the lecture, it is essential that the handout be given out about one week in advance. A hierarchic organization of headings and sub-headings is usually most suitable, because the students need a basic framework rather than details. Because the information is new to the students its clarity is essential.

3. A lecture guide

A third kind of handout is used to guide students through a difficult lecture. Lecture guides are particularly appropriate when the topic is complex or the students have learning difficulties (Lazarus, 1988). Since we have already seen in the last chapter that students' own notes are frequently inadequate and often inaccurate, lectures don't have to be very difficult or complex to merit a lecture guide.

It is not essential to distribute a lecture guide a week before, but it is advisable to let the students look it over before beginning to lecture. This enables them to see the whole topic before any one part is considered. It may be given out the previous week if preparatory reading is required, but, if it is a difficult topic, references will need to be simple and well chosen in order not to discourage or confuse the students.

(a)   How much detail?

The question arises, "How much detail should a lecture guide contain?". In an experiment by Northcraft and Jernstedt (1975), students with lecture outlines did better than students given either complete notes or lecture scripts. Other research on this point is inconsistent and unexpected. Morgan *et al.* (1988) found in one experiment but not in another, that a list of headings was better than headings and a summary of key points.

Possibly student variables explain the inconsistencies. Lambiotte and Dansereau (1992) projected word lists, outline notes or concept maps when playing tape-recorded lectures. Though all scores were low, lists of concepts were most effective for students with high pre-knowledge of the subject. But the opposite was true for students with little pre-knowledge and for those who were less confident. (Lambiotte *et al.*, 1993). There are also some indications in experiments by Frank (1984) and Kiewra and Frank (1988) that students more dependent on their environment need fuller handouts than those who are 'field independent'. There may also be subject differences. It is to be expected that more detailed handouts will be an advantage in subjects, such as the physical sciences, where accuracy is important. In subjects, such as the humanities, where independence of mind is encouraged much earlier, an outline of the lecture structure and key points is sufficient stimulus.

Although Kiewra *et al.* (1988) is an exception, there is evidence (Collingwood and Hughes, 1978; Hohn *et al.*, 1990; Morgan *et al.*, 1988; Siegel, 1973) that complete notes and even lecture scripts result in more detailed learning when review and revision are possible before tests. This is hardly surprising, but of course, revision is a different purpose for handouts than a lecture guide. When the test was immediate, Hohn *et al.* (1990) found no difference in the achievement of knowledge and application of principles between complete and skeleton handouts. Complete notes are too much to read as a lecture guide, but allow more thorough revision later.

(b)   Blank spaces.
The apparent conflict when lecturers have both these two purposes, can be reconciled if lecture guides are laid out spaciously showing the organization of the lecture and with blank spaces between sections for students to add their own notes and comments. In this way students actively build up their own notes for revision purposes; the lecturer knows that students go away with the essentials; some of the pressure of note-taking in lectures is removed; details can be noted that would otherwise be missed; and some of the divided attention between note-taking and listening is relieved.

Collingwood and Hughes found this technique more effective than relying wholly on students' notes. On the other hand, since copies of the lecturer's detailed notes were better revision for a delayed test, the students' additions may not have been detailed enough. Layout affects this. Hartley (1976) found that students with widely spaced handouts took more notes than others.

(c)   Sentence completion.
Another device is to leave gaps in sentences for students to fill in key words during the lecture. Hartley used a sentence completion technique and found that students' recall of those particular facts benefited. Recall of other points was not improved. Accordingly, lecturers using this technique should make sure the gaps exercise students' minds on the points they particularly want them to know.

(d)   Questions.
In effect, sentence completion handouts pose questions to students which they must answer by listening to the lecture. Clearly handouts could be devised with other kinds of question, in particular the questions the lecturers intend their lectures to answer.

Research investigating this technique shows it to be highly effective (Rickards and McCormick, 1988; Chmielewska, 1976; Facinelli, 1982). I shall deal with handout questions to promote thought in the section after next.

(e)   Advantages.

Isaacs (1989a) reports that the reason for handouts most commonly given by lecturers is that they outline, summarize or explain a topic. The advantage of this use of handouts is that even the least able students carry away an accurate record of the major points, whereas Hartley and Cameron (1967) reported that, even from a lecture of average difficulty, the proportion noted of what the lecturer thought important varied from 21% to 73% at different times. Further confirmation of this point will be unnecessary for lecturers who find their statements are sometimes distorted in examination answers.

(f)   Disadvantages.

Its disadvantage is that, having openly committed themselves to a certain plan, the lecturers are less free to change their approach during the lecture, and when, as often happens with a difficult topic, a lecturer needs to go more slowly, there is a temptation to cover the ground set out on the handout rather than to teach it. Paradoxically, it is the experienced lecturer who is sensitive to non-verbal feedback who is most likely to experience these difficulties. Lecturers who perform rather than teach are less often aware of this kind of problem. One solution is to take the class into one's confidence, describe the difficulty as a teaching problem (not as someone's fault), and explain why, or ask whether, a change of plan is appropriate. 'I don't seem able to make this point clear. In view of its importance when we come to deal with.....do you think I ought to spend longer on it now even though it means I shall not reach....today?'

Taking the class into one's confidence is not only a valuable strategy in many lecturing situations, it is an intrinsic feature of good student rapport; but authoritarian lecturers, and those lacking self-confidence in their knowledge or teaching ability, find it a difficult technique to use.

4. To save note-taking

Some lecturers give handouts that summarize their lecture so that students do not need to take notes. In that case they could serve most of the same functions as note-taking (Figure 10.2). Handouts are obviously useful in situations where note-taking is impossible. These include illustrated lectures in which important information is given in semi-darkness, practical demonstrations when the student is standing, and lectures that for some reason are never delivered. They are also a useful safeguard for bad lecturers (but this remark should not discourage new lecturers from using them). If lecturers teach with a large amount of informal class discussion, or easily get off the point of their own accord, these handouts provide anxious students with some comfort. In some circumstances they can be used to relieve the pressure of time on the lecturer. They offer freedom to fan the flames of student interest in one point with less worry about the neglect of another.

If understanding is improved by diagrams, lecture time can be saved by their inclusion. (There is an important exception to this when drawing the diagram is used as an active method of teaching it. This method is quite common and is often especially effective when the diagram is slowly built up from simple elements rather than presented in its complete, and possibly complex, form.) Rather surprisingly, Chmielewska (1976) found that handouts consisting of pictures, questions, key points, and headings were most effective in that order. Presumably the importance of pictures is subject specific.

The advantages and disadvantages of summary handouts are similar to those of a lecture guide, but they raise questions of how far students should take notes for themselves and the value of lectures in which notes cannot, or need not, be taken - questions to which there is no one answer.

Research on the relative advantages of students taking their own notes or being given partial or complete notes, is ambiguous; but on balance it pays to give handouts. In Table 11.1, I assume, unless the reports state otherwise, that students were able to take notes in lectures in the normal way.

We have already seen that the study by Northcraft and Jernstedt favored partial handouts. Similarly Linda Annis (1981) found that students receiving a full set of notes did less well on essay and multiple choice tests, than those taking their own or adding to partial notes. There was no interaction with preferred study techniques. She interprets this as showing the benefits of having to encode subject matter during lectures. Students originally preferring to take their own or to receive full notes, later switched their preference to partial notes.

On the other hand Rasor (1980) reports significant correlations between the use of fully prepared notes during lectures and students' course completion rates.

Table 11.1 On balance it pays to give handouts

HO = Handouts
N-t = Students' note-taking

Studies favoring handouts

1	Collingwood & Hughes (1978)	Teacher's detailed notes v. N-t; Outline notes v. N-t	Delayed achievement test
2	Facinelli (1982)	HO worksheets v. Lecture;	Five tests in 15 week semester
3	Fisher & Harris (1973)	Lecturer's notes v. N-t;	3 week delayed recall
4	Kaul (1976)	HO+discussion v. Lecture+limited discussion;	Attitude change
5	Kiewra (1985)	HO v. N-t;	Facts learned
6	Rasor (1980)	Prepared notes v. None;	Course completion rates
7	Rickards & McCormick (1988)	HO of pre questions v. N-t; v. No notes;	Depth and number of concepts recalled
8	Smith (1984)	HO v. "No notes";	Comprehension

Studies showing no significant difference

1	Annis (1981)	Partial HO v. N-t;	Essay and MCQs
2	Rickards & McCormick (1988)	HO of pre questions v. HO+N-t;	Depth and number of concepts recalled
3	Tucker (1989)	Structured HO v. teacher's notes	One week delayed quiz
		v. students' notes	Two week delayed exam
4	White & Chavigny (1975)	Lecture+audiotape summaries v. Lecture;	Mid-term and final exams

Studies favoring student note-taking

1	Annis (1981)	Full HO v. N-t;	Essay and MCQs
2	Fisher & Harris (1973)	Lecturer's notes v. N-t;	Free recall and MCQs
3	Henk & Stahl (1985)	HO v. N-t;	Recall

Freyberg (1956) has described an experiment in which some students took no notes, some took them either in full or in outline, and others were issued with a duplicated summary. Both on an immediate test, and after two weeks, the first group showed the best retention of information. However, when given the opportunity to revise their notes, those that had them not only performed significantly better than the first group, but obtained higher scores than on the immediate test. Thus although it is sometimes claimed that note-taking aids concentration and learning, in this instance notes were only of benefit if used on a later occasion. Psychologically, we may say that note-taking was an aid to memory only when the consequent interference was compensated by rehearsal. In Freyberg's experiment the group with the handout did best of all after revision - perhaps because their notes were more accurate and contained fewer omissions. If this interpretation is correct, handouts to save note-taking could be used selectively for difficult topics.

This kind of handout may be made available only at the end of a lecture, but it is arguable that, like the previous type, students should have the opportunity to make comments and additions. Lectures are clearer if handouts are distributed at the beginning provided some time is immediately given for students to look them over.

5. To stimulate thought

Handouts containing questions, tests or theoretical issues are useful to stimulate thought. Provided the students answer the questions or debate the issues on their own, this kind of handout is particularly useful where it is necessary to give an expository account and there is no lecture time for teaching the important patterns of thought. For this reason it is sometimes used with large classes with whom little individual or small-group discussion is possible. If given out a week before, students may have the questions in mind, and recollect their initial thoughts about them, during the lecture, and the lecture may have added interest if it allows students to check their answers. The difficulty is to make sure that students think about the questions before the lecture, but feedback techniques may provide some check on this, and Elton (1970) has shown that self tests may be used successfully with first year undergraduate science courses. And I have already mentioned in the last chapter, Alison King's report (1992) that students posing questions for themselves at the beginning of a lecture, learned and remembered more in the long run, than students who took their own notes or who were given summary handouts.

The kind of questions asked should depend upon the kind of thought patterns the lecturer wishes to teach. The important point is that not any question will do. The questions may require the application of principles, powers of observation, skills in using books and source material, the analysis of data, the use of judgement and possibly the need for originality or some other kind of thought process. Therefore, the construction of the question will require some understanding of students' thought processes and this is not always easy to obtain.

The simplest rule is to give tasks that practice the skills students are intended to learn. In an experiment by Facinelli (1982), one group of students was given bibliographic instruction in lectures; another had additional worksheets containing exercises to find information in dictionaries, manuals, encyclopedias, bibliographies, indexes, biographies, catalogs and journals. Five pre-tests and post-tests over a 15 week semester showed significant benefit to the group with worksheets.

It is frequently difficult to encourage student motivation in large classes. The provision of questions from past examinations may provide an attainable goal and thereby enhance it. Since many examiners give high marks to students who display a breadth of view, it is useful to include hints in the form of supplementary questions which force the students to connect issues which would otherwise have remained unrelated in their minds. This is especially true with younger students with whom the objective is to teach new patterns of thought rather than to practice partially established ones.

6. To guide and stimulate reading

Reading lists are amongst the most common handouts, but are frequently not carefully thought out. The same lecturers may give careful consideration to the presentation of written information on their subject, but when the information is concerned with references the same care is not observed. Yet the amount of student learning at stake may well be greater in the latter case. Indeed, if there is no significant difference in the rate of learning from reading and other presentations (Dubin and Taveggia, 1968), and students spend longer reading recommended references than in any other learning activity (Hale Report, 1964; Saunders et al., 1969), the preparation of reading lists is worth considerable effort.

It is difficult to generalize for all subjects, but the important functions of reading lists are usually to guide and stimulate the students to read. These are quite different from those at the end of books or journals which are frequently to permit the public verification of data and the acknowledgement of sources. Consequently, the way they need to be presented is quite different. A long list of references may inform students of what exists, if they bother to look it through, but it is more likely to discourage. If the reading for a whole course is given at the beginning, in the belief that students will welcome the freedom to plan their work, the students' reaction is often to delay getting down to work, or to seek the security of a standard text and neglect journals and other original work. This may lead to a concentration on understanding facts at the expense of a spirit of inquiry, criticism, the excitement of originality and other "higher level" objectives.

Therefore, while not rejecting the use of a short initial reading list to inform students of 'books to buy', 'reference books' or 'basic books' (for those who have forgotten required basic knowledge), it may help if it is short enough to make its guidance practical, if the function of the recommendations is made explicit, and if it is supplemented with more stimulating references through the course when their novelty will be attractive.

Many lecturers give guidance on the relative importance of references by using a system of asterisks; it is also helpful, but less common, to suggest the degree of difficulty or the order in which they should be read. Where a knowledge of technical terms would save reading time, the provision of a glossary handout is useful, particularly if different recommended authors use the same term with different meanings, or different terms for the same thing. These confusions can cause the student endless frustration, while, being familiar with their subject, lecturers can sort them out relatively easily if they look through their recommendations as the list is made.

A second cause of student frustration is the inability to find the recommended sources. This may sometimes be avoided by giving the college library classification, since librarians do not always classify volumes in the way that others expect, and the books associated with some subjects may be very dispersed. Time can be saved if availability of reading is assured. Most college libraries will now stock photocopies of articles in heavy demand when requested and others will temporarily classify popular volumes as 'for reference only'. In the long run these precautions make the lecturer's job easier, because well-read students understand better and are easier to teach.

Students' understanding is frequently better if they have read a variety of viewpoints, but, until they know the subject, they cannot guide their own reading in this respect. The lecturer can give this guidance and stimulate considerable interest if comments or questions are added to each recommendation. These may draw attention to bias or important points.

It may be objected that, in the interests of scholarship, lecturers should let their students make their own judgements on what they read, and that they should learn to select what is important for themselves. I agree with this, but do not think it is a serious objection. The guidance suggested in the previous paragraph applies to the beginning of the course, and is to help students guide themselves later. It is arguable that students will be able to make better informed and more difficult judgements by the end of a course, if the results of early spadework can be achieved in less time. The objection is rooted in the belief that students who are spoonfed never learn to use a knife and fork, but this is not necessarily so. The reverse may be true when the food they are given (knowledge) is the basis on which later skills depend, and the development of academic skills has a particularly interactive character of this kind.

Preparation and Use

Although the preparation and use of handouts depends on their purpose, there are some considerations that are nearly always applicable.

1. Stages in preparation

(a)   Envisage its effect in context.
Handouts are an integral part of the teaching methods used during a period of teaching. They are not, or should not be, an adjunct. So the first step is to envisage the period of teaching as a whole. What are its objectives? And what part will handouts play in achieving them? In other words, what will be the effect of the handout in its context?

(b)   Decide when it should be used.
Considering how a handout is to achieve certain objectives will answer the next question - how and when should it be used? If it is an advance organizer (see page 86) it will need to be given either before the lecture or at its beginning. If the latter, time must be given for students to read it before the lecture starts.

If it is to help students follow the lecture, it will also need to be given before the beginning of the lecture and referred to as the lecture proceeds. If it is only given at the beginning without students having the opportunity to read it before the lecturer starts speaking, students will listen and read with divided attention. That is a recipe for ineffective lecturing.

Some lecturers give a summary handout at the end of a lecture in the belief that it gives opportunity for repetition and rehearsal. In practice this creates a dilemma for students. Should they take detailed notes during the lecture knowing that essentials will be duplicated more accurately in the handout to come? Or should they take no notes, rely on the handout, and listen to the lecture avoiding the usual conflict between noting one point and listening to the next? Much depends on how detailed the follow-up handout is. Only the lecturer knows that. So, if lecturers insist on delaying distribution until the end of the lecture, to remove this dilemma, they should give advice on the students' best strategy.

When a handout, such as a diagram, relates only to part of a lecture it might be given during the lesson. It might be thought that this would be a disruption. It might be if the distribution is not well organized with a little forethought, but we have seen that there are advantages in lecture breaks.

(c)   Decide its structure.
The organization of a lecture handout will normally correspond to the organization of the lecture itself. Anything else might be confusing. However I should not be too

dogmatic on this point. Pre-lecture handouts as levelers may introduce concepts without covering the ground of the lecture. And post-lecture handouts might be used to show that a topic could be viewed in quite a different way.

(d)   Pilot a draft.

Prepare a draft and check it out with a colleague. Piloting on a sample of students is a good idea unless the handout can only be understood in the context of a lecture they have not heard.

(e)   Revise, produce and distribute.

Revise the handout in the light of feedback. Check it for errors, not least word processing errors. Produce a few more than you should need - somehow they are always needed. Make sure you file a copy with your own lecture notes and overhead transparencies. Plan how you intend to distribute them (eg put a small number at the end of each row of students).

(f)   Evaluate.

It is not normally necessary to make a formal evaluation, but it is useful to get some feedback from the students. It is also a good idea to write evaluative comments on the file copy so that changes can be made before the handout is used another time.

2. Paper

It is usually intended that students should keep handouts; therefore it is necessary to produce them on paper to fit their files. If various kinds of 'handout' are used (e.g. lecture summaries, instructions for practical work, bibliographical references, and question sheets) duplicating paper of different colors will facilitate quick and easy reference for students.

3. Layout

The layout of handouts requires careful thought. A blank wall of prose is normally to be avoided (unless, of course its purpose is to present literary quotations rather than notes). Sufficient space for students' additions and comments often helps them to think because the two sets of ideas can be related more easily when set out together.

4. Timing

In the investigation by MacDonald and Romano (1983) lecturers underestimated the value of layout and summaries. Female students were particularly inclined to neglect poorly presented handouts; and MacDonald and Romano say, if they are not well presented, lecturers should work through them in class.

When should handouts be distributed? A clear conception of their purpose largely answers this question. Handouts as a leveler need to be given a week before the lecture. Those to state objectives, save note-taking or act as a lecture guide must be presented at the beginning of the lecture at the very latest. Those to stimulate thought and reading could be collected by students at the end. McDougall *et al.* (1972) found that students given a handout before a lecture out-performed others on a test immediately afterwards, but were not significantly better in an examination 7 weeks after the end of the course. Once again the revision function of notes and handouts compensated for the immediate disadvantages of poor teaching technique (not receiving the handout earlier).

5. Availability

There are always some students who fail to receive a copy at the same time as the others. Therefore, it is usually advisable to duplicate more than one per student, to ensure the availability of copies (perhaps from a departmental secretary) during the following weeks, to retain at least one copy (with errors boldly corrected in red) for one's own use, and if future reduplication is likely, to make sure the master copy is not destroyed.

6. Ensuring their use

Handouts are more likely to be read if they are an integral part of a course than if they seem to be addenda. This may be achieved by the addition of relevant examination questions, the inclusion of one or two essential references and their use during teaching periods, especially practicals.

MacDonald and Romano (1983) found that students don't read handouts unless there is intrinsic motivation to do so. Freshers and part-time students tend to leave them until revision for examinations; and then they rely on them heavily. The higher the level of student, the less reliance they place upon handouts. Older students were more likely to read long handouts, but were more discriminating about what they read. Most students preferred handouts that gave some scope for activity.

Training in reading

While it is not the purpose of this book to discuss students' reading skills, they are relevant to the extent that students' learning is frequently the product of an interaction between lectures and their reading. Secondly, lecturers expect students to supplement their lectures by this means. Furthermore when training in reading skills is given as part of a college course, it is often conducted in a lecture situation.

The failure of most colleges to provide training in reading to learn is, in my opinion, little short of a disgrace. While it is probably true that some commercial training courses have made exaggerated claims for the increases in speeds and comprehension by their methods, the average gains far outweigh the costs. Reading speeds over one thousand words per minute (wpm) after training have frequently been reported but after looking at data from many institutions, Poulton (1961) found that the average reading speed was between 160 and 280 wpm before training, and between 340 and 500 wpm afterwards. These figures represented increases of 40 per cent - 130 per cent. If we assume a mean of 85 per cent interacting with a mean improvement of 10 per cent in comprehension scores (MacMillan, 1965), the gain in efficiency is just over 100 per cent. However, this figure may be optimistic. There is evidence of some regression after the completion of such courses except when motivation is high (where there are even some reports of further improvements e.g. Berry, 1965). A practice effect may operate on the post-reading tests used and there may be other imponderables.

Supposing therefore we arbitrarily reduce the improvement rate to 50 per cent, this would mean that one third of the time spent in reading could be saved. To put that another way, if we suppose students are on a three-year course, their training course in reading would have to exceed the whole of one year's reading time in reaching a 50 per cent improvement, before one could say that the training was not worthwhile.

If we imagine students on a three-year course who read eleven hours per week during two 15 week semesters but never during vacations nor at any time in the rest of their life, they would need to make less than 3 per cent improvement in reading efficiency after 30 hours' tuition before we could say that the time spent training them to read faster was not saved by increased efficiency.

These calculations ignore the special requirements when reading specific subjects. Eighty-one per cent of the students in a university psychology department claimed that instruction in how to read experimental reports would have been helpful. It seems reasonable to expect that specialist literature should require a specialist training, yet few university departments see such training as an intrinsic part of the development of their subject.

Efficient reading is not simply a matter of speed. The training should include familiarization with a technical vocabulary, reading to get the main idea of a passage, the extraction of details, the application of principles, the testing of inferences and reading to evaluate. Techniques for skimming and identifying the structure of a passage are of vital importance. The earlier these skills are taught before the establishment of bad habits, the better. When detailed handouts are given, annotation by underlining key words is quicker than writing notes and quick to review later. Ayer and Milson (1993) found it no less effective, though Howe and Godfrey (1977) did, possibly because selecting words to highlight was more of a distraction than an aid to memory in the short time allowed.

The present inefficiency in reading is a luxury we do not want and cannot afford. Short courses in conjunction with subject departments need not subtract any time from the specialist disciplines. They could ease teaching, raise academic standards and help students, but until the will is present, the necessary staff will not be appointed.

Conclusion

A theme running through this section has been the need to prepare the design and manner of distribution of handouts according to their purpose. To ask the purpose of a handout seems a fairly obvious step before its preparation, yet in practice it is easily overlooked.

The need to teach study techniques such as reading skills is an extension of the same principle. If students arrive at college after careful coaching but with little experience of independent work, they will require training to work efficiently on their own.

12. Styles of Lecturing

Stylistic descriptions and their limitations.
1. What style is.
2. The paucity of research.
3. Personal factors as dimensions of styles.
4. Traditional styles amongst disciplines.

Dimensions of description.
1. Management of information.
2. Familiarity and clarity of language.
3. Styles reflecting the relative certainty of subject matter.
4. Educational values as determinants of style.

Stylistic descriptions and their limitations?

Books like this too easily leave the impression that there is only one right way of lecturing. There may be some wrong ways, but there are many right ways. If everyone lectured the same way, students' academic diet would be very monotonous. Idiosyncratic styles are to be welcomed provided they are effective. Much of this book describes what makes a lecture effective.

A question for lecturers to answer is, 'What is my usual style?'. It is a question of self awareness so that the perceptions and reactions of audiences can be understood. Answering that question is a step towards a mature self evaluation.

1. What style is

Lecturers' styles consist of the common characteristics and frequency of the techniques they employ and the way those techniques are combined. For example lecturers may write on a blackboard frequently or not at all. Obviously that is a matter of frequency. They may also write clearly, quickly, in block capitals, with yellow chalk and so on. These are characteristics or 'qualities' of their writing technique. They may combine this technique with techniques of making a key point, giving examples, explaining, lowering the voice, audience observation etc., each of which have their own frequency and characteristics. It will be evident that whilst all the elements of any technique could be enumerated with difficulty, the number of techniques is great, and the number of their possible combinations into styles is astronomic.

It follows that any description of lecturing styles first involves selecting both techniques and particular characteristics of them. Just as important, it involves not selecting a million others. Since neither techniques nor their characteristics are sharply defined, there is then a process of classification.

The selection is usually arbitrary. Every chapter of this book mentions techniques and their qualities that could be relevant.

Any description of a lecturing style is wholly constrained by this selection. The data is typically gathered through questionnaires. A 'principal components analysis', or 'factor analysis' is used to detect factors underlying responses, and then a cluster analysis groups together individuals for whom each of the factors are of similar importance. It is said of computers, 'Garbage in: garbage out'. The same might be said of factor and cluster analyzes, or indeed, any statistical treatment of data. The choice of observations or data collected wholly determines the techniques and their characteristics that constitute a description of style.

Given the limitations, there are two broad approaches. One is to attempt global descriptions by gathering as much information as possible on whatever seems important, and then analyzing it statistically. The other is to restrict data to particular techniques and characteristics so that the resultant styles are explicitly linguistic, traditional, subject centered, values driven, or what ever the particular restriction is. The relevance of such selective descriptions depends upon what they are used for. Self-enlightenment, improvement, evaluation or adjustment to particular audiences are all possible purposes.

2. The paucity of research

The study of lecturing styles is in its infancy. There is no generally agreed classification. There are studies of students' learning styles, and research into styles of teaching in general, such as student-centered and subject-centered teaching; but there has been very little research into specific styles of lecturing. What there is, is largely dependent on the subjective opinions of students in questionnaire studies. There are very few objective studies using direct observation by trained observers. And with the exception of the study by Bakhtar and Brown (1988), the range of observations in these studies is very restricted.

Dudley-Evans and Johns (1981) thought there are three lecture styles: reading, rhetorical and conversational. They pointed out that these styles involve quite different lecture signals. Whilst the rhetorical style might be more appropriate in arts subjects, the choice of these styles probably reflects personal preferences.

3. Personal factors as dimensions of styles

It might be thought that personality factors would be determinants of lecture style. Surely, for example, the confident and the timid will have different approaches. Maybe they do; but there is remarkably little confirmation from research. Indeed there is very little research on this point, and what there is does not paint a consistent picture. Possibly the number of relevant variables is so great that no one factor, or group of factors, shows up strongly.

Another possible reason for inconsistencies is that even if the personal characteristics of lecturers determines their styles, it is the interaction with those of the students that will determine any measurable outcomes; and since students differ, they will not all interact the same way. Arguably different students will flourish with different styles. Katz (1990) found that students with a reflective learning style did better on problem solving tasks following lectures; those with a more active learning style needed discussion or more involvement than passive listening. However Cavanagh *et al.* (1995) showed no advantage for students with a reflective learning style, though their recommendation that lecturers should cater for a variety of styles, and therefore involve the students in a variety of ways, is a repeated message in this book.

In one study (Winocur *et al.* 1989) regardless of their sex, lecturers with a friendly style were perceived by students as more effective, confident, professional and approachable. Whether they were in fact more effective was not reported. Indeed educational seduction is a well recognized phenomenon (Chapter 14) but there is some confirmation from Kelly and Kelly (1982). They interviewed nine professors who had won teaching awards and found that on the whole they were older, came from non-affluent families, had a strong academic preparation and motivation for a teaching career and questioned the priority of research in salary and promotion criteria. Their styles were characterized by enjoyment, enthusiasm for the subject, humor, theatrical performance, a good command of language and its delivery, and involvement of students through questions and discussion.

4. Traditional styles amongst disciplines

The relative privacy of lectures means that the only role models that many faculty have are those who lectured to them in their student days perhaps some years ago. Not only does this produce a very conservative profession, but the inbreeding within subject disciplines means that teaching styles are characteristic of academic subjects. Indeed anyone who has observed lectures on a range of disciplines across several continents can testify that there is more in common stylistically between, say, biochemistry lectures in Indian, European and American medical schools, than with biochemistry lectures in the chemistry departments of the same universities.

These conservative stylistic traditions within disciplines still need to be researched. They are not always a function of the subject matter. Nor are they based upon objective evidence of what is effective. For example, philosophers want students to consider specific propositions, but it is remarkably rare for philosophy lecturers to display the propositions on an overhead projector or chalkboard, or to stop lecturing and let the students consider them either individually or in groups. The convention is that the philosopher keeps tight control by responding immediately to any contribution a student makes. This inhibits thought in a discipline that, almost above all others, aims to promote it.

Dimensions of description

We have seen that the number of dimensions could be infinite. In seeking awareness of their own style, lecturers might choose any of them. What follows is confined to published studies and is not intended to restrict the scope of lecturers' self awareness.

1. Management of information

The best and most global study of lecturing styles was carried out by Bakhtar and Brown (1988). To choose their data they noted similarities and differences of style and discussed them with a few faculty. After piloting a questionnaire asking faculty what is important when lecturing, they got a 65% return rate and responses from over 50 subject specialisms which they classified into humanities, social science, science and engineering, and biomedical. The questionnaire included self-reports and open ended questions on good and bad lecture techniques. Although wide ranging, most of their items were concerned with how lecturers manage the information content of their lectures - its preparation, organization, language, sources, presentation, assessment, and so on. Factor analysis revealed six aspects of lecturing: information giving, structuring, a sense of purpose, visual techniques, self doubt/confidence, and attention to presentation techniques such as asking questions, quoting and using repetitions.

The factors clustered into five lecturing styles which they labeled: exemplary (26%), amorphous (23%), oral (18%), visual (26%) and eclectic (9%). Bakhtar and Brown found no relation between group membership and either seniority or length of experience. If this implies that lecturers do not change and develop their techniques throughout their working lives, it lays stress upon the importance of initial training. You are invited to consider whether your own and others' lecturing styles fit any of these groups.

Exemplary lecturers appeared to follow the advice given by the majority of respondents. Around one-third of lecturers in humanities, social and biomedical sciences were in this cluster. They are confident, well organized, use a variety of oral and visual techniques, structure their lectures and lecture notes clearly with headings and sub-headings, and inform students of their objectives and future topics. Less significantly they recapitulate and link previous lectures, outline the organization of the present one, raise questions at the beginning and end of lectures, use visuals and quotations to illustrate points, and provide handouts and advice on note-taking. Overall they strive to promote thought and understanding, not just factual information.

The amorphous group are the most distinctive. They are confident, but vague and poorly prepared. They are the least likely to tell students their objectives, lecture organization, future topics, examination topics, or how to take notes. They approve of lecturer training, but don't think they personally need it. Around 30% of scientists and engineers in Bakhtar and Brown's sample were in this cluster.

As their name suggests, oral lecturers scarcely use the chalkboard, overhead projector or any other visual aid. They are to be found (particularly amongst scholars in arts and humanities, 34%) using and possibly quoting several sources, and relying almost exclusively on their own verbal fluency to expound them. Accordingly they don't prepare in detail on paper; headings, subheadings and brief notes are all they require.

Visual lecturers are strongly represented in science and engineering subjects (43%). They are most inclined to rely on one text, prepare full notes and spend much of the lecture writing (calculations and proofs) on the chalkboard or overhead projector. More than other groups they are inclined to give more information than students can absorb at the time. They may summarize on completing a topic, but because topics do not fit neatly into 50 minute lectures, these summaries are often in the middle of a lesson.

Lastly the eclectic group was the smallest in Bakhtar and Brown's survey (9%). They use a variety of techniques but lack confidence in using them. Indeed in an earlier research paper (Brown, Bakhtar and Youngman, 1984) they were called 'self-doubters'. They don't write their objectives down, but like all the other groups except the amorphous lecturers, they claim to think about them.

In a more restricted enquiry, Bakhtar and Brown (rightly in my view) place some emphasis on the organization of lectures when discussing styles. They briefly described the classification hierarchy, problem centered, chaining, comparison and thesis lecture forms, and then asked lecturers which they used most often. With the exception of humanities (48%), all used the classification hierarchy around 60% of the time. Problem centered (20%) and chaining (18%) were each the second most used by about a third of the lecturers. Comparison and thesis lecture forms were said to be used very little.

Two other studies have focussed on how lecturers manage their information. Rather than investigate lecture styles and then see which is most effective, Albanese *et al.* (1991) asked students which lecturers they rated high and low, and then compared the styles. Differences in student involvement and the clarity of introductions and organization emerged as most important. Clarity, organization and student involvement also emerged as the important stylistic factors for students, regardless of their age and sex, in a study by Ross (1989). These two studies tend to confirm Bakhtar and Brown's emphasis upon organization.

2. Familiarity and clarity of language

Lecturers differ in linguistic style. Lectures are more difficult to understand when the style of language is unfamiliar. Bernstein has shown that lower social groups are relatively disadvantaged because they speak with much more simple sentence constructions than their teachers. Even lectures in American Sign Language show different styles in their syntax, lexical choice, speech rate, pausing and intonation (Shaw, 1987).

Linn (1973) describes several varieties of English: the 'frozen style' of written documents, the academic or 'formal style' that faculty expect students to write, the 'casual style' between friends and acquaintances, and the 'intimate style' between friends and lovers. He says the language of black Americans lies somewhere between the last two and is characterized by ellipsis, jargon and slang. The typical linguistic style of lecturers is 'formal' and maintains a social distance too great for a fully supportive climate to develop. On the other hand, if lecturers try to use a linguistic style that is not their own, they are quickly perceived as insincere and not genuine.

Familiarity is one important aspect of a lecturer's language. Clarity is another. Land (1981) used three video-recorded lectures of 20 minutes with the same information, but varying in the number of vague expressions and uninformative phrases. Students' learning and ratings of clarity were both related to the lecturer's accuracy of language. In a later experiment (Land and Combs, 1982) Land varied the amount of unexplained content in 15 minute video-recorded lectures. When there was "none" the lecturer was perceived as clearer in explaining, more confident, serious, better prepared, less nervous and more knowledgeable in the subject.

Hiller (1969) found a lecturer's vagueness and students' acquisition of knowledge correlated negatively (-0.48 and -0.59). He therefore confined a later study (Hiller, 1971) to the spoken indications of conceptual vagueness and concluded that when lecturers lack knowledge they suffer stress and adopt stylistic behaviors to defend themselves. These relationships are represented in Figure 12.1.

In general both lecturers' emotions and their knowledge of their subject influence their lecture techniques, particularly the clarity or vagueness of their language. The techniques, or their consequences, may also affect feelings so that a spiral effect is created. In particular, where lecturers lack knowledge (because they have insufficient, are confused, uncertain or can't remember) they are afraid to express themselves. The resulting defensiveness, anxiety and low self-esteem may make the confusion, uncertainty and information retrieval far worse. The fear to express oneself leads to a variety of linguistic techniques described as non-specific equivocation, such as excessive cautiousness or simplified statements (Hiller, 1971). Similarly Carlsen (1993) found that scientists teaching unfamiliar topics in schools tended to talk for longer periods and ask rather low level questions.

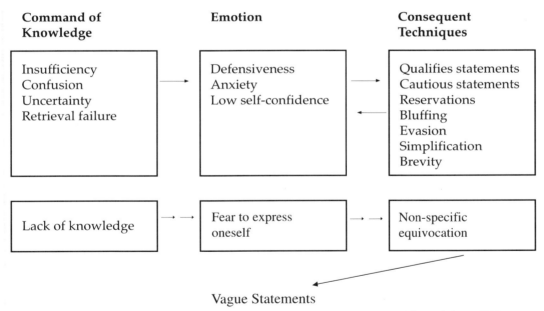

Figure 12.1 The impact of ignorance and emotion upon vagueness. (Adapted from Hiller, 1971.) Arrows indicate direction of cause to effect.

3. Styles reflecting the relative certainty of subject matter

The influence of conservative traditions and lecture content could result in lecture styles varying with subject disciplines. The styles of explanation could be different. Influenced by Bakhtar and Brown, Behr (1988) also obtained responses from lecturers. He classified the results into four styles: Information Providers and Dramatic, Structured and Visual Presenters. With the exception of engineers, the majority of every subject group saw themselves as structured presenters. One wonders whether their students would see them the same way.

Although Behr's sample was not large, his data shows a tendency for subject disciplines to stand in a certain order with regard to lecturing styles. According to Schachter *et al.* (1991, 1994) lecturers in natural sciences, social sciences and the humanities, in that order, are more likely to fill pauses with 'uh', 'er' and 'um' because humanists have a wider vocabulary, therefore more words to choose from

	% of Respondents			
	Structured Presenter	Dramatic Presenter	Information Provider	Visual Presenter
Engineering	20	-	-	80
Science	47	8	-	45
Health	40	10	15	35
Commerce & Law	45	21	17	17
Humanities (Social Sci)	50	20	17	13
Arts and Languages	61	22	7	10

Figure 12.2. Tendencies towards styles for subject disciplines

and more possibilities of what the next word should be. Language in the natural sciences is more precise, so there are fewer options for the lecturer and less hesitation is needed. A similar order appears on many other apparently different measures: for example what students expect from lectures (Smithers, 1970); numerical - verbal emphasis within disciplines; the vocational orientation of students (with the possible exception of scientists); and personality dimensions such as authoritarianism - independence of mind, dogmatism - open mindedness, convergent - divergent thinking, and anxious introversion - stable extroversion. Ramsden (1992) shows the same sequence with regard to evaluation data.

Very much more study is needed, but so far it looks as if the certainty of the subject matter taught is more definitive of teaching style than a concern for teaching itself. Though different, these measures all reflect the degree of certainty in the disciplines. They reflect a discipline orientation.

4. Educational values as determinants of style

The order as associated with an educational orientation is not quite the same. Ratings of educational values, an interest in educational research, or expertise in teaching commonly show a slightly different order: health, engineering, physical sciences, commerce/law, social sciences, languages and arts (Ramsden, 1992).

However, using a different questionnaire, Falchikov (1993) did obtain five factors to do with teaching: qualities necessary in a lecturer, a positive attitude to teaching, a negative attitude to teaching, responsibility for students, and beliefs about the best way to teach and learn. On the basis of these factors Falchikov identified seven groups of faculty:

(i)   *A group pro student autonomy with a student focus* believe students should take responsibility for their own learning and teachers should turn them into thinkers.

(ii)   *Traditionalists* who think their job is important and satisfying, and is to communicate, to impart knowledge, and to help students pass exams.

(iii)   *The pro student autonomy group with a faculty focus* believe their job is satisfying, and is to develop students and to be enthusiastic.

(iv)   *A group under pressure* think students learn by finding out, solving problems, taking responsibility for their own learning, and going to the library. Faculty need to communicate, have more time to prepare and create a supportive environment. They find their job stressful.

(v)   *Senior faculty* like course development and think there is no best way to teach, students should take responsibility for their own learning, and have an open outlook.

(vi)   *Professionals* contribute to their discipline, want promotion and be a team member.

(vii)   *Defensive traditionalists* are subject centered, and keep abreast of their subject. They think there is too much emphasis on research, their job is to impart knowledge and to maintain standards of discipline.

Innovators tended to be amongst groups (i) and (v). Scientists tended to be traditionalists with less emphasis upon higher levels of intellectual and ethical development (Perry, 1970).

Conclusion

Lecturing styles is an area ripe for research. Millions of people have observed and discussed differences in lecturers' styles, yet remarkably little is known about them with objective detachment. What is known seems to indicate the importance of organization and language.

13. Ways of Obtaining Feedback

Non-verbal communication.

1. Arrival of students.
2. Seating position and student groups.
3. Students' reactions.
4. Styles of note-taking.

Verbal feedback.

1. Questioning technique.
2. Mechanical means of response.
3. Help with individual work.
4. Buzz groups.
5. Submitted work.
6. Step-by-step lecture.
7. Record of answers in a problem-based course.
8. Prepared answers.
9. Interpolated questions from students.
10. Questions from groups.

Conclusion.

One of the most serious criticisms of the lecture method is that the lecturer has no feedback on his performance, and students have no knowledge of the amount and accuracy of their learning. Beard (1967) has drawn an analogy with two kinds of evaluation in industry. The first consists in the assessment by inspection of completed work; while the second monitors the production process in order that continuous improvements may be made in its efficiency. In manufacturing processes the second is regarded as the more important, but in education great emphasis is placed on the final examination and less on the process of teaching and learning. What is required is for the effectiveness of a lecture to be evident at the time so that corrections can be made if necessary. This is the importance of feedback.

This is confirmed by psychologists who have shown the importance of feedback for learning and the performance of other tasks (Annett, 1969). The lecture is a form of one-way verbal communication such that neither the lecturer nor his audience has adequate knowledge of what they are doing.

There are three broad solutions. Lecturers may rely on non-verbal communication from the students. They may abandon the exclusive use of the lecture method by obtaining verbal feedback, or they may evaluate their effectiveness after the lecture either from the opinions of students and other observers or from indicators of students' learning. Evaluations after the lecture, whether from direct observations or students' learning, will be considered in the next chapter. This chapter is concerned with feedback during the lesson itself.

Non-verbal communication

The observation and interpretation of the non-verbal behavior of students in the lecture situation is an essential skill for good teaching. The new lecturer cannot expect to acquire it fully in his first three years; some probably never do, and remain oblivious of missing anything. It is essentially learned by practice. Observation of students during other people's lectures by sitting to one side near the front may provide practice without the additional need to concentrate on the lecturer's subject matter.

The first task is to make informed 'guesses', about the students' emotions and attitudes. (I say 'guesses', because one can never know what they are for certain. Many students have learned the art of maintaining a fixed expression which hides their thoughts and feelings.)

1. Arrival of students

Do the students arrive as a group, or dribble in, in ones and twos? This may give an indication of the relationships amongst the class and may therefore reflect the degree of cohesiveness in the group as a whole. If the teaching methods require work in groups for discussion or practical activities the social structure of the group may be important.

Do they arrive on time? Are notebooks opened ready for the lecture or are they reluctantly pulled out of a bag with an 'Oh well, I suppose we had better...' attitude once the lecture has started?

2. Seating position

Where do students sit? If they sit at the back it may indicate a distant relationship between the students and the lecturer so that two-way communication is more difficult. This will affect the willingness of students to ask questions when they do not understand, and the ease with which the lecturer can obtain responses or contributions from the class. Thus, these relationships impose limitations on the teaching techniques that can be used. How has the lecturer's manner affected these relationships? Obviously if the lecturer is aggressive or pinpoints individuals with questions, the students are likely to retreat, but usually student-lecturer relationships are more subtle than this so that individuals react differently and the sensitivity of the lecturer to the reactions of individuals needs to be acute.

It is very useful to observe differences between students and groups of students. Who is independent in his judgement and who looks sideways for the support and agreement of others? Are there individuals who indicate the general mood of the class? If so, it is useful to recognize these barometers early in a course.

Look at Figure 13.1. A has come, not only to listen to the lecture, but also to watch everyone else. If he is a student, not an inspector or an academic colleague, he may be a bit of a loner.

B is what used to be called 'a swot'. He is intent on doing well academically to the exclusion of his wider education, the development of his social skills and what else the university can offer. (In tests out of 10, Giles *et al.* (1982) found that students in the front, middle and back rows scored 8.00, 7.16 and 6.81 respectively.) In section 4 below, I recommend observing the note-taking of typical students near the front, in order to judge the pacing of the lecture and the clarity of its organization. B is not one to observe for this purpose.

C are a courting couple. They seem a bit wrapped up in each other. If they have shared their tasks for private study, and have only one set of notes between them, they will be in difficulties if they quarrel and split up before the examinations.

The students around D and E form a group. It is difficult for a lecturer to observe every student when there are more than 30 in a class. The reactions of students in the group will be strongly influenced by the group leader. But which is the group leader? It is likely to be either D or E. Other group members will sit where they can observe the leader and take their cue from him. So the leader won't be in the row behind; nor is he likely to be at the end of the group in the row in front. So for this group of seven students, the lecturer can get feedback most efficiently by observing either D or E. Another way to identify the leader is to observe this group when they arrive. Others will observe and follow where the leader intends to sit. For this reason he may well be the second or third member to come through the door.

Many students who want to enjoy other things, think they are least likely to be observed if they sit in the back row. This is a mistake. They are much less noticeable if lost in the crowd. Experienced lecturers use eye contact to engage the attention of students in the back row.

Finally we may notice that G has taken a seat near the back door because he wants to get away fast and be first in the lunch queue or borrow the only library copy of the book you have just recommended. If you want him to hear administrative announcements, make them at the beginning of the lecture.

These examples are, of course, anecdotal, but they should give the beginning lecturer some feedback about students from their choice of seating position.

3. Students' reactions

How alert and responsive are the students? The speed of their reactions reflects their interest and speed of comprehension. How far do the emotions of the students reflect the emotions of the lecturer? Because humor is an expression of the emotions, reactions to the lecturer's jokes are a particularly sensitive indicator of the lecturer-student relationship. A very wide range of emotions and relationships can be expressed in laughter. These are frequently signs of the limits of student tolerance. Is the reaction appreciative, is it spontaneous? If there is no reaction, communication is minimal.

What reactions are shown on the students' faces? Are they attentive, tired, sullen, rebellious....? Do they look at the lecturer or avoid his gaze? Do they look for non-verbal communication from the lecturer? If this kind of feedback is difficult to obtain from some students because they never look up from their notes, pointing to visual aids at

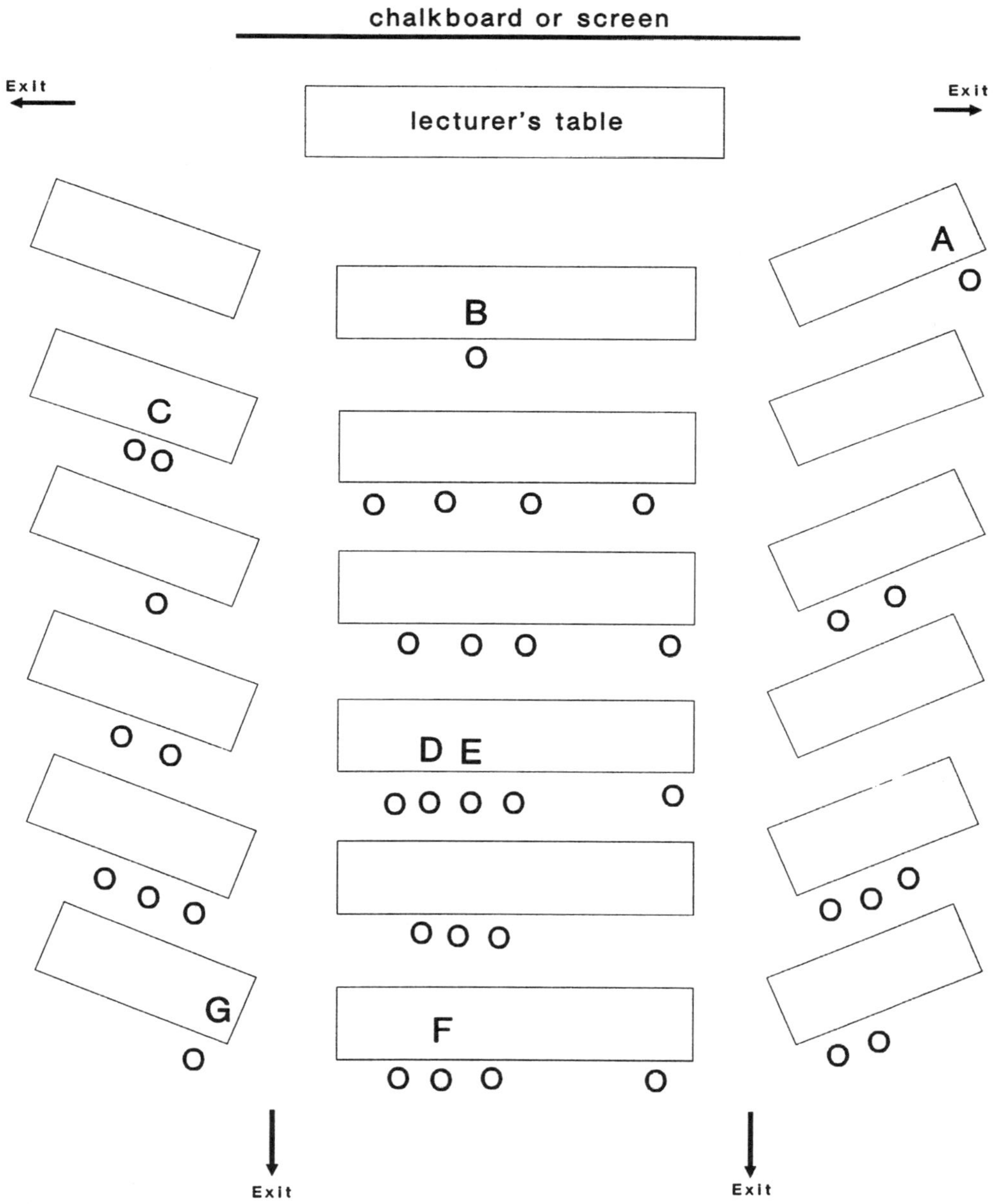

Figure 13.1 Seating positions in a lecture theatre.

the front of the class and using such words as 'this', 'these', 'here', and 'now watch' will force the students to look up. The lecturer may slow the pace momentarily to give students time to look up, and himself time to observe their left-over facial expression which often gives a sign of their recent feelings. Subsequent pauses give the students 'thinking time' and the lecturer time to see how they use it.

4. Styles of note-taking

Attention should be paid to what students note. Student who always write too much may be lacking in self-confidence which should be boosted in tutorials or group discussion. Noting everything frequently indicates an inability to select what is important. This may have many causes - lack of background knowledge, poor critical ability or the lack of clear organization by the lecturer. The first requires a carefully planned course of reading; the second, practice in applying knowledge and solving problems in written work, discussion or private study; and the third, itemization of points under headings on the blackboard or screen as the lecture progresses.

It is worth noticing - by looking for the spacing of headings and the presence of numbers in the margin or inset from it - how far the students' notes reflect the organization of the lecture. (This is not to say that they always should. The best students may reorganize the lecturer's information in their own way; or they may know the facts already and only note their reactions. It is for the failure to grasp any organization at all that the lecturer should be vigilant.) If these observations are related to a student's written work, it is possible to get some understanding of how a student deals with information, his thought processes, and possibly his general study habits.

These observations are also essential to the timing within a lecture. If lecturers want the students to listen with undivided attention they should wait until students have finished noting one point before going on to the next. Yet it is quite common for lecturers to proceed apace, regardless of what the students are doing. This may easily happen with new lecturers who are nervous; but if they can take a firm grip of themselves and pause (which may not be easy) the pause can be used to steady themselves.

Verbal feedback

About 5% of the students interviewed by Marris (1964), complained of lecturers who resented or evaded questions. If lecturers want immediate verbal feedback from the students they must stop their own exposition to obtain it. Once students have begun to give and receive feedback, the lecturer's job is relatively easy. The difficult task is breaking the ice both with the class as a whole and with particular individuals. The suggestions that follow are neither exhaustive nor infallible. They are techniques that some lecturers have found useful. Much depends on the personal feelings of those involved.

1. Questioning technique

Because questioning is the form of language that requires a response, lecturers requiring feedback are likely to use a questioning technique. But it must also be remembered that questions are threatening stimuli. They produce a fear reaction. Using pulsemeters, I have found that the heart rate of students in a tutorial group increased by 5 to 10 beats per minute in the first thirty seconds after a tutor asked a question. The heart rate of students who spoke increased by 10 to 70 beats per minute. It seems reasonable to think that answering questions in the presence of a lecture audience would be an even more stressful situation. This awaits further investigation, but it is interesting that in both group tutorials and lectures, I have found that students' heart rates rise appreciably when their neighbors speak.

Two tentative conclusions may be drawn: the questions and the ways in which they are asked should produce minimal psychological stress; and to obtain feedback from those students for whom a 'public response' would be too stressful, the lecturer will need to adopt a less direct technique. Questions requiring personal reactions, personal opinions or the application of personal experience such that the answers are unlikely to be wrong, are, paradoxically, the least incriminating. They are also useful in that they easily permit supplementary questions leading to the development of the topic. Psychologically speaking, if student feedback is to be encouraged, their responses need to be rewarded. Consequently the lecturer's manner is of vital importance. Therefore the relevance of a lecturer's first question is less important than its emotional climate.

2. Mechanical means of response

Some teachers have developed techniques to obtain feedback 'in private'. Lecture theaters can be wired for electrical responses to a panel only seen by the lecturer. Such panels may give individual or collective responses.

Lecture theaters with networked computer terminals for each student allow much more sophisticated presentations and responses. More significantly they allow sophisticated analysis of individual students' responses such that follow-up tuition and counseling can be more personally directed than in the past.

Using a much less costly device Taplin (1969) supplied Air Force trainees with two-and-a-half inch cubes with differently colored faces so that answers to multiple-choice questions could be shown privately by students, each holding his own cube in cupped hands so that only the lecturer could see the color selected to correspond with his answer. Dunn (1969) has used colored cards more cheaply for the same purpose with medical students. Harden *et al.* (1968) devised 'An audience response card' with five colors covered by paper flaps, which could be shown in fourteen combinations permitting relatively complex multiple choice questions to be answered.

For example, during a lecture on goiter the following question was asked:- Iodine deficiency:
(i)   may result in goiter,
(ii)   results in hypothyroidism,
(iii)   is commoner in the winter,
(iv)   is associated with low urine iodine excretion,
(v)   results from a deficiency of meat in the diet.
(correct answers (i) and (iv))

When a significant proportion of the class answered (ii), the lecturer realized that his lecture had not sufficiently stressed that in most countries iodine deficiency is rarely severe enough to cause hypothyroidism. Harden et al found that the preparation of questions and the organization of the lecture took more time, but that the result was more interesting and more effective teaching. Taplin, too, found that the preparation of questions took time, but that without this feedback he would have assumed more understanding from his students than would have been justified. This assumption is more common than to underestimate students' knowledge.

3. Help with individual work

It is, of course, possible to set problems for students to solve individually in the lecture situation while the lecturer goes round to help those having difficulty. This is a useful technique which can promote thought and help the lecturer to know his students as well as provide feedback on students' understanding, but it can cause resentment if students come expecting only to listen, think the lecturer is not doing his job, or do not appreciate the value of immediately applying the principles they have just learned. Consequently, as with all techniques that break the long-established habits of teaching, its purpose must first be explained to obtain student assent.

4. Buzz groups

An alternative feedback technique is to give the problems to small buzz groups of two to six members to discuss for two to five minutes before reporting their answers (Chapter 19).

5. Submitted work

Some lecturers set problems to be solved before the next lecture or tutorial group, but, as we have seen, rehearsal and feedback are not as effective when delayed as when given immediately, during the lecture itself (Chapter 4). Furthermore, motivation frequently wanes during the ensuing week unless the obligation to complete the work is reinforced strongly.

6. Step-by-step lecture

What I call the 'step-by-step lecture' method consists of three to ten short periods of exposition by the lecturer each followed by class discussion under the lecturer's general control. The student activity, frequent feedback, opportunities for rehearsal, the periodic relaxation from concentrated listening and the consequent reduction of retroactive interference make this a very useful method with classes up to thirty and with difficult subject matter that is best built up in stages.

Koo, Wong and Tam (1993) compared traditional lectures and lectures based upon a handout with spaces and problems. Interaction with the lecturer was monitored every 5 seconds. Students spent 13% of the time on the problems at intervals through the lectures and 33% in discussion with the teacher immediately thereafter. There was no difference in their learning as measured by an objective test of factual information after 3 weeks; but they might have found a difference if they had tested more thought. Students strongly favored the interactive method.

7. Record of answers in a problem-based course

McCarthy (1970) used a variation of this method by basing his course around problems projected on a screen and which were each attempted by the students and discussed by the teacher before proceeding to the next. The questions were also supplied on a handout with space for students' notes so that a complete record of the course could be maintained. There was little formal lecturing. The method was quite popular with the students, but like Taplin (1969), the teacher over-estimated students' knowledge and had to slow his pace considerably.

8. Prepared answers

Elton (1970) provided the first year physical sciences course at Surrey University with full lecture notes and space for additions together with self-tests. Possession of the notes did not discourage attendance at lectures which became occasions for feedback on test performance, rather than the reception of information for the first time. Almost half the students did the tests either 'always' or 'frequently', while only 7% 'never' did.

Instead of lecturing, MacManaway (1970) circulated complete lecture scripts together with questions and assignments designed to extend thinking and comprehension in sociology. Feedback was obtained by contact with seven or eight discussion groups during the first half hour and then by general discussion following group reports. This method was appreciated by the majority of students and only 13% would have preferred some form of lecture.

9. Interpolated questions from students

It is quite a common practice for lecturers to deliver their lecture and only ask if there are any questions at the end. However, it will already be clear from what has been said about reducing retroactive interference, the provision of opportunity for rehearsal, the immediacy of feedback for motivation and the effect of a change of stimulation or change of activity on the decline in students' attention, that it is better to avoid long periods of uninterrupted exposition. Furthermore, students may be embarrassed to ask questions about the early part of a lecture if doing so implies they have not understood the rest, while if the later part of a lecture is to be understood, it is the lecturer's duty to ensure these questions are answered before that point is reached. In any case, the effect of retroactive interference in a paced situation is sufficiently strong that students frequently forget questions they would have liked to ask. Delaying the opportunity for questions fails to take advantage of the temporary initial interest in a point. Asking 'Are there any questions?' at the end, frequently means the same as 'If there aren't any questions we can all go', and at some times in the day it takes a strong-willed student to respond. Consequently questions are often only asked by the more able and dedicated students, while feedback is required more from those with difficulties. It may be controversial, but in my view, few periods of exposition by a lecturer should exceed twenty minutes to half an hour without some feedback or other variation in method.

If the lecturer wishes to elicit questions and contributions from a class it is usually not a good idea to give the student carte blanche by asking 'Are there any questions?'. It is usually better to direct questions to an important issue on which feedback is desired.

If there are still no questions it is useful for the lecturer to have supplementary open questions: 'Did you find Smith's explanation convincing?', or 'Do you think this fact is surprising?'. When a student answers this sort of question it is possible to ask him 'Why?' and his explanation will give valuable feedback on his understanding.

10. Questions from groups

A useful way to obtain feedback is to instruct buzz groups (Chapter 19) to ask at least one question each. This has the advantages that foolish and time-wasting questions are eliminated by fellow students who answer them; students who are too shy to speak in a lecture class may be willing to pose a question in a small group; and many students are willing to ask a question when they discover they were not the only ones who did not understand, or who disagreed with, a particular point.

If further anonymity is required the questions may be written on paper and either passed forward to the lecturer or collected when visiting each discussion. In either case it saves time and leads to a more orderly presentation if the questions can be grouped appropriately. Because a number of buzz groups usually ask similar questions, this technique is useful for lecturers to find out which part of a topic is most difficult and thus requires most careful explanation. (Conclusion, Chapter 9.)

Conclusion

Some of the techniques that require greatest skill in obtaining feedback are derived from a lecturer's observation of his class. The sensitive lecturer notices the slight frown, the hesitation for thought, the smallest expression of puzzlement and a student's stare at his notes that is longer than usual. These often signify thoughts about the lecture and if the lecturer can tactfully elicit them, it may be possible to develop the lecture topic in a way that is particularly meaningful to that class. Thus, it is the combination of techniques that leads to good teaching, not their use in isolation.

14. Evaluation of lectures

There's a debate about what approach to take

Make a preliminary enquiry.

Get professional help to observe and describe.
    1.   Who are the professionals?
    2.   Difficulty in facing oneself.
    3.   Procedures and principles of consultation.

Students' opinions.
    1.   The need to obtain students' opinions.
    2.   Devising the questionnaire.
    3.   What should be evaluated?
    4.   The potent variable in students' opinions.
    5.   Students' opinions are reliable.
    6.   The validity of students' opinions is modest and inconsistent.
    7.   Conclusion.

Assessment of learning objectives achieved.
    1.   Recognition of key points.
    2.   Memory of a simple stated relationship.
    3.   Making simple inferences.
    4.   Application.
    5.   Analytical thought.
    6.   Synthesis.
    7.   Evaluation.
    8.   Attitudes.
    9.   Conclusion.

Conclusion.

There's a debate about what approach to take

The logic of this chapter is slightly different from the others. In other chapters I have tried to combine research, common sense and experience to paint a picture of generalizations lecturers can apply in their own teaching. In this chapter the aim is to suggest generalizations about particulars. That is to say, how to find out characteristics of a particular lecture or lecturer in order to impove them.

    What methods should be used? There are any number and the answer depends upon your paradigm of inquiry. Amongst educationalists, this has been a matter of debate. Being a debate, too often a method, or sequence of methods, has been presented as opposed to others, rather than recognizing that they all have their merits depending on what you want to find out.

On a traditional approach a lecture is evaluated by testing the students' learning to see how far the lecturer's objectives have been achieved. Students' learning is a fundamental indicator of the lecuer's success. This is sometimes described as a scientific paradigm as if it used experimental testing of a hypothesis in order to increase confidence in a generalization. It is nothing of the kind. Firstly, as made clear in sections 4 and 5 of Chapter 3, that is not the way generalizations are made about teaching. And secondly, as I've just said, establishing generalizations is not what these evaluations are for any way.

The assessment of learning can have some objectivity, but it has its limitations. It does not evaluate whether the objectives were sufficient or worth while. The criteria are sometimes imposed by the evaluator, not negotiated with those evaluated. They take no account of the students' aims. A lecture might teach all the knowledge etc. that the lecturer intended, but have such disastrous side effects, for example on students' motivation, as to render the lecture a failure in a wider context. There are always subsidiary aims and standards of this kind that normally go unspoken. Furthermore, the assessment of students alone does not tell the lecturer where or what improvements are needed, or what to do about them. Some critics will go further and say that a lecture should be conceived as a social event governed by all kinds of unacknowledged rules and rituals. A lecturer's and students' intentions and values can only be understood in a social context.

Accordingly it is argued that a lecture cannot be evaluated in an objective way detached from its context, but only *interpreted* from within a sub-culture. On this view a lecturer's behavior, and the students' response, can only be interpreted in the light of their intentions, perceptions and the whole background of their knowledge and assumptions. Hence these interpretations are necessarily subjective. An independent evlauator cannot observe them. All the evaluator can do is to help the lecturer and students to *reflect* on what they did, why they did it, and what they would want to do differently on another occasion. Helping others to reflect may involve some *negotiation*. Alternatively, by working to clarify their assumptions, rules, understanding and values, the evaluator may behave more like a counselor than a researcher. Such an inquiry will go wider than what happens in the lecture room. For example, it will include reflection on administrative processes and how knowledge is organized in their minds.

There are several variants of these subjective approaches. Their critics will point out that we all have coherent and consistent self-deceptions and illusions about ourselves, what we do, our reasons for doing it, and out social perceptions. You don't have to study Freud to know that, because lecturers feel exposed, they have all manner of defense mechanisms that only a full blown psychoanalysis will reveal.

It will be clear that both objective and subjective methods have their limitations. The things that can be evaluated are legion and complex in their interactions. Subjective methods can range more widely than objective assessments. So it probably pays to start with the more subjective approaches and use them diagnostically to *progressively focus* on particular areas for improvement. My advice is keep it simple.

Preliminary inquiry. First of all carry out a preliminary inquiry. Let this be descriptive and potentially diagnostic like the open-ended questionnaire in Figure 14.1. Very likely that will tell you as much as you need to know.

Consultation. If it doesn't, and you want to inquire in more detail on more specific points, if possible consult someone professionally engaged in evaluation work. A deeper inquiry is a research task. If educational evaluation is not your field, no one should expect you to be 'expert' at it. Depending on what you want to know, the consultant could use any of many different research techniques. To describe them would take another book. This chapter can only sample two of them:

Students' reflections and opinions. Questionnaires are by far the most researched and commonly used methods.

The assessment of learning objectives achieved. Although there are several kinds of objective test, truth functional tests were specifically desgned for assessing the effectiveness of lectures.

Make a preliminary enquiry

First it is necessary to decide what is to be evaluated. There are so many aspects of lecturing and what goes on in lecture rooms that it is impossible to evaluate all of them simultaneously. Even if one could, the evaluation process would so disturb the lecture itself as to render the evaluation invalid. Any evaluation is partial. Inevitably there is a selection process. Being preliminary before any objective evaluation, the selection is necessarily impressionistic. Consequently, right at the beginning, there is a loss of objectivity in all evaluations, quite apart from whether the data itself and its interpretation are subjective. The subjective selection of what to evaluate runs the risk that unimportant aspects will be given undue weight and important aspects will be omitted.

One way to reduce this risk is to give students a preliminary open-ended free response questionnaire of the kind shown in Figure 14.1. Covering only one side of the sheet of paper, it is quick to produce and administer. It needs no professional evaluator.

The first question seeks an overall judgement which helps to interpret later responses. However there is a trap to be avoided in its interpretation. Lectures are multi-faceted. Different students will use different criteria. Therefore responses should be treated individually, not averaged or treated statistically in other ways. To a point this caution goes for any rating scale. The more specific the scale, the more objective it can be. This scale is particularly general. The comments may indicate an individual's criteria.

If the lecturer and the students are trying to achieve different things, they will get nowhere working in conflict. Question 2 checks this out.

Questions 3 and 4 are diagnostic. Question 4 elicits details for self improvement or further investigation. More important, question 3 shows the strengths that can be built

Figure 14.1 Form for a preliminary enquiry

LECTURE EVALUATION

In order to help me to improve my lectures, please complete the form below. Your response will be treated as strictly confidential and anonymous. Please do not put your name on the paper.

Poor Good

1. What is your overall opinion of this lecture
    compared with lectures generally
    Place an X in the appropriate box.
    Please comment.

    Poor   *Good*

2. State your objectives in attending this lecture. How far have they been achieved?

3. Give two things you liked about the lecture.

    a)

    b)

4. Give two things you disliked about the lecture.

a)

    b)

5. If I was to teach this topic again, what changes do you recommend I should make?

upon and which should not normally be restricted by changes for improvement. Demanding itemized points encourages thought and brevity. I often ask for three of each, but not more. With responses from a whole class, it is usually clear where I need to improve, and what the good points are that I should not remove when doing so.

Question 5 is designed to encourage constructive responses and can be the springboard for discussion later.

As I said, this form can be administered by the lecturer and is usually sufficient. If further enquiry is required, it is generally best to get professional advice.

Get professional help to observe and describe

To some people, seeking help may feel like an admission of failure. Not a bit of it. It is a sign of strength, honesty and commitment.

1. Who are the professionals?

The question arises, who should you consult - who are the professionals? In institutions where someone is appointed for staff development there should be an established facility.

Yet few people are expert in lecture observation. Even college of education tutors who are called upon to help student teachers have frequently had little preparation for the task. Their assessments are known to correlate badly with estimates by their first headteachers, subsequent headteachers and vocational promotion (Wiseman and Start, 1965). Presumably some experience of teaching is an advantage, but it is also possible to have too much, so that the experience of learning to teach is remote. Similarly, to be a good lecturer could easily be a handicap in appreciating the difficulties of others, just as being good at mathematics does not necessarily enable one to teach it. An athletics coach need not be better than his athlete at athletics, but he needs to be some good as a coach. Being able to do something is different from knowing what to do and getting others to do it.

Relying on subjective experience is not enough. Aspects of 'experts' personalities will affect their judgements. For example, Cicirelli (1969) has shown that supervisors with differing scores on tests of creativity, observed and used different features of student-teachers' behavior. Their diagnoses and assessments were consequently different. Less creative supervisors tended to give specific recommendations on how teaching could be improved, while creative supervisors were more concerned with overall objectives, planning and organization.

Consultants should have a good knowledge of lecture research and have tested and trained their subjective impressions against independent objective criteria. Too few staff developers have undergone this discipline. One exception is Cartmell (1971) who was able to observe fourteen behaviors which correlated highly with his judgement of a good teacher. He video-recorded the behavior of 60 trainee lecturers and correlated 23 aspects of their performances with subjective judgements of their merit on a numerical scale, course marks, Eysenck's Personality Inventory, an 'Occupational Interest Questionnaire' and other tests. Trainees rated in the top 30% tended to be younger, stable extroverts who were interested both in people and the job. Those in the middle 40% were not so extroverted, and the lowest 30% were not so interested in teaching. There was a significant correlation between overall course marks and the observations of the video-recorded teaching; but whether this is best explained by the 'halo-effect', trainee motivation, or some other common cause, it is difficult to say.

2. Difficulty in facing oneself

It is still relatively rare in colleges and universities for lecturers to invite educationalists or other colleagues to their lectures. In the long run it seems doubtful whether this isolation benefits anyone. Discussion of techniques and difficulties is most practical when there are observations in common.

Lecturers may hesitate to invite colleagues because they fear being judged by others. Most faculty are sensitive about their reputations. But confidentiality and reciprocal observations could be conditions of the invitation. In any case, it is better to have a reputation based on careful observation than casual remarks and hearsay gossip.

However, the fear of observation is not as simple as this. Few lecturers take the opportunity to make audio or video recordings of their lectures privately, confidentially and available to themselves alone (Beard, 1970). Yet in most institutions the opportunity exists. Thus the fear of visitors comes partly from a difficulty in facing oneself. Once this difficulty has been overcome, it is easier on later occasions provided the delay is not too long.

If you do video record yourself, encourage 6 to 10 students from the class to take time out and view it with you. My experience is that in the informal situation students not only comment on lecture technique, they ask a lot of questions about lecture content which help them and show the lecturers in detail where the lectures could improve. More important, the cooperative relationship fostered, lasts until and beyond the students' graduation. Why? Because both the lecturers and the students have trusted the other where they feel vulnerable - their incompetence and their ignorance respectively.

3. Procedures and principles of consultation

In my work as a consultant there are typically eleven steps in the evaluation process:

(a) Lecturer approaches consultant.

First I am approached by a lecturer usually in casual conversation and often more by a hint rather than a direct invitation. It is not I who makes the first move, nor will I respond to requests by the head of department or other administrators to 'inspect' one of their staff. Trust is of the essence. The lecturers' consent or willingness are not enough; they must actively want the available support. Since the casual context is usually unsuitable to take the conversation further, I usually arrange a time and place where we can meet privately.

(b) Progressive focus on information required.

At that meeting my task is to narrow down to exactly what the lecturer wants and needs. Essentially what I hope to provide is information. It might be about any of the things mentioned in this book, for example how the lecturer uses handouts or lecture

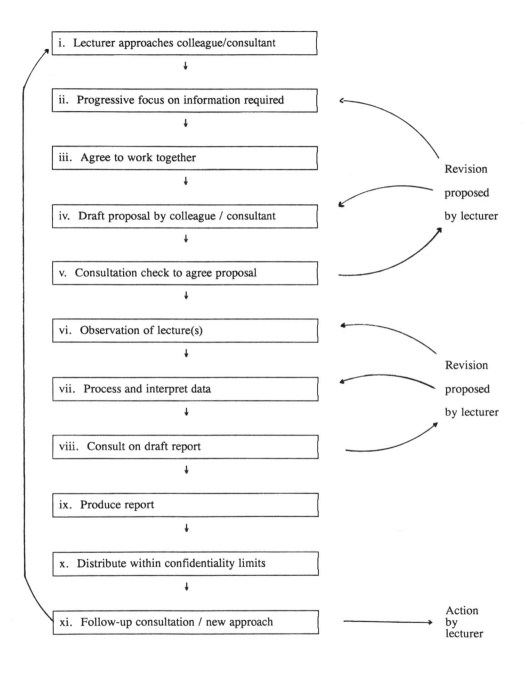

Figure 14.2. Typical sequence of professional evaluation.

signals, how key points are presented, lecture speed, what techniques are used to maintain attention, and so on. To provide information about conceptual vagueness is tricky because that information is close to the lecture content of which I am ignorant. (Figure 12.1).

Lecturing is so complex I cannot undertake to evaluate, or even observe, everything. If what lecturers want and my perception of their needs are different, I may need to use some counseling skills. In particular I shall need to empathize with their feelings and clarify the problems if there are any, without controlling them. Teaching situations are conflict situations. Part of the clarification process is to recognize the conflicts the lecturers must face. I am not seeking to change their styles, but I may create opportunities for lecturers to consider changes for themselves. The conversations are often also an educational process for us both.

(c) Agree to work together.
I need to employ some negotiation skills. Essentially we are working towards a 'contract'. As with any consultant I may need to recognize that I am not the best person to help. But if we agree to work together (and it is a joint undertaking, not a one sided operation) it usually finishes with me promising to draft a proposal within a week for the lecturer's approval.

(d) Draft proposal.
The draft proposal is like a mini research proposal. Indeed that is its ethos. So far as possible (and in many respects it is not possible) the evaluation should be a scientific investigation. Its aims, procedures, observation instrument(s), and methods of data processing and interpretation are briefly specified. By 'scientific' I don't necessarily mean the narrow sense of hypothesis testing. On the contrary, what I usually attempt is a description, firstly that the lecturers will accept as reasonably objective, (in the sense that others, including the lecturers, would make the same observations), and secondly that the lecturers will be able to interpret for themselves. Lecturers are more likely to act upon their own interpretations.

Very often the proposals are to confirm or quantify some behavior reported in the preliminary survey. Recording will enable the lecturer to confirm my observations. Providing the lecturers are willing for me to attend, I make paper and pencil notes against either the precise time or the counter number on the recorder.

The most common instruments are the student rating questionnaire and some more direct and objective assessment of student learning. These are dealt with in the next two sections of this chapter.

(e) Consultation check to agree proposal.
There is a consultation to make sure all involved agree on what is to be done, including who else, if anyone, will receive copies of the eventual report. As Figure 14.2 shows, if changes are agreed, certain steps in the consultation process are recycled.

(f) Observation of lecture(s).
Once agreement is reached, the observation instrument will be produced and used in the lecture(s) agreed. The instrument is not necessarily anything very sophisticated. Usually it is a list of behaviors to observe. When observing teaching I try to remember

the principle that different lecturers are good in different ways; so consultants and colleagues should look for talents that can be developed, rather than faults to be corrected.

Observing the behaviors of students is more difficult partly because lecture theaters are not designed to observe the audience, and partly because pertinent behaviors come and go so quickly that there is no time to focus cameras or even scribble a note.

(g) Process and interpret data.
As in any investigation, when the data has been gathered, the consultant, as the researcher, will process and interpret the data.

(h) Consult on draft report.
As a professional consultant I reckon to produce a written report. A lecturer's colleagues would probably not do so. They would go straight to step (k).

I invite lecturers to correct any factual errors and suggest revisions. Very occasionally, the lecturer has wanted something changed because, if it got into the hands of Professor X or Dr. Y in a different context, it would be interpreted very differently. In practice most lecturers see it as their integrity not to change what I have written, but if they do, we jointly go over the data and my interpretations of it.

When I think lecturers are very sensitive I consult them on interpretations of observed facts before I write them into the report. In other words I write the report up to and including the 'Results' section, but we talk about the discussion section before I write it.

I also need to check at this stage that my recommendations are feasible and acceptable. To some extent my recommendations are negotiated. I am conscious of the principle that there is no one right way to give a lecture and that variety, not a model, is to be encouraged. So I try to elicit from lecturers what they see as their talents; or, if modesty forbids them, at least find out the techniques with which they would feel most comfortable. These are the abilities that need to be extended and developed into new techniques to overcome, or compensate for, any difficulties. For example, it is no use trying to develop powers of oratory for a lecturer who is shy and sensitive. Far better, develop that sensitivity into a caring and meticulous teacher. Then both kinds of lecturer can be valued for their distinctive contribution.

(i) Produce report.
Once agreed, the final report is produced.

(j) Distribute within confidentiality limits.
It is distributed or made available on request only as previously agreed. When other people have contributed to the research and that may include students, I operate a convention that copies should be available to the contributors; but this must have been agreed at step (e).

(k) Follow-up consultation/new approach.
Follow up consultations are very important. Have the lecturers implemented the recommendations? Do they want any help in doing so? Would they like a follow up investigation to monitor changes?

Even before asking these questions, a most constructive follow up is to enlist the support of students in a three way meeting between the students, the lecturer and the consultant. Theoretically the consultant chairs the meeting, but such meetings are always most constructive if they are very informal with a free interchange of ideas between students and the lecturer.

Students' opinions

It is hard to think of an area of educational enquiry that has been more heavily researched than this one. There are literally thousands of studies. Though most are concerned with teaching in general rather than lectures in particular, it is impossible to give here all the lessons to be learned from them.

1. Reasons for obtaining students' opinions

Gathering students' opinions is by far the most common method to evaluate lectures, yet there is a curious logic about seeking them. In most consumer surveys, researchers use questionnaires and interviews to find out something about the consumers, not the product. The qualities of the soap powder, or what ever the product is, can be studied by more scientific methods. But in the case of teaching it is assumed that student surveys tell us, not something about the students, but about the teaching. It depends on the question asked. Yet it is hard to see any difference in principle from the methods used to find out about consumers. The truth is, there are lecturers, students and interactions between them. Students' opinions will reflect all three. Surely the corresponding way to study the qualities of a lecture is to observe, classify, experiment, interpret or whatever else scientists do.

So why seek students' opinions?

(a) One argument is that the customers are always right.

Except that we all know they often are not. This view has been most forcibly expressed by Johnson J. A. (1967): 'It is often the individual student who knows best whether or not he is learning. It is the student who knows best when he cannot understand or already knows what is being discussed. It is the student who knows whether a course is stimulating him to learn more about a subject or whether it is boring him to death. .... It is the student who can best evaluate when he is beginning to integrate the process of learning with the problems he continually confronts in life.' We shall see later that each of these four claims is highly contentious. I shall argue that although students' opinions of specific lectures are reliable in the sense that they are consistent, and although they are undoubtedly the authority on some matters, on others the validity of their opinions as measured against objective tests remains uncertain. Nevertheless, they are useful impressions to obtain. Students' evaluations of lecturers and courses are statistically reliable but evidence of their validity is also at present inconclusive.

(b) Complex judgements are possible.

It can be argued that objective tests of lecture effectiveness are highly selective, but the human mind is wonderful. It makes countless complex evaluations every day. The range of factors unconsciously considered in any one such judgement are much greater than could be listed in any reasonably sized objective test. Different factors and their interactions in the lecture situation should be given different weight in different circumstances. Objective tests are not flexible in this way and the most sophisticated statistical techniques cannot do justice to complex interactions in a classroom.

(c) Superficially, subjective opinions are easily gathered.
Questionnaires with rating scales are quick to administer to a captive audience at the end of a lecture. They neither arouse the opposition of students nor the anxiety that they personally are being tested. The data is numerical giving the false impression that it represents quantities, rather than qualities and value judgements. With that impression go a collection of statistical assumptions when the data is processed by readily available computer programs. Numerical data also gives the impression that it can be used to compare lecturer X with lecturer Y, even when they teach different subjects to different students. Opinions are not measures. They are pointers to areas that could benefit from further study.

(d) The observer effect is removed.
The presence of observers or the knowledge that one is being tested may interfere with the teaching situation itself. Arguably students' opinions are less open to this kind of uncertainty principle.

(e) Valid opinions.
Insofar as ratings by students are indications of their opinions, they are necessarily valid. (Whether they are valid indications of lecture effectiveness is a question we must consider later.) A lecturer cannot afford to neglect student reactions, for even if students are at first incorrect in believing that Professor Y's lectures are of little value, the consequent decline in motivation will make their judgement a self-fulfilling one, especially if their disenchantment results in absenteeism.

In my opinion it is the fifth reason that should carry greatest weight. It is part of a constructive dialogue of mutual cooperation between lecturer and students each to assist the other, not a matter of passing judgement, praise or blame. Compared with the lecturer's subjective impressions, the use of questionnaires is more systematic than chance verbal or non-verbal feedback. It also obtains data from a larger proportion of the students.

For constructive dialogue, it is advisable to obtain some knowledge of students' reactions after about one-tenth of the course has been completed. Because courses are so varied the figure of one-tenth may require modification, but the third week in a one-year course, or the end of the second week of a 15-week semester, is a suitable time. It should be borne in mind that the purpose of student evaluation is to modify a course to suit the students' needs. Thus, to leave it much later allows little time to make adjustments, and makes established habits and routines difficult to break. Because the end of one course and the beginning of another is frequently a time for replanning, there should normally be a further evaluation at the end of the course. Whether intermediate ones are used will depend on whether they can serve a useful purpose for the students.

2. Devising the questionnaire
Accepting, therefore, that lecturers should adopt some form of evaluation by students, what method should be used? Interviews are time consuming. The preliminary enquiry

uses open, free response, and fairly comprehensive questions. That may discourage their further use. Rating scales are by far the most common method.

The use of rating scales will not make the judgements objective; they merely substitute a number of subjective judgements for more comprehensive ones. But they may ensure that students consider a range of criteria and provide quasi-numerical estimates on which it is thought that a more general opinion should be based. Even so the halo effect is likely to operate. (This is a distortion such that an opinion on one issue influences ratings on other items.) For example Rugg found that ratings of army officers showed less variation when the instructors were previously known to the judges (Rugg, 1921, 1922). This suggests that lecturers are more likely to obtain guidance on specific features of their teaching techniques if they invite relative strangers to assist them.

There are other factors to consider when devising the questionnaire. Students who are not used to rating scales are sometimes apt to opt for the middle positions, especially if there are only three from which to choose. For this reason I prefer a six-point, or even an eight-point, scale, but this is not the usual practice. Anonymity is essential, and if follow-up comparisons are to be made later, pseudonyms can be used to match responses. It is important to ensure that the evaluation is completed by all students, otherwise the personality factors affecting the selectivity of response, would probably give an unbalanced impression. I therefore recommend that questionnaires are completed during class time. It is also advisable that space should be left for free comments and time made available for follow-up discussion if the full meaning of the ratings is to be apparent.

3. What should be evaluated?
The choice should be guided by the purpose of the evaluation. These might be (i) to improve lectures, (ii) to assess the lecturer, possibly to inform personnel decisions, or (iii) in some cases, to help students choose courses. In this book I am primarily concerned with improvement. Improvement is only possible if the lecturer is so motivated, if the evaluation provides relevant information, and if alternative lecturer behavior is possible.

The preliminary enquiry should indicate what areas may need further study. In other words it is best if student evaluations are purpose designed to throw light upon particular problems experienced by a specific lecturer or group of students.

However, all too often evaluators take, or adapt a questionnaire designed by someone else. An implicit assumption of this approach is that there is a standardized set of model criteria to which the lecturer should conform. With a little thought most people would regard this assumption as false. Students and universities need variety, not conformity.

Where did the set of model criteria come from? Very often out of the original evaluators' heads. Typically a very long list is prepared on a five point rating scale and given to a very large sample of students to evaluate a large number of lecturers. Numerical values are given to each point on the scales and a factor analysis to identify the factors underlying students' judgements, is carried out. Items contributing strongly to the main factors are then included in a shortened questionnaire, though typically even this questionnaire is long. Factor analysis assumes, possibly correctly, that students' opinions are based on relatively few underlying factors. The exclusion of any item not associated with any of the main factors assumes that it is not important, or at least, not important for students in their opinion. But some poorly associated items could be very important (eg audibility). Because it only takes one element of a lecture to vitiate the whole, a similar problem could arise when a crucial item is absorbed within a factor. Again, my advice is 'Keep it simple'. Statistics can mislead.

Two broad factors constantly recur in published reports: one concerns subject matter; the other, personal relationships. With this in mind (notwithstanding my cautions that evaluations should be purpose designed and simple) where an evaluation is general, rather than focussing on specific aspects of lecturing, intending evaluators would be wise to include items related to these two factors - or at least have reasons when not doing so:

(a) Clarity of subject matter.
This factor might include items on lecture organization, its speed, the clarity of its purpose, visual aids, summaries, effective use of time, lecturers' knowledge of their subject, and their care in preparation. Items contributing to this factor are typically related to issues discussed in Chapter 4 and parts 1, 3 and 5 of this book.

(b) Rapport.
This includes a wide range of items to do with the interaction between lecturers and their audience. The items are more to do with feelings than subject matter (stimulating interest being both). They include personal style, questioning techniques, opportunities for discussion, inspiring interest, responsiveness to the audience and general personal characteristics. In this book Chapters 5, 6, 12, 13, 14 and part 4 are particularly relevant.

Most researchers find more than two factors depending on the balance of items included, but they can usually be classified under these two headings. For example Feldman (1976) reviewed a large number of studies and concluded that students are consistently concerned with the following eight factors:

Clarity	Enthusiasm
Stimulation of interest	Friendliness
Preparation	Helpfulness
Knowledge of subject matter	Openness to others' opinions

(c) Global value judgements.
A small number of researchers (Cranton and Smith, 1990) have also found a factor consisting of global value judgements; for example ratings on how much was learned, the significance of the content, lecture effectiveness, interest generated and overall value.

Of course, the factors obtained are only as good as the original list. It is strangely rare for lecturers to consult their students about items that might be included in student evaluation questionnaires (though the preliminary enquiry does). To do so would foster a spirit of mutual help. Hodgson and McConnell (1985) used personal construct theory to elicit areas of concern to students rather than the preconceptions of lecturers.

Students were asked in what way two lecturers were alike but different from a third. The criteria thus elicited were students' mental constructs. When classified, the nine most important were:

Criterion construct	Times mentioned	Criterion construct	Times mentioned
Content of lecture	61	Lecturer's enthusiasm for subject	32
Lecturer's attitude to students	59	Pace of lecture	27
Structure and organization of lectures	51	Lecturer's knowledge of subject	20
Stimulation and maintenance of interest	46	Lecturer's ability to put subject over	14
Encourages student participation	32		

A second stage of the project elicited further criteria: Students' general attitude to the lecturer; Students' perceptions of the lecturer; Ease of note-taking; Use of audio-visual aids; and Clarity of explanations. Though Hodgson and McConnell's sample was heavily weighted towards the social sciences, in the present context their study has the advantage that it focussed specifically on lectures, not other teaching methods.

4. The potent variable in students' opinions

I suggested earlier that students' opinions of lectures may reflect characteristics of the students as much as the characteristics of the lecture or lecturer. There is not much evidence to suggest that the age or sex of students are related to their ratings; nor is the sex of the lecturer. Ratings tend to be more favorable when students' have an interest in the subject, have opted to attend the lectures or take the course, and found them a challenge. There is a slight tendency for ratings to be higher when they are anonymous, when the purpose of the evaluation is known, when the lecturer is present and when the lecturer has a distinguished reputation for research. Inconsistent findings have been obtained to show higher ratings for more senior professors, when students expect or have obtained good grades, and for lecturers in arts and humanities compared with sciences and engineering. There is some reason to think that small classes and very large ones are preferred to classes around 40 or 50.

Caution should be observed when interpreting these generalizations. They are partly based upon ratings of courses of which lectures were only a part. On the other hand it could be argued that this is reasonable because opinions of lectures cannot be separated from their social and institutional context. The large number of students involved results in low correlations being statistically significant even when the variable has little if any effect upon the rating. In any case correlations do not imply causes; so it does not necessarily follow that ratings of lectures are biassed by these student characteristics. Even if they were so biassed, the bias would be reasonable if the students' characteristic genuinely influenced their learning.

This catalog might lead you to think that evaluators can ignore the characteristics of students who express opinions about their teachers. Needless to say this is not true.

The question is, 'What characteristics are important and what, if anything, do lecturers need to do about them?' Look at Table 14.3. Different students expect different things from their lecturers, but, except for the two items in italics, there is a common

Figure 14.3 Per cent of students rating lecturers' characteristics as 'Essential' or 'Desirable' (Smithers 1970a and b)

	Engineers	Life Sciences	Physical Sciences	Arts & Soc Sci
Slow enough to take full notes	87*	82*	66#	62#
Talks around brief notes	19*	27	25	35#
Provides essential as a framework	46*	70#	56*	81#
Takes distinctive line on unresolved problems	20*	37	38#	47#
Gives references	81*	89	90	92#
Enjoys lecturing	78*	82*	61#	66#
Likes students	76*	70	61#	57#

	Extroverts	Introverts
Entertaining	71*	53#
Appears confident	87*	70#

	Unstable	Stable
Stimulates independent thought	82*	97#
Presents all sides of a controversy non-committally	50*	68#
Slow enough for full notes to be taken	80*	65#
Sets attainable standard	74*	56#

	Unstable introverts	Other students
Reads out notes relevant to the exams	71*	44#
Allows exercise of the imaginations	53*	79#
Takes a distinctive line on controversy	24*	48#
Explores ideas not in the textbooks	59*	77#

	High Dogmatism	Low Dogmatism
Sets clear objectives	85*	64#
Sets attainable standard	83*	51#
Gives summary handout	57*	38#
Prepares thoroughly	93*	77#
Keeps to the point	76*	57#
Links with other work	91*	64#
Uses appropriate visual-aids	49*	25#
Clear blackboard organization	70*	49#

* is significantly different from # at the 5% level

dimension underlying the differences. Some students crave certainty: they want facts, clear objectives, a full set of notes, and attainable standards. Others tolerate uncertainties, controversies and ambiguities; they welcome a framework, but want to explore ideas and do their own thinking.

Similar contrasts, but with different labels, can be found in the work of other researchers. Marton and his disciples (1984) have described as having a 'surface level approach' students who want lectures to cover the ground, who concentrate on memorizing detail, and who expect to find the 'right' answer to questions. These contrast with students adopting a 'deep approach' who are concerned with a lecture's central point, what lies behind the argument, what it boils down to, the logic of the argument, getting the whole picture and challenging the conclusions. Parlett (1970) described 'syllabus bound' students who only study what they are required to study, want the lecturer to give clear instructions, do not often question things they hear from professors in lectures, and are more focussed on exams than interested in their discipline. 'Syllabus free' students on the other hand, explore ideas not mentioned in lectures, try to think of a better way of doing something than described in a lecture and generally display independence of mind. Perry (1970) also describes freshers starting their university careers believing it is the job of lecturers to dispense truths, and finish regarding lecturers' knowledge and values as contextual and relative. Feldman and Newcomb (1973) cite over 30 studies showing students becoming less authoritarian, dogmatic, ethnocentric and prejudiced during their time at college.

Two implications are of interest. First, in most disciplines it is the duty of faculty to try to wean students away from craving dogma towards a rational independence of thought. This will best be achieved by placing students in small groups where their own ideas are tested and where they must confront the views of others. In the lecture room, this is best achieved by using buzz groups, not by lecturing.(Chapter 19).

Second, whilst I accept that the variable I have described is multidimensional, its relationship to students' evaluations of lectures (or indeed of lecturers and courses) has been curiously neglected. The personalities of lecturers have not. Yet these researches suggest craving for certainty may be the most potent variable. It could also be a variable that might invalidate students' evaluations because, if too many students are seeking the wrong thing from lectures, namely the certainty of indubitable knowledge, the criteria for their evaluations would be inappropriate.

5. Students' opinions are reliable

There is no doubt that students' evaluations of teaching are highly reliable in the sense that they are consistent. This has been found repeatedly in research for over 70 years. (Remmers, 1934; Heilman and Armentrout, 1936; Guthrie, 1954; Lovell and Haner, 1955; Remmers's review, 1963; Spencer and Aleamoni, 1970; Harvey and Barker, 1970; Costin et al.'s review, 1971; the series of articles by Feldman, 1976-79; Marsh, 1984; and Murray et al., 1990; to name but a few.) The reliability coefficients are consistently in the range 0.7 to 0.9 whether the same students rate a lecturer more than once, or different students rate the same lecturer.

In fact the consistency can be galling. One lecturer obtained ratings on 44 criteria and then, using this detailed information, spent two years working hard to improve his lectures. When he gave the same rating scale to a later cohort, he was dismayed to find that the ratings hardly changed at all. The correlation would only have occurred by chance once in 2000 times (Foy, 1969).

6. The validity of students' opinions is modest and inconsistent

The validity of students' ratings of lectures is far more doubtful. No account would be complete without mentioning studies in educational seduction. An actress was introduced to a class of education and health professionals as the distinguished educator, Dr. Myron Fox. She gave a lecture almost devoid of content on an unfamiliar topic in an enthusiastic and expressive manner using eye contact and every conceivable non-verbal skill. The lecturer was rated highly not only for personal expressive qualities, but also for the lecture content (Natfulin *et al.*, 1973).

Though the study was criticized for having no control group, a poor evaluation instrument and a rather brief lecture, confidence in the validity of students' opinions has never been quite the same ever since. Replications have adopted a standard 3 X 2 design with three levels of lecture content and two of expressiveness; and have assessed students' learning and opinions. Their broad conclusions are that expressiveness affects students' opinions and has a small effect upon learning; whilst the content affects learning with only a small effect upon students' opinions (e.g. a meta-analysis by Abrami *et al.*, 1982). As mentioned in Chapter 6, expressiveness increases student motivation; but if other incentives are introduced, particularly before the lecture, overall motivation is not further enhanced (Marsh, 1984).

The validity of students' judgements will depend upon what they are judging. There are some matters on which they are the authority. If students tell me they cannot hear what I say or cannot read what is projected on the screen, I should not normally doubt them. If they tell me they don't understand the point I'm making I believe them; when they tell me they do, experience has made me more skeptical. I reckon I'm a better authority on the latter.

Ratings are much more likely to be valid with reference to variables to which they are logically or theoretically related. For example we might expect responses to 'The lecturer is inspiring' to be valid with reference to students choosing further courses with that lecturer, but much less valid, for example with reference to how often the lecturer gives handouts as a lecture guide. That is why ratings should be specific. Specific ratings are also give more direction for lecturers seeking to improve their techniques.

In other words the question 'Are students' opinions valid?' begs the question 'Valid for what purpose?' The most obvious way to test the validity of students' opinions of lectures is to argue that the purpose of lectures is student learning and to correlate students' ratings of their learning with objective tests of their learning. But things are not that simple.

The results of that procedure give remarkably inconsistent and contradictory results. Consider Professor Smith's lectures. Most of his topics are moderately difficult.

The more gifted students gain satisfaction by responding to the challenge. The less gifted struggle, know they are struggling, and get a little frustrated. Consequently the gifted students rate 'I learned a lot from this lecture' favorably and score well on an objective test. Less gifted students rate that item unfavorably and score badly on the test. The result? - a positive correlation between ratings and test scores. The following week's lecture is on an easy topic. The gifted students say 'I knew all that already', rate it low and score highly on the test. Less able students say 'Thank God at last I've understood something', rate the lecture highly, but still score much lower than their peers on the test. The result? - a negative correlation. (Figure 14.4.) Clearly the invalidity here results from variables amongst individual students.

However, multisection studies using class averages, rather than scores for individual students, are not vulnerable to this criticism provided differences between class sections are controlled and the size of class sections is sufficiently large for individual variables to even out. Most multi-section studies evaluate courses rather than lectures specifically; but these, too, give inconsistent results. Abrami *et al.* (1988, 1990) found over 40 such studies together with six reviews of them. The reviews came to markedly different conclusions. For example, Cohen (1981) said 'The present meta-analysis provides strong support for the validity of student ratings as measures of teaching effectiveness. Teachers whose students do well on achievement measures receive higher instructional ratings than teachers who do poorly'. By contrast, seeing widely varying validity coefficients, Dowell and Neal (1982, 1983) said 'The literature can be seen as yielding unimpressive estimates of the validity of student ratings'. In

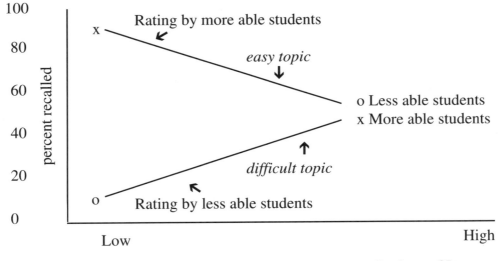

Figure 14.4 One explanation for inconsistent validity studies

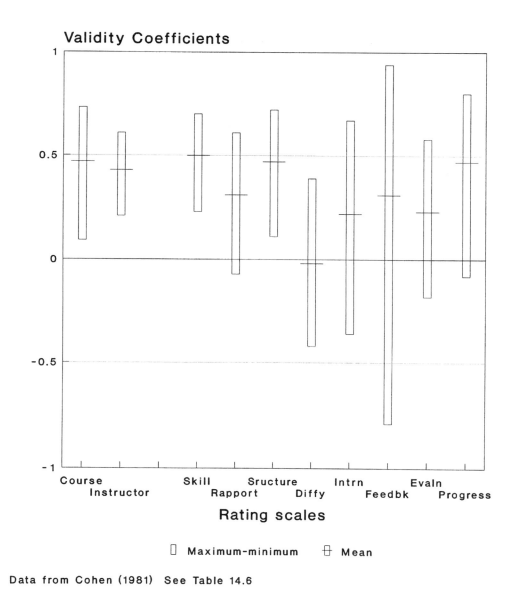

Validity Coefficients

Rating scales

☐ Maximum-minimum   ⊟ Mean

Data from Cohen (1981) See Table 14.6

Figure 14.5. The unreliability of validity coefficients.

their later paper they said student ratings are 'indicators of student satisfaction rather than teaching effectiveness'.

Abrami, d'Appollonia and Cohen (1990) reworked Cohen's data. Cohen (1981) had classified the validity coefficients relative to student achievement from studies he reviewed into 10 categories, 2 general (course and instructor) and 8 rather more specific:

Table 14.6. Factors in Cohen's meta-analysis

	Factor	Typical item	Av. validity coefficient
1.	Course	This is an excellent course	.47
2.	Instructor	The instructor is an excellent teacher	.43
3.	Skill	The instructor has a good command of subject matter	.50
4.	Rapport	The instructor is friendly	.31
5.	Course Structure	The instructor uses time well	.47
6.	Difficulty	The instructor assigns difficult reading	-.02
7.	Interaction	The instructor facilitates class discussion	.22
8.	Feedback	The instructor keeps students informed of their progress	.31
9.	Evaluation	The examinations are fair	.23
10.	Student progress	I have learned a great deal on this course	.47

Not only did Abrami et al now regard these average validity coefficients as modest, but as Figure 14.5 shows, the coefficients were very wide ranging. They therefore concluded it was premature to say that students' evaluations of teaching are valid. They also concluded that because the correlations between the 10 sets of validity coefficients were low, it is both conceptually and empirically reasonable to analyze these factors separately. This reinforces my advice not to try to evaluate everything at once.

The validity of students' opinions can also be tested against other criteria than student learning. For example the invalidity of students' opinions have also been found with respect of their judgements of lecture speed. A tape-recorded 45 minute lecture in three parts was played to three groups of students such that each group heard different parts spoken at different speeds. Half the students perceived no differences in speed, although the fastest was twice the speed of the slowest, and only 10% placed the three parts in the correct order of speed (Bligh, 1974). In another experiment, expressed intention to read more about a lecture topic had no bearing on whether they actually did read about it, even though it may have indicated the degree of initial interest aroused by the lecture.

7. Conclusion on students' opinions
It will be seen from the evidence cited that the chief correlates of students' opinions of lecturers are features of their own personalities, courses and learning strategies. It is always dangerous to step from correlation to causation, but if we assume that their personalities and course interests affect their judgements, this would explain their highly significant reliability but modest and varied validity where other independent

measures have been obtained. In other words, students' opinions of their lectures may reflect the nature of the students as much as that of the lectures.

It does not follow from this that lecturers need not bother to seek students' opinions. Quite the contrary, if students' personalities are unlikely to change very quickly, it is lecturers who may have to change their techniques, because it is the lecturer who initially controls the teaching situation. To do this appropriately they will need to know students' reactions. Thus the chief purpose of ascertaining students' opinions of a lecture is to help the lecturer help the students, not to pass judgement on the lecturer. It is for this reason that they are useful early in a course and when planning the next.

Assessment of learning objectives achieved

If the opinions of students are rejected as invalid, the most satisfactory way to evaluate a lecture's effectiveness will be to test the students' learning directly. This may be done by one-word answer tests of the key points or multiple-choice questions, but the first may produce a reaction of 'We're being treated like school children' and the second takes a considerable time to prepare if the 'distracters' (the false answers) are to be suitably plausible and if a variety of objectives are to be tested. The first may be avoided if the purpose is carefully explained; then the students too, can obtain feedback by marking their own answers (which also saves the lecturer's time) and anonymity is preserved when answer sheets are handed in. (If questions are given on a handout it is advisable to duplicate a few spares as there are usually some students who wish to take a copy away with them.)

Before going any further, you are asked to imagine that Chapter 4 has been presented to you as a lecture. You are then invited to fill in the questionnaire on page 186.

This test design, devised as a research tool to study the relative effectiveness of presentations such as lectures and lecture scripts, is called a 'Truth-Functional Test' because in principle the statements may be constructed so that they have a particular relationship in truth -functional logic to statements given in the presentation (Bligh, 1970b, 1974). This means that, not only may it be objectively marked, but unlike most other tests, it is objective in its construction. Furthermore the logical relationship can be varied to test different kinds of thought and rebuts the criticism often made of objective tests that they don't.

1. Recognition of a key point
Question 1 tests recognition of one key phrase. In other words it tests the memory of a 'key point' that was made. It only tests one idea.

2. Memory of a simple stated relationship
Question 2 tests recognition of a reason that was presented (See figure for Question 2). That is, it tests memory of a relationship between two ideas - the fact that one is the reason for the other. It will be seen that the cause and the effect have been reversed in the question. This kind of inversion is one of the most common errors in reasoning by

If you have read Chapter 4 you are invited to attempt the following questionnaire. All the questions consist of a statement. You are asked to say whether you 'agree' 'disagree' or 'don't know'. Please work briskly. If you do not know it is quicker to say so. If you have some idea, but are not certain, it is better to guess.

Place an X through the circle of your choice.

	Agree	Don't Know	Disagree
1. Repetition consolidates learning	O	O	O
2. One reason why words in the middle of a list suffer from proactive and retroactive interference is that they are not remembered so well	O	O	O
3. The capacities of long term and working memories provide evidence that they are different in kind	O	O	O
4. If you practice playing table-tennis with your right hand, your left hand game will improve	O	O	O
5. All evidence for there being two kinds of memory has been obtained by psychologists observing other people and animals	O	O	O

6. A and B are matched groups

Group A	(1) Memory task	(2)	(3) Test of memory task
Group B	(1) Memory task	(2) Undemanding dissimilar task	(3) Test of memory task

	Agree	Don't Know	Disagree
The results of the above experimental design could reasonably be claimed to demonstrate the effects of rehearsal	O	O	O
7. No experiment on forgetting can rule out the effects of retroactive interference	O	O	O
8. Lecturers' understanding of STM should enhance their empathy for students taking notes in lectures	O	O	O

Thank you

Figure 14.7 An example of a "Truth-Functional Test". The preferred answers appear at the of this chapter.

Recogition of reason presented in Question 2.

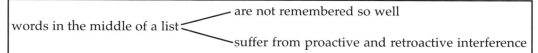

words in the middle of a list — are not remembered so well — suffer from proactive and retroactive interference

students who find it difficult to distinguish between the truth of statements and the validity of the reasons for them. The strongest variable in these tests is the subject matter. Using a question like this immediately after a lecture, only 41% got it right when correction had been made for guessing (Bligh, 1974).

(This particular question also assumes some knowledge of how the terms 'proactive' and 'retroactive interference' are used, but, since a person could confuse them and still get this question correct, it does not require a knowledge of their precise meaning.)

3. Making simple inferences
Question 3 tests the ability to make a relatively simple inference and remember it.

(i) 'there is a limit to the number of items one can hold in working memory at once',
(ii) 'there does not appear to be a limit to the number of ideas in long memories';

he is then expected to assume that:

'the difference between there being a limit and no limit is a difference in kind',

and infer that:

'working and long term memories are different in kind'.

It should be noticed that Truth-Functional Tests require students to relate meanings of presented propositions, not their precise words. Just as question 2 tested more than recognition, question 3 tests more than memory of a relationship. It tests simple comprehension because it requires the ability to manipulate presented information in certain simple ways. Immediately after a lecture using the words of Chapter 4, 37% were judged to have answered a question like this correctly when corrections for guessing were made.

4. Application
Question 4 tests the ability to apply the information that has been acquired. Thus it requires more than relating ideas that were given; it requires the student to relate examples that were not presented, to general principles that were. In this case the principle given was summed up in the phrase 'practice of one skill affects the performance of similar skills'. The student has to select the principle as relevant, then apply it. Questions to test application essentially consist of supplying an instance of a generalization that was presented. In tests given to students 85% got this question right

after corrections for guessing. (However, this item illustrates a problem. The pre-test score was positive and therefore had to be subtracted to assess learning.)

5. Analytical thought

Logically, questions like question 5 require that the students check whether 'All A is B'. Question 5 requires the student to check through the five kinds of evidence presented and ask of each kind, 'Is it obtained by observing other people and animals?' It therefore assumes that students will remember all instances of A (i.e. the kinds of evidence). It is an analytical mental process because the student must consider a characteristic (i.e. B) of all instances of A. Because the characteristic in this instance is a methodological one, it is more abstract that many analytical questions and could be said to require some judgement in addition to analytic thought. In addition to 'All A is B', statements of the forms

'Some A is not B'
'Some A is B' and
'No A is B'

will test analytic thought.

Because critical thinking often requires checking all the instances of a concept, these analytical questions are very useful in training students in critical thought, as well as being an indication of the thought processes permitted by lectures.

6. Synthesis

To answer question 6 students must ask themselves 'If I want to demonstrate the effects of rehearsal, what experimental design will I need?' To answer this they will require a creative act (by which I do not mean 'original' except in the sense of being original to the individual). It is a constructive process of making a decision or proposal. In this sense it may be described as 'synthetic'. If they come to the conclusion 'I must have two matched groups, one that can rehearse and one that cannot, and then compare results', they will first need to analyze the design given in the question to see if it fits their requirements, and then check whether necessary controls are observed.

This type of question is difficult because it requires analytical thinking in addition to the synthetic process. It is also difficult to set because highly critical students may see weaknesses in the proposed design and therefore reject it. Although this kind of student will compensate on the analytic and judgmental questions, it may seem unfair to penalize them for this virtue here. In some respects it is true to life that the critical mind is uncreative, and if this is so, perhaps one should not be too apologetic for the weakness; but it is a weakness nonetheless and this is inevitable since creativity cannot be well tested by any question that admits only one correct answer.

Nevertheless, the frequent use of this kind of question may help to detect students with potential research ability more easily than by using projects which, when time permits only one or two in a course, are less reliable. The essential feature of these questions is to relate one's own ideas to ideas given in the presentation. This is difficult to do during a lecture. In fact, after adjustments for guessing, virtually no student got this item right after a lecture. This illustrates once again that thinking in lectures is either difficult, rare or both. It also lends support to Truth-Functional Tests as a less vulnerable research tool, to the criticism that the thought takes place during the test rather than during the period assessed.

7. Evaluation

Question 7 requires different kinds of analyzes and generalizations. For example, it requires a conceptual analysis of 'retroactive interference' to appreciate that

(i)   'it refers to psychological events that follow the memory task'.
(ii)   'testing will follow the memory task'.

After considering experimental situations a further generalization is necessary to infer that,

(iii)   'retroactive interference will always occur before testing in experiments on forgetting'.

Having inferred that,

(iv)   'retroactive interference takes place in all experiments on forgetting', the statement in the question will be judged incorrect.

8. Attitudes

Question 8 is a test of attitude yet it poses as a question of fact. Clearly this book has failed if the reader is unsympathetic to this attitude. The important point here is that attitudes and values may be tested alongside cognitive skills, and this may produce a more genuine result if students are not conscious that their values are being examined.

The purpose of describing these eight types of question is to show that feedback on a variety of lecture objectives may be directly obtained by a form that is apparently uniform in design. The types here correspond with levels of thinking in Bloom's Taxonomy of Educational Objectives (1956), but there is, in principle, a far wider range that could be assessed. Practice is required in designing the questions of different types because most lecturers are not used to thinking in these terms. They are easy to mark and quick to administer. The test is amenable to marking by computer if required.

The provision of a 'Don't Know' category and a marking scheme such that 2, 1 and 0 are respectively awarded for a correct answer, don"t know and an incorrect answer, can help to decrease guessing. In any case the proportion of incorrect answers to 'don't knows' will give an indication of how far a student risks a 'guess' (a caution-risk factor).

Although in general the more complex thought processes are more difficult, this is by no means always true. The familiarity and abstractness of the concepts involved are important variables here. Students tend to agree with the statements given, therefore questionnaires of this kind should have an equal number of preferred agreements and disagreements with each type of question.

9. Conclusion on assessment of objectives

The Truth Functional Test provides a method of testing a wide range of objectives directly. Like all such checks on lecture effectiveness, the cooperation of students should be sought. The tests also have a worth while teaching function by practicing students' thought in a variety of patterns, and there is room for much further development of the technique for this purpose.

Conclusion

The evaluation of teaching is probably the most heavily researched and controversial area in the study of education. Obviously not all is about lecturing; even so, I am conscious that I cannot do justice to the controversies within the scope of this book. There are many relevant principles. Here are some underlying this chapter.

- Involvement: Let lecturers initiate and be involved and consulted throughout;
- Purpose: Be explicit about the purpose of the evaluation;
- Priorities: Let improvement take priority over personnel and funding decisions;
- Competence: Get 'expert' advice;
- Relevant: Tailor make the evaluation to achieve that purpose, not something else;
- Individualized: Don't use pre-packaged evaluations; satisfy the individual's needs;
- Sampling: Evaluate over time and courses;
- Multimethod: Use several methods;
- Criteria: Use some open-ended questions;
- Objectivity: Be cautious about opinions;
- Timing: Early evaluation allows time to put things right.

Preferred answers to questions in Figure 14.7
1.   Agree
2.   Disagree
3.   Agree
4.   Disagree
5.   Disagree
6.   Agree
7.   Disagree
8.   Agree

15. Overcoming Common Difficulties

The use of inappropriate teaching methods.
    1.   Diagnosing the difficulty.
    2.   A possible solution.

Teaching at the students' level.
    1.   Diagnosing the difficulty.
    2.   Possible solutions.

Nerves.
    1.   Consequences of the difficulty.
    2.   Possible solutions.

Speed.
    1.   The consequences of going too fast.
    2.   Possible solutions.

The problem of large audiences.
    1.   Diagnosing the difficulty.
    2.   Diminishing the difficulty.

Conclusion.

It is easy to find fault with lecturers. Because lecturing is an art no one style suits everyone and probably no conscientious lecturer is ever wholly satisfied with his teaching. What is required is an understanding and diagnosis of the lecturer's difficulties coupled with constructive suggestions to overcome them or to make the best of them.

The purpose of this chapter is 'to diagnose and suggest', with reference to common difficulties of new lecturers not touched on elsewhere. However, since difficulties are frequently personal, the suggestions made here are a little 'hit and miss' for the needs of the individual reader.

The use of inappropriate teaching methods

One of the most common mistakes by lecturers is to use the lecture method at all. For objectives classified as 'the presentation of information' we have seen that the lecture method is no better than any other and it is less effective for the promotion of thought and for changing attitudes.

Broadly speaking, available evidence suggests that reading, tape recordings, video-tapes, summary handouts, programmed texts and discussion methods are all as effective as lectures in teaching information, and, if self paced, may be more effective with classes of mixed ability.

1. Diagnosing the difficulty

Yet one must appreciate lecturers' difficulties. Because they have no other model, or experience from which to draw, they are likely to conceive of their role in terms of the kind of behavior exhibited by their teachers. The architecture of many lecture theaters makes the use of any other teaching methods extremely difficult. (Heads of expanding colleges are frequently blissfully unaware that they commit their teaching staffs to decades of inappropriate teaching methods when they accept an architect's plans.) Students' expectations and other social factors pressurize 'lecturers' to 'lecture'. There are psychological constraints to 'play it safe' because unknown methods are accompanied by fears of unforeseeable problems with unknown solutions. The choice of appropriate teaching methods is not difficult for those who have had some training for the task, but few lecturers have done more than attend a course for a few days. (Even the training for teaching in schools experienced by most college of education lecturers gives little guidance in recently developed methods in the teaching of adults.)

In short, the diagnosis of this difficulty is the lack of professional training. When the complex combination of skills required by a lecturer is appreciated, few will dispute that it is needed. Unfortunately it is often not appreciated. (N.B. This book only touches on one teaching method of a possible thirty that a lecturer might need to use, and apart from a knowledge of teaching methods, most lecturers require a knowledge of how to specify objectives, student selection techniques, the selection and use of assessment techniques and possibly some knowledge of administration and student counseling.)

Table 15.1. Some common teaching methods and appropriate objectives

Teaching Method	Category of primary objectives
Audiotapes	
These may be played to a whole class or individually	Guide practical work Variation of presentation method Knowledge of information Self-awareness Demonstration (e.g. of social interaction)
Brain-storming	
An intensive discussion situation in which spontaneous suggestions as solutions to a problem are received uncritically	New ideas (creativity) Problem solving Decision making

Buzz groups

Groups of 2-6 members who discuss issues
or problems for a short period, or periods,
within a lesson

Encourage reticent students
Group cohesion   Feedback
Consolidate memory by rehearsal of facts
Learn terminology by use
Thought (at all levels) Arousal
Training in discussion techniques

Case discussion

Real or simulated complex problems are
analyzed in detail for students to suggest
their own solutions or decisions

Understanding complex
inter-relationships
Application of principles

CCTV

Knowledge of information and skills
Self-awareness

Computer Assisted Instruction (CAI or CAL)

Not strictly a single method. Computers may
be used in many ways to present information,
set tasks and obtain feedback

Knowledge of facts Computing skills
Thinking and problem solving skills
Feedback to student and lecturer

Controlled discussion

Teaching in which students may raise
questions or comment, but the general
direction is under the teacher's strict control.
This is normally used after a presentation
method with a class, not a group.

Knowledge of facts
Understanding (including "revision")
Feedback

Counseling

Students voluntarily consult a trained tutor,
doctor or welfare officer about their private
or academic problems

Very varied
Student welfare

Demonstrations

The teacher performs some operation exemplifying a phenomenon or skill while the students watch (A presentation or reception method)

Observation skills
Knowledge of principles
Knowledge of physical skills

Films

Knowledge of information and skills
Development of attitudes

Free-group discussion (FGD)

A learning situation in which the topic and direction are controlled by the student group; the teacher observes and facilitates only when necessary

Observation Change in attitudes, feelings, human relations
Self-awareness
Willing to receive and consider new ideas

Group Tutorial

A period of teaching devoted to a single student

Individual development of student thought, especially at higher levels
Asks questions Gives reasons
Feels for others

Horseshoe Groups

Groups (normally 4-12 members) with a specific task which is discussed

Evaluation Decision making
Analytical thinking
Know how to apply principles

Individual task

Usually this consists of a problem to work out in class, but it could consist of other activities performed by each individual separately

Active learning
Involvement by all
Problem solving

Lecture

A period of more or less uninterrupted talk by
the teacher (not necessarily a complete lesson).
In effect "lecture" is defined here in terms of
the psychological conditions it implies

Knowledge of information
Obtain general background of a topic

"Practicals" and Laboratory work

Observation
Manual skills
"Scientific thinking"

Programmed learning (various)

Usually a text containing questions each of
which must be answered before proceeding

Knowledge of information
Simple problem solving

Projects

Very varied but commonly an exercise
submitted on paper as a result of practical
skills connected with the subject

Information skills: knowledge of,
how to seek, application of,
organization of, illustration of
Skills of presentation

Reading

Knowledge of information
Some thinking
Ability to seek and select information

Role-play or "sociodrama"

Students are given certain social roles and
freely dramatize them in a group, i.e. they
act out their specified role
Attitude change

Empathy
Work off tensions
Self-awareness

Seminar

Group discussion introduced by the
presentation of an essay or other work

"Critical" thinking
Ability to present an argument
Thought at all levels

Simulation and games

Teaching in which a real situation is duplicated in its essential features perhaps in the form of a game or a problem. The participants adopt an appropriate role or status, if possible.

Empathy Work off tensions
Self-awareness
Attitude change
Vocational skills

Step-by-step discussion

Teaching by a carefully prepared sequence of issues and questions to draw out the required information from students

Knowledge of facts
Understanding (especially logical argument or developmental sequence)

Step-by-step lecture

A lecture organized around 3-10 topics, each of which is talked about for a few minutes followed by discussion or other activity

Knowledge of information
Routine problem solving

Syndicate method

Teaching where the class is divided into groups of about 6 members who work on the same or related problems with intermittent teacher contact and who write a joint report for the critical appraisal of the whole class

Skills in seeking and organizing information
Develop teamwork; Committee skills
Interdisciplinary application
Decision making
Presentation skills

Synectics

A development of brain-storming in which special techniques, such as choosing group members from diverse backgrounds, are used to produce a creative solution to the problem

Creativity including creative problem solving and decision making

---

Tape-slides (various)

As for audio tapes except that the attached projector or viewer is used for visual teaching

Knowledge of information, especially visual information
Observation

Television

Knowledge of information and skills
Development of attitudes

T-group method

A method of teaching self-awareness and
interpersonal relations based on therapeutic
group techniques in which individual
members discuss their relationships with
each other

Sensitivity in human relations
Self-awareness, especially of
feelings, motives

---

2. A possible solution

The selection of the appropriate teaching method requires, first, an analysis of the
teaching objectives in terms of the psychological change required of the students,
second, matching a method to the objectives, and third, the ability to carry out the
method. This requires a knowledge of psychology, especially occupational psychology,
that few lecturers possess. Yet since most new lecturers are more than busy preparing
the subject matter of their courses, even fewer are placed in a position to spend time on
further study.

Although this book cannot provide the professional training, Table 15.1 lists a
number of teaching methods at present in use in Further and Higher Education together
with the objectives they are said to achieve. If the reader says, like some others when
shown this list, 'I've never heard of some of these teaching methods', perhaps this is
further evidence in support of the diagnosis.

Teaching at the students' level

1. Diagnosing the difficulty

The second major difficulty of new lecturers is to get down to the students' level of
understanding. Some new lecturers, feeling a little unsure of their knowledge, over
compensate by a display of erudition. Others conscientiously feel that it will benefit the
students if they are told everything they need to know. Thus the problem is both level
and quantity.

This is the problem of trying to teach too much. However you measure it, studies
show that students learn less than half of what a lecturer says (McLeish, 1968).
McKeachie (1963) has shown that, up to a point, if you try to teach less, students learn
more. It is a particular problem for lecturers who have recently been students
themselves. Having usually been good students they modestly fail to appreciate that the
average student does not find the subject as easy or as interesting as they did. A
characteristic of good students in examinations is that they are able to display a lot of

knowledge and thought in very few words. This compact style is an excellent skill for timed examinations to be read by professors familiar with the subject; but it is almost the opposite of what is required when teaching. New lecturers may be tempted to think that they know what it is like to be a student because they have recently been one; whereas they only know what it is like to be a good one. They have read widely and become so immersed in their subject that they are aware of neither their assumptions nor that the concepts they use every day are unfamiliar and complex to their students. More especially they are unaware of the time required for these concepts to be built up.

Table 15.2. Three levels of concepts used in lectures

Level A	Level B	Level C
Familiar concepts 100%	New concepts defined in terms of level A 80%	New concepts defined in terms of level B 20%

Consequently it is a common mistake of new lecturers to demand too great a conceptual development from their students in one lecture. Using truth-functional tests after lectures, I have found that students score around 80% on tests of new concepts (Level B) that were defined in terms of already familiar ones (Level A), but only about 20% on tests of new concepts described in terms of other ones new that day (Level C). See Table 15.2 below. Notice that understanding a new concept is not an 'all or nothing' process. If it was, we might expect students to score around 64% on Level C concepts (i.e. 80% of 80%). A thorough understanding involves linking the concept to many others.

2. Possible solutions

As we saw in Chapter 9, a lecturer cannot make all possible links for students. Students must make them for themselves. They can do very little for themselves while the lecturer is bombarding them with more information. The solution is for the lecturer to stop lecturing and give students an opportunity to make links.

The students can do this if they are allowed to use level B concepts in discussion or problem solving so that Level B language moves towards assimilation with that of level A. If assimilation in the lesson was 100% possible (which of course is most unlikely) Level B concepts would become Level A and Level C concepts would become Level B with around 80% scores, not 20%.

Thus, the use of discussion in small groups (4 at the most) between short periods of lecturing may partly overcome this difficulty. If the lecturer moves amongst the class the level of students' understanding can be guaged and misconceptions corrected when the lecture is resumed. In this way lectures build upon discussion.

The temptation to teach too much was mentioned in Chapter 4. McKeachie (in Gage, 1963) and Erskine and O'Morchoe (1961) have reported that students learned more when told less. Gane (1969) and Taplin (1969) found that the use of questions to obtain feedback after each stage of a lecture, prevented them from racing ahead of the class. Indeed, it is to be expected that all feedback techniques will be possible solutions for this reason.

New lecturers who transfer the compact examination style of their student days to their lectures, need to learn how to elaborate a point as described in Chapter 8. They will find it easiest to practice the 'General Form' first because its elaboration phase is explicit and the timing of the lecture (frequently an underlying anxiety) is easiest with this form.

Nerves

1. Consequences of the difficulty

Lecturing causes teachers more anxiety than any other part of their job. From measures of heart rate, cortisol excretion and subjective anxiety Houtman and Bakker (1987, 1991a and b) concluded that lecturing is ego threatening and imposes both psychological and physiological stress, particularly at the beginning. It was greater in simulated lectures than during the real thing. Whilst the symptoms decreased over a 3 month period in which the lecturers gave at least 20 lectures, the rank order between them hardly changed.

Although they may have other causes, a large number of lecturers' common difficulties have their origins in early lack of confidence. The bad habits resulting from nerves become embedded in their style long after beginners' nervousness has disappeared. Consequently it is advisable to face these difficulties in the first few weeks of teaching. Some hide self-consciously behind a hand in front of their face, others mumble for fear of embarrassment at what they say, and most of us have mannerisms. Because fear of the class prevents some lecturers from looking at the students, they continuously look down at their notes or sideways out of the window. Others, for fear of being tongue-tied, write out their whole lecture and usually read it with a monotonous voice, which is also the result of the same nervous tension. Unfortunately when the 'eyes down' manner of reading results in inflexible and inappropriate remarks, or when the consequent failure to observe students' reactions results in a more evident adverse response, the lecturer retreats yet further into the security of his over prepared notes, or builds a defensive mental barrier between himself and the class, so that the problem is only exacerbated. Some people blame the students when they don't understand. Others show false bravado. Marris (1964) suggests that the failure to invite questions is sometimes based on the mistaken belief that lecturers should never admit their ignorance, or the mistaken fear that their prestige will suffer if they display any lack of knowledge. Speaking too fast is also sometimes caused by nerves, but this difficulty is so common that a special section will be devoted to it.

2. Possible solutions

These consequences seem like a list of students' criticism of their lecturers. Yet we have seen that a critical attitude only makes matters worse. Criticism is inappropriate. What is needed is an appreciation of the difficulty. Correction of faults too often implies that there is only one way of giving a lecture. Nervous lecturers need reinforcement of their good points with suggestions on how these strengths can be used to achieve the teaching objectives. This is possible because nervousness is, itself, a good sign. It shows that the lecturer is concerned about students' reactions.

Most university lecturers overcome the adverse effects of nervousness in their first few months of teaching. Indeed, we saw in Chapter 12 that amorphous lecturers become complacent. Two research groups have developed confidence building techniques for those who are less fortunate. Weaver and Cotrell (1985) describe 'imaging' as a process whereby a picture of the self is imagined and 'scanned' rather like reviewing experience of an event. This produces a series of self-revealing images. After deciding what self image the lecturer would like to project, images are selectively sensitized. Weaver and Cotrell say that neural impulses, bodily movements and lecture problems associated with fear are reduced.

In a series of articles Stanton (1978, 1979) reports using relaxation training, positive suggestion and success visualization with a total of 58 lecturers as well as student teachers. More than 75% reported increasing self confidence and were rated as such by students, whilst controls showed little improvement and even some deterioration. Success visualization involved lecturers 'seeing' themselves performing in the way they would like to perform. Positive suggestion improved physical and mental health, increased energy levels, the ability to cope, calmness, concentration, and feelings of contentment, well-being and self confidence.

The second ingredient of early nervousness is usually a lack of information on what the student reaction is. It is a fear of the unknown. Therefore, one solution is to find out by obtaining feedback in one or more of the techniques previously suggested. If nerves are derived from feeling inadequate it is unwise to pretend to be more adequate than one is. Students appreciate an honest and open person.

Nervous tensions normally require an outlet. Surgeons reputedly obtain this by expressions of bad temper, and school teachers by supposedly confident displays of aggression towards their pupils; but neither of these would be acceptable when lecturing. If this energy can be displaced into an enthusiasm for the subject, or the vigorous exposition of a theory, the lecturer will have the support of a good proportion of the students surveyed by Marris (1964), Smithers (1970a and b) and the NUS Commission (Saunders *et al.*, 1969), especially arts students.

A common cause of nervousness is simply that some lecturers do not like to be the center of attention. They can avoid this for some of the time and have an opportunity to gather their composure if they use buzz groups or other forms of small-group teaching within the lecture situation. Thus the use of alternative teaching methods can give some relief (Part 4).

Speed

1. The consequences of going too fast

Going too fast is a common difficulty and it is one to which new lecturers are particularly prone. In fact it is very rare for students to complain that a lecturer is going too slowly. For example, when Geller *et al.* (1975) manipulated lecture speeds and asked students to press electric feedback buttons when they were too fast or too slow, students hardly ever indicated that the speed was slow.

Empirical evidence on the effects of listening speeds is occasionally ambiguous, yet the model depicted in Figure 15.3 may reconcile apparent conflicts. This model supposes that lecture speeds may be increased up to a certain point without serious losses in effectiveness, but that after this point there is a rapid decline. The critical word speed is hypothesized to depend on the cognitive difficulty of the lecture and the tests used.

According to this model, less able students and lectures requiring thought will show a decrement in test scores at slower speeds than intelligent students and lectures with easy subject matter.

Actually this model applies to other lecture variables too. For example, if you gradually remove techniques of clear explanations (e.g. lecture signals, itemization, blackboard build up, etc) there will be little effect at first. But then test scores for the least able students will suddenly fall. Then scores for average students will plummet. Finally, when your lecture organization is poor and your explanations are abysmal, even your best student won't understand.

Why do their scores decrease suddenly? The answer, once again, is that understanding consists of linking ideas. When students understand one idea it is linked to others; and so they understand the others too. But when the links are not made, the ideas at either end of the links are not so easily retrieved from memory, even if they were stored in the first place. Why? - because memory tends to be by association of ideas. Retrieval uses the links. Teaching and learning are all about making links, not storing facts in isolation.

Orr (1968) has suggested that the critical presentation speed is about 275-300 wpm. This is two or three times faster than normal lecture speeds, but Orr's generalization is probably based on experiments using situations cognitively easier than lectures. Furthermore, these speeds are obtained by mechanical compression of tape-recorded speech. (In most cases measures to correct the change of pitch were taken.) But comparisons of virtually identical lectures given live and on tape suggest that the critical speed of live lectures for answering questions requiring thought may be at nearly half the speed of tape recorded speech (Bligh, 1970c). Using 80 university students Reid (1968) found the decrement occurred after 325 wpm, that comprehension was superior when grammatically simple speech was used, and that grammatical complexity interacts with subject matter. Certain generalizations may be inferred from his experiment. If you wish to lecture fast, it is better not to use unnecessary words, to use the active, rather than the passive voice, to put 'if, - when - because' clauses at the

Test scores

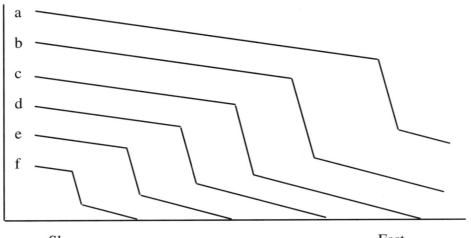

Figure 15.3. Model to depict the effects of increasing lecture speeds. Curves a-f are for tests of increasing cognitive difficulty

beginning of sentences and to keep sentences short. If it is always desirable to maximize comprehension, this advice is probably applicable to all lectures.

Grobe and Pettibone (1975) varied the speed of lectures from 102 to 145 syllables per minute (spm). Whilst none of these speeds is high, they found that attention increased, and disruptive behavior decreased, at the higher speeds. Curiously, Pettibone and Martin (1973) reported that noise levels in university classrooms were lowest at the mean speed of 134spm, greater at slower speeds, and greatest at higher speeds. Aiken *et al.* (1975) showed that higher speeds (240wpm compared with 120wpm) results in a 'terse' note-taking style which does not favor memory. At higher speeds the time taken to note a point interferes with more information. Recall was best when no notes were taken and the lecture was given twice at 240wpm. The first lecture probably acted as an advance organizer for the second.

Other variables have been demonstrated by Friedman and Johnson (1968), Sticht (1968) and Woodcock and Clark (1968) who showed that intelligence, especially verbal ability, is an important variable. Orr (1968) demonstrated the role of practice routines in learning to comprehend speeded speech, and motivation may have been an important factor when Barabasz (1968) found no effect on recall and retention scores when lectures were speeded from twenty-one to fourteen minutes. (However the critical point may not have been reached.) The changes in speed required for variations in lecture objectives have already been mentioned (Bligh, 1970c, 1974) - if you want students to think, go slower.

2. Possible solutions

(a) Use short periods of lecturing.

These research findings still leave some ambiguity. Why should students complain so persistently that lectures are too fast when experimental work suggests that they may be speeded considerably without loss of comprehension? One obvious point is that most experiments did not describe situations in which the listener took notes. Another is that, with the possible exception of Barabasz's, the passages used were very much shorter than a typical lecture and concentration may be possible for short intensive periods. Indeed, initial slight increases in retention following moderate compression of speech have also been interpreted as the result of less trace decay owing to the shorter time taken for delivery. Therefore, if lecturers who tend to go too fast use only short periods of lecturing interspersed with student rehearsal, some consolidation of memory may be achieved to produce a very intensive, but effective, learning situation. Ideally, throughout a period of an hour, the sections of lecturing should be progressively shorter whereas those with rehearsal, should lengthen.

(b) Maintain the length of pauses.

A further clue to resolve this ambiguity may be found in the work of Miron and Brown (1968). Instead of using mechanical speech compressors, they read passages at three different speeds and compared the proportion of time spent in phonation (actually speaking) and in pauses between words and at the end of sentences. They found that as speakers speed their delivery, they disproportionately decrease the total pause time. Slower speeds with longer pauses permitted superior comprehension. If we bear in mind the role of interference of a memory trace (Chapter 4) and the need for rehearsal, it would seem that if lecturers wish to increase their speed of speech they should take care to maintain the length of pauses at the end of sentences and especially after major points. Thus the variation in speed, and the timing of pauses, are significant factors affecting the comprehension of lectures.

(c) 'The general form'.

The use of 'the general form' for making a point is recommended for new lecturers because, by using repetition it lengthens the time spent on each point.

(d) The lecture guide.

The use of lecture summary handouts with headings, essential points and space for additions is useful for the lecturer who cannot slow himself. Reference to this technique has already been made. (The Lecture Guide, Chapter 11).

(e) Feedback techniques.

Finally, if lecturers do talk too fast, amends can only be made if they first find out the points that were lost and then fill in the gaps. For this reason feedback techniques are essential for the rapid lecturer.

The problem of large audiences

1. Diagnosing the difficulty

As pressures upon teachers grow, the problem of large classes is becoming a major difficulty. There is a belief that large classes are less effective than small ones. A recent study (Gibbs, 1996) seems to confirm this with regard to enrolments on courses. But when the criterion is the amount of information learned in lectures, there is a large amount of evidence that this belief is false. For example, Hudelson (1928) has reported 59 comparisons of learning in small and large lecture classes. Although most of the results showed no significant difference, 46 of the 59 favored the larger classes, and so did the majority that were significant. This finding has since been repeated many times with substantially the same results (Rohrer, 1957; Camorosano and Santapolo, 1958; Nelson, 1959; Macomber and Siegel, 1960; de Cecco, 1964). In most of these studies small classes ranged from 20 to 30 students, while large ones were over 60. Two-thirds of the lecturers in the Dorward and Wiedemann study (1977) thought the maximum size for efficient teaching is 40.

McKeachie (1963) and Meredith *et al.* (1982a) have claimed that large lectures tend to be inferior when the criteria used are more concerned with thinking and attitudes. Since management of personal interaction is more difficult in large classes and small classes are more 'intimate', this is probably true; but so far I have found very little empirical confirmation. It is true that Siegel, Adams and Macomber (1960) found fairly consistent differences favoring smaller classes when the criteria included thinking, problem solving and changes in attitude, but the differences were slight and for none of these criteria was there a consistent significant difference. Smith (1996) found the same when teaching the application of simultaneous equations in economics.

In contrast there have been many studies of the effects of class size at school level. After a meta-analysis, Glass (1987) concluded there is not much difference between the outcomes of classes over 30; but with classes smaller than 30 the advantages are greater, the smaller the class. More important, the effects are cumulative with more hours of instruction. The same broad conclusions may not apply to non-stop lectures, but if they do not apply to varied teaching methods at college level, one might ask why.

The expectation of a difference arises when one only considers the lecturer's task. If the two situations are considered from the point of view of the individual student, the lack of difference is hardly surprising. When listening to a speaker, the fact that a certain number of other people are doing the same thing does not greatly change the student's mental activity. Consequently the kind of psychological objectives that can be achieved remain the same.

It is the teacher's role that is changed by increases in class size; the changes in the students' role are relatively slight. Some research by de Cecco (1964) throws an interesting light on this. When he asked students and lecturers in a direct way whether they preferred large or small lecture classes, they both claimed to prefer the smaller ones. But when students answered a questionnaire containing a large number of items about particular classes not apparently related to their size, the students showed no preference for one or the other. Meredith and Ogasawara (1982b) and Marsh *et al.* (1979) also report that size is only weakly related, if at all, to perceived educational outcomes and satisfaction with the lecturer.

If large and small classes are equally effective, does the difficulty lie in the fact that lecturers do not like teaching large ones? Startup (1977) reported that lecturers who valued informal feedback from students were more satisfied with small classes. Some saw themselves as thinking out loud and were indifferent to class size! Certainly, (i) the range of teaching methods that can be combined with lecturing is progressively restricted with increases in size; consequently (ii) the compensating demands upon lecturing technique are greater if the problems of attention and motivation are to be overcome.

2. Diminishing the difficulty

(a) Use buzz groups.
The demands upon technique are mostly derived from the difficulty of obtaining both verbal and non-verbal feedback. Obviously with larger classes there are more people to observe, a smaller proportion can speak, and fewer will have the courage to do so (Stones, 1970). Of the methods suggested in Chapter 19, only buzz groups give a satisfactory sample of feedback when students number more than one hundred; and even this method may be restricted.

(b) Personal projection.
There are also less obvious difficulties. When the distance of members of the audience from the speaker is greater, it is more difficult to establish eye-contact. This in turn affects timing, humor, facial communication and many conversational cues of which we are seldom conscious.
To overcome this it is necessary for speakers to project their personalities. This may require some confidence and dramatic ability, particularly at the beginning. A certain amount of light-heartedness can release the tension, make the lecturer more relaxed so that his personality is displayed, and let the audience feel free to react. On the other hand large lectures tend to be more formal and students expect them to be. Consequently attempts to break the formality by flippancy or casualness are risky tactics that can bring disrespect and poor attention if not handled with care.

(c) Sentential pauses.
A useful tip is to pause a little longer at the end of sentences than one might do with a smaller class. Use the opportunity of the pause to look around the class, gauge reaction and, where possible, get eye contact. If you see a furrowed brow at the back, ask the

student by name whether they have understood and re-explain or otherwise have a brief exchange of conversation. This sends a message to all students that they are not lost in the crowd and that their non-verbal behavior is noticed. It keeps a personal touch and it breaks the formality of the lecture acceptably.

(d) Maintaining attention.

It is more difficult for students to concentrate in a large lecture. A periodic review (or 'taking stock') of the lecture so far, helps students grasp the overall structure of the lecture and fill in gaps where their attention lapsed. Since we saw in Chapter 4 that the attention declines in the middle of lectures and the lecturers cannot be sure how well they have been understood, it is sometimes suggested that the density of information should be less at that time. As we saw in Chapter 5, a buzz group or some other change of activity helps to maintain attention. Warning the class at the beginning that you intend to introduce an activity also creates pressure to concentrate. The activity could be very brief, such as completing a line in a calculation.

Inviting a colleague to form a duo and share the lecture is another way to introduce variety (see reference to Betts and Walton 1970).

(e) Inviting questions.

Because students are less likely to ask questions or interrupt in a large lecture, members of buzz groups can be given the task of answering each other's questions. Those that cannot be answered by group members should be written on a sheet of paper and passed to the front for the lecturer to deal with. This avoids any embarrassment of students expressing ignorance to a large audience and it enables the lecturer to deal with similar problems at the same time. Obviously it is also useful feedback.

(f) Slower on key points.

Another tip is to speak slower on key points. The different routes by which sound rebounds in a larger room results in it being less distinct. Ideally the vowel sounds in words need to be a little longer and the consonants more distinct, but it is difficult to do this consciously without speech training. If, however, every sentence is spoken slower, attention in a large class is much more difficult to maintain.

Lecturing skills can be learned

It is sometimes said that good lecturers are born, not made. Don't despair. There is now good evidence that this is not true. No doubt as in other fields of human endeavor, some people are more gifted than others, but lecturing skills can be learned.

Some skills are more easily learned than others. Sixty-five lecturers gave pairs of explanations which were video-recorded. Trained independent observers rated them without knowing which were given first, and which were second (Daines and Brown,

1983). All skills showed improvement, particularly openings, organization, the use of audio-visual aids, creating interest, and global ratings. Lecturers were less successful in improving their endings and in taking account of their audience. Linguistic analysis showed significant improvements in sign-posting and linking; and some improvements in focussing attention, audience awareness, and reducing stumbles, hesitations and incomplete sentences.

The skills most easily acquired included the use of examples, appropriate vocabulary, diagrams, audio-visual and other materials; summarizing; selecting appropriate content; focussing attention on important points; setting the stage for the explanation and repeating main points. The least learnable features were changes in the lecturers' style; verbal fluency; the elimination of digressions; the use of metaphors and explaining links; and displays of enthusiasm, flexibility, and interest.

The most difficult skills relate to affect (i.e. feelings, attitudes and motivation). Using reflection-based decision making in a teaching laboratory, Klinzing (1988) was not only concerned with lecturers developing clarity, interest and a social climate, but with four skills of non-verbal expressiveness that communicate affect. These were gestures, voice delivery, facial expression (including eye expression and eye gaze), and posture and movement (including movement in the room). The training consisted of preparing, giving and discussing a lecture in a group of 7; hearing a lecture on theory and research on non-verbal behavior; practicing and imitating each of the four skills; discriminating emotions shown in pictures; and finally a repeat lecture in the group of 7. Ratings on adjective scales showed improvement in all domains.

Margaret King (1973) found that new university teachers were more anxious about lecturing than anything else. Fox (1980) found their principal concerns were to do with assessing their own teaching and development. Either way, we cannot be surprised that 75% of lecturers are apprehensive before video feedback sessions to improve their lecturing (Cryer, 1988), even though these sessions are always the most highly rated afterwards. Cryer recommends that participants are reassured by first seeing others lecturing on video, and themselves in discussion. I always give lecturers the first opportunity to criticize themselves and run a convention that favorable comments should always precede any adverse criticisms. From observing lecturers for many years I am acutely aware that behaviors to overcome difficulties in their first three lectures become habits that last a life time. I therefore strongly recommend that lecturers get help right at the start of their careers, even if they think they don't need it.

Conclusion

The problems of lecturing covered in this Chapter are ones that most lecturers share at some stage in their career. There is no use pretending that they have ultimate solutions. All lecturers can do is make the best of a bad job. I hope the above suggestions are helpful, but I suspect some of them are easier to make than to carry out.

16. Lectures for the Promotion of Thought

Stimulating thought.
1.   Choose a suitable lecture form.
2.   The use of questions.

Making thinking easier.
1.   Visual display.
2.   Use handouts.
3.   Pre-reading.
4.   Speed

Conclusion.

I have argued in Chapter 2 that the typical descriptive lecture is unsuitable for the promotion of student thought. The argument was based firstly on experimental findings that 'thought objectives' are not achieved and secondly on psychological grounds that lectures do not provide a situation in which much thought may take place.

However, when making suggestions for new lecturers, the practical situation in which they are frequently placed must be faced. It is no good blaming principals, professors or departmental heads. The new lecturer may have to face the immediate problem of taking large classes for a course with no follow-up seminars and in which it would be irresponsible not to have objectives including student thought.

Therefore, the question must be posed, 'How can I promote student thought in large classes?' The answers should take account of the psychology of thinking and this, presumably, will either involve a lecturing technique different from those used in the experimental studies, or the inclusion of discussion techniques (Part 4).

Stimulating thought

1. Choose a suitable lecture form
A 'descriptive' lecture mostly consists of the presentation of information and is likely to conform to the hierarchic form of classification, a chain of narrative, or some combination of these. But we have seen that in a problem-centered lecture, a chain of argument or the presentation of a thesis, the student is required to think in order to follow the reasoning. Since thinking is learned by practice, if lecturers are in situations in which they must lecture rather than arrange student discussion or other active learning, it is these forms that should be used for the promotion of thought.

In other words, if the objective is to teach students to think, the provision of information, although necessary, is not enough. When teaching students to solve problems Corman has shown that a knowledge of how to go about them is more important than a knowledge of the principles to be used. This is a pertinent study because it is often assumed that if students are told about the principles of a subject, they will know how to use them. Corman (1957) tested students on their ability to solve problems after he had systematically varied the amount of information they had been given. The information was of two kinds. One was about the principles to be applied; the other was concerned with the methods students should use to apply the principles and to discover the solutions. Application and discovery require thought. For most students their ability to solve problems varied directly with the amount of information they were given on the method of approach. Students who had scored highly on intelligence tests were better able to apply a knowledge of the principles and did less well than others without it. Less able students were only able to cope with a limited amount of information about the method, and whether they were told about the principles made no difference to the number of problems they could solve. This experiment illustrates the maxim 'Teach students what they need to know, not something different'. Students who were given guidance in methods of thinking were better at thinking. It sound obvious, but it cannot be done if the lecturer does not have clear objectives.

2. The use of questions
The most common device to promote thought is to ask questions, and this may be done in a number of ways. Where students are supplied with networked computer terminals, lecturers can monitor individual and group responses. Questions in lectures may be rhetorical, and although these do not compel activity from the student it is the nature of our language that they stimulate it, particularly if followed by a brief silence. We are conditioned to try to answer questions that are asked even if we have been trained not to shout the answer. In a well controlled experiment Sime and Boyce (1969) inferred that questions raised the level of attention because the learning of concepts about which no questions were asked showed greater improvement in classes with questions than in classes in which students had none to answer.

In general, questions should be those that require the specific kind of thought stated in the teacher's objectives. Hunkins (1967, 1968) asked only analytical and evaluative questions of one class and only factual questions of another. Subsequent tests showed no difference in the groups' abilities in questions requiring knowledge, simple comprehension, application and synthesis of facts, but significant differences in the predicted direction in the students' abilities to analyze and evaluate.

Testing, or apparently testing students' factual knowledge in public will almost invariably provoke an undesirable reaction, for no-one likes to be placed in a position where they may display their ignorance. Students will not be discouraged if they are asked for their personal opinions or personal reactions, firstly because their answers cannot be wrong and secondly because they feel respected if their opinions are considered worth hearing. Supplementary questions to elicit clarification of an individual's viewpoint are often necessary for the rest of the class, but so long as answers are accepted for consideration there need be no feeling of intimidation. Intimidation should normally be avoided at all costs; because of the manner of some school teachers, fear reactions are more common amongst students than lecturers might expect. In my opinion acute sensitivity to slight changes in students' emotive reactions is essential to good teaching.

Provided lecturers know precisely what they are trying to do, it is not difficult to use student replies to open up and develop a lecture topic. If, whatever students reply, lecturers can relate it to their objectives, their objectives can in turn be related to what is already in the students' minds (i.e. the students can 'understand').

Less personal questions can be set as essay titles, as discussion topics, or for individual answers on handouts (Elton, 1970). Uren (1968) has described a technique of raising a question for discussion before the lecturer expounds upon it. He found that, by thinking, the class was able to suggest most of the important points the lecturer would have raised. As a result students' thought was encouraged and the lecturer was able to synthesize the suggestions and develop the topic further than he otherwise would.

A variation on this technique is to ask each student to work individually on a problem before resuming a class discussion approach or formal lecturing. Obviously

Figure 16.1. A guide for students to generate questions
(Adapted from King, 1991)

How are - - - and - - - alike?
What is the main idea of - - - ?
What would happen if - - - ?
What are the strengths and weaknesses of - - - ?
In what way is - - - related to - - - ?
What values are assumed by - - - ?
How does - - - affect - - - ?
What is the function of - - - ?
What principle is applied when - - - ?
Compare - - - and - - - with regard to - - - .
What causes - - - ?
How does - - - tie in with what we learned before?
Which one is the best - - - and why?
What are the possible solutions for the problem of - - - ?
Who are the major authorities in this field? What are their central propositions?
Do you agree or disagree with the statement - - - and why?
What do I(you) still not understand about - - - ?

---

some of the benefits of attending lectures are to listen to experts and to meet fellow students, and both these are denied if individual work is over-used; but the technique can maintain student attention, provide a change of activity, direct student thought and provide welcome feedback for both student and teacher when the answer is explained.

The use of buzz groups is described in Chapter 19. They may provoke thought in a specific direction provided their task is carefully thought out and the purpose made clear to the students.

A most important technique has been developed by King. She developed a set of question stems with gaps such as those shown in Table 16.1. Students were each required to generate three questions by inserting appropriate concepts or lecture content in the gaps. This technique not only provided a degree of learner autonomy; it demanded critical thinking and thought at a meta-level with reference to the topic of a lecture. King (1989, 1991) compared the comprehension scores for students who (1) answered each others' questions and their own in buzz groups of three members; (2) only answered their own questions; (3) reviewed a topic in a buzz group discussion; and (4) reviewed the topic individually. Students working on questions (1 and 2) out-performed those reviewing the material (3 and 4). She also compared (1) and (3) with a group like (1) except that the students could not use a guide like Table 16.1 to generate the questions (King, 1990). Although this group did better than (3), (1) displayed more critical thinking. A further report (King, 1994) showed that students who generated and answered their own questions performed better than those who answered the same questions generated by others.

	Worked individually	Worked in buzz groups
Answered student generated questions	2	1
Reviewed lecture material	4	3

Figure 16.2.   The conditions of King's experiments.

Making thinking easier

Thinking involves holding more than one idea in the mind at once in order to relate or distinguish them. These processes employ short-term memory. But we have seen that short-term memories have a limited capacity. Therefore one way to make thought possible is to reduce the load on the students' short-term memories.

It is because thinking imposes an extra load that the conditions required to promote thought are more exacting than those to allow students to remember and note information. Consequently, in addition to trying to stimulate thought, much of the lecturer's task will consist of making thinking easier. Both are necessary. (Some lecturers call this 'spoon-feeding' - an emotive expression - but there is no point in expecting students to do what numerous studies have shown they cannot normally achieve, without attempting to make the task easier.)

1. Visual display

We have already seen that the relatively permanent visual display of information, using the blackboard or overhead projector, is one way of doing this.

2. Use handouts

Another method already mentioned is the use of handouts not only containing the necessary information (perhaps in summary form) but arranging it appropriately together with the problem(s) being discussed. When used in this way the function of the handout is to provide a substitute for student note-taking and to redirect attention to the issue that requires thought. It was suggested that if the handout is distributed a week before, the students could become familiar with the basic information and lecture time could be saved; but in this case the lecturer must rely on the novelty of the problem, rather than a new subject, to arouse interest. Also with difficult subject matter prior distribution may not always be advisable, although it has the advantage that student attention is less likely to be distracted from the lecturer to the handout at the wrong time.

3. Pre-reading

A further suggestion is to set reading the week before; but if this is adopted certain precautions should normally be observed. The lecture will fail if the students do not do the reading unless the lecturer has plans for this contingency. Therefore, these contingency plans must be made in addition to the intended lecture. (It is not enough to say 'If I do my bit, I expect the students to do theirs'. This attitude does not face the reality that not all students act in their own best interests. Consequently, teachers have a managerial role. They are not simply someone who produces information for the students to assemble in their minds; they need to have a view of the whole learning process. This includes anticipating difficulties in the way that an industrial manager may anticipate human problems affecting the production process.) But to do this alone is defeatist. Students will read as required if they want to, and if they can. Thus the task is partly to arouse motivation. One way to do this is to read short extracts as 'trailers' that arouse interest, summarize the major points, or stimulate humor. Another way is to make it clear that full benefit from next week's lecture cannot be obtained without preparation, and when the time comes explicit reference to the prescribed texts will provide psychological reinforcement of their preparatory behavior.

The references must be available, easy and short. If they are not easily available the lecturer may 'tie' the books in the library, ensure the provision of a suitable number of photocopies (perhaps also tied in the library) and, where appropriate, make sure the local bookshop can satisfy a sudden demand (e.g. of Scientific American offprints).

The readings need to be in sufficiently easy language, not to require an introductory lecture. Articles and books with summaries are useful. If the reading is longer than six to twenty pages (obviously this varies tremendously with the subject, size of page, and so on) a substantial proportion of the class will not have read it by the following week. This should be avoided. Like the breaking of New Year resolutions, once students fail to live up to their intentions they will find it difficult to keep good study habits. It is better to set too little, and to lecture to a class with a known uniform background, than to set too much. If students fail to read, there is little a lecturer can do to make them. It is better to make sure that they never fail in the first place.

A useful compromise is to summarize the reading at the beginning of the lecture selecting what is relevant to the central problem to be considered and without implying that the summary is complete or, indeed, that it is a summary. (If students come to believe that the summary is complete, they may not do the required reading.)

The summary may also be used as a framework by students who found the reading difficult, consequently close observation of individual class members at this time (e.g. whether they take notes) is a useful way to discover the lazy and less able. Assuming the required reading was a key reference, re-reading and the borrowing of photostat copies available in class, may be advised, particularly when combined with horseshoe groups (Chapter 19).

4. Speed
It has already been mentioned that a very important factor affecting the amount of student thought that can take place in a lecture is its speed. In an experiment I gave the same lectures at three different speeds to three groups and then tested the students not only on their gain in knowledge and simple comprehension of the subjects, but also in their ability to analyze, resynthesize, evaluate and use the information to solve problems. Although there was no difference between the groups in their ability to recall information and display simple comprehension of it, students who heard a lecture at its slowest speed did significantly better on questions requiring more thought (Bligh, 1974). Since students require time to think, especially when presented with new information, this result may not seem surprising, but it is none the less important if 'the promotion of thought' is one of the lecturer's objectives.

Conclusion
Lectures are not usually effective in teaching students to think; this objective is better achieved by using lectures in conjunction with other methods as suggested in Chapter 19. If these are not possible, a problem-centered lecture form, a chain of argument or the presentation of a thesis are suitable forms of organization. Thought may also be encouraged by the use of questions and techniques to reduce the load on students' short-term memories.

17. Lectures to Teach Attitudes

The lecturer's task in teaching attitudes
1. Acquisition of attitudes.
2. Change of attitudes.

Strategies in the presentation of information.
1. Students' initial attitudes.
2. Stating possible conclusions.
3. Previous education.
4. Order of presentation.
5. Credibility of lecturer.
6. The amount of attitude change advocated.
7. Personality of the student.
8. Summary of strategies.

The lecturer's task in teaching attitudes

It is the purpose of this chapter to suggest some ways in which attitudes may be taught by lectures. It is not concerned with philosophical questions of what attitudes ought to be taught or whether we ought to teach them at all. In many vocational subjects such as law, medicine, education and business studies certain professional attitudes and values are assumed to be necessary. Therefore, if students do not possess these when they enroll, they will need to be taught; and although it has already been argued that lectures are not the best method for these objectives, teachers are sometimes forced to use the method.

There is a second class of attitude objectives where one is concerned, not so much that the students possess a specific attitude, but that they do have an attitude towards a particular thing, and that they can justify it rationally. For example, whatever attitude students have towards Sartre's plays or the theory of continental drift, they may be required to support it by argument.

There is a fundamental difficulty in the teaching of attitudes which does not arise in the teaching of information and which consequently normally demands a different approach. Factual information is usually absorbed following some kind of presentation, but attitudes are not something external to the student, they are based on emotions and therefore cannot be absorbed from outside. They are predispositions for dealing with information that is presented; they cannot, themselves, be presented by a lecturer. They are a kind of internal coding system. Thus a change in attitudes must originate from the student. In this sense, attitudes cannot be taught; it is the teacher's task to engineer the situation so that the students will acquire or change them for themselves. Information alone is not likely to change attitudes. The lecturer must appeal to some emotion the students already possess.

1. Acquisition of attitudes

Engineering this situation commonly has two stages. The teacher may first make the student aware of a need, then provide the means of satisfying it. This pattern is familiar in advertising except that, while the lecturer's audience is often captive, an advertisement must first attract attention. This is frequently achieved by means of some device quite irrelevant to the product, but thereafter the pattern is recognizable. Motives such as maternal affection, social status and sexual attraction are aroused, and a product is offered which may satisfy them.

This process may be thought of as objectionable in the educational field although it is a normal feature of human conversation; but it seems to me to be acceptable provided it is not coupled with deliberately restricted information. It is the restriction of information that is antithetical to education, not the appeal to students' motives. To teach students to seek information and express opinions are important educational objectives. Thus at the beginning of a lecture in medicine or education the lecturer may point out the needs of the patient or child to arouse certain motives in the student. Attitudes may be formed when these motives are associated with the information and techniques taught.

2. Change of attitudes

Attitudes may be changed when they are inadequate to deal with information presented. The inadequacy may be of two kinds:

(a) Change resulting from inadequate information.

The students may have no relevant attitude or system for coding presented information. If they have never read any of Sartre's plays and know little or nothing about them from other sources, they will look for any attitude that makes sense of the new information. This may be an irrelevant prejudice against the French or an irrational respect for the lecturer. Students are likely to agree with their friends or people they admire even though the source of their admiration and friendship may be quite irrelevant to the issue for agreement (Tannenbaum, 1953). The ignorant are more suggestible than the knowledgeable.

(b) Change resulting from conflicting information.

If new information cannot be reconciled to two attitudes, a person may change one or both. For example, if a student held favorable attitudes towards the Labor unions and the Republican Party, but was told that many people in the Republican Party supported what he believed to be anti-union legislation, his favorable attitudes towards one or both may change. Complete rejection of a previous attitude is unlikely. The student is likely to take up an 'in between position' which may be nearer the unions or the Republican Party according to the relative strengths of his previous attitudes; he may attach reservations to these principles or establish a higher order principle to deal with the conflict. Thus attitudes may develop and become more complex by successive modification. It is this process for which free-group discussions are particularly suitable (Barnett, 1958; Abercrombie, 1960).

Because it is difficult for people to face up to conflicts in their own ideas, it is necessary in the lecture situation where individuals do not have to explain their inconsistencies, to state issues very clearly so that they cannot easily be repressed. Yet, if the clarification is achieved by over-simplification, the students' reconciliation of attitudes may easily be naive. The consequent need for both clarity and detail makes it very difficult to achieve a change of students' attitudes by lecturing.

The second situation, (b), is more common in student learning and everyday life; but the first has particular importance here, both because students are constantly having to cope with new areas of knowledge and because lectures are essentially situations in which information is presented.

(c) Change resulting from threatening information.
The effects of threatening presentations are ambiguous. The information that smoking will result in a slow and lingering death has had remarkably little effect upon people from all walks of life and all levels of intelligence. The consequence is delayed. The threat of one or ten years imprisonment will make little difference to the incidence of crime. The consequence is delayed and uncertain. Three groups of students heard lectures varying on the dire consequences of dental neglect and what they should do to prevent it. Those who heard the most severe lecture expressed most anxiety immediately afterwards, but took least remedial action later. Those with least threat acted upon it most.

It seems that severe threats don't bear contemplation. We put up defenses to prevent being disturbed by the message. However there is reason to believe that strong appeals will have an effect if they threaten our loved ones, the topics are relatively unfamiliar, the individuals have high self-esteem or low vulnerability and the source is credible.

Strategies in the presentation of information

The degree to which students' attitudes will change following the presentation of information will vary with their initial attitudes, their previous education, the order in which the information is given, whether both sides of an issue are presented and are considered, the credibility of the lecturer, the amount of change advocated, the personality of the student and, no doubt, many other factors.

1. Students' initial attitudes
If students' initial positions are unfavorable to the lecturer's arguments, they will change their attitudes more if both sides of an argument are given; but if their initial positions are favorable, these attitudes will only be strengthened by the presentation of their point of view (Hovland, Lumsdaine and Sheffield, 1949). When favorable students heard arguments on both sides of a question no signs of change were observed. Presentations of information alone did not result in permanent changes unless coupled with a decision the students had taken for themselves.

These findings suggest the need to be aware of students' initial attitudes, and this may be obtained by the use of discussion methods at the beginning of a lecture, but if that knowledge is obtained by requiring an expression of their opinion, this act of commitment may result in a less open mind. When it is remembered that adults have subtle ways of concealing their attitudes it will be realized that the lecturer requires considerable sensitivity to the feelings of students by using non-verbal means of feedback during the initial class discussion. This can sometimes be done by getting the class to raise issues rather than give answers. The lecturer will frequently sense the initial attitudes by the way issues are raised and selected. If the questions are translated into neutral language as they are written on the board, commitment is avoided.

2. Stating possible conclusions

The importance of decision making in the formation of attitudes may lead one to suppose that students will acquire appropriate professional attitudes if the lecturer states facts and then leaves students to draw their own conclusions. This may be true of able students, but where subject matter is difficult or unfamiliar, a statement of the conclusion produces the necessary comprehension for attitude change. Hovland and Mandell (1952) presented identical arguments favoring devaluation to two groups except that the argument's conclusion was omitted for the second group. Devaluation is a complex subject and they found twice the number of people changed their attitude in the favored direction in the group that heard the conclusion. Since students in lectures are required to understand difficult and unfamiliar information which they cannot easily relate it is probably better for lecturers to state the conclusions that can be inferred from their lectures.

Some lecturers (not to mention some newspapers) claim that it is their duty to present 'facts' rather than state a conclusion, and leave the students to make up their own minds. The validity of this claim will vary with the lecturer's objectives, but the facts and the words in which they are expressed are necessarily selected and we shall see that attitudes are learned as much from a teacher's personality as from the conclusions stated. Therefore, paradoxically, if lecturers wish to be impartial it is sometimes necessary for them to state their point of view.

3. Previous education

If complete impartiality is impossible and it is more effective to make possible inferences explicit, should both sides of issues be considered? The answer to this question seems to depend on how far previous education has taught people to look at both sides before making a judgement. Because students in Higher Education are capable of some critical thinking (which is usually to be encouraged) it seems reasonable to expect lecturers to present both sides of an argument. Hovland, Lumsdaine and Sheffield (1949) found that while less educated soldiers were persuaded by a one-sided argument (on the probable length of the war against Japan), those with more education took balanced arguments more seriously.

Lumsdaine and Janis (1953) found that those who had previously heard both sides of a question were more resistant to change in later group discussion. This may be relevant to a current problem in the training of teachers. There is a tendency for teachers to become more authoritarian and less child-centered in their first year after training while their lecturers in the colleges think that this is a retrograde change. The lecturers may, therefore, need to take steps to face their student teachers with the difficulties and arguments against the approaches they advocate. Indeed students may react unfavorably if well-known contrary arguments are not considered. The failure of a lecturer to consider contrary arguments arises from the fear that the arguments may be convincing. But students are more likely to react unfavorably if such arguments are familiar but remain unmentioned, than to be convinced by arguments presented by one who does not believe them.

4. Order of presentation

Granted that it is usually better to consider pro and con arguments in a lecture, in which order should they be considered? This is known as the primacy-recency question. Provided the student is not warned about the fallibility of first impressions (Cohen, 1964), the argument presented first is more likely to be convincing if the students have no previous knowledge and it fixes their orientation to the subject or, if, unlike later presentations, it does not compete with previously formed ideas. On the other hand, the most recently presented ideas may be more convincing if they interfere with the memory of earlier ones, or students are wavering between two equal arguments.

Not surprisingly, the first argument is most effective when the audience is tired or not very interested. Janis (1957) found that the first argument presented for or against participation in civil defense was more persuasive as measured by the readiness of listeners to volunteer. Miller and Campbell (1959) found that the first presented argument was most effective when both are presented on the same occasion whether students were given a post-test immediately or after one week. But if the two sides of an argument are presented one week apart and immediately tested on the second week, recency is stronger than primacy.

With people already possessing an opinion, McGuire (1963) has shown that attitudes change more when points they favor are presented first. If non-favored points are presented first the students seem to listen with 'but....' on their minds. They seem to resist contrary points until their own have been expressed. Because the students are emotionally involved, and attitudes are partly the product of emotions, this is a more powerful factor than those previously considered. Since it is difficult to know the range of students' views in one class, it may often be advisable to start a period with class discussion after raising a question, and only then go on to lecture (if necessary for complete treatment of the question) rather than start by a lecture which produces resistance.

Cohen (1964) reports that if, after hearing only one side of a controversial issue, listeners make a response which publicly indicates their position on an issue, they are less likely to change their minds. This effect does not operate if they anonymously fill in a questionnaire. This is worth bearing in mind when dealing with student protest or other forms of negotiation. (Politicians, too, sometimes find it difficult to change their minds in public.) On one occasion when I sought the cooperation of a class for introducing an innovation in teaching, one vocal member at once declared dogmatically that he would not cooperate. The reasons for his impulsive reaction need not concern us, but it was necessary during ensuing discussion to make him feel there would be no loss of face by withdrawing from his publicly stated position. It was necessary to make it clear that he was not regarded as finally committed and that no one would notice if he changed his mind. (e.g. First, 'the door had to be kept open', and secondly, it was necessary to draw attention away from the individual by dissociating viewpoints and personalities.)

5. Credibility of the lecturer
The persuasiveness of a lecture will vary with the credibility of the lecturer, and Hovland, Janis and Kelley (1953) have shown that the credibility of 'communicators' (not necessarily in a lecture situation) is the result of their expertise, trustworthiness, fairness and intentions as perceived by listeners. Of these, fairness was found to be more important than expertise and intent. Aspects of the person that were irrelevant to the subject as appearance, prestige, prowess in sport and membership of a minority group, were also found to be influential. Tanner (1968) has shown that a lecturer's influence is enhanced by the support of a student 'confidante' or an 'expert'. In short, lecturers are more likely to be believed if they are perceived as 'a good guy' by their students. Academic expertise is not the only, or even the most influential factor; the effectiveness of lecturers in achieving attitude objectives is strongly influenced by their relationship with their class.

6. The amount of attitude change advocated
Up to a certain point the degree of attitude change will increase the greater the change required, but beyond that point, at first little, and then no change, is obtained (Cohen, 1964). It is as if there are limits to individuals' credulity and when the limit is reached they refuse to yield an inch.

This implies that if lecturers require a big change in the attitudes of their audience, they will have to design their programs in small steps; and since not all their audience will change by the same amount, the size of the steps will need to be progressively smaller.

Cohen reports that the limits of credulity vary with the credibility of the source of information. With respected and credible teachers, the greater the discrepancy between the students' views and those presented, the greater will be the shift in attitudes. With doubtful or less credible lecturers, the degree of resistance increases as the discrepancy increases. Aronson, Turner and Carlsmith (1963) demonstrated this by giving students accounts which were attributed either to T. S. Eliot or to a fellow student, and carefully graded as estimates of the value of a literary work. As the praise said to be given by T. S. Eliot increased, so the estimates of the work's value increasingly exceeded those expressed in a pre-test. When the same praise was said to have come from the fellow student, changes in attitude increased up to a point, but then decreased. It should be noticed that, as in a lecture situation in which students can make no contribution, the opinion of the 'information source' could not be changed or further elaborated. The reverse is true when attitudes are expressed in student tutorials or group discussion.

However, Cohen has suggested that the advantage of high credibility is nil after three weeks. He explains this in terms of dissociation of information from its source, or the interaction of experimental subjects in discussion. This is not to say that there is no attitude change at all, but that those who record big changes revert towards their original position in time.

7. Personality of the student

The degree of attitude change in students also depends on their degree of 'persuasibility'. Hovland and Janis (1959) have suggested a personality trait of 'persuasibility' with seven characteristics.

(a) Low self esteem.

Students who hold themselves and their opinions in low esteem are more likely to change their attitudes by persuasion. Positive correlations were obtained between measures of attitude change and scales based on self-rating questionnaires administered by Janis and Field (1959).

(b) Perceptual dependence.

Witkin (1962) has shown that some students tend to perceive themselves with reference to their physical environment more than others who perceive themselves and relations between objects independently. These differences correlated with the Rorschach, and other personality tests. Students who are dependent on the environment are more easily persuaded.

(c) Other directedness.

People who are inner directed in that they have strong personal motives and goals, are less easily persuaded than those who are weak willed.

Cohen (1964) argues that people who are isolated seek social contact and are therefore more suggestible. This is consistent with the work of S. E. Asch (1951) and others on the power of group pressures for conformity.

(e) Authoritarianism.

Some psychologists have suggested there is an authoritarian-democratic dimension in our personality which is capable of measurement. People at the authoritarian end of this scale not only give orders to their inferiors, but more willingly accept them from their superiors than those with democratic attitudes. Cohen suggests that they accept presented attitudes more readily than 'democrats' in the way that they more readily accept orders. Since lectures, when compared with discussions, are authoritarian situations, this is consistent with Smithers' finding (1970a) that dogmatic students (as measured by the Rokeach Dogmatism Test) prefer to be given very direct guidance.

(f) Richness of fantasy.

People with a good imagination are most easily convinced.

(g) Sex.

Hovland and Janis (1959) suggested that the acquiescent social role of women makes them more persuasible than men, who display more variable changes in attitude; but whether this generalization is applicable now is more doubtful.

The small but positive correlations between personality tests and changeability of attitudes may be explained by a combination of three processes: fear of social disapproval, feelings of inadequacy and motivated gullibility. The first could be described in terms of group pressure or conditioning. For example, the desire for approval can be rewarded, and attitudes strengthened, by saying 'Good' (Hildum and Brown, 1956; Singer, 1961). The role of conditioning and group pressure is also confirmed by Scott's finding (1957) that students proposing the opposite view to the one they actually believed showed greater attitude change if their side won the debate. But the implicit principle of 'learning through activity' suggests that this process is not very applicable in lectures.

The effect of feeling inadequate is illustrated by (b), (c), (d) and (e) above; and motivated gullibility is related to (a) and (f). Students also have a need to impose meaning and organization on experience. Cohen (1964) has demonstrated that students with a high need for cognitive clarity, sometimes called 'sharpeners', may change their attitudes to achieve it. Paradoxically therefore, with this particular kind of student, increasing ambiguity and lack of clarity in a lecture could force them to change their attitudes more than a clear one, provided that the lecture was not so obscure that nothing could be sharpened. However, obviously in view of the difficulty of obtaining this balance, and the fact that not all students are 'sharpeners', vague lectures are not to be recommended. The important point is that students who work hard to reconcile opposing views display greater attitude change than others. Lectures themselves do not provide a time for this work, but they may provide the viewpoints.

Summary of strategies

In Chapter 2 it was argued, on the basis of experiments in teaching, that the lecture method is relatively inappropriate to teach values or to change attitudes. The more analytical findings of psychologists referred to in this chapter confirm, and to some extent explain, this relative unsuitability. If, however, teachers are obliged to use the lecture method, there is some evidence that they will be more effective if they are fair-minded, present more than one point of view, consider the students' viewpoints first (perhaps by asking their opinions), present their own conclusion first if the students do not already have one, and require some reconsideration of the issues within three weeks at the most.

Part 4
Alternatives when Lecturing is Inadequate

18. The Lecture Method Alone is Rarely Adequate

Psychological reasons.
1. Feedback to students and lecturer is needed.
2. Rehearsal needed.
3. Avoid interference and negative transfer.
4. Encourage "deep processing".
5. Reduce the intensity with self-pacing.
6. Active learning is better.
7. Maintain high levels of attention.
8. Foster motivation by activity.
9. Accept and use human nature.
10. Teach thought and feeling by discussion.
11. A mix of methods is best to teach information too.
12. Match the mix of learning styles.

A general educational argument.
1. Different kinds of objectives are best achieved by different methods.
2. Teachers usually have different kinds of objectives in any one lesson.
3. Therefore the objectives of any one lesson are usually best achieved by different methods.

Conclusion.

Chapter 2 showed that there are many methods just as effective as lectures. In principle any of them could replace lectures. But this book is not about other methods. They have their defects too. Part 4 is about combining other methods with lectures to compensate where lectures are inadequate.

Using evidence already presented, I shall argue in Part 4 that the inherent defects of the lecture method mean that, on its own, it is rarely adequate. Therefore, if not replaced, it will need to be combined with other methods in some way.

Accordingly, in this chapter I shall first review the reasons why the lecture method alone is rarely adequate. In Chapter 19 I shall describe a number of teaching methods which can be used with lectures; and then, in Chapter 20, briefly suggest some ways in which they may be combined.

It must be emphasized that the statement, 'The lecture method alone is rarely adequate', does not imply (as is sometime misconstrued) that the lecture method is rarely appropriate. The lecture has a place, but the place it is given is often too prominent. Surveys show that lecturing is still the dominant teaching method, yet lecturers themselves yearn for more variety. (Strasser and Ozgur, 1995.) My point is that the heavy reliance placed upon lecturing and its frequent use as an all-purpose method are unjustified in the light of evidence as to what it can achieve (Chapter 2) and the psychological limitations of students (Part 2).

Psychological reasons

Much of the information given in the early chapters of this book comes together in this short chapter. We have seen, particularly in Chapters 2, 4 and 5, that there are strong psychological reasons for supposing that the sole use of the lecture method for 50 minutes or an hour is ineffective. The following reasons for using a variety of teaching methods in the same period of teaching are not in any particular order, but I believe they add up to a powerful case for variety in each lesson.

1. Feedback to students and lecturer is needed

The importance of feedback in learning, and in pacing the teacher, has been stressed (see in particular Chapter 13); but verbal feedback is not obtained unless a lecturer stops lecturing and permits some form of response from the students. Weaver and Cotrell (1985) have described what they call 'Mental aerobics'. During a lecture students are asked to take half a sheet of paper and write their reactions to the lecture thus far. This technique encourages feedback, expression, involvement, criticism, insight and higher levels of thinking. The buzz group and horseshoe group methods are also particularly effective for two-way feedback. (See Chapter 19.)

2. The need for rehearsal

The lecture without pause or interruption does not permit students to rehearse what they have learned. Quite the opposite; one part of a lecture may interfere with memory of another. Rehearsal is important to consolidate their memory traces (to 'fix it in their minds'), to develop concepts by their use (see page 46), to relate different items of information, and to obtain a view of the whole topic being considered. (See also Ruhl and Suritsky, 1995 page 58 and Ruhl *et al.*, 1990.) After the lecture is too late. Furthermore, as Kelly and O'Donnell (1994) amongst others, have shown, students who review lecture notes in pairs or small groups are more comprehensive than individuals in their approach. They extract, elaborate and restructure the information better. That being so, when is better for short small group reviews than during the lecture period itself?

3. Avoid interference and negative transfer

Furthermore, because the concepts used in a lecture are likely to be similar, "negative transfer" (see page 49) is more likely to cause confusion than if opportunity is provided for students to clarify what they have heard. The longer you lecture without a break, the longer will be the period damaged by retroactive interference.

4. Encourage 'deep processing'

Thus an early opportunity to reconsider and organize the information before it is forgotten, will make it mean something in terms of the students' background knowledge, and thereby reduce the amount to be remembered. (Chapter 4). Without an opportunity to digest what has been said, there is information overload, information is lost and 'deep processing' is impossible.

One way to reduce information overload and facilitate reorganization of material is to use an advance organizer. This could be a short buzz group to consider a problem before you lecture on it. Brant *et al.* (1991) found that students using a computer simulation as a framework for understanding before formal instruction, did better than those who used it as a synthesis afterwards. They understood the lecture better.

Browne *et al.* (1995) complain of a disparity between faculty intent and practice in their failure to promote critical thought at graduate level. They recommend interrupting lectures by asking questions, introducing controversy, devising test instruments and integrating knowledge across the curriculum.

5. Reduce the intensity with self-pacing

The tendency for many lecturers to go too fast results in psychological interference, while the interspersed use of self-paced teaching methods such as short periods of discussion may reduce the intensity of learning demanded.

6. Active learning is better

It has long been known that active methods of learning are more effective than passive ones. Indeed conference papers demonstrating the fact no longer reach the research journals. (Collard, 1994; Drew, 1990; Troisi, 1983.) It's no longer news. While the amount of activity involved in listening to lectures is a relative question and can be considerably increased if students are trained in how to listen, the method remains a relatively passive form of learning. As long ago as 1931, experiments by Bane and others, showed that retention of information presented in lectures is worse in delayed tests of recall than when the same information is taught by more active methods such as discussion. This was not the case on immediate tests.

One technique is to give students a photocopied extract from a research journal to criticize during a lecture pause. Most lectures consist of secondary material, not the lecturer's own research. Most textbooks are the same. Too many university students rely solely on these secondary sources. In addition to demanding active thought and judgement, this technique can initiate students' use of the research journals. (Pennington, 1992)

Bonwell and Eison (1991) recommend pauses in lectures for brief demonstrations, ungraded written exercises as precursors to discussion, feedback, debates, role-playing, problem solving and for students to consolidate their notes.

7. Maintain high levels of attention

The lecture method is relatively poor for maintaining attention. Compared with the uninterrupted lecture, variations in teaching methods will usually provide greater

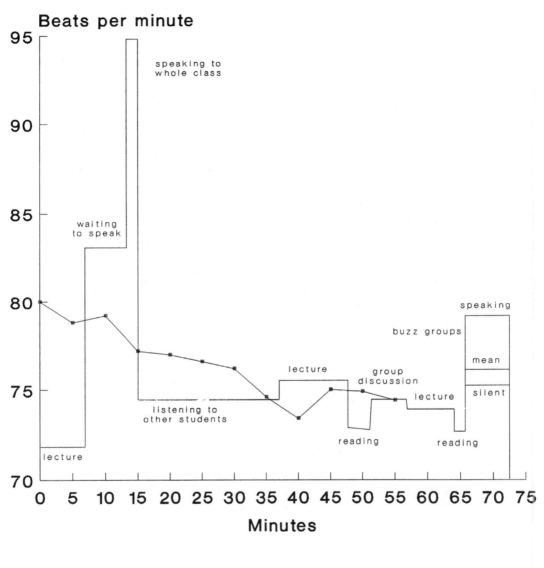

Figure 18.1 Mean heart-rates during two teaching periods

novelty, more arousing auditory stimuli, changes in posture, and opportunities to take occasional microsleeps without serious loss in efficiency. The importance of novelty in teaching methods was demonstrated when Little (1964) found that lectures supplemented by periods of programmed learning were popular with students for the first three weeks of a course, but not thereafter, because programmed learning demands even more concentration than lectures. Several times after significant points were made in a lecture, Hollingsworth (1995) instructed students to discuss for 2 minutes what they thought was most important. Compared with a control group, these students listened more attentively and although their advantage was insignificant on a delayed test, they scored significantly higher on an immediate posttest.

There is no one measure of arousal that is entirely satisfactory, but heart-rate gives some indication and is relatively easy to obtain with the use of 'pulsemeters'. Figure 18.1 shows the heart-rate for four military personnel aged about 45 in a group of 12 during two lessons. During the lecture there was a relatively smooth decline in a curve remarkably like that suggested by Lloyd (1968) (see page 56). Three weeks later the teacher used a variety of methods and, after the relatively stressful situation in which each student spoke to the rest of the class, there was no general decline. Indeed the group as a whole were probably as alert during buzz groups after sixty-five minutes as they had been for most of the previous hour.

8. Foster motivation by activity

In contrast to the performance of a solitary lecturer, the provision of problems and ways of involving the students fosters motivation. Involvement motivates; passive listening does not. Furthermore, naturalistic studies (Hert-Lazarowitz *et al.*, 1981) show that, although social interactions between students do occur in lectures, lecturers do not use this social motivation constructively to enhance learning.

9. Accept and use human nature

Small group discussions are natural; lectures are not. It is human nature to talk and to socialize. The lecture method stifles the desire for self-expression instead of using it, and it disregards the natural desire for social interaction, especially with one's peers.

10. Teach thought and feeling by discussion

We saw in Chapter 2 that thought and feeling are best encouraged by methods other than lectures, particularly discussion. Cognitive skills, such as the ability to apply principles, to analyze or synthesize complex data, to take decisions or to make fine judgements, require active learning before the memory of detail received during a short period of lecturing, dies away. Thus intellectual development in a subject requires mixing the cognitive processes involved. Unless special care is taken, the lecture method normally places students in a position in which they are only concerned with one process - the acquisition of information. But education is about developing thought and feeling, not just stuffing heads full of facts. Galotti (1995) instructed pairs of students to develop an argument about how many kinds of thought they observed in their partner, for example geometric analogies, moral dilemmas, deductive reasoning and 'everyday' reasoning. Using a combination of lectures, small groups and class discussion, one objective was to develop students' critical thinking, creativity and models of thought.

11. A mix of methods is best to teach information too

By definition, a variety of teaching methods entails a greater variety of stimuli than a single one. Because varied stimuli maintain arousal levels we might expect varied teaching methods to maintain arousal better than unremitting lectures. I compared three teaching methods all using identical words (lectures, audiotapes and reading) with a mixture of the three. Certainly students scored better on Truth-functional tests after the mixture and the scores for reading and audiotape showed the attention decrement, even though I must admit the lectures did not (Bligh, 1974).

12. Match the mix of learning styles

If students differ in the methods by which they learn best, and teachers should adapt their methods to maximize their effectiveness, it seems reasonable to think that teachers should use a variety of methods to cater for the differences between students. This is not easy to do in a systematic way because of the difficulty of knowing specific students' needs; but it is a further reason for adopting a general policy of using a variety of methods.

Over the past 75 years there has been surprisingly little research directly focussing on how lecture effectiveness relates to personality differences. There is reason to believe that anxious introverts, students with a more favorable disposition towards authority, and students who are reflective and theorists, rather than activist and pragmatic, prefer lectures to more participative methods; but the relative strength of their preference is not reliably matched with greater learning from lectures compared with other students.

With reference to reading and independent study, Marton and others have distinguished students with a disposition to memorize facts from those who are more thoughtful. It might be thought that the former would feel more comfortable in lectures than some other methods, but whether teachers should give them the diet they prefer, is another matter.

A general educational argument

Apart from the specific inadequacies of lectures which may be compensated by its combination with other methods, there is a general educational argument for the use of varied teaching methods within a period of teaching. Briefly summarized, this argument is:
(1) Different kinds of objectives are best achieved by different methods.
(2) Teachers usually have a number of different kinds of objectives in any one lesson.
(3) Therefore the objectives of any one lesson are usually best achieved by different methods.

1. Different kinds of objectives are best achieved by different methods

Much of the argument to establish this proposition depends upon the premise that students learn best by active methods involving the desired behavior. In other words the best way to teach people to analyze data is to place them in situations where they have to analyze it; the best way to teach students to put their thoughts in words is to use methods that require them to express themselves; the best way to teach them how to apply their knowledge is to let them apply it; and so on.

The truth of this principle is particularly evident in practical skills. The details of a lecture-demonstration are soon forgotten unless rehearsal is followed by practice. Similarly, while it may be true that to learn facts they must first be presented, if understanding and thinking involve actively relating one fact to another, students will need to be given a task which has been consciously planned to include this activity. Again, although some suggestions have been made for when a lecture method has to be used, attitudes cannot easily be taught by any form of presentation method. What the teacher has to do is to provide situations in which students will consciously consider and apply their attitudes. It is only when they express their attitudes in relation to others, that many students become aware of what their attitudes are, so that they may begin to consider them more objectively. This may require problem-solving or decision-making situations but the lecture is essentially a method that inhibits expression by the students. (Free-group discussion, role-play, T-groups and counseling are also suitable for achieving attitude objectives but cannot be used so easily in a lecture room).

In one way this premise may be thought so obvious that it requires no argument. In so far as one lecture is like another, it seems reasonable to expect that they will produce similar effects. To expect to teach practical skills from one lecture and attitude change from another using the same basic techniques, seems unduly optimistic; yet the reliance on the lecture method in some institutions makes this kind of assumption.

2. Teachers usually have a number of different kinds of objectives in any one lesson

It cannot be proved that teachers usually have a number of different kinds of objectives in any one lesson, because one cannot know what most teachers' objectives are. I can only appeal to the readers, if they are teachers, to consider their own objectives for themselves. There would be something odd about saying 'I want the students to know these facts but I'm not bothered at the moment whether they understand them or see how they are related to things I've said in other lectures', or, 'I want them to be able to conduct this experiment, but I shan't worry about their scientific attitude'. It seems obvious that one must teach these things on the same occasion. Similarly in many subjects it would be educationally unsound to separate considerations of theory from practical application.

3. Therefore the objectives of any one lesson are usually best achieved by different methods

If 1. and 2. are accepted it seems to follow logically that the objectives of any one lesson are usually best achieved by different methods.

It will be seen from both the psychological reasons and the educational argument that discussion methods provide important combinations when used with lectures. Therefore in the next Chapter particular attention will be paid to discussion methods with special reference to the objectives they may achieve.

Conclusion

Taken altogether, the arguments are very strong for mixing lectures with other methods within the same period of teaching. This is not just theory. There is a host of unpublished documents available through ERIC (the Educational Resources Information Center) which attest the importance of variety. (Zacharakis-Jute, 1983; and Couch, 1983 on Guided design; Osterman, 1985 on feedback; Drew, 1990 on peer teaching; Bonwell and Eison, 1991 on pauses, demonstrations and ungraded exercises; Browne *et al.*, 1995 on critical thinking; Campbell and Lison, 1995 on simulations; Ransdell, 1992 on computer activities; Collard, 1994 on role playing, games, debates and lectures based on students' questions; and Scott, 1996 and Orlosky, 1996 on cooperative learning techniques in science and mathematics lectures; to name only a few.)

There are others, outside the scope of this book, where the alternatives involve no lecturing at all. (Hubbard, 1990, on tertiary mathematics.) These will increasingly use computer disseminations.

In short, not only the dominance of lecturing, but the presumption that teachers and visiting speakers will lecture, must cease. The alternatives are practical; and it is some of those practicalities we must now consider.

19. Teaching Methods to use with Lectures

Buzz groups
   1.   Possible methods.
   2.   Possible objectives.

Horseshoe groups.
   1.   Method.
   2.   Possible objectives.

Controlled discussion.

Lecture-discussion method.

The case study method (case discussion).

Short talks by students.

Audiotapes and reading.

Computer facilities in lecture rooms.

Conclusion.

In this Chapter I shall suggest a number of teaching methods that can be used in a lecture room, but they probably cannot all be used in any lecture room or with any students. Therefore the readers will need to select those that are practicable in their circumstances. Nonetheless, it is hoped they will suggest new methods and new combinations of methods and that the reader will jot down their ideas as they come to mind. (If left until later they may be forgotten because the rest of the chapter, being similar information, may induce retroactive interference.)

Jot down ideas here:

Buzz groups

Buzz groups are seldom used in college teaching. My purpose here is to encourage lecturers to consider their use more often; and to suggest when they are appropriate. To this end there are two broad themes: the use of buzz groups is possible in a wide variety of circumstances; and they may be used to achieve a wide variety of objectives.

1. Possible methods

Buzz groups are groups of two to six members who discuss issues or problems for a short period, or periods, within a lesson. If used within a lecture situation the most common method is to ask alternate rows to turn round to face the row behind (Figure 19.1). This may be difficult in a steeply terraced lecture theater or where high backed chairs are fixed tightly together in rows. In this case the groups may consist of two or three members in the same row. Notice it may be necessary to ask one or two students to move to a group.

In either situation there should not normally be more than three in the same row if those at the ends are to be able to see and hear each other with ease. Another reason is that, to keep the overall noise level down, it is advisable where possible to ensure that the maximum distance between any two members of the same group is less than the distance between groups.

If it is desirable to vary the composition of the groups, those who did not turn round the first time may do so the second, while part of the front row moves across to form a group with the rest (Figure 19.1). If the seating position is uncomfortable the length of a 'buzz' period should be short.

If the problem set is one where students may have very individual viewpoints, such as are frequent in philosophy and literature, smaller groups will offer each student a better opportunity to develop their own thinking and have it considered by others.

To ensure that every individual has something to contribute to a group and it has no idle passengers, the task can first be set individually. As soon as the first students seem to have finished, or even sooner, suggest that they compare their answers with their neighbors'. Then encourage others to do so, sooner rather than later. In this way buzz groups are introduced without being proclaimed as a new teaching method - a useful technique if it was thought that some students might resist the method.

Tasks should be focussed and specific. (e.g. 'List three reasons for ... ?', not, 'Why do you think ... ?') Listing tasks have the advantage that the teacher can see the length of lists from a distance without invading and disturbing groups. Break down big tasks into smaller steps. This requires the teacher to analyze the thought processes expected of the students. It is usually, but not necessarily, better if they involve concrete familiar examples from which the lecturer can then go on to draw general or more abstract principles. (Jenkins in Gibbs, 1992.)

Although discussion techniques are amongst the most difficult teaching methods for a teacher to learn, buzz groups are amongst the easiest and they may be the basis for developing other methods. They are popular with students; they may be used in either formal or informal settings with 6 to 360 students; they are flexible in that they do not

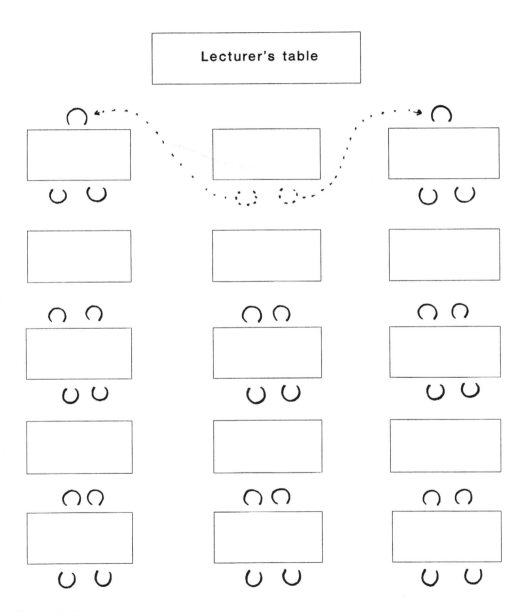

Figure 19.1. Buzz groups in a typical classroom.

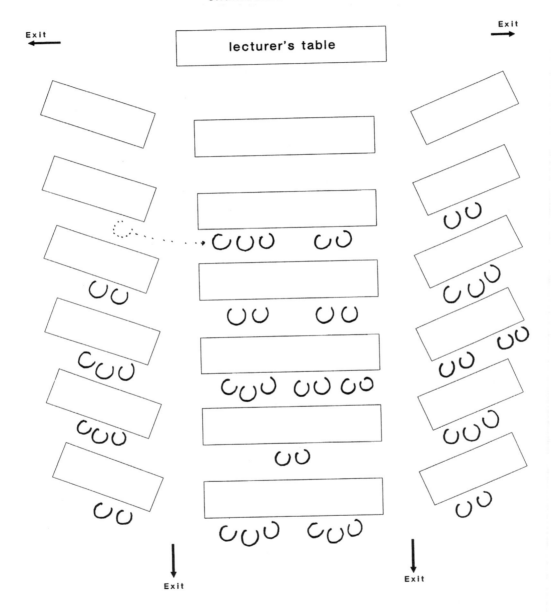

Figure 19.2. Buzz Groups in a steeply terraced lecture theater

necessarily require elaborate preparation and may take as little as half a minute of class time depending on their objective. Consequently they may be used in a relatively 'impromptu' fashion if the need arises. Furthermore they may be adapted for a variety of objectives.

It is important to realize that groups need not buzz for a long time. Even a task lasting 30 seconds, such as writing the next line of a calculation or jotting a personal opinion, is sufficient to rearouse an audience. (Figure 5.6.)

In fact it is quite a good idea, particularly when first introducing the method to students, to pressure them by saying, 'I will only give you 2 minutes to discuss this' and then say after 1 minute, 'You've had half your time'. This teaches them that activity is demanded and that a business-like and committed approach is required. Your classes are no place for students to hang around. Di Vesta and Smith (1979) compared giving three 2 minute pauses in a 21 minute lecture, with 6 minute pauses either before or after the lecture. The pauses were filled with group discussion, individual review or an irrelevant puzzle. Interspersed pauses with group discussion was the most effective as judged by free recall and cued recall tests immediately and 2 weeks later. The post lecture pause with group discussion or individual review came next. The irrelevant puzzles before, or interspersed within, the lecture interfered with learning. (See also Ruhl and Suritsky, 1995, referred to on page 58, who also used 2 minute pauses to great effect.)

2. Possible objectives
(a)   Clarification.
Lecturers who think they may not have 'got their point across' may set a problem or task for the students to work at in twos or threes. The problem should be simple but require a knowledge of the point in question. The objective here is clarification. It may be achieved either by the students teaching each other, which they may be able to do more simply than the lecturer who is an expert, or by the lecturer when the solution is demonstrated afterwards.
(b)   Feedback.
Lecturers will obtain feedback on the effectiveness of their teaching if, in the same situation, they visit those groups that seem to be having difficulty, or receive suggested solutions from the class before demonstrating their own. By choosing a suitable task, feedback on the whole lesson can be obtained quite quickly.
(c)   Consolidation of understanding.
'I understood it at the time, but I don't now', is not an uncommon remark from students writing up experimental work or doing revision. What was required was some consolidation of the learning and understanding that took place. Almost any discussion situation could provide this, because all provide an active learning situation and use of the information taught, but buzz groups have a particularly important role because they may take place immediately following the initial learning situation such as a lecture, and before substantial forgetting takes place ('Factors influencing memory', Chapter 4). Since the students in this case understand the information, the task should be more

difficult than for 'clarification'. It may require the student to relate different parts of a lecture together or to common experience.

(d)   To use concepts and terminology.

The same kind of tasks will teach new concepts and terminology provided the students can only perform the tasks by using the concepts. We saw in Chapter 4 that the articulation and rehearsal of information assist its memory. The ineffectiveness of presentation methods alone for learning terminology may be demonstrated if you read three pages of a dictionary and then test yourself to find the proportion of meanings you can remember only one day later.

There is another powerful reason for using buzz groups to teach terminology. Imagine three levels of concepts A, B and C. A is expressed in terms of the student's everyday language. B is defined in a lecture in terms of A. And C is defined in terms of B. On an immediate post lecture test students typically score 100% for A, 80% for B and 20% for C. As students use B words in a buzz group, they shift to become more like A - they become part of the student's everyday language. Consequently words which were level C shift towards level B. Their comprehension shifts from 20% towards 80%. Consequently lecturers will be far more effective if, before using C level words, they initiate buzz groups that will use B level words.

(e)   Practice specific types of thought.

The ability to think is best acquired by practice. It is part of the job of the teacher to provide the opportunity. This requires the design of situations in which the student must apply, analyze and evaluate information. Buzz groups provide one such situation, although horseshoe groups, seminars and group tutorials probably allow more thorough thought if there is more time and greater diversity of opinion. Problem-solving situations may teach the application of information. Questions such as 'What is the difference between....?' and 'In what way are .... similar?' require analytical thinking. Discussion of evaluative statements or simply listing the merits and demerits of a theory, may teach evaluative thinking. (The question "What are the merits of ....?" is sometimes neglected in favor of a more destructive form of critical thinking. Both have their place in education. The former may be important for developing an appreciation of research and its difficulties.)

If we suppose that Chapter 4 is an account of a lecture (although the way points are made would be unsuitable if spoken), the lecturer has only described brain processes and presented a list of factors causing forgetting and factors aiding memory, together with some applications to teaching students. The audience have not been made to think about these factors or use the concepts, nor has any attempt been made to consolidate their learning of them. When students can be made to analyze the concepts for themselves all these objectives may be achieved. For example a lecturer may form buzz groups and give them the following task: 'If you think about the concept of 'motivation' as it affects memory, you will realize that I could have classified it as a factor aiding memory just as easily as a factor causing forgetting. 'Interference', on the other hand, could only be classified as a hindrance to memory. Look at each of the other factors I mentioned and decide which is like 'motivation' in this respect, and which is like 'interference'.'

(f)   Teaching relevance.

Relevance may be encouraged by providing a task that has definite criteria of its completion. Problem-solving tasks are usually suitable. A handout, placed in the middle of each group, with a succession of short problems each with space for their answer, will provide a physical focus of attention and criteria of relevance. However, irrelevance may spark off creative and original solutions. If creativity is one of the course objectives perhaps the students will first need to be taught to distinguish between problems that have definite solutions and those that do not.

(g)   Release tensions. Just as individual tutorials and counseling provide a confidential situation between a member of staff and a student, buzz groups provide a confidential situation between a small number of students. Yet, unlike the college refectory or the union bar, they are within the total teaching situation. They provide the immediate reaction of students to the teacher and teacher-student interaction is immanent. Consequently they possess unique properties in their group dynamics which the teacher can use. Buzz groups may be used to release tensions because everyone has the opportunity to express them. The discipline of listening to lectures prevents the release of these tensions; the energy needs to be constructively channeled; consequently the use of buzz groups is a particularly valuable technique for bad lecturers! They may be used to work off examination nerves that prevent attention to any kind of class teaching, but horseshoe groups are usually even better.

(h)   Respite for anxious lecturers.

Buzz groups may also be used to give the flustered teacher breathing space. No doubt in the best of all possible worlds the teacher is never flustered; but some new teachers in universities, thinking that they must lecture all the time, find that if a lecture starts badly they are unable to recover the situation. It is sensitive lecturers who easily go from bad to worse in this way. The use of buzz groups can give them time to think and recover their composure. Furthermore group work is precisely the kind of teaching in which their sensitivity is an asset.

When buzz groups are used in this way the objective is an immediate one in terms of class management. It is only indirectly related to the long term objectives of the course, but such secondary objectives are nonetheless important in the long run too.

(i)   Confidence for reticent students.

The same confidentiality and release of tension may encourage reticent students to put their ideas into words. They are therefore more likely to be listened to, heeded and accepted by a small group. Each of these gives encouragement. With the prior agreement of their group, they are more likely to risk a contribution to the whole class at the reporting back stage or in a larger group. Since most forms of student assessment and selection place a heavy emphasis on verbal ability, and 'the ability to express oneself' is an important objective of most teaching, buzz groups have an important role with sensitive students. Since their patterns of college behavior (which may be quite different from their behavior at home) are probably established in their first semester, buzz groups may be particularly important at that time.

(j)   Building supportive relationships.
This conclusion is reinforced if buzz groups are used to foster a cohesive class spirit. While few people make a large number of friendships quickly, a buzz group places up to six students on speaking terms with each of the others in quite a short time. The observant teacher will be able to notice if these relationships continue outside the classroom. Assuming students do not always sit in the same seats, the network of relationships may be broadened by the frequent use of the method. The speed with which it establishes friendships is important for short and sandwich courses. It is useful for evening classes and non-vocational courses where students frequently come for the social contact as much as the social culture, and where student numbers are important. Early friendships are also important for the full time student away from home for the first time. Signs of 'homesickness' are difficult for the teacher to observe, but the work of Student Medical Officers suggests that it is more frequent than many teachers suppose.

Thus it is important to see teaching methods in their social and emotional roles, as well as their academic context. Buzz groups can satisfy the need for social interaction. They may not be possible in all circumstances, but they are in a great many. Most teachers will have some of the above objectives at some time, and buzz groups are an appropriate method of achieving them. It therefore seems probable that most teachers should at some time consider using them.

Horseshoe groups

1. Method
A horseshoe group may be an amalgamation of two buzz groups and could vary in size from four to twelve members. The larger the group, the shorter the time it will take to answer problems which demand special knowledge, skills, or particular procedures, because the necessary expertise is more likely to be found in the groups. If the answer to the problem is a matter of opinion, consensus will, on the average, be obtained more quickly in a small group, as there will be less variation of opinion to be reconciled (Klein, 1961). In most cases a group of six is very convenient. Groups larger than this may break into smaller conversation groups for at first short, and then longer periods of time, unless there is a leader, the problem supplies a sense of common purpose, or the seating arrangement creates a tightly knit group.

By definition, a discussion group is arranged so that each member may interact face to face with every other member (Abercrombie, 1978). Obviously in these groups the seating arrangement is in the shape of a horseshoe (Figure 19.3). Chairs are normally arranged in a 'C' or 'U' shape with the opening facing either the center or the front of the room. The central opening enables the teacher to stand in the middle of the class, listen to the progress of each of the groups and unobtrusively join each group to give help as needed. This is made easier if there is a vacant chair in position at the opening (+ in Figure 19.3) so that the teacher closes the circle, making it more intimate, when joining the group. The arrival of the teacher can easily kill discussion. To avoid this enter the group at the students' eye level. Do not stand towering above them. Crouch if necessary. And avert your gaze avoiding eye contact for two or three interchanges of conversation.

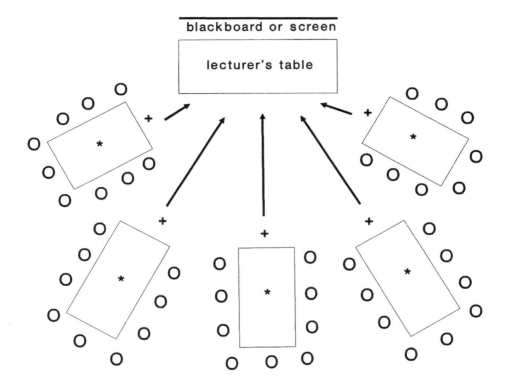

Figure 19.3. The arrangement of furniture for horseshoe groups

The front facing openings, as in Figure 19.3, can be used in a similar way and have the additional advantage that the teacher may stop the discussions to explain a difficult point from the front with the use of the blackboard or other visual aids. It is a useful arrangement for alternating formal teaching with group work; and if the problems are written on the board rather than separately for each group, the students may refer to them as they go along. Provided there is a table in the center of the 'C' for specimens and notes, the flexibility in teaching method offered by this seating arrangement is very convenient for any teacher who possesses a variety of teaching skills, and who is sufficiently sensitive to student reaction to know when to change method and what method to use. The horseshoe group method is a particularly good one for getting to know the students when the size of the class is less then forty and is never taught in small groups at any other time.

One caution should perhaps be observed: the teacher should make sure that the sides of the 'C' are not long and straight so that those at one end cannot see those at the other. As with buzz groups, three per straight side is the maximum because it is possible to lean forward to see past one person, one's neighbor, but not past two people.

It should be noticed that this method requires careful planning. Thought must be given to the arrangement of the furniture. Time must be allowed for introducing the problems, visiting each group, preferably more than once, and pooling the findings of the class at the end if necessary. 'Introducing', 'visiting' and 'pooling' each require different teaching skills (e.g. clear, succinct and interesting statement of a problem; sensitivity to both individual and group reactions; astute chairmanship).

The preparation of the problems often requires considerable thought if they are to develop student thinking in a specified direction. Figure 19.4 illustrates a series of problems given to student teachers of physical medicine. The objective was to make them aware of philosophical assumptions in the treatment of patients. Formal lectures and group tutorials had not achieved this with previous students who failed to see the relevance of philosophy. Horseshoe groups succeeded. Readers are invited to place themselves in the position of these student teachers, answer the questions, compare their answers with those of another person and find the reasons for any disagreements there may be. These reasons may either be assumptions themselves, or point to assumptions. If assumptions were not made explicit in the discussions, it was the teacher's role to elicit them on his 'visits' and during 'pooling'.

Notice the technique of focussing thought. Most of the questions require very short, even one word, answers; but, taken together, they raise big issues. A series of precise questions helps students to focus on their dilemmas or precise points of disagreement. Judging from an experiment by Hinkle and Hinkle (1990), this is more effective than setting an essay on the lecture topic (and certainly takes less grading time). They compared 'focused freewriting' with 'focused thought'. Both improved comprehension, but the focused thought group was superior on a test one week later.

2. Possible objectives
The major objective of teaching using horseshoe groups is that the students should think. Whether the precise kind of thinking is analytical, creative, evaluative or applies general principles depends on the problem given (see page 15).

A second objective is to provide an opportunity for 'feedback' from the class to the teacher.

There are five kinds of problems than can be set to a horseshoe group and it is easier if these are introduced, broadly speaking, in this order:

(a) Seeking information.
There is the task to search for information including an element of selection and organization of the information that is found. This may be set with the objective of

teaching facts and their organization, but it may also be set with the objective of teaching how to find facts and how to use available literature of the subject. This second objective is very important for students at the beginning of a course, and it may be that this task is suitable for buzz groups whose members know each other fairly well. In this latter case the groups should feel free to go to the library and other sources of reference during the period, and come back at a certain time to report their findings. I shall call this type of horseshoe group a 'mini-syndicate' since it only takes part of one lesson and no formal written report is required. A lively method to acquaint up to 30 students with relevant literature available in the college library is to borrow about one hundred books for the duration of the lesson, arrange them about the room, and set problems which may be answered by using specific references given on the problem sheet. If reporting back is delayed until the following week and the books have to be returned at once to the library shelves before the students have finished their task, they usually use the library catalogs to complete it. This method is more effective than giving a bibliographical handout for an essay, because their appetite is whetted, they know what they are looking for and there is allegiance to the group to finish the job. Syndicate method may also be introduced by this means.

If one has a larger group and is more concerned with the first objective, especially the organization of facts, it saves class time to set specific reading before the lesson so that the students are expected to arrive having both read and selected appropriately. Much of the lesson is then concerned with organization and the consequent understanding of facts from different viewpoints.

It may be that not many lessons need to be spent on this kind of objective at university level as university students have often learned these skills at school, but in colleges with less able students, possibly a considerable part of a course will consist of teaching students how to find out information. These skills are essential to any other kind of independent work on which so many professions depend.

(b)   Convergent thinking.
The groups may be asked to work out a problem that has a correct answer. The term 'problem' should here be interpreted very widely. It may consist of interpreting facts or identifying the cause of some phenomenon of the specific subject of which students have some previous knowledge from lecturers or pre-reading. Hence this kind of horseshoe group is normally used in conjunction with other teaching methods. It requires a knowledge of facts and use of the general principles of the specific subject.

The usual objectives of this kind of discussion are to consolidate the knowledge of general principles, to teach how to apply them and to teach students how to relate their knowledge of facts to principles. These three objectives are relevant to all levels of Higher Education.

Using over two hundred subjects, Gore (1962) formed two experimental classes to compare the effectiveness of lectures and horseshoe groups of three or four students each given job sheets. In addition to the usual sources of information, films and visual aids were available for the horseshoe groups on request. Changes in group membership were permitted. The job sheets were also given to the students in lecture classes, but

---

1.   Is it true that you/students/patients can sometimes choose to do one action rather than another?

2.   Does choosing involve selection from various possibilities?

3.   Is it a scientific assumption (an assumption made by scientists) that all physical events in the universe are completely caused (by what has happened before)?

4.   Is this assumption valid?

5.   If some processes/events are completely caused and some are not, which are not?

6.   Are all human actions physical processes?

7.   Is all neural activity some kind of physical process?

8.   Are all human actions completely caused?

9.   If 'No' to Question 8.

       (A)   Which is not?

       (B)   Is it possible to have physiological theories?

       (C)   Is physiotherapy possible?

10. If 'Yes' to Question 8.

       (A) '   Is there a possibility of a person not doing what he in fact does?

       (B)   Can a person choose to do one thing rather than another?

11. Does having 'professional/moral' standards or principles assume it is possible to choose one action rather than another?

12. If 'Yes' to Question 11, is there a conflict between having professional/moral standards/principles and believing scientific evidence?

Figure 19.4. A series of problems for physiotherapists in horseshoe groups

they had to be done outside lecture time. The performance of the horseshoe groups was significantly superior on tests at the end of the course, on delayed tests of retention of information, and on the answers to the job sheets themselves.

(c)   Divergent thinking.

One may also ask the groups to work on a problem with a number of possible answers. For example, there may be a number of possible interpretations, causes or explanations of a given set of facts. In many ways this kind of discussion has the same objectives as those mentioned in (b). But since there are a number of possible answers, it has the additional objective that students should be aware of, and understand, different points of view. Because of this, the form of the discussion is often quite different from that where there is a correct answer. Where there is a correct answer, the form of the discussion will converge towards that answer. Anything that does not do so many be eliminated by the participants as irrelevant or incorrect. Where there are a number of possible answers, the discussion will have a number of possible strands running at the same time. Consequently the task of the group will be much more difficult. If the students do not do so, the teacher must relate the alternative answers either when the groups are visited or when students report their conclusions at the end. The teacher must try to preserve a balance between the different answers that are put forward. This requires an open, clear and flexible mind. The teacher must make sure that the alternative answers are laid out clearly side by side either on paper or on the blackboard so that the differences and similarities can be understood easily. Flip charts or poster papers can be used for this, though I often get students to itemize their points on overhead projector transparencies.

(d)   Judgement, discernment and criticism.

A fourth kind of problem may require the students to make an act of judgement. Once a number of possible answers are laid out before the students, they can then decide which is the best. For example, students may be asked to evaluate a theory. In these cases there may be a judgement commonly accepted by the experts in the field, which the teacher wishes the students to infer by the same reasoning.

Insofar as there is an accepted answer, the discussion techniques here may be similar to that in (b), although the criteria for the judgement are much wider because they will often involve the use of principles, such as the principles of scientific method, which are outside the empirical science. These principles are frequently not those that can be looked up in a textbook before the lesson. They are principles of reasoning which the teacher cannot necessarily expect the students to have learned from lectures or reading before they come to the class. Consequently they often require a questioning technique to make the students think behind their everyday judgements. This technique involves posing a number of questions that crystallize and polarize the central issues so that the answers by the students will form a closely reasoned argument. The best questions are those with Yes/No answers but these take a lot of thoughtful preparation (see example given). In this respect the technique is more subtle than in (b).

(e)   Revision and planning exam answers.

Horseshoe groups have a very useful function in revision and preparation of students for essay examinations. They provide an outlet for pre-examination nerves that seems relevant to the student, while the presentation of yet more information in lectures only provides more to be anxious about. The urgency of the pre-examination situation enables horseshoe groups to be used with larger classes than at other times. The limitation in size is usually dictated by the furniture, space and general physical provision rather than the number of students. The problems set require the group to plan answers to examination questions in about fifteen minutes each. The teacher may present a specimen plan, conduct a brief period of pooling the groups' ideas, or, if there is time and the groups have been given different questions, visit each group to improve their 'model answers'. Used in this way horseshoe groups are particularly good for helping students see the breadth, and possible interpretations of questions, and to suggest ways of organizing the answers. They provide a suitable opportunity to discuss examination technique.

Teaching with horseshoe groups is a useful technique, but the problems, their answers and the general organization of the class require thoughtful preparation and a variety of teaching skills.

Controlled discussion

Most teachers practice controlled discussion (sometimes called 'Class discussion') in which points or questions are raised from the lecture floor. The usual objectives of this method of teaching are clarification on matters of fact and the development of lines of thought and interest that have been stimulated. Smeltzer and Watson (1983) showed that students listen more closely when they know there is going to be class discussion on what a lecturer is saying. Most teachers use this form of discussion after periods of lecturing, but it can easily fall flat if the lecture was not stimulating.

In my opinion controlled discussion is not at all easy, and it is made all the more difficult by the fact that its defects are not always apparent. Although it involves some feedback, not every member of the class is able to contribute, consequently there is always the possibility that serious misunderstandings and interesting view-points are not revealed. This may be exacerbated by the fact that those who have understood the lecture least, are least likely to ask questions or expose their misunderstandings to correction. There is also a tendency for particular 'personality types' to be vocal, and others to be silent. It can be difficult to ensure that the points raised permit a balanced consideration of the subject. In some cases it is difficult to get the discussion started. As suggested elsewhere (Verbal feedback, Chapter 13) this can often be achieved by asking questions requiring personal reactions or other relevant information on which the audience, not the lecturer, has special knowledge. These questions do not have wrong answers that can be corrected by the lecturer and class members need not fear correction or serious contradiction.

Although it is common practice, I think it is nearly always unwise to go straight from lecturing to controlled discussion. Even in public meetings it is far better first to give a few moments for silent reflection and review, or buzz group consideration of what points to raise. These moments for consideration remove factual misunderstandings and raise the level of discussion.

A genuine discussion atmosphere is more likely to develop if the teacher takes opportunities not to reply to points raised, but motions for further contributions from the audience.

Lecture-discussion method

This method essentially consists of obtaining the key points from the class and the teacher providing further elaboration, technical re-expression and necessary detail. The teacher raises general questions before any lecturing, and writes the students' key points on the blackboard or overhead projector to give a summary as they go along. As each point is raised the lecturer adds or seeks detail. For example, if we imagine that the sections on 'memory', 'attention' or 'handouts' in this book were each to be the subject of a lesson using the lecture-discussion method, most of the major points would be provided by the collective contributions of a class in answer to such questions as 'When do you find it easy to remember things?', 'What things keep you alert?', or 'When do you think handouts are most useful?'. As the discussion proceeds the teacher may change the wording of the questions to give different emphases and elicit different points, (e.g. 'When do you find you can concentrate most?', 'What keeps you that way?', 'Are there some situations in which you are always more drowsy than others?', 'Why is that?') and then gradually re-express the questions in more general, abstract and technical language if this is necessary (e.g. 'What general factors affect alertness?', 'What are the variables of arousal?'). In this way a class can find themselves involved in a conversation using technical language which they did not know when they walked into the room .

The key points may be written on the board in the order in which they come, but if there is a preferred or logical order they may be written up as they come but suitably spaced for later insertions.

This is a very effective method of teaching, for a number of reasons. It makes the students think; it forces them to relate the subject to their personal experience, background knowledge and practical examples if suitable questions are asked; because the key points are expressed in the students' words the teacher can be relatively sure they understand; students as encouraged when their points are accepted; it forces the teacher to proceed at the pace of the class and to go slower on more difficult points, and by using class involvement and various voices it maintains attention very well.

The method may be used without so much elaboration by the teacher when findings of buzz groups or horseshoe groups are reported back to the whole class (when they are 'pooled').

Because not all groups will organize their reports in the same way, it is usually better for the teacher to have a checklist of points to be brought out and to write them on the board (or overhead projector) in their most logical order.

Another variation is to elicit as many points as possible from the class first without much elaboration and then proceed to give a prepared lecture which draws them all together. This is useful where the topic is difficult and lecturers want to be able to relate what they say to the students' background knowledge and their ways of expressing it, as much as possible. It is therefore useful for developing a subject or 'going a little deeper'. When another teacher lectured on a closely related topic and it is difficult to know exactly what was said, what slant was taken and what was neglected, this variation can help to relate the two topics together. In the same way it is useful before a practical to revise theoretical work covered a long time ago.

The case study method ('case discussion')

This method has some similarities with the horseshoe group except that it is not always conducted as a group method. Essentially it consists of a detailed study of a particular example (what the example is an example of, obviously depends on the subject). It usually involves consideration of an actual example requiring the synthesis of a large amount of different kinds of information, and the making of recommendations or decisions. It is applicable in law, medicine, education, business studies, politics, English or any subject that studies the making of decisions. Because it is appropriate for the study complex interactions of principles, it could be used by teachers in almost any subject. It is useful for demonstrating the application of principles and for practicing the analysis of complex situations (Kletz, 1970).

If we consider political decisions, or examples of medical or architectural recommendations, it also has value in showing students what they do not know, and in some cases, what they cannot know. In this way it may teach students to reserve their judgement and to recognize the need to seek further information. Provided the cases are well chosen so that students must select certain items of information and use them to make particular inferences the case-study method can make some impact on students who display superficial thought or easily jump to conclusions.

Lecturers sometimes fear that if discussion groups are formed without the presence of a subject expert, mistakes will be learned and go uncorrected. This is not so provided the task or problem is designed with sufficient focus (Davis *et al.*, 1994). Davis et al found no difference in students' tests scores and satisfaction between groups led by experts and non-experts. Indeed experts tend to dominate groups; and students then wait for the experts to give the answers rather than thinking for themselves. Consequently, teachers and other leaders are a nuisance; they get in the way and prevent intellectual development.

The skills of task design at the micro level are insufficiently understood by many teachers. Many present problems that are too big. The technique of presenting a sequence of smaller problems that together make up a larger one, can direct the focus. To use this technique the lecturer needs to analyze the larger problem into a series of smaller steps. Figure 19.4 gives an example. It is quite different from saying, 'Discuss the problem of freewill and determinism'.

To use case studies in this way requires very careful preparation. If the case is not a genuine one, it is easy either to overlook important details, or to include some that are inconsistent. It is impossible to generalize for all subjects, but very commonly the kind of information given includes a history of the case and a description of the conditions that exist at the time the decision has to be taken. Whether these conditions are physical, emotional, economic, social or of any other kind will obviously depend upon the subject and the kind of case. The way in which the information is provided may be made as similar to the practical situation as possible. In medicine, education or law they may consist of the patient's notes, the child's records or a client's file. The students may be given these together with a problem to be discussed in groups before general class discussion; or the teacher may distribute the information for individual perusal for, say, three minutes, and then conduct an inquiry by the lecture-discussion method. In either method, it is useful to have obtained photocopies of the documents on acetate transparencies so that they may be shown using the overhead projector. If there is no one illustration that all may see, and to which the lecturer may point, the lecturer is liable to spend many minutes saying 'You will see this is mentioned two-thirds the way down the third page. Have you all got that? No? Well it's....'. When students have found the place the lecturer can obtain no eye contact by which to make discussion flow.

Because case-studies require students to use a large amount of information, if it is conducted by small group discussion it is useful from the teacher's point of view for students keep a record of their discussion so that the teacher can check which items of information have been considered.

Short talks by students

The use of student talks have been recommended for use in engineering and medical faculties (Henderson, 1970) but it is equally useful in training for any profession requiring oral skills (e.g. education, law, management, social work) or where vivas form part of the system of assessment.

Once the method is accepted by the students it is usually fairly successful, but it requires cautious introduction and it can "flop" badly if the innovation is made without consulting the students first. Students expect lecturers to lecture and any sudden attempt to reverse the roles without an explanation of how they benefit requires some psychological adjustment. Even after tacit acceptance the failure to turn up when it is their turn, may indicate a submerged mild 'trauma'. The difficulty of adjustment can be minimized by not requiring more than ten minutes' exposition (they frequently over prepare and speak for too long) and by making the occasions informal.

The teacher needs skills in working for an emotional climate in which the audience is appreciative and wants to learn from what is said. The choice of topics is therefore crucial.

Each talk requires follow-up class discussion in which the good points of the talk are reinforced. If criticism of the content is necessary this may be done after dissociating the point from the speaker. Occasionally a student will abuse the occasion, but, provided class members as a whole accept the method, they will deal with the abuse more effectively than the teacher.

Audiotapes and reading

It may be objected that all these methods take too long compared with the lecture, but this objection as it stands is incomplete. One may say 'They take too long to achieve X, Y and Z compared with the lecture', but as soon as the objection is clearly stated in terms of objectives achieved, its inapplicability becomes obvious if the lecture method cannot achieve X, Y and Z; and this is the case with the alternative methods so far suggested.

However, the problem remains of how to achieve all the course objectives in the time available. Since we have seen in Chapter 1 that other presentation methods, such as audiotapes, videotapes and reading, are equally effective for retention and comprehension of information (Bligh, 1970; Frank and Lesher, 1971; Greene, 1934; Joyce and Weatherall, 1957), class time could be saved by making these available at other times. The provision of handouts and reading has been mentioned elsewhere and they are widely used but the provision of audio and videotapes in college libraries has received scant attention and finance. If audiotapes are accompanied by a slide viewer and earphone attachments, they may provide illustrated lectures at any time, as often as necessary and at the students' preferred pace. They are suitable for revision, the method is cheap and if well used, it is thorough. They are invaluable for foreign students with language difficulties.

Apart from problems of copyright, the chief difficulty with audio and video presentations in lectures lies in their over-use. When over-used, attention is generally poor, caused, at least in part, by lack of interpersonal interaction. Used with discretion they have an important place. Videos can repeatedly illustrate and demonstrate processes that cannot be shown in a lecture theater (e.g. a surgical operation, interviewing techniques, deep sea fish, high temperature and pressure reactions, etc).

Videotaped lectures are not normally popular with students (Firstman, 1983), but they are acceptable when mixed with other methods. As ever, the secret is variety. When Sox and others (1984) interrupted videotaped lectures for questions and discussion, the mixture proved more popular with students than uninterrupted traditional lectures. Sox et al recommend the technique when expert lecturers are not available. Smeltzer and Watson (1983) found that a group viewing video-demonstrations during lectures asked more questions and wrote better lecture summaries than students receiving a traditional uninterrupted lecture. The latter took more notes.

Lectures introducing practical work are frequently ineffective because students have to remember everything in advance. Audiotapes in the science laboratory may be used for repeated instruction. Goodhue (1969) reports that not only could students using tape-slides dissect a rat in one hour when it previously took three, but they made fewer errors. Carre (1969) thought students accepted responsibility for their own learning when placed in a self-paced situation. Harris (1971) used an audio-tutorial supplement in engineering and found no difference from instruction supplemented with written scripts. Able students preferred the tapes and less able students, the scripts.

There is some evidence that audiotapes are more effective if accompanied by questions (the same is also true of live lectures) and they are more popular if a variety of voices is used (Frank and Lesher, 1971). Most lecturers find that if they record their lecture, they need to prepare it more thoroughly, but this may be a comment on the lecture method as much as the use of audiotapes.

Computer facilities in lecture rooms

Computer facilities are increasingly available in lecture rooms. Where an LCD (liquid crystal display) is placed on an overhead projector, the lecturer can show the result of calculations or other computer processes. In principle this is another technique to present information. It is a useful visual aid. It is not an alternative to the lecture method and is not likely to teach more than information. Accordingly no more will be said about its use here.

Computers offer a different teaching method and one which may achieve higher cognitive objectives when students have networked terminals and may be set problems or other tasks that demand thought. As with other methods considered in this chapter, the kind of thought taught depends upon the task designed. As with some other methods of presenting problems, there is some evidence that learning is better if the problems are tackled in pairs, or first individually and then in pairs.

Where computer equipped lecture rooms are different is in their opportunities for feedback both to the lecturer and to the student. Consider a class in statistics in which the lecturer has taught a particular technique and then sets an example for the students to work out. The teacher can tune in to each student's (or student pair's) terminal to check their progress and, by implication, get feedback on the effectiveness of the lecture. The teacher may also get feedback on the percentage of students giving the same answer to a question. This could be coupled with an audio facility, as in a language laboratory, by which the teacher can guide individual students (or pairs) over their difficulties. In contrast, Nager (1983) has described a computer assisted feedback system using electronic index cards to interact with students' ideas in answer to subjective examination questions. Campbell and Lison (1995) have devised computer simulations to reflect the real world complexity of even interpersonal skills and to provide rapid self assessments to students on their performance.

It is a short step to adapt this facility for interaction over the World Wide Web and combine it with distance methods of presentation such as audio or television. As we saw in Chapter 2, hitherto, the disadvantage of distance methods of lecture presentation has been their inability to teach thought and affect. Computer supported lecture theaters make distance teaching of higher cognitive skills much more possible. The teaching of affect remains difficult, however.

Conclusion

Lectures are inadequate because they do not teach thought or affect well, and for many students they hold attention poorly after about 25 minutes. The alternatives in this chapter attempt to solve these problems. The art in their use lies in how they are combined with lecturing. We must now consider this.

20. Some Combinations of Teaching Methods

1.   Lecture - Buzz groups - Horseshoe groups - Controlled Discussion.

2.   Buzz group or Horseshoe groups - Lecture.

3.   Brainstorming - Lecture.

4.   Lecture - Buzz groups - Practical - Buzz groups.

5.   Lecture - Unsuccessful Class Discussion - Buzz groups.

6.   Lecture - Buzz groups - Brains trust.

7.   Step-by-step lecture (i.e. alternating lecture-discussion).

8.   Lecture - Individual problem solving - Reading.

9.   Mini-syndicates - Debates.

10.   Lecture - Audiotape alternately.

11.   Lecture - Audiotape and group tutorial.

       Conclusion.

In theory there is an infinite number of ways in which these teaching methods may be combined. The task facing new lecturers is to decide and invent combinations suitable for their purposes. The purpose of this chapter is to liberate them from the pressures of conformity and tradition by giving examples of some combinations and the objectives they may achieve.

1. Lecture - Buzz groups - Horseshoe groups - Controlled Discussion
Have you ever been to conferences where no one confers? - They spend all their time listening to lectures. The audiences do not engage with the enthusiasms of the speakers because they are given no opportunity to do so. The chairpersons conceive of discussion only as opportunities to respond to the speakers, not as an opportunities for people to discuss amongst themselves. They have not heard of buzz groups and would be afraid of losing control if they used them. The result is that the mixing of minds is not as thorough as it might be. Strangers don't get to know each other so well as they might.

The sequence suggested in the heading above elicits immediate reactions to the lecture and produces a much more lively controlled discussion. Maybe the terraced lecture theater does not permit genuine horseshoe groups; but the essential technique, where the architecture allows, is to merge, or reconstitute, pairs of buzz groups, thus widening the circle of contacts for conference members.

If you want a lively conference, chairpersons must be trained, attenders should be forewarned of the technique, and timetables must allow for it.

2. Buzz group or Horseshoe groups - Lecture

The most common way of using buzz groups or horseshoe groups is first to lecture and then to set up discussion groups on the assumption that the lecture has provided some stimulus and information. But, as with controlled or class discussion, where the objectives are to make students think and to relate a subject to their previous background, it is often a good idea to present the central issue of a lecture to the students first so that they try to solve the problem using their background knowledge. After a period of 'pooling' in which the students' suggestions are written on the board (or overhead projector), the teacher may give the prepared lecture making sure to relate it to the students' suggestions wherever appropriate. Bearing in mind that the objectives include the promotion of thought which normally requires a slower speed of delivery, this combination allows a subject to be covered relatively quickly for several reasons. The students have turned their mind to the problem; the pooling has provided a common background; and the lecturer does not have to remind them of the basic groundwork, since not only has the discussion done this, but feedback enables the lecturer to start at the students' level of understanding. Thus, in spite of the belief that discussion groups take a long time and that lectures can 'cover the ground' quickly, in terms of these objectives, this combination is a time-saver.

3. Brainstorming - Lecture

A variation on this combination, when the intention is to teach creative problem solving and open-mindedness, is to use a "brainstorming" technique during the initial discussion. This consists of introducing some time pressure by allowing only a few minutes, and instructing students to concentrate on making as many suggestions as possible, however implausible, and not to view them critically at this stage. The theory behind this is to throw together as many ideas as possible so that a chance association which produces the creative solution is more probable. However, although the ideas produced by the group in this way may be more original and creative than those by other methods, there is conflicting evidence on how far a sustained course using brainstorming techniques results in greater individual creativity (Taylor, Berry and Block, 1958; Parnes and Meadow, 1959).

The use of time pressure when a group is introduced to group techniques in lecture situations is valuable to instill a businesslike approach. Because students like to feel they have achieved a lot in a short space of time, this approach is important to the success of innovations.

4. Lecture - Buzz groups - Practical - Buzz groups

Buzz groups in practical classes can be useful to clarify the students' task. If the period begins with lecturing to provide information and is followed by horseshoe groups or buzz groups to plan an activity or experiment, the organizational crisis that often occurs when practical work begins, can be avoided because the different groups will be ready to start at different times. The groups may reassemble at the end of the period to evaluate and coordinate their results before 'writing them up'.

Minutes	Lecturer or student activity.
0-10	Task on OHP directs students as they enter to pick up course guide, a 9-page lecture handout, and to arrange the seating so they can sit in groups of 2-3 and get to know each other.
10-15	Task requires student groups to interpret graphs showing decline of student attention in a conventional lecture and the impact on student attention of the structured lecture used in the course.
15-25	Lecturer gives his interpretation of the graph and uses it to explain how the course will be taught and what he expects them to do during class sessions.
25-35	Task requires groups to interpret a quote from Wittgenstein and explain its relevance to geography.
35-45	Lecturer analyzes quote and shows its relevance to the course themes which are set out in the course guide.
45-55	Task requires individuals to write answers to questions on the lecture handout. The questions require them to draw upon their common sense knowledge of Britain's changing geography.
55-65	Task require individuals to compare answers.
65-80	Lecturer draws upon what he has overheard, but his analysis takes it beyond common sense knowledge. Using students' statements he shows that it is possible to give very different interpretations of Britain's geography.
80-90	Task to write the quote from Wittgenstein in the students' own language and explain its relevance to the course. They are warned that the lecturer will not go over this task and the course guide shows that it was on last year's exam.
90-110	Students and lecturer take a break
110-120	Task requires students to analyze a set of quotes that give contrasting definitions of geography as a discipline and emphasize very different processes as explaining geographic patterns.
120-130	Lecturer interprets these quotes and links back to the quote from Wittgenstein.
130-140	Task. Lecture handout includes part of the introduction to the course textbook. Task requires students to analyze the authors' view of geography, which processes they will emphasize and which they will neglect.
140-150	Lecturer reiterates the text's central viewpoint and introduces alternative perspectives.
150-160	Task to analyze a brief extract from a book with a contrasting interpretation.
160-170	Task which requires students to write a summary of the whole session.
170-180	Lecturer emphasizes the role of the textbook in the course and introduces a task which requires students to work outside class to answer questions relating to the first chapter. They are told next week's session will be based on the answers.

Figure 20.1. Analysis of a 3-hour structured lecture. (Jenkins in Gibbs, 1992)

5. Lecture - Unsuccessful Class Discussion - Buzz groups

Buzz groups can also be used after a lecture to get the teacher out of difficulties in the subsequent class discussion. The opportunity provided for reticent students has been mentioned, but they also provide an opportunity for everyone to have their 'say' when too many wish to speak. They may also be used to 'cool it' if personal acrimonies intrude, by separating the contestants. They may be used in the same way if there is a conflict over which topic should be discussed.

6. Lecture - Buzz groups - Brains trust

When subject matter is non-controversial and does not raise issues that can easily be discussed, or when students are unwilling to express their difficulties in class discussion, buzz groups may be instructed to agree on a question they wish the lecturer to answer, to write it on a sheet of paper and pass it anonymously to the front. If some of the questions show lack of understanding on the same point, this technique provides useful feedback on the teacher's effectiveness in addition to clarification of the lecture. Instead of the teacher, it is sometimes possible to have a small panel of students, lecturers or research students to answer the questions.

This technique is also useful in an industrial context when new proposals are considered. By contrast, in a mass meeting the individual worker is a spectator rather than a participant, and cannot put critical questions to the management anonymously. Furthermore, individual opinions are less likely to be distorted when passed directly to the panel than when presented by a representative in meetings at successive levels of the industrial hierarchy.

7. Step-by-step lecture (i.e. alternating lecture-discussion)

Alternating short periods of lecture and discussion (any of the kinds mentioned) may be used to regulate the pace of a difficult chaining lecture or one that requires particularly close reasoning such that the next step must not be taken until the previous one is fully understood.

A variant of this approach by Jenkins (Gibbs, 1992) is shown in Figure 20.1. Students' attention and active participation were maintained for 3 hours with a 20 minute break. Notice that time was taken to explain and justify the methods being used. Tasks are tightly focussed whilst allowing individuality. Initial doubters later recognized that they had been made to work and think intensively, and they had learned to think more independently and critically. Having experienced this class, students were not likely to ignore the instructions to prepare for the next.

8. Lecture - Individual problem solving - Reading

One way of facilitating personal development in a subject when tutorials are not possible, is to present a problem sheet of the kind shown in Figure 19.4 coupled with a detailed set of references (giving precise page numbers) which the students may consult in the lecture room in the way that was described for mini-syndicates (except that students may work individually). For example, a lecturer may begin by outlining the theoretical positions that may be taken on a certain topic (e.g. the theories of light, the origins of matter, or an aesthetic judgement) and then present a sheet of questions either of the multiple-choice type, or of the kind with distinct alternative answers shown in Figure 19.4.

Students are required to read certain passages according to their responses to the individual questions. Thus each student follows an individual path of reading as if on a branching program, so that competition for specific texts decreases when there is diversity of opinion.

However, although this combination may achieve very worthwhile objectives in difficult circumstances, it requires a great deal of careful preparation by teachers who know their subject very thoroughly. Furthermore, because of its branching nature, it is difficult to pull together all the strands or use them as the basis of further teaching. It is therefore most appropriate at the end of a series of lectures. Alternatively this combination may be used to make horseshoe groups go deeper into a subject by using reference books.

9. Mini-syndicates - Debates
Student speeches can be combined with horseshoe groups if one member of a group is asked to give a fairly formal report on its decisions. If two groups are mini-syndicates with the task of finding evidence for or against a proposition or hypothesis, the reporting back can be turned into a kind of debate. But because this requires students to look at only one point of view, it is educationally questionable unless some other method is used to preserve a balance. For example, some compensation is obtained if each group is required to sum up the other's case.

10. Lecture - Audiotape alternately
The technique of using more that one lecturer as a form of 'team teaching' employed by Betts and Walton (1970) has already been discussed (page 52). If staff time-tables do not permit this form of cooperation, the use of tape-recorded voices to provide alternative viewpoints and a varied auditory stimulation can sharpen distinctions and maintain attention; but this technique can easily be over-used.

11. Lecture - Audiotape and Group tutorial
Assuming two rooms are available, classes of up to twenty-four can be divided after a fifteen to twenty minute lecture so that one half may have a group tutorial with the lecturer on what they have heard, while the other hears a tape-recorded lecture for another fifteen to twenty minutes. After this time the tape-recorder and lecturer change rooms. This combination permits feedback on learning to both the students and the lecturer, while in view of the normal decrement in attention in a uniform situation, it is possible that the total amount of information conveyed by the lecture and tape-recording would be no less than by a 55 minute lecture.

Conclusion

The purpose of Part 4 has been to persuade the reader that it is usually better to use a variety of teaching methods in a 'lecture' period.

All the combinations of teaching methods suggested have been successfully used, but whether they are applicable to other situations can only be decided by the teacher concerned. Factors that may influence this decision are considered in the next chapter, but it must be emphasized that their effectiveness, like that of any single method, depends on the goodwill of the students, and although it is possible to prepare the students' minds the week before, goodwill is established over a longer period of time.

Part 5
Preparation for the Use of Lectures

21. Thinking the Lecture Through - Rough Preparation

The sequence of decisions

1. Questions about the college and departmental organization.
2. Decide or modify objectives.
3. Decide suitable teaching methods.
4. Select the most suitable teaching methods.
5. Decide the "key points" and organization of subject matter.
6. Decide how the teaching time is to be organized.
7. Decide student preparation and follow-up.
8. Decide detailed teaching techniques.

Conclusion.

Having discussed lecturing techniques, it is now necessary to suggest how a lecturer with no previous experience should prepare to use them. Yet this is not easy. There is plenty of room within the suggested techniques for variations in style. Different people prefer to prepare in different ways and there may be differences between subjects. What follows is a checklist for a series of decisions, but they may have to be varied selectively in the light of the reader's particular needs and approach.

The sequence of decisions

1. Questions about the college and departmental organization
It will be assumed here that the course has already been planned, at least in broad outline. In practice what most new lecturers have to teach is more or less imposed on them either directly by the head of department or indirectly by an examining board or vocational needs. Visiting lecturers are frequently given a topic. New lecturers soon discover, if it is not immediately obvious, that many of the most important decisions about their courses have been taken without much consultation with them. It is not the purpose of this book to discuss overall course design and course objectives, but the new lecturer may find it helpful to answer certain questions.

What are the limits of the constraints imposed? In what area does the lecturer have freedom to take decisions? These may include selecting specific topics from a wide syllabus and deciding the order in which they should be tackled.

Frequently there are less tangible constraints, involving the customary organization of teaching, which are not formally binding and may easily be accepted without thinking, but which should at least be recognized if not questioned.

New lecturers may also consider which decisions will need the cooperation of their students.

In other words the new lecturer normally has to ask, 'What is the system in which I am to work and what is going to be my role in it?'

2. Decide or modify objectives

Assuming the course objectives and syllabus have been decided, the teacher's first task with reference to a specific period of teaching is to select the objectives to be achieved at that time. They should be expressed in terms of what the students should be able to do at the end of the period (i.e. their achievement should be testable in principle). It is a good idea to jot them down in rough because nearly all other stages depend on these decisions. (When I have given an unsatisfactory lecture, which is more often than I sometimes care to admit, the root of the trouble is frequently inadequate preparation at this stage because these decisions take time for careful thought. While I cannot be sure that others make the same mistake, they may when time is short).

Although in principle course objectives should not require modification, in practice they usually do. In fact courses and teaching usually seem to be better if they are constantly being modified to suit particular circumstances, provided an overall view is maintained.

3. Decide suitable teaching methods

If the teaching methods that could achieve these objectives are written down, the teacher may stop himself from assuming that one particular method must be used. Reference to Table 15.1 on pages 192*ff* may help to guide this decision.

We have seen, especially in Parts 2 and 4, that a variety of methods is probably needed.

4. Select the most suitable teaching methods

There are three sets of factors that may influence these decisions: the limitations of the teacher, the students and the physical conditions.

Obviously teachers should choose methods that they have a reasonable chance of being able to use satisfactorily (where the criterion of satisfaction is the achievement of the objectives). Like most social skills, learning to teach involves using the talents one has, rather than trying to be what one is not. No teacher will teach equally well by all methods and most of us would consider ourselves unskilled in the majority of them. The different skills and personality traits required by different teaching methods make conflicting demands. For example, the extrovert lecturer who commands the attention of his audience by occasional showmanship, may have difficulty in finding the empathy required of a counseling tutor.

This is not to say that teachers should stick with a few methods. It is to say that they may need to plan a course of self development in the use of all appropriate methods. Because five to ten years is a realistic time for such a program, heads of department have an important role when planning the opportunities given to their staff.

The limitations of the students are imposed by their expectations and previous experience. New lecturers cannot know what these are for a few weeks, until they have used feedback techniques (Chapter 13). Because part of the teacher's job is to train students in new learning skills, teachers will need to plan a program of development for them too. This responsibility is not always appreciated by teachers in universities and colleges. Thus the selection of a teaching method may be partly influenced by its place in a sequence of teaching designed (amongst other things) to train students how to study, listen and learn.

Finally, because the physical conditions impose limitations upon the teaching methods that can be used, it is helpful to look at the room allocated and check on the timetable for feasible room changes that could overcome these limitations when necessary. For example, the unsuitability of a steeply terraced lecture theater for the flexible use of horseshoe groups might be overcome with a simple room change. (The tendency for administration to dictate the educational process should, in my opinion, be vigilantly restrained.)

A second reason for looking at the room is that preparation is easier and more practically orientated when teachers can imagine themselves in the room with the facilities it offers.

Check the size and surface of the blackboard and see if there are available screens; if so, do they obstruct the board so that they cannot both be seen at once? A look at the lighting and blackout facilities may save later embarrassment if any kind of projectors are to be used. Not knowing where the light switches are can be disturbing for an inexperienced lecturer. In particular, if a dimmer is provided so that notes may be taken, it will affect the speed at which slides may be shown and the silences that are necessary. If unavailable, a longer and more careful recapitulation is necessary for each illustrated point, and the number of slides that may be shown at one time is restricted. Thus important features of timing are affected.

What teaching aids are available, how long are their flexes and where are the power points that serve them? Where will the overhead projector be to avoid obscuring anyone's vision and how great will be its magnification? This will affect the size of letters and density of colors on prepared acetates.

What is the shape of the room and can the furniture in it be rearranged if desired? Will you be in a raised position and will you be behind a large bench so that there is a barrier between you and the class? These things affect rapport and the amount of spoken and non-verbal feedback that can easily be obtained. These in turn affect the use of class discussion, questioning and the selection of other techniques.

Will you be seen by all the class and will you see what all members of the class are doing? (N.B. The latter question is concerned with more than being able to see them.)

5. Decide the key points and organization of subject matter
Let us now assume that having considered these factors the 'teacher' has decided to use the lecture method either on its own, or with other methods. (Hence I shall now refer more to the 'lecturer', 'lecture' and 'audience' than the 'teacher', 'period' and 'class'.)

Whether the key points or the lecture organization is decided first will depend on the lecturer's objectives. If the objectives consist of teaching information it is probable that the most important items (key points) will be decided first so that they can then be organized in a simple way.

This is not always the case, however, because there are some instances when the requirements of a latter part of the course make it advisable that information should be arranged in a particular way. (Again we see a need for an overall view of the course.) To take an over simple example, it may be easier for students of geography to compare two regions that were originally described under similar headings in lectures. The example is more pertinent if applied to comparing the merits of various methods of bridge construction or the similar initial symptoms of subsequently contrasting diseases. On the other hand if the objective is to encourage varied patterns of thinking, perhaps the geographical descriptions should be fundamentally different in approach.

Where the objectives require a chaining structure this usually imposes itself so that the lecturer is left with the task of deciding the key stages to be emphasized.

Similarly, when the objective is to stimulate thought during the lecture period, a step-by-step lecture form with questions (Chapter 20), or a problem-centered lecture organization, usually impose themselves so that the selection of key questions or key points in the problem's solution are usually the second group of decisions.

Where the major objective is a change or development of certain attitudes the key points will be decided during preparation and the order of presentation will only be decided during the teaching itself when the knowledge and initial attitudes of the students become clear during an opening period of class discussion. Thus where attitude change is the major objective, the lecture organization is probably left flexible and only brought together in a pre-determined way in the final lecture summary.

Whatever the form of lecture organization, it is useful to jot down the proposed arrangement of key points as soon as these decisions are taken, in order to clarify the overall plan.

6. Decide how the teaching time is to be organized
This involves a host of decisions which depend upon the organization of subject matter. We have seen that it is advisable to use a variety of teaching methods; what is to be the timing of these and how are they to be organized?

Active learning is more efficient than passive learning; what activity will the students undertake and how will they become involved in it? ('What are the students going to do?' is a more crucial question for the lecturer than 'What am I going to do?')

The importance of immediate rehearsal and feedback has been emphasized; how are these to be facilitated?

How is student attention to be maintained and what inherent motivation is there in the subject? If little or none, what interest can appropriately be aroused?

7. Decide student preparation and follow-up
What previous knowledge is required? If the lecturer assumes some knowledge, what preparation, such as pre-reading, is expected of them and how is it to be organized?

If it is not possible to teach all that is necessary during a lecture what follow-up will be required? Are there the available resources for all students to do what is required?

Will either the preparation or follow-up require questions, essays or other tasks to be set? How are the preparation, the lecture itself and the follow-up related to seminars or other teaching?

In short, what is the total activity required from the students to achieve the objectives associated with a particular lecture?

8. Decide detailed teaching techniques

Many teaching techniques, as distinct from methods, cannot be prepared because they are the spontaneous expression of the lecturer's personality. Nevertheless it is particularly important for the new lecturer to attempt to cultivate an ideal as near to perfection as possible because early standards of technique quickly become habitual. It is quite possible for the first few lectures to influence subsequent teaching style for the rest of a teacher's life. Consequently careful thought and sound guidance are invaluable at this stage.

How is the lecture to be introduced? Some people like to write down their introductory statement verbatim. Since it should not be read, I find this inhibiting, inflexible and unnatural when the time comes, but I sometimes note the germ of an idea. The introduction usually serves to suggest an attitude against which later information is set.

How is the blackboard work to be arranged? It is sometimes useful to leave one part for ad lib explanations. How is other visual apparatus to be used? (See Chapter 8.)

When it is difficult to think of examples illustrating the key points, some lecturers write them down, whenever they come to mind, on a small "jotting pad" with tear-off sheets that can be placed in the appropriate places in their lecture files. Because, in some subjects, the examples can turn a dull lecture into an interesting one, this habit can avoid latent difficulties.

What exam questions could be based on the lecture topic? If the lecturer sets no assignments, exam questions can guide students' thinking, especially if the lecturer uses class discussion to elicit the range of relevant information and how it may be applied.

Conclusion

Much of what this chapter is trying to develop is the lecturer's self image. An essential part of lecture preparation is to imagine oneself doing the job. Answering the many questions in this chapter will help to achieve that.

22. Writing the Notes

1. When?
2. Key points.
3. Objectives and introduction.
4. Elaboration.
5. References.
6. Reminders about procedure.
7. Task design.
8. Equipment required.
9. Handouts.
10. Preparing the conclusion.

Having thought the lecture through and made some rough notes, the next stage is to prepare the notes for use during the lecture, if necessary. How this is done is largely a matter of personal taste and each lecturer usually develops his own style. Therefore I shall describe a method I use, which the new lecturer may adopt, modify or reject according to how far it suits his particular lecturing style.

1. When ?
Contrary to most of the advice I have ever been given, although I may prepare in rough, I usually find it better not to prepare lecture notes more than a week in advance. If I do, my intentions do not take the class reaction to the previous lecture into account; the lecture lacks spontaneity; and details of approach (which cannot always be noted) are sometimes forgotten.

2. Key points
I do not always use the same form of preparation although there are common features. Because Coats and Smidchens (1966) have shown that lecturers are more effective when they speak around a few points than when a lecture is read, the most important feature for me, is the layout of the 'key points' with headings and sub-headings. These form the basis of the blackboard or projected summary. They also serve to jog my memory of each successive point when necessary. Because I need to see them during the lecture I write them boldly, uncrowded by other notes, and preferably large enough to be recognized (not necessarily read) when standing at the chalkboard in case I forget the wording of a key phrase. For this reason I use plain paper because lines are too narrow and detract from clarity. (N.B. Because they are designed to be read from a distance of ten to twelve inches typewritten notes are certainly too small.) So that I can find my place quickly the key phrases are the only words written between one-and-a-half and four inches from the left hand side of the page (Figure 22.1).

3. Objectives and introduction
I do not always write out my objectives separately because these are often virtually the same as a knowledge of key points, but I usually do when the objectives are concerned

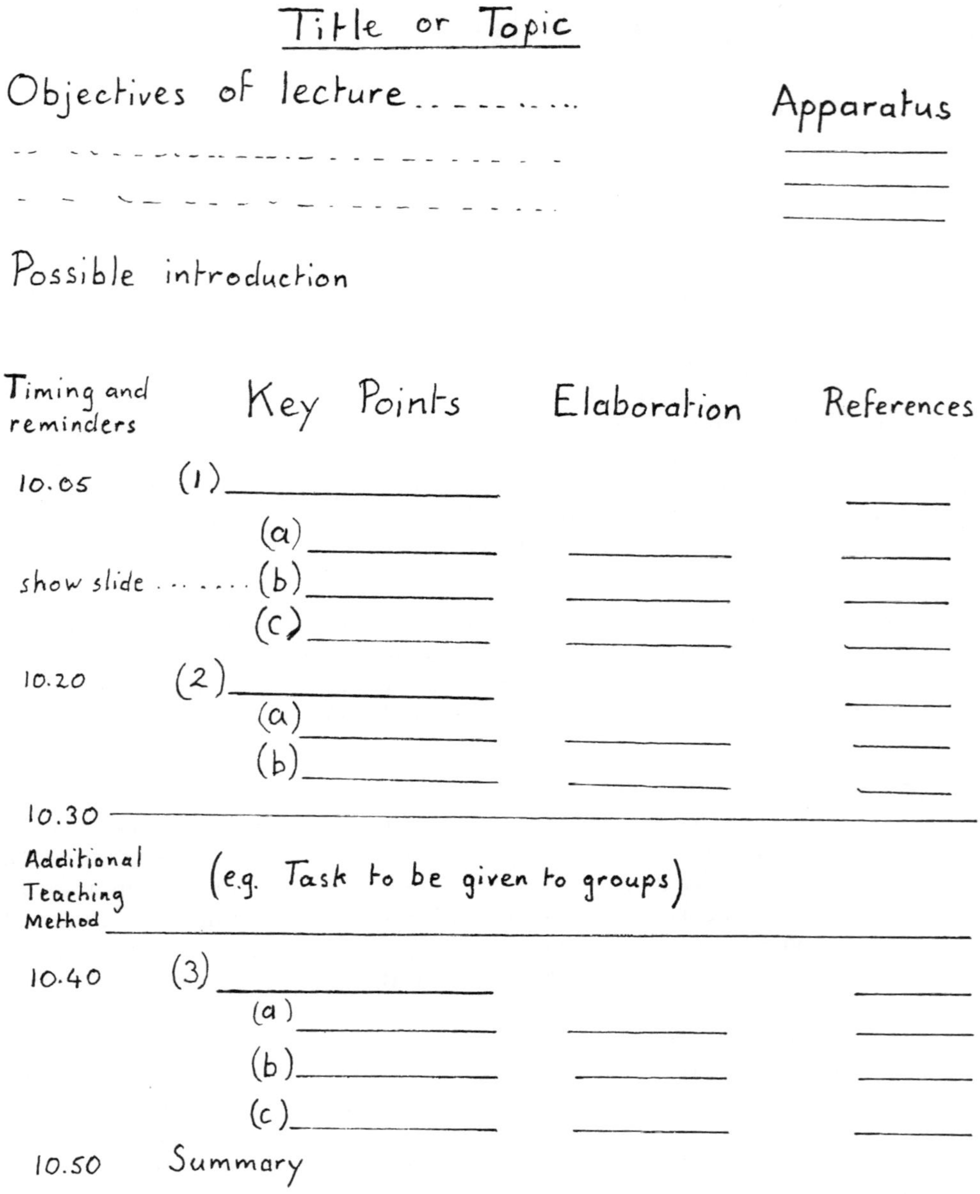

<u>Title or Topic</u>

Objectives of lecture.........   Apparatus
-- `` `----------------------- -   ———————
- - `-- ---------------- ----   ———————
                                                   ———————

Possible introduction

Timing and reminders	Key Points	Elaboration	References
10.05	(1)_____		_____
	(a)_____	_____	
show slide	(b)_____	_____	_____
	(c)_____	_____	_____
10.20	(2)_____		_____
	(a)_____	_____	_____
	(b)_____	_____	_____

10.30 ————————————————————————————————————

Additional Teaching Method ___ (e.g. Task to be given to groups) _____

10.40	(3) _____		_____
	(a)_____	_____	_____
	(b)_____	_____	_____
	(c)_____	_____	_____
10.50	Summary		

Figure 22.1 A possible schema for the preparation of a lecturer's notes

with promoting thought and attitudes, in which case I write them across the top of the first page as a constant reminder.

Any jottings for the introduction, such as a quotation, I also write near the top, usually in a smaller hand. But there is a trap to be avoided here. Be prepared to ditch your prepared introduction at the last moment if it does not feel right. That witty anecdote you thought would get everyone's attention and bonhomie could achieve the opposite if the joke falls flat. It's a matter of sensing the mood of the class when the time comes.

4. Elaboration

Examples and other details of elaboration are usually written on the right-hand half of the page opposite the appropriate key points, in the form of odd words to jog my memory. If there are any that are important, or that I know I tend to forget, I sometimes underline them lightly with a red ball point pen so that I may find them quickly.

5. References

On the right-hand edge of the page I write bibliographical references in different colors according to their use. Those that I wish to recommend to the students during the lecture are sometimes written in a bright color. These may include references to handouts, but sometimes those are in a different color signifying that I wish students to refer to them at that time and that I must bring my own copy to the lecture. References that indicate my own sources of information are written in a more subdued color; they are not used during the lecture unless I cannot answer a question, but they are useful if I wish to refer to my lecture notes on a later occasion or if I wish to check on detail.

6. Reminders about procedure

The left-hand margin is reserved for reminders about procedure, but is usually left blank. If timing is important, I may write what I reckon the time will be when I reach certain key points. Because there are dangers in such self-imposed restrictions, this is exceptional; but it could be useful for a beginner inexperienced in knowing how long particular explanations take.

If some form of reorganization of the room is required in the middle of the lecture for the use of small groups or visual aids, a reminder to myself shortly before the time can sometimes save a moment of confusion. By writing the number of a color transparency in the margin, it is easier to select the right slide at the right time.

The variations in teaching method may also be noted in the left hand margin if there is any likelihood of the notes being used on a later occasion. For example, I might remind myself in the left hand margin, to refer to a handout at a particular point, because I know that is the sort of thing I tend to forget.

7. Task design

Tasks given to students when using alternative methods, need careful thought. The wording of questions given to a buzz group, horseshoe groups or to open class discussion are worked out in terms of their psychological effects (such as the thought required, the objectives achieved and the probable class reaction) and noted across the width of the page.

8. Equipment required
When experienced teachers forget to bring a teaching aid to the lecture theater, they usually know how to manage; but it can be very disturbing for new lecturers. If I require items of apparatus that I am likely to forget to take, I sometimes list them in green at the top right hand corner of the first page.

If you will need the help of a laboratory assistant, maybe you should review your notes and make a request the previous day (or whenever). I tend to work a lot at home, so I need to check the list the previous night. (If I leave it till breakfast I'll forget; as in most families, there's too much going on to remember.) The list also permits a quick last minute check before going to class.

9. Handouts
One master copy of handouts that are an essential part of the lecture may be filed in my lecture notes if the folder is not made too voluminous as a result. This is useful because I usually prefer to mark them for easy reference to important points during the lecture. What is more, in broad principle I wish to have anything of this kind in front of me if the students can also refer to it.

10. Preparing the conclusion
In lectures to teach information I do not write a conclusion because it usually consists of standing at the chalkboard and reviewing the lecture summary written on it.

Lectures to promote thought usually require problems to be re-posed, and a reminder of reading or other work students may do to decide their own answers. In other words, rather than facts, I try to let the students go away with questions in their minds and some directions as to how the questions may be answered. These, too, are usually written elsewhere in the notes and do not need to be written again.

Conclusions to lectures primarily concerned with attitudes are superficially similar to those concerned with stimulating thought in that the issues are restated, but then I attempt to set out the alternatives with sentences of the form, 'If A then X, but if B then Y' so that students are left to choose between 'X and Y rather than A and B'. In other words the alternative conclusions are stated, not only the issues or problems considered.

There is a further, important, reason why I do not prepare the conclusions of my lectures. Very few lectures ever go exactly according to plan. I nearly always find that I need to modify my intentions as a result of verbal or non-verbal feedback so that a prepared conclusion is rarely the precise thing that needs to be said.

The fact that lectures do not go as intended does not imply that preparation is not worthwhile. Quite the contrary, preparation needs to be broader than the ground that may actually be covered. Some contingencies need to be anticipated. Purists may say that a plan that has to be changed is not a good one, but in practice one cannot plan for every contingency in a complex interactive process; and when lectures go exactly as planned it may be more pertinent to question the lecturer's sensitivity to audience reaction. If 'planning' implies some inflexibility, good lectures may be 'prepared' but not 'planned'.

23. Lecturing for the First Time

This chapter is a quiet word for beginners, but more experienced lecturers may like to check out their approach. Because it is a rather tense occasion, new lecturers, who have to go in front of a class for the first time, sometimes welcome very direct suggestions on what to do. Some have found the following suggestions helpful.

For lecturers who keep some of their lecture materials at home, it is worthwhile to glance at the list of apparatus (Figure 22.1) just before going home the previous day, to check on what will be needed.

If you read through your notes ten minutes to a quarter of an hour before going to class, the key points and overall organization will be fresh in your memory. In this way a glance will be sufficient to remind you of each successive point during the lecture, so that you are not concentrating on your notes when you should be attending to the reactions of the students ('Non-verbal feedback', Chapter 13). The preview also gives a reassurance of knowing where you are going so that the lecture easily flows from point to point.

On entering the room and reaching the lecturer's table, notes and other apparatus need to be arranged for easy use. In particular, lecture notes need to be raised so that you will not easily lose visual contact with the class.

Most new lecturers start talking too soon. It is normally better to wait for a class to become quiet than to ask for silence, and when silence is obtained it is important to wait a few moments longer. This will seem a very long time indeed if you are a nervous baptismal lecturer, but you can use it to steady yourself, and without implying an atmosphere of discipline, it places the responsibility for silence on the audience, sets the standards of attention the lecturer demands, allows the class time to adjust mentally to the task ahead and raises the level of expectancy and sense of occasion.

Coats and Smidchens (1966) have shown that eye-contact is important in establishing rapport with a class, and while personal interaction is important during the lecture, new lecturers sometimes find it easier to establish at the beginning, before part of their attention is directed toward their subject and their notes.

Some beginners realize that inaudibility is a common fault and over-compensate at first, then find that their mouth becomes dry and their voice does not last. A glass of water can help, but some lecturers watch the reactions of the students at the back and adjust their voice accordingly.

We have seen that in the desire to appear confident it is easy to go too fast. Nevertheless students are more likely to work well through the whole course if a 'businesslike' tone is set from the start. Thus there is a need to be brisk without being hurried. This may be achieved if the re-expression and elaboration of each point is carefully prepared so that while further details are being given, the few key points are being persistently driven home. (Chapter 8.) In this way the lecture may command attention by seeming to move forward, while teaching is thorough because the movement is not too great. A working atmosphere can quickly be created by setting a small amount of work to be completed by the second meeting; but the work must be feasible, bearing in mind that students may not yet have bought basic textbooks, and library facilities may be limited. To give a handout to be read by the second lecture is one way of achieving this. If students discover they need not do such work, the working atmosphere is lost. Notice how Jenkins (in Gibbs, 1992) avoids this trap at the foot of Figure 20.1.

It is fairly obvious that to stimulate students to work from the beginning of the course, major objectives of the first few weeks are to arouse the interest of the class and convince students that they can learn what is necessary. Because people like doing things at which they feel successful, to obtain confidence and motivation, students need to feel they have learned something. Whether they have actually learned anything is less important than motivation at this stage because most information learned in the first few weeks is likely to be forgotten by the end of course examinations.

Many teachers begin their course by defining their subject, defining some of the common terms involved, and then perhaps giving a short history of the development of the subject. This approach may be all right for a textbook, but it is inappropriate for lectures. These things do not inspire students, and the significance of the history is often incomprehensible when the background issues are not known. It is not enough to provide a framework of ideas; the ideas are unintelligible if they cannot be related to the students' background knowledge. Consequently a problem-centered lecture, where the problem is concerned with a broad spectrum of the principles of the subject applied to an everyday situation, is suitable.

With classes of less than forty new lecturers will enjoy teaching much more if they can get to know their students personally. It is well worthwhile to spend an afternoon looking at their college application forms for their personal, rather than their academic, background. This is particularly valuable for helping students with personal difficulties.

When you have begun to speak, your mind will be on what you are saying and how the audience reacts. Like a musician, actor or sportsman you will become yourself through becoming thoroughly involved in what you are doing. Consequently a conscious application of earlier advice at this stage risks producing a stiff and unnatural performance. For this reason it is not desirable to make further suggestions here that you should remember to apply once the lecture has started.

24. Conclusion: The Use of Lectures

1. **What lectures can be used for - Part 1.**

2. **Factors and techniques in their use - Parts 2 and 3.**

3. **When lectures are not so useful - Part 4.**

4. **Preparing for their use - Part 5.**

The title of this book is deliberately ambiguous. It considers two questions: 'What can lectures be used for?' and 'How should they be used?'

1. What lectures can be used for - Part 1.

It is concluded that they can be used to teach information, including the framework of a subject, but an expository approach is unsuitable to stimulate thought or to change attitudes.

2. Factors and techniques in their use - Parts 2 and 3.

While it is not normally possible to establish rules of lecturing technique, some suggestions are made in the light of psychological and experimental evidence, on ways of organizing information, teaching a single idea, using handouts and feedback techniques, and overcoming common difficulties. In each case preparation is required to follow these suggestions.

3. When lectures are not so useful - Part 4.

It has been argued that the limitations of the lecture method commonly necessitate its use in combination with other teaching methods. The way methods are combined also requires preparation in the light of the objectives to be achieved.

4. Preparing for their use - Part 5.

Thus answers to the second question require decisions at the time of preparation in addition to those concerned with the selection of subject matter.

Appendices to Chapter 2

Appendix to Table 2.1. – Lectures are as effective as other methods to teach information, but not more so

This table summarizes reports of comparisons between lectures and other methods. Three items of information are given for each comparison: the author(s), the methods compared and the measures used. The criterion of significance is that results would have occurred on less than 5% of occasions by chance. Obviously I cannot claim that the literature survey is complete. In particular there are around 200 comparitive studies of traditional teaching with both television and PSI (Personalized Sytem of Instruction). These have been omitted. See Chapter 3, Reservations, with regard to PSI.

The classification of teaching methods

Some explanation is needed for the classification of teaching methods used in this, and later tables. Teaching methods can vary in a multitude of ways. There is no single dimension on which they can all be distinguished.

I regard a lecture as a period of more or less continuous exposition when teaching. I admit the phrase 'more or less' introduces some vagueness, but that corresponds to the way the word is used. Although necessarily defined in terms of what the teacher does; in practice it sets psychologically what the students are expected to do.

PSI uses five principles, four inherited from programed learning as used in the 1960s: the principles of small steps, self paced active learning, early feedback on performance, individual support with personal contact, and progress to the next unit of work being conditional upon previous mastery. Methods I have classified as related to PSI have at least three of these characteristics, and mostly four or all five. My inclusion of 'Individualized instruction' under this heading is the most contentious because authors' use of the term is often unclear. I have assumed it adopts at least the middle three principles.

Discussion occurs when students make a spoken contribution and get a response. This criterion would include a student asking a question in a lecture and getting an answer. That may stretch the definition of 'discussion' too much, but Chapter 5 shows that such an incident has significant psychological effects upon the attention of all students. We simply have to accept that teaching methods are continua. Any attempt to cut a line between them will be arbitrary in some respects.

'Enquiry' assumes that students have to obtain or seek information, but it cannot exclude their being presented with some too. It might be regarded as an element within 'Independent study'. It is only presented as a separate method here when experimenters have done so.

'Independent study' could include many psychologically different activities depending on the subject of study. In particular, reading a history book is very different from doing mathematical calculations. I have assumed that the dominant activities are reading and writing. This is intended to exclude laboratory practicals and workshops.

The 'Other methods' heading mostly includes other methods of presenting information (eg. audio, TV, computers, etc). Strictly, computer assisted learning is not a single method. Computers are tools that can be used in many different ways.

Key to this and other Tables in this Chapter

CAL	=	Computer Assisted Learning	MCQ	=	Multiple choice questions
D	=	Discussion	Q & A	=	Question and answer
Demo	=	Demonstration	Q	=	Questionnaire
L	=	Lecture	TF	=	True-False tests
Lab	=	Laboratory methods	R	=	Reading, private study or independent study
PL	=	Programmed Learning	TV	=	Television
PSI	=	Personalized system of instruction (Keller Plan)			

Studies showing lectures less effective for teaching information

Lecture versus PSI related methods

1	Abbott & Falstrom (1977)	L v. PSI	Statistics achievement
2	Badia et al (1978)	L v. PSI.	Less able students quicker mastery
3	Cross & Semb (1976)	L v. PSI	Low performers on 100 item test
4	Drake (1987)	L v. PSI	3 exams and 5 month delayed test
5	Gray et al (1986)	L v. PSI	Higher cognitive retention
6	Hedges (1975)	L v. PSI	Content on this and later courses
7	Hinrichsen (1975)	L v. PSI	More A and B grades
8	Ostrow (1984)	L v. PSI	Exam immediate & 3 month delay
9	Swartz (1986)	L v. PL	American College Math Test
10	Riedel et al (1976)	L v. PSI.	Posttest
11	Sheehy (1989)	L v. PSI	Achievement test in algebra
12	Coldeway et al (1974)	L v. PSI v. Contingency management	Course work and final exam
13	Rysberg (1986)	L v. L+unit tests+proctors	Mastery
14	Ehlers (1986)	L v. Mastery teaching	Students <21 or with feeling
15	Lee and McLean (1978)	L v. Mastery approach	Achievement scores
16	Jernstedt (1976)	L v. PL	Essays
17	Randels et al (1976)	L v. PL+TV	Theoretical knowledge
18	Taber (1974)	L v. Individualized instruction	Course work final exam
19	McCue (1973)	L-D v. Individualized instruction	Achievement criteria not clear
20	Watson (1983)	L v. Individualized instruction	Pass rate

Lecture versus Various Discussion methods

1	Bane (1925 and 1931)	L v. D	Delayed recall
2	Beach (1960)	L v. Class D	Less sociable students MCQ L v. Tutorless small-group D More sociable students on MCQ
3	Bond (1956)	L v. D	Delayed test
4	Erskine and Tomkin (1963)	Two Ds v. nine Ls	Objective tests, total time
5	Gerberich and Warner (1936)	L v. D	Less able students on MCQ tests, matching true/false questions and examinations
6	Gore (1962)	L v. Problem-centered groups	Final examinations, retention tests, job sheets.

7	H.C.Smith (1955)	L v. Syndicates	Achievement test, not clearly specified
8	Huffaker (1931)	L v. D	Immediate and delayed tests of recall
9	Kirby (1931)	L v. D	Immediate and delayed tests of recall examinations
10	Rickard (1946)	L v. D	Delayed recall test
11	Walker (1986)	L v. D	Vocabulary and written material
12	Ward (1956)	L v. D	Understanding of information by more able students
13	Gibb (1993)	L v. Teach to learn	Knowledge retention
14	Fontenot (1996)	L v. L+Cooperative learning	Science achievement test
15	Carter (1995)	L v. L + D	4 week delayed 20 item MCQ
16	Beilin and Rabow (1979)	L v. L+D	Scores on final exams by whites
17	Dawson (1956)	L+Demo v. Problem-solving groups	Test of recall of information
18	Abdul-Munim (1988)	Video L v. Video panel/D	7 mostly memory tests

Lecture versus Independent study

1	Cormier (1976)	L v. R	Retention test
2	Dorsel (1976)	L v. R	Comprehension
3	Siegel (1973)	L v. R	Examination
4	Singagra and Lopez (1989)	L v. R	Learning styles, note-taking clarity of expression
5	Thompson (n.d.)	L v. R	Notes taken
6	Williams et al (1957)	TV L v. R	Retention immediately and after 8 months
7	Holt (1973)	L-Demo v. Independent Study	Cognitive gains while developing psychomotor skills
8	Wells (1982)	L v. Independent Study	Business maths
9	Wilson B. K. (1993)	L v. Independent Study	Academic performance (unclear)
10	Parsons (1957)	L+D v. Correspondence	Gains on delayed MCQ test

Lecture versus Enquiry methods

1	Awodi (1984)	L v. Enquiry	Scientific method, test scores
2	Sage (1971)	L v. Enquiry method	Concepts in electronics
3	Yadav (1984)	L v. Guided discovery	Objectives achieved
4	Selim & Shrigley (1983)	L v. Discovery methods	Recall
5	Specht and Sandlin (1991)	L v. Experiential learning	Quizzes after 6 weeks
6	Tuttle (1930)	L v. projects	Objective test for students with previous knowledge

Lectures and Other methods

1	Gonzalez-Menendez (1985)	L v. Demo	15 day recall
2	Rai (1976)	L+D v. Demo+D v. Practical fieldwork+D	PDT
3	Yadav (1982)	L v. Demo	Knowledge
4	Maier (1957)	2 L-Demo + D v. 1 L-Demo + Lab	Exam scores for L-Demo + Lab
5	Shahabudin (1987)	Problem-centered L v. Recalled facts	Clinical experiences
6	Greenberg & Jewett (1985)	L v. Case presentation	Gain scores
7	Higgins and Boone (1990)	L v. CAL	Test of retention
8	Lowery (1988)	L+D v. CAL	Mastery, time, cost
9	Williams (1996)	L v. CAL	Grades
10	Stanton (1994)	L v. CAL	Time taken

11	Vincent (1985)	L-D v. CAL	Delayed test, 18% less time
12	Lowery (1989)	L-D v. CAL	Time and cost
13	Roberts (1994)	L+Lab v. CAL for low pretest students	
			A predictive technical concept
14	Hicks (1996)	L+practice v. CAL	Gains, esp less able students
15	Harris (1984)	L-D v. CAL	East Texas Progress Safety Test
16	Chen (1995)	L+Lab v. CAL/Simulation	
			Time spent
17	Isaacs (1973)	L v. Precision teaching	MCQ
18	Odubunmi and Balogun (1991)	L v. Lab	Males and low achievers on posttest
19	Smith (1987)	L v. L+Lab	Nelson Biology Test Form E
20	Dubes (1987)	L v. Posters	3 week delayed test
21	Rankowski & Galey (1979)	L v. Multimedia	Achievement, spatial relations
22	Downes (1995)	L+Demo v. Multimedia	Gain scores about injections
23	Schoenbaum (1996)	L v. Multimedia+CAL	Posttest
24	Sherman (1975)	L v. Mixture of methods	Knowledge gains
25	Hoffman (1974)	L v. Audiotape + team teaching	
			State Board Nursing Exams position in Nat. League
26	Damsgeegt (1982)	L v. L+Behavior Modification	
			Recall of BM principles
27	Brinson (1989)	L v. Game	MCQ and T-F tests

Studies showing no significant difference

Lectures versus PSI related methods

1	Baker (1974)	L v. PSI	Essays immediate and delayed
2	Cross & Semb (1976)	L v. PSI	Average and high performers on 100 item exam
3	Grant (1983)	L v. PSI	Biology Achievement Test
4	Tatum and Lenel (1985)	L v. PSI	Final exam, average course grade retention after one year
5	Collard (1987)	L v. modified PSI	Achievement x age sex race GPA
6	Ertwine (1984)	L v. Thayer Method(paced PSI in class)	
			Quizzes, exams, homework
7	Jumpeter (1985)	L+Demo v. PSI	Achievement and opinions
8	Jernstedt (1976)	L v. PL	Short answers
9	Johnson K. A. (1967)	L v. PL	MCQ Short written answers
10	Anaemena (1986)	L v. PL	Basic electronics (test unclear)
11	Magoulis (1986)	L v. L+PL	MCQ in accountancy
12	Whitson (1983)	L v. PL	Pre and Posttests
13	Shine (1983)	L-Demo v PL	Digital computer arithmetic
14	Curry (1984)	L-D v. Individualized Instruction	
			Covariate on pretest
15	Heller & Dale (1976)	L+D v. Competency Based Instruction	
			Gains
16	Bourgeois (1996)	L v. Peer tutoring	Mathematics scores
17	Robinson (1995)	L v. peer tutoring	Home assignments, class tests

Lectures versus Various Discussion methods

1	Bane (1925 and 1931)	L v. D	Immediate recall
2	Becker & Dallinger (1960)	L v. D	Factual knowledge
3	Carlson (1953)	L v. D and L v. L-D	Gains on test of knowledge
4	Benson (1996)	L v. L+D in small groups	
			Claydon course exam: knowledge

5	Diflorio (1996)	L-D v. Cooperative learning
		MCQ
6	Randolph (1993)	L-D v. Cooperative learning
		Introductory biology
7	Robinson (1995)	L v. Cooperative learning Home assignments, class tests
8	Smith D.L. (1995)	L-D v. Cooperative learning Knowledge test
9	Andrews (1996)	L v. Cooperative learning + CAL
		Mechanics Baseline test + exam
10	Dutt (1994)	L v. 2 weeks' Cooperative learning
		quizzes
11	Courtney et al (1994)	L v. D (Cooperative learning)
		MCQ
12	Dubes (1987)	L v. D	3 week delayed test
13	Fitzgerald (1960)	L v. D	Objective tests
14	Gadzella (1977)	L v. D	Essay exams
15	Gerberich & Warner (1936)	L v. D	Heterogeneous groups on exams, MCQ tests, matching true/false Q
16	Gotke (1931)	L v. D	Immediate and delayed tests
17	Guetzkow et al (1954)	L v. D	Misconception tests and USAF standard exam
18	Hill (1965)	L v. D	Concepts and principles
19	Hudelson (1928)	L v. D v. Q&A sessions	Type of test not specified
20	Rickard (1946)	L v. D	Recognition of facts
21	Robbins (1931)	L v. D	Immediate and delayed recall
22	Rohrer (1957)	L v. D	Terminology, facts and principles
23	Ruja (1954)	L v. D	Tests of knowledge on two out of three courses
24	Smith J.P. (1954)	L v. D	Recognition of facts
25	Spence (1928)	L v. D	Tests of facts
26	Ward (1956)	L v. D	Retention of information by more able students
27	Bills (1952)	L v. Student-centered D	Objective tests
28	Di Vesta (1954)	L v. Student-centered D	Knowledge of principles
29	Eglash (1954)	L v. Free-group D	Examinations
30	Jenkins (1952)	L v. Free-group D	Standard examination
31	Johnson and Smith (1953)	L v. Free-group D	Test on terminology and facts
32	Gauvain (1968)	L v. Seminar	MCQ and essay exams
33	Casey and Weaver (1956)	L v. Small-group Ds	Objective tests
34	Barnard (1936)	1L and 2Ds per week v. 3Ls
		MCQ
35	Beach (1960)	L v. Class D	MCQ
36	Erskine and Tomkin (1963)	Two Ds v. nine Ls	Essays
37	Churchill (1960)	L-D and Private study v. Small groups
		MCQ
38	Churchill and John (1958)	Small L-D group v. large L class
		Objective test
39	Connolly (1992)	L+D v. D	1/3 groups posttest
40	Leton (1961)	L v. Case Discussion	Tests of knowledge, not clear
41	Tillman (1993)	L-D v. Case Discussion	Course content
42	Carter (1995)	L v. Case study method	Immediate 20 item MCQ
43	Watson (1975)	L v. Case study method	Knowledge of principles
44	Watts (1977)	L v. R+D	Sex Knowledge and Attitude Questionnaire
45	Wieder (1954)	L-Demo v. Free-group D	Objective tests
46	Deignan (1956)	L+D v. L+Student-centered D
		MCQ and sentence completion
47	Haigh and Schmidt (1956)	Teacher-centered v. Student-centered
		Horrocks-Troyer test

48	Joyce & Weatherall (1957)	L v. D v. L+Practicals v. L+R
		Short answer tests and MCQ
49	Lifson et al (1956)	L v. L+D	MCQ on facts
50	Palmer and Verner (1959)	L v. D v. L+D	MCQ
51	Beilin and Rabow (1979)	L v. L+D	Scores on facts and final exams for ethnic minorities
52	Ott (1996)	L v. Expert-led reflective D
		Physiologic concepts
53	Patton (1955)	Student-centered teaching v.
		Measures not clearly described trad. teacher-centered teaching
54	Husband (1951)	Large L [Av 200] v. small L [av 55] +questions + D
		Hourly quizzes and final examinations

Lectures versus Independent study

1	Bligh (1970a)	L v. R	MCQ on terms, facts
2	Bligh (1974)	L v. R	TFT on terms, facts
3	Gadzella (1977)	L v. R	Essay exams
4	Jha & Baral (1973)	L+D v. R	Retention
5	Mueller (1974)	L+D v. R	Unit exams
6	Northcraft & Jernstedt (1975)	L v. R	Objective exams
7	Russell & Bryant (1987)	L v. R	Posttest gains
8	Simpson (1982)	L Reading v. Cued reading
		Immediate 1 week delayed test
9	Williams et al (1957)	L v. R	Immediate and 8 month retention
10	Beach (1960)	L v. Independent Study	MCQ
11	Diemer and Mazzocco (1974)	L v. Independent Study	Scores of personality types
12	Moore (1994)	L v. Independent Study	Certificate exam of Gas Assoc.
13	Rooney (1994)	L+D v. Independent projects
		Gain scores on nursing issues
14	Merrill (1995)	L+Demo v. Independent Study
		Knowledge of cardiac support
15	Elsberry (1995)	L v. Self-paced learning	Grade Point Averages in physics
16	Guetzkow et al (1954)	L v. Private study	Misconception tests and USAF standard exam
17	Fitzgerald (1960)	L v. private study	Objective tests
18	Jone N. W. (1980)	L v. Self paced learning	End of course exams
19	Parsons (1957)	L-D v. Correspondence	Gains on MCQ immediate test
20	Oines (1971)	L-Demo v. Self-paced instruction
		Pre to post test knowledge gains
21	Farquhar (1986)	L v. Problem-based guided study
		Standardized tests

Lecture versus Enquiry methods

1	Specht and Sandlin (1991)	L v. Experiential learning
		Immediate quizzes
2	Newman (1996)	L v. Problem Based Learning
		Exam, information gathering
3	Howerton (1987)	L+Lab v. Guided discovery
		MCQ
4	Masuhara (1984)	L+Practice v. Guided Design Problems
		Immediate and delayed tests
5	Emese (1993)	L-D v. Discovery	Time taken
6	Onyejiaku (1982)	L v. Discovery methods	Non-analytic students' retention of maths

Lecture and Other methods

1	Bligh (1970a)	L v. Audiotape	MCQ on terms, facts
2	Bligh (1974)	L v. Audiotape	TFT on terms, facts
3	Hendrix (1968)	L v. Audiotape	Course grades
4	Simpson (1982)	L v. Audio	Immediate 1 week delayed test
5	Biegert and Withrow (1978)	L v. Tape-slides	50-item MCQ
6	Harding et al (1981)	L v. Tape-slide	Retention
7	Laurie (1976)	L v. Slide-tape	Objective test
8	Laurie (Jnr) (1976)	L v. Tape-slides	Information acquisition
9	Garren and Gathmann (1974)	L + Lab v. Audio-tutorial	Unit tests and final exam
10	Belzer and Conti (1973)	L v. Audio-tutorial	Tests scores and final exam
11	Stokley (1990)	L v. Audio-visual instruction	Delayed test
12	Miller and Jackson (1985)	L v. multimedia	Pre-test, post-test of information
13	Peterson (1974)	L v. Multimedia	State Board of Nursing exams
14	Watkins (1996)	L v. Multimedia	Allied Health Studies
15	Blackwood and Trent (1968)	L v. TV lecture	Knowledge gain scores
16	Conlin et al (1971)	L v. TV lecture	Knowledge recall comprehension
17	Ellis and Mathis (1985)	L v. TV	Test performance
18	Keeble & Weinman (1986)	L v. TV	Immediate recall
19	Nay (1975)	L v. TV	Questionnaire
20	Parsons (1957)	L-D v. TV L	Gains on MCQ immediate test
21	Pohl et al (1982)	L v. TV	MCQ exam
22	Siegel (1973)	L v. Video	Examination
23	Sox et al (1984)	L v. Tutored video instruction+Q & A	Final exam
24	Tomm and Leahy (1980)	L v. TV v. TV + D	Criteria not clearly specified
25	Firstman (1983)	L v. TV + D	Scores of more able students
26	Axeen (1967)	L v. CAL	Amount of knowledge
27	Fleschsig and Seamans (1987)	L v. CAL	Learning information
28	Gerardo (1986)	L v. CAL	Learning Fortran
29	Higgins and Boone (1990)	L v. L+CAL	Test of retention
30	Howard (1986)	L v. CAL	Immediate and delayed tests
31	Schroeder & Kent (1982)	L+Lab v. CAL	Achievement test
32	Tabar (1990)	L v. CAL+ interactive video	Test on nutrition unclear
33	Whitaker (1990)	L v. CAL	57 item objective test
34	Elliott (1986)	L-Demo v. CAL	Immediate and 3 week posttest
35	Whitson (1983)	L v. CAL	Pre and Posttests
36	Van Scoder (1986)	L v. CAL	Posttest on respiratory theory
37	Reddy (1989)	L v. CAL	Wilsondisc test
38	Stanton (1994)	L v. CAL	Test and topic unclear
39	Wilson L. E. (1993)	L v. CAL	5 knowledge tests thro' semester
40	Lowery (1989)	L-D v. CAL	Maths
41	Roberts (1994)	L+Lab v. CAL	A predictive technical concept
42	Flexer (1978)	L v. Lab	Exams 6 month retention
43	Odubunmi and Balogun (1991)	L v. Lab	Females and high achievers on posttest
44	Pigford (1974)	L-Demo v. Lab	31 MCQ and 5 short answers
45	Gonzalez-Menendez (1985)	L v. Demo	Immediate recall
46	Adame (1986)	L v. Content involving style, interactive	Knowledge of sex
47	Falvo et al (1991)	L v. Role-modelling	Questionnaire/test
48	Dieterle (1985)	L v. Simulation	Knowledge tests

49	Cooper (1995)	L v. Simulation	Posttest in social studies
50	Nay (1975)	L v. Modelling	Questionnaire
51	Saunders (1988)	L v. L+Guided clinical practice	
			25 item MCQ Diagnostic Rating
52	Shahabudin (1987)	Problem-centered L v.	Facts covered Clinical experiences
53	Tomm and Leahy (1980)	L v. Practice interviews	Criteria not clearly specified
54	Kazanas and Frazier (1982)	L-D v. Performance based instruction	
			Retention
55	Metz (1987)	L v. "Interactive instruction"	
			17 of 19 measures
56	Gross (1985)	L-D v. Active musical experience	
			Knowledge and discrimination
57	Earl (1993)	L v. Accelerative learning	
			Immediate and 30 day delay

Studies showing lectures are more effective for teaching information

Lectures versus PSI related methods

1	Friedman et al (1979)	L+D v. PSI	Final exam
2	Fox (1986)	L v. PSI using CAL	Content exam final grades
3	Jernstedt (1976)	L v. PL	MCQ
4	Khan (1983)	L v. PL	Physical geography (test unclear)
5	Bhushan & Sharma (1975)	L v. PL v. L+PL	Criteria unclear
6	Hull and McClay (1965)	L-D v. PL	Knowledge gains
7	Walton (1986)	L v PL	Acquisition of English Grammar
8	Watson (1983)	L v. Individualized instruction	
			delayed retention

Lectures versus Various Discussion methods

1	Bloom (1953)	L v. D	Stimulated recall of attention to simple comprehension
2	Gadzella (1977)	L v. D	MCQ
3	Gerberich & Warner (1936)	L v. D	More able students on MCQ tests, matching true/false questions and examinations
4	Guetzkow et al (1954)	L v. D	University exams
5	Jha & Baral (1973)	L+D v. D	Retention
6	Ruja (1954)	L v. D	Tests of knowledge on one of three courses
7	Spence and Watson (1928)	L v. Class D	Objective tests
8	Ward (1956)	L v. D	Retention and understanding by less able students
9	Walker (1986)	L v. D	Recall and comprehension
10	Beach (1960)	L v. Tutorless D	Less sociable students on MCQ
11	Burke (1955)	L-D v. 'student-centered' free group D	
			Exams and Course work
12	Beilin and Rabow (1979)	L v. L+D	Scores on facts by whites
13	Byers and Hedrick (1976)	L v. D (small group)	Test scores/exams
14	Connolly (1992)	L+D v. D	2/3 groups posttest
15	Beach (1960)	L v. tutorless small group D	
			Less sociable students on MCQ
16	Brooks (1993)	L v. Cooperative learning Knowledge gain scores	
17	Smith D.L. (1995)	L-D v. Cooperative learning	
			Time spent in private study
18	Asch M.J. (1951)	L-D v. 'non-directive' free group D	
			MCQ, Essay examinations

19	Dawson (1956)	L-Demo v. problem-solving groups
		Test of recall of information
20	Barnard (1942)	L-Demo v. problem-centered D
		Tests on specific information
21	Marr et al (1960)	L v. quizzing of teacher by students
		Course tests, final examinations
22	Metz (1987)	L v. "Interactive instruction"
		2 of 19 measures

Lectures versus Independent study

1	Ripple (1963)	L v. R	Immediate and delayed test
2	Brooks (1993)	L v. Private study	Knowledge gain scores
3	Paul (1932)	L v. private study	Time spent
4	Greene (1928)	L v. R	Completeness of notes taken
5	Gadzella (1977)	L v. R	MCQ
6	Corey (1934)	L v. R	Immediate recall on true/false, completion and short answer tests
7	Brooks (1993)	L v. Private study	Knowledge gain scores
8	Houghton (1994)	L v. Correspondence	Gain scores in test
9	Camp (1993)	L v. Self paced Lab	Maths

Lecture versus Enquiry methods

1	Onyejiaku (1982)	L v. Discovery methods	Analytic males' retention
2	Morris (1930)	L v. Problem projects	Course grades for pairs matched on previous grades
3	Newman (1996)	L v. Problem Based Learning
		MCQ

Lecture and Other methods

1	Watkins (1996)	L v. CAL	Allied Health Studies
2	Siegel (1973)	L v. Audio	Examination
3	Brantley (1974)	L-Demo v. Audio-tutorial course work
		Achievement test
4	Stokley (1990)	L v. Audio-visual instruction
		Immediate test
5	Sullivan et al (1976-77)	L v. TV	Posttest
6	Keeble & Weinman (1986)	L v. TV	Recall after 2 weeks
7	Firstman (1983)	L v. TV + D	Scores of less able students
8	Watts (1977)	L v. Audio-visual instruction
		Knowledge gain about sex
9	Watts (1977)	L v. Multi-media	Sex Knowledge and Attitude Q
10	Fodor (1963)	L v. No teaching	Gains in tests of knowlwdge
11	Gulo and Baron (1965)	L v. Irrelevant activity	MCQ
12	Gulo and Nigro (1966)	L v. Irrelevant task	MCQ
13	Hancock et al (1983)	L v. Decision orientation	Content
14	Peterson & Ridley (1984)	L+Demo v. Film modelling v.
		Info on procedures and equipment attention control
15	Long (1987)	L v. Clinical simulation	Tests of information
16	Brinson (1988)	L v. Game	MCQ and T-F tests
17	Solomon et al (1964)	Learning of facts related to a lecturing
		MCQ style of teaching
18	Thrasher (1972)	L v. Student team teaching
		Knowledge - criteria not clear
19	Bussett (1965)	L + D v. Film + D v. Bulletins + D Knowledge gained by adults
20	Brinson (1988)	L v. Game	MCQ and T-F tests

Appendix to Table 2.3 – Lectures are relatively ineffective to stimulate thought

This table summarizes reports of comparisons between teaching methods where the criteria of effectiveness include student thought. As in Appendix Table 2.1, in most cases three items of information are given: the author, the methods compared and the measures used. The criterion of significance is 5%. The intention is to show the overall pattern of findings. Because the reports do not always describe the teaching methods and measures in detail, caution should be observed in generalizing from individual reports. Abbreviations and the criteria for classifying teaching methods are the same as given at the top of the Appendix to Table 2.1.

Studies showing lectures are relatively ineffective to stimulate thought

Lecture versus Various Discussion methods

1	Asch M.J. (1951)	L v.'Non-directive' free-group D	
			Breadth of thinking, consider more than one authority
2	Bloom (1953)	L v. D	Stimulated recall of thinking
3	Bond (1956)	L v. D	Decision making
4	Brinkley (1952)	L v. Group D	Stimulated recall of thought
5	Guetzkow et al (1954)	L v. D	McCandless Test of Scientific Attitudes, analytical thinking
6	Katz (1990)	L v. D	Problem solving with active learning style, time taken
7	Lam (1984-5)	L v. D	Depth of questions
8	McKeachie & Hiler (1954)	L v. D	Application of knowledge
9	Perkins (1950)	L v. D	Application of knowledge
10	Rickard (1946)	L v. D	Giving examples of generalisations
11	Ward (1956)	L v. D	Understanding by more able students
12	Cabral-Pini (1995)	L v. Cooperative learning	
			Understanding a case study, Flexible, creative (2-yr case study)
13	Mohr (1996)	L v. Cooperative learning	
			Cognitive Complexity Index
14	Smith D.L. (1995)	L-D v. Cooperative learning	
			Application questions
15	Gibb (1993)	L v. Teach to learn	Application of knowledge
16	Jensen (1996)	L v. Experiential learning	
			Skills of Kolb's learning cycle
17	Hingorani (1996)	L v. Case study + CAL	reasoning, criticism, problem identification/solving, decisions
18	Tillman (1993)	L-D v. Case Study	Problem solving, reserved judgement, multiple perspectives
19	Self et al (1989)	L v. L+Case D	Moral reasoning
20	Khoiny (1995)	L v. Problem Based Learning	
			Critical thinking
21	Burns and Jones (1967)	L v. Lecture-tutorial	Sharper focus in written work more intense communication
22	Johnson and Smith (1953)	Instructor-centered v. Student-centered	
			Reasoning and creativity tests, case analysis

23	Gibb and Gibb (1952)	L-Demo v. 'Participative action groups'
		Role flexibility in thinking
24	Dawson (1956)	L-Demo v. Problem-solving groups
		Problem solving
25	Erskine and Tomkin (1963)	Two Ds v. Nine lectures Oral examinations
26	Sawyer & Sawyer (1981)	L v. Microcounselling Decision making
27	Watson (1975)	L v. Case study Application of principles
28	Carpenter (1956)	Ls, films and Demos v. Small-group D
		Problem solving, scientific thinking
29	Barnard (1942)	L-Demo v. Problem D Problem solving and scientific attitude

Lecture versus Independent study

| 1 | Brinkley (1952) | L v. R v. Indiv. classwork |
| | | Stimulated recall of thought |

Lecture versus Enquiry methods

1	Sage (1971)	L v. Enquiry method Problem solving in electronics
2	Selim & Shrigley (1983)	L v. Discovery methods Application of science
3	Fielding et al (1983)	L v. Discovery methods Personal opinions
4	Gunzenhauser (1989)	L+Lab v. Experiential learning
		Integrates knowledge, reduced preconceptions
5	Newsome (1990)	L v. Guided Design Problems, plan patient care

Lectures and Other methods

1	Canelos & Ozbeki (1983)	L v. PSI Difficult problems
2	Newsome (1989)	L v. "Guided design" Nurses' clinical problem solving
3	Ross and Wasicsko (1983)	L+R v. Classroom observation
		Application of principles
4	Nay (1975)	L v. Modelling+Role play
		Application of principles
5	Long (1987)	L v. Clinical simulation Application of process
6	Gist (1989)	L v. Cognitive modelling
		Quantity and diversity of ideas
7	Greenberg & Jewett (1985)	L v. Case presentation Planning treatment
8	Randels et al (1976)	L v. PL+TV Problem solving
9	Smeltzer and Watson (1983)	L v. L + Video-demo Students asked more questions quality of summaries
10	Millett (1969)	L v. L + Video Student-teacher translation tactics
11	Bligh (1970a)	L v. Audiotape MCQ testing synthesis and evaluation
12	Taylor (1987)	L v. L+CAL Seeking information

Studies showing no significant difference

Lecture versus Various Discussion methods

| 1 | Bloom (1953) | L v. D   Stimulated recall of application of knowledge |

Lecture versus Independent study

1	Bligh (1970a)	L v. R MCQ on analysis, synthesis evaluation and application
2	Bligh (1974)	L v. R TFT on application, analysis, synthesis and evaluation
3	Cormier (1976)	L v. R Problem diagnosis, goal setting

Lecture versus Enquiry methods

1	Emese (1993)	L-D v. Discovery v. Discovery+graphic calculators
		Computation and transfer

Lectures and Other methods

1	Canelos & Ozbeki (1983)	L v. PSI	Problems of average difficulty
2	Bligh (1974)	L v. Audiotape	TFT on application, analysis, synthesis and evaluation
3	Cormier (1976)	L v. Slide-tape	Problem diagnosis, goal setting
4	Harding et al (1981)	L v. Slide-tape	Statistical problems
5	Conlin et al (1971)	L v. TV lecture	Application of principles, analysis and synthesis
6	Dixon & Judd (1977)	L+D v. CAL	Performance in statistics
7	Gerardo (1986)	L v. CAL	Learning Fortran
8	Zsiray (1984)	L v. CAL	Library information retrieval
9	Chen (1995)	L+Lab v. CAL/Simulation	Boolean algebra
10	Sadatmand (1995)	L v. CAL	Algebra problems
11	Newman (1996)	L v. Problem Based Learning	Decision making
12	Hancock et al (1983)	L v. Decision orientation	Watson Glaser, Critical Thinking Appraisal
13	Long (1987)	L v. Clinical simulation	Problem solving
14	Smith H.C. (1955)	3 Classes varied in strictness of control	Problem solving
15	Bookman & Iwanicki (1983)	L+D v. No teaching	Problem solving
16	Ross and Wasicsko (1983)	L+R v. Controls	Application of principles
17	Smith (1987)	L v. Lab v. L+Lab	Criticism. Watson Glaser Test

Studies showing lectures are relatively effective to stimulate thought

Lecture versus Various Discussion methods

1	Katz (1990)	L v. D	Problem solving with reflective learning style, time taken
2	Millett (1969)	L v. Unstructured D	Student-teacher translation tactics

Lecture versus Independent study

1	Zsiray (1984)	L v. Independent reading	Library information retrieval

Lecture versus Enquiry methods

1	Fielding et al (1983)	L v. Discovery methods	Application of principles

Lectures and Other methods

None

Appendix to Table 2.4. – Lectures are relatively ineffective for changing attitudes and values

The key for abbreviations is the same as at the head of the Appendix to Table 2.1.

Studies showing lectures are relatively less effective

Lectures versus Discussion methods

1	Barnard (1942)	L+Demo v. Problem-centered D	
		Scientific attitude	
2	Bennett (1955)	L v. Consensus + Indiv decisions in D	
		Expressed willingness to volunteer	
3	Bovard (1951)	Teacher-centered v. Student-centered	
		Application of principles	
4	Casey and Weaver (1956)	L v. D	Minnesota Teacher Attitude Inventory
5	Courtney et al (1994)	L v. D (cooperative learning)	
		Self efficacy.	
6	Gibb and Gibb (1952)	L v. 'Participative action groups'	
		Role flexibility and self insight	
7	Johnson & Smith (1953)	L v. Free-group D	Democratic attitude scale
8	Kelley & Pepitone (1952)	Instructor-centered v.	Ratings of empathy by peers. Student-centered
9	Levine and Butler (1952)	L v. Group decision	Objectivity in supervision of employees
10	Lewin (1943)	L v. D	Behaviour in response to persuasion
11	Metz (1987)	L v. "Interactive instruction"	
		Felt challenged	
12	Mitnick & McGinnies (1958)	L v. D	Delayed attitude test
13	Pederson (1993)	L v. D (Debate)	Understanding suicidal factor
14	Pelz (1958)	L v. D v. control	Implementation of decision
15	Pennington et al (1958)	L v. Group decision by D	
		Opinionnaire	
16	Walton (1968)	L v. Seminar	Willingness to see patient, understand their
			emotional attachments
17	Wanlass et al (1983)	L v. D	Greater tolerance
18	Connolly (1992)	L+D v. D	1/3 groups' questionnaire on retirement
19	Diflorio (1996)	L-D v. Cooperative learning	
		sense of responsibility to others	

Lectures and Other methods

1	Leblanc (1996)	L-D v. Simulation	8 week delayed attitude to elderly
2	Dresner (1989-90)	L v. Simulation game	Game behavior
3	Teevan & Gabel (1978)	L v. Role play	Ratings of empathy, Lister Helper Response
			Inventory
4	Kipper & Ben-Ely (1979)	L v. Psychodrama	Accurate Empathic Scale
5	Selim & Shrigley (1983)	L v. Discovery methods	Scientific attitudes
6	Taylor (1987)	L v. L+CAL	Questionnaire
7	Huthaifi (1989)	L v. CAL	Computer Anxiety Index
8	Walton (1986)	L v PL	Attitude of Arabic speakers to discipline
9	Lee and McLean (1978)	L v. Mastery approach	Attitude improvement

Studies showing no significant difference

Lectures versus Discussion methods

1	Becker & Dallinger (1960)	L v. D	'Liberal democratic' attitudes
2	Bennett (1955)	L v. D	Willingness to volunteer
3	Corey (1967)	L v. D	Authoritarianism, perception of self and others
4	Di Vesta (1954)	L v. D	Leadership skills
5	Eglash (1954)	L v. D v. Free-group D	Rokeach Dogmatism Scale
6	Hill (1960)	L v. D	Liberal attitudes and tolerance of ambiguities, insight
7	Johnson and Smith (1953)	L v. Free-group D	Social sensitivity
8	Kriner & Vaughan (1975)	L v. Structured D L v. Unstructured D	Attitude to drugs
9	Leton (1961)	L v.Case D	Minnesota Teacher Attitude Inventory, Shoben's Parent Attitude Survey
10	Boroffice (1992)	L v. L+D	Attitude to patients
11	Connolly (1992)	L+D v. D	2/3 groups' questionnaire on retirement

Lectures and Other methods

1	Collard (1987)	L v. modified PSI	Aiken & Draper Maths Attitude Scale
2	Barresi & Gigliotti (1975)	L v. No teaching	Pre-post questionnaire no change
3	Kipper & Ben-Ely (1979)	L v. Reflection	Accurate Empathic Scale
4	Russell & Bryant (1987)	L v. Reading	Attitude to mentally retarded
5	Wanlass et al (1983)	L v. L+D v. L+L review	Reduced anxiety
6	Watts (1977)	L v. R+D v. multi-media	Sex Knowledge and Attitude Questionnaire
7	Schoenbaum (1996)	L v. Multimedia+CAL	Attitude posttest
8	Watkins (1996)	L v. Multimedia v. CAL	Allied Health Studies
9	Miller (1996)	L v. CAL	Attitude Towards Women Scale
10	Harrington et al (1990)	L+Demo v. CAL	Computer anxiety
11	Anderson (1982)	L-D v. Values clarification	Survey of Interpersonal Values
12	Bargainnier (1996)	L v. "Active leaning" (unclear)	Condoms as arousing/exciting
13	Leblanc (1996)	L-D v. Simulation	Immediate attitudes to elderly

Studies showing lectures are relatively more effective

Lectures versus Discussion methods

1	Gerberich & Warner (1936)	L v. D	Tests of liberal attitudes
2	Pederson (1993)	L v. D (Debate)	Care for others
3	Wanlass et al (1983)	L v. D	Reduced anxiety
4	Benson (1996)	L+L v. L+D in small groups	Claydon responsibility scores

Lectures and Other methods

1	Costanzo (1992)	L v. Practice	Confidence
2	Kipper & Ben-Ely (1979)	L v. No teaching	Accurate Empathic Scale
3	Wanlass et al (1983)	L v. No teaching	Reduced anxiety

Appendix to Table 2.5. - Lectures are relatively ineffective to stimulate interest in a subject

The key for abbreviations is at the top of the Appendix to Table 2.1.

Studies showing lectures are relatively ineffective to stimulate interest

Lectures versus Discussion methods

1	Asch M.J. (1951)	Lecture v.'Non-directive' D	
		Amount read	
2	Byers and Hedrick (1976)	L v. D (small group)	Greater interest better attendance for D
3	Courtney et al (1994)	L v. D (cooperative learning)	
		Motivation	
4	Geiger (1996)	L v. Cooperative learning groups	
		Engagement with set task	
5	Winteler (1974)	L v. Seminar	Motivation

Lectures versus Other methods

1	Gray et al (1986)	L v. PSI	Interest in the course
2	Sheehy (1989)	L v. PSI	Opting for more maths courses.
3	Rysberg (1986)	L v. L+unit tests+	Less dropout D with proctors
4	Lee & McLean (1978)	L v. L+Mastery	Attitude to subject
5	Taylor V. (1977)	L v. Individualized Instruction	
		Higher completion lower dropout	
6	Rankowski & Galey (1979)	L v. Multi-media	Attitude to subject
7	Williams (1996)	L v. CAL	Course completion
8	Taylor (1987)	L v. L+CAL	Questionnaire, attendance, seeking information
9	Brantley (1974)	L-Demo v. Audio-tutorial coursework	
		Dropout	
10	Hendrix (1968)	L v. Audiotape	Student dropout
11	Milton (1962)	L v. No teaching	Purchase of books

Studies showing no significant difference

Lectures versus Discussion methods

1	Smith D.L. (1995)	L-D v. Cooperative learning	
		Gable-Roberts subject interest Q.Motivated Learning Strategies Q.	
2	Austin (1996)	L v. Cooperative learning	
		Attitude to mathematics	
3	Geiger (1996)	L v. Classroom discourse	
		Engagement with set task	
4	Firstman (1983)	L v. TV + D	Expressed interest dropout rates

Lectures versus Other methods

1	Keeble & Weinman (1986)	L v. TV	Interest, notes taken
2	Flexer (1978)	L v. Lab	Attitude to maths
3	Belzer and Conti (1973)	L v. Audio-tutorial	Attrition rates
4	Oines (1971)	L-Demo v. Self-paced instruction	
		Changes in attitudes to astronomy	
5	Kazanas and Frazier (1982)	L-D v. Performance based instruction	
		Attitudes to subject	
6	Stanton (1994)	L v. CAL	Motivated Learning Strategies Q

| 7 | Dixon & Judd (1977) | L+D v. CAL | Attitude to subject (statistics) |

Studies showing lectures are relatively effective to stimulate interest

Lectures versus Discussion methods

| 1 | Firstman (1983) | L v. TV + D | Attendance rates |

Lectures versus Other methods

1	Houghton (1994)	L v. Correspondence	Interest in the course
2	Caston (1996)	L v. Variety of methods	Attendance
3	Reddy (1989)	L v. CAL	Wilsondisc attitude survey

Appendix to Table 2.6. – Lectures are less popular with students than other methods

Because this table summarizes students' subjective judgements rather than the performance of experimentally controlled groups in specific conditions, the influence of cultural factors on these findings is likely to be stronger than on those reported in the other tables in this chapter. For the Key to abbreviations see Appendix to Table 2.1.

Lectures less popular with students than other methods

Lectures versus PSI related methods

1	Ostrow (1984)	L v. PSI	Immediate preference
2	Tatum and Lenel (1985)	L v. PSI	Preference for PSI in questionnaire
3	Johnson et al (1975)	L v. PSI	Withdrawal rates, student evaluations
4	Jumpeter (1985)	L+Demo v. PSI	Slight preference
5	Gray et al (1986)	L v. PSI	Perceived learning, satisfaction, self esteem, reduced anxiety
6	Coldeway et al (1974)	L. v. PSI	Student ratings v. Contingency management
7	Rysberg (1986)	L v. L+unit tests+D with proctors	Course evaluation
8	Robinson (1995)	L v. Reciprocal peer tutoring	Satisfaction with course
9	Johnson K. A. (1967)	L v. PL	PL took half the time for same learning
10	Jernstedt (1976)	L v. PL	Believed more learning(wrongly), flexible
11	Taylor V. (1977)	L v. Individualized Instruction	Attitude questionnaire
12	Taber (1974)	L v. Individualized Instruction	88% say choose Indiv. Instruction again

Lectures versus Discussion

1	Walton (1968)	L v. Seminar	Rating teaching and knowledge acquired
2	Winteler (1974)	L v. Seminar	Questionnaire
3	Hale Report (1964)	L v. Seminars v. Tutorials	Questionnaire survey
4	McLeish (1968 and 1970)	L v. Seminar v. Tutorial	Agree/disagree questionnaire
5	Stones (1970)	L v. Seminar v. Tutorial	Questionnaire on preferred method
6	Saunders et al (1969)	L v. Seminar v. Tutorial	Ratings as 'very effective', preferred amount of time spent on the methods, criticisms of teachers
7	Ott (1996)	L v. Expert-led reflective D	"Useful, helpful, enjoyment"
8	Burns and Jones (1967)	L v. Lecture-tutorial	Anonymous questionnaire

9	Metz (1987)	L v. "Interactive instruction"	
			Preferred method
10	Lam (1984-5)	L v. D	Interaction, teacher & student sociability, sharing experience
11	Andrews (1996)	L v. Cooperative learning + CAL	
			Enjoyment
12	Austin (1996)	L v. Cooperative learning	Enjoyment, preferred learning groups
13	Mackie (1973)	L v. Student-centred D	Content, instruction, achievement
14	Flood Page (1970)	L v. Small groups v. D	Mean rank order for 'efficiency' and 'enjoyment'
15	Reid-Smith (1969)	L v. Syndicate groups	5-point rating scale
16	Khoiny (1995)	L v. Problem Based Learning	
			Questionnaire, group interview
17	Benson (1996)	L v. L+D in small groups	
			Preference ratings

Lectures versus Other methods

1	Frank and Lesher (1971)	L v. Audiotapes	Prefer the variety of voices on tape
2	Garren & Gathmann (1974)	L + Lab v. Audio-tutorial	Time saved - additional courses possible Ratings on questionnaire
3	Hoffman (1974)	L v. Audiotape + team teaching	
			83% preference on questionnaire
4	Denton et al (1982)	L v. TV	Quantity of information presented.
5	Sox et al (1984)	L v. Video + D + Q & A	Ratings
6	Sherman (1975)	L v. Mixture of methods	Prefer large class with mixture
7	Axeen (1967)	L v. CAL	Less time by students less time by teachers after preparation which took more
8	Whitson (1983)	L v. CAL	Attitude towards instruction
9	Schroeder & Kent (1982)	L+Lab v. CAL	Favorable attitude
10	Saunders et al (1969)	L v. Practicals	Ratings as 'very effective', preferred amount of time spent on the methods, criticisms of teachers
11	Hale Report (1964)	L v. Other methods	Questionnaire survey
12	Marris (1964)	L v. Other teaching methods	
			Standardized interview
13	Isaacs (1973)	L v. Precision teaching	Enjoyment
14	Flood Page (1970)	L v. Demo	Mean rank order for 'efficiency' v. Project lab work and 'enjoyment',
15	Flood Page (1970)	L v. 'Class teaching' and essay	
			Rankings of 'efficiency'
16	Cook (1987)	L v. Self paced multimedia	
			Perceived effectiveness (wrongly)
17	Schoenbaum (1996)	L v. Multimedia+CAL	Satisfaction with delivery method
18	Wilson B. K. (1993)	L v. Independent Study	Kelly's Adjectives Rating Scale interesting and practical

Lectures are as popular with students as other methods.

Lectures versus PSI related methods

1	Friedman et al (1979)	L+D v. PSI	Course completion
2	Collard (1987)	L v. modified PSI	Attrition and dropout
3	Sprenkle & Gillmore (1975)	L v. Mastery Courses	Mastery Instruction Student Rating Form
4	Jone N. W. (1980)	L v. Self paced learning	Satisfaction with course
5	Curry (1984)	L-D v. Individualized Instruction	Attitude to course

Lectures versus Discussion

1	Powell (1988)	L v. D	Self concept scores
2	Reid Smith (1969)	L v. Seminar	5-point rating scale
3	Tillman (1993)	L-D v. Case Study	Course evaluation

Lectures versus Other methods

1	Harding et al (1981)	L v. Tape-slide	Learning system
2	Pohl et al (1982)	L v. TV	Preferred method given
3	Sox et al (1984)	L v. Tutored video instruction	
			Ratings
4	Damsgeegt (1982)	L v. L+Behaviour Modification	
			Attitude to BM
5	Dobson (1987)	L v. Handouts	Ratings of information imparted
6	Flood Page (1970)	L v. 'Class teaching'	Rank order for 'enjoyment'
7	Gauvain (1968)	L v. Factory visits	Postgraduate questionnaire
8	Flexer (1978)	L v. Lab	Evaluation of teaching
9	Gross (1985)	L-D v. Active musical experience	
			Preference
10	Downes (1995)	L+Demo v. Multimedia	Attitude to laboratory experience
11	Brinson (1989)	L v. Game	Judged effectiveness (mistakenly)

Lectures more popular with students than other methods.

Lectures versus PSI related methods

1	Born & Whelan (1973)	L v. PSI	High PSI withdrawal rate (26%)
2	Hinrichsen (1975)	L v. PSI	Stated preference and less lecture dropout
3	Jone N. W. (1980)	L v. Self paced learning	Higher enrolment for course

Lectures versus Discussion

1	Gauvain (1968)	L v. Seminars	Questionnaires to postgraduates

Lectures versus Other methods

1	Bligh (1974)	L v. Audiotapes	Preference ratings
2	Denton et al (1982)	L v. TV	Prefer L for note-taking
3	Firstman (1983)	L v. TV + D	Course evaluation
4	Dobson (1987)	L v. Case study+role-play+	
			Ratings of information imparted clinical interviews+visits
5	Houghton (1994)	L v. Correspondence course	
			Administration perceived as more responsive
6	Flood Page (1970)	L v. Essay work	Mean rank order for 'enjoyment'
7	Thrasher (1972)	L v. Student team teaching	
			Student teaching very unpopular
8	Holmes (1988)	L v. Computer based training	
			Instructors resist poor management support
9	Elliott (1986)	L-Demo v. CAL	Preference
10	Caston (1996)	L v. Variety of methods	Perceived opportunity to succeed

Appendix to Table 2.7. – Personal and social adjustment should not normally be the major objective of lectures

The key to abbreviations is the same as at the top of the Appendix to Table 2.1.

Lectures are less effective to teach personal and social adjustment than other methods

1	Gray et al (1986)	L v. PSI	Reduced anxiety in communication
2	Dziadosz et al (1977)	L v. PSI;	Less anxiety on Anxiety Achievement Test, State-Trait Anxiety Inventory, Test Anxiety Scale
3	Diflorio (1996)	L-D v. Cooperative learning	
		Interview: student relationships	
4	Cabral-Pini (1995)	L v. Cooperative learning	Decreasing math anxiety, inter-racial relations
5	Courtney et al (1994)	L v. D (Cooperative learning);	
		Reduced anxiety	
6	Heverin (1993)	L v. Communication and Problem	
		Marital adjustment Solving (Premarital relationships)	
7	Klein (1983)	L v. Experiential learning	Self efficacy; conflict managemt
8	Camp et al (1994)	L v. Problem based learning;	
		Zung Self-Rating Depression Scale	
9	Asch M.J. (1951)	Ls v. Free-group D;	Minnesota Multiphasic Personality Inventory
10	Wieder (1954)	L-D v. Free-group D;	Covert prejudice on California E-F Scales, measures of 'conventionality' and 'authoritarian-aggression'
11	Dresner (1989-90)	L v. Simulation game;	Social influence
12	Long (1987)	L v. Simulation;	Sympathy for rape victims
13	Earl (1993)	L v. Accelerative learning	
		Confidence in appraisal skills	
14	Wilson B. K. (1993)	L v. Independent Study	Spielberger's State-Trait Anxiety

Lectures and other methods are equally effective to teach personal and social adjustment

1	Bechtel (1963)	L v. Small group D;	Allport Vernon Lindzey Study of Values Bill's Index of adjustment
2	Ruja (1954)	L v. D;	Emotional Stability
3	Brooks (1993)	L v. Cooperative learn v. Private study	
		Health/alcohol locus of control	
4	Wieder (1954)	L-Demo v. Free-group D;	
		Minnesota Multiphasic Personality Inventory and Bill's Index of Adjustment	
5	Timmel (1954)	L v. Group Project v. No teaching;	
		Minnesota Personality Scale	
6	Newsome (1989)	L v. "Guided design"	Nurses' clinical anxiety
7	Young (1986)	L-D v. Audiotapes	Coping and decreasing stress
8	Williams (1996)	L v. CAL	Self concept

Lectures are more effective to teach personal and social adjustment than other methods.

1	Erlich (1979)	L v. D;	Anxiety reduction
2	Wanlass (1983)	L v. D	Decreased sexual guilt

3	Yorde & Witmer (1988)	L+D v. Relaxation by EMG	
			STAI and SSS - stress reduction biofeedback;
4	Tuohimaa et al (1993)	L v. No teaching;	Self report before cadaver dissection.

Appendix to Table 2.8. – Lectures are relatively ineffective to teach behavioral skills

The key to abbreviations is the same as at the top of the Appendix to Table 2.1.

Studies showing lectures less effective to teach behavioral skills than other methods

Lectures versus Practice of skills

1	Saunders et al (1975)	L+D v. Microteaching;	Questioning skills
2	Teevan & Gabel (1978)	L v. Role play;	Counselling skills
3	Willis & Gueldenpfenning (1981)	L v. Skills Practice;	Tutoring skills
4	Evans et al (1989)	L v. Workshop practice;	Interview skills
5	Falvo et al (1991)	L v. Role-modelling;	Simulated patient interaction, communication
6	Flanagan et al (1979)	L v. Role play;	Parents' time-out procedure
7	Hale & Camplese (1974)	L+D v. Mastery method;	Student talk, teaching skills
8	King K. (1980)	L+D v. Modelling;	Teaching skills, eg praising, paraphrasing
9	Adams et al (1980)	L v. Role Play;	Behavior modification techniques
10	Heverin (1993)	L v. Communication, Problem	
			Non-verbal skills Solving (Premarital relationships)
11	Bookman & Iwanicki (1983)	L+D v. Practice problems;	
			Problem solving
12	Costanzo (1992)	L v. Practice;	Interpreting cues.
13	Mussnug (1984)	L v. Competency Based	Visualization; psychomotor skills Vocational Education

Lectures versus Observation

1	Kubany and Sloggett (1991)	L v. Active observation v.	Classroom management
			Passive observation;
2	Randels et al (1976)	L v. PL+TV;	Interviewing, observational skills
3	Brown (1996)	L+R v. Video	Nutritional behavior
4	McGuire (1984)	L v. Video	Use of open-ended questions
5	Millett (1969)	L v. L + Video	Student-teacher translation tactics

Lectures versus Other methods

1	Gray et al (1986)	L v. PSI	Communication skills
2	Connolly (1992)	L+D v. D;	1/3 groups' involvement in preretirement education, behavior change.
3	Courtney et al (1994)	L v. D (cooperative learning);	
			Social cohesion.
4	Howerton (1987)	L+Lab v. Guided discovery;	
			Ability to read computer programs
5	McMinn et al (1991)	Expt 2 L v. CAL;	Use of nonsexist language in 1/3 essays
6	Stenehjem (1986)	L+Demo v, CAL;	Fewer errors in printing practical
7	Mason (1996)	L-D v. Independent Study	
			Texas Academic Skills Prog
8	Merrill (1995)	L+Demo v. Independent Study	
			Cardiac life support skills
9	Earl (1993)	L v. Accelerative learning	
			Soft interpersonal skills

Studies showing lectures equally effective to teach behavioral skills as other methods.

Lectures versus Practice of skills

1	Tomm & Leahey (1980)	L+Demo v. Make your own Demo;
		Interview skills
2	Walker (1985)	L-D v. Role play v. T-Groups
		Verbal; rhetorical sensitivity
3	McGuire (1984)	L v. Role play v. Video Items interview elicited No. words spoken by
		patient
4	Tait (1993)	L v. Role playing (modelling)
		Analogue coding grief facilitation
5	Talbert et al (1975)	L v Modelling v. L+Modelling;
		Teaching techniques
6	Austin & Grant (1981)	L v. L+self video Interview skills with and without feedback;
7	Heverin (1993)	L v. Communication, Problem
		Verbal skills Solving (Premarital relationships)
8	Saunders (1988)	L v. L+Guided clinical practice
		Nurses' physical assessment

Lectures versus Observation

1	Austin & Grant (1981)	L v. L+Demo; Interview skills
2	Tom & Leahey (1980)	L+Demo v. D+Demo; Interview skills
3	Willis & Gueldenpfenning (1981)	L v. Demo; Tutoring skills
4	Flanagan et al (1979)	L v. TV Demo v. R; Parents' time-out procedure
5	Buckley et al (1981)	L v. TV; Clinical skills
6	Pohl et al (1982)	L v. TV; Administration of a medical examination
7	Yorke (1977)	L v. TV; Students' classroom performance
8	O'Neill (1990)	L v. Videodisc Volker Nursing Process Test
9	Swezey et al (1988)	Videotaped L+ practice v. Interactive CAL v. Non-interactive videodisc;
		Electromechanical maintenance
10	Cook (1987)	L v. Self paced multimedia
		Clinical compliance rates
11	Downes (1995)	L+Demo v. Multimedia Nurses' injection skills
12	Koniak (1982)	L-Demo v. Audiotutorial Nursing assistants' skills

Lectures versus Other methods

1	Bennett (1955)	L v. Consensus + Individual
		Acted on willingness to volunteer decisions in D
2	Powell (1988)	L v. D Assertiveness
3	Powell (1987)	L v. D; No change in self concept behavior
4	Diflorio (1996)	L-D v. Cooperative learning
		Interpersonal skills
5	Connolly (1992)	L+D v. D; 2/3 groups' involvement in preretirement
		education, behavior change.
6	Riggio & Throckmorton (1987)	L v. No teaching; Interview skills
7	McMinn et al (1991)	Expt 1 L v. No teaching; Expt 2 L v. CAL;
		Use of nonsexist language. 2/3 essays
8	Seal and Swerissen (1993)	L v. L+prompts v. Contro v. L+prompts+contract;
		Self-reported safety behaviors.
9	Kuna (1975)	L v. L+R; Verbal counseling skills
10	Flexer (1978)	L v. Lab; Effectiveness of student teaching

Studies showing lectures more effective to teach behavioral skills than other methods

Lectures versus Practice of skills
None

Lectures versus Observation

1	Kuna (1975)	L v. L+R+Demo;	Verbal counseling skills
2	McFarland (1982)	L v. D v. Demo	Hazard identification

Lectures versus Other methods

1   Klentz and Beaman (1981)   L v. Mass media campaign;
                                                              Reports of shop lifting
2   Kubany and Sloggett (1991)   L v. Brief instructions v. No teaching;
                                                              Classroom management
3   McMinn et al (1991)   Expt 2 L v. No teaching; Use of nonsexist language in 1/3 essays
4   Millett (1969)   L v. Unstructured D;   Student-teacher translation tactics
5   Benson (1996)   L v. L+D in small groups
                                                              Claydon responsible behavior

References and Bibliography

Abbott, R. D. and Falstrom, P. (1977) Frequent testing and personalized systems of instruction. Contemporary Educational Psychology, July vol.2 no.3 pp.251-257. 269

Abdul-Munim, A. M. (1988) Dissertation Abstracts International, vol.50/03A p.607. 270

Abercrombie, M. L. J. (1960) The Anatomy of Judgment, Hutchinson. 44, 92, 103, 216, 238

Abercrombie, M. L. J. (1978) Aims and Techniques of Group Teaching, Society for Research into Higher Education. 18

Abrami, P. C., Cohen, P. A. and d'Apollonia S. (1988) Implementation problems in meta-analysis. Review of Educational Research vol.58 no.2 pp.151-179. 182

Abrami, P. C., d'Apollonia S. and Cohen, P. A. (1990) Validity of student ratings of instruction: What we know and what we do not. Journal of Educational Psychology vol.82 no.2 pp.219-231. 182, 184

Abrami, P. C., Leventhal, L. and Perry, R. P. (1982) Educational seduction. Review of Educational Research, Fall vol.52 no.3 pp.446-464. 181

Abrami, P. C., Perry, R. P. and Leventhal, L. (1982) The relationship between student personality characteristics, teacher ratings and student achievement. Journal of Educational Psychology vol.74 pp.111-125. 181

Adame, D. D. (1986) Instruction and course content in sex knowledge and attitudes and internal locus of control. Psychological Reports, February vol.58 no.1 pp.91-94. 274

Adams, G. L., Tallon, R. J. and Rimell, P. (1980) A comparison of lecture versus role-playing in the training of the use of positive reinforcement. Journal of Organizational Behavior Management, Summer vol.2 no.3 pp.205-212. 280

Adams, J. A. (1955) A source of decrement in psychomotor performance, Journal of Experimental Psychology, vol. 48, 390-94. 56

Aiken, E. G., Thomas, G. S. and Shennum, W. A. (1975) Memory for a lecture: Effects of notes, lecture rate, and informational density. Journal of Educational Psychology, June vol.67 no.3 pp.439-444. 122, 123, 132, 202

Albanese, M. A., Schuldt, S. S., Case, D. E. and Brown, D. (1991) The validity of lecturer ratings by students and trained observers. Academic Medicine, January vol. 66 no.1 pp.26-28. 152

Anaemena, E. I. (1986) A comparison of andragogy and pedagogy as instructional methodologies toward cognitive achievement in basic electronics in technical colleges of Anambra State of Nigeria. Dissertation Abstracts International-A vol.47 no.03, September p.874. 271

Anderson, T. G. (1982) The effect of a values clarification process on students at Northern Montana College. Dissertation Abstracts International-A vol.43 no.04, October p.1076. 281

Andrews, S. (1996) The effects of a constructivist learning environment on student cognition of mechanics and attitude toward science: a case study (attitudes toward science).

Dissertation Abstracts International-A vol.56 no.08, February p.2981. 272

Annett, J. (1969) Feedback and Human Behaviour, Penguin. 156

Annis, L. F. (1981) Effect of preference for assigned lecture notes on student achievement. Journal of Educational Research, Jan-Feb vol.74 no.3 pp.179-182. 140, 141

Annis, L. F. and Davis J.K. (1977) The effect upon preferred and non-preferred method of various study techniques and cognitive style on recall and recognition. Paper presented at the American Educational Research Association. New York. Available from Prof L Annis. 124

Argyle, M. and Henderson, M. (1985) The anatomy of relationships, Penguin Books. 108

Aronson, E., Turner, J. A., and Carlsmith, J. M. (1963) Communicator credibility and communication discrepancy as determinants of opinion change. Journal of Abnormal and Social Psychology, vol.67 pp.31-6. 219

Asch, M. J. (1951) Nondirective teaching in psychology: an experimental study, Psychological Monographs, vol.65 no.4 pp.1-24 (whole no.321). 275, 277, 282, 285

Asch, S. E. (1951) Effects of group pressure upon the modification and distortion of judgments, in Guetzkow, H. (ed.) Groups, Leadership and Men, Carnegie Press pp.177-90. 14, 18, 220

Austin, D. A. (1996) Effect of cooperative learning in finite mathematics on student achievement and attitude. Dissertation Abstracts International-A vol.56 no.10, April p.3868. 282

Austin, M. F. and Grant, T. N. (1981) Interview training for college students disadvantaged in the labor market: Comparison of five instructional techniques. Journal of Counseling Psychology, January vol.28 no.1 pp.72-75. 287

Ausubel, D. P. (1968) Educational Psychology, a cognitive view. Holt Rinehart and Winston, New York. 17, 86, 134

Awodi, S. (1984) A comparative study of teaching science (biology) as inquiry versus traditional didactic approach in Nigerian secondary schools. (Volumes I and II). Dissertation Abstracts International-A vol.45 no.06, December p.1707. 270

Axeen, M.E. (1967) Teaching library use to undergraduates - comparison of computer-based instruction and the conventional lecture. Illinois University, Urbana. ERIC ED014316. 274, 283

Ayer, W. W. and Milson, J. L. (1993) The effect of notetaking and underlining on achievement in middle school life science. Journal of Instructional Psychology, June vol. 20 no.2 pp.91-95. 147

Baddeley, A. (1996) Human memory: Theory and practice. Lawrence Erlbaum Associates. 34, 35, 38, 42, 103

Badia, P., Harsh, J. and Stutts, C. (1978) An assessment of methods of instruction and measures of ability. Journal of

Personalized Instruction, September vol.3 no.2 pp.69-75. 269

Baggett, J. L., Jnr (1994) A comparison between the use of different concept maps as advance organizers to supplement a unit on photosynthesis in a community college biology course. Dissertation Abstracts International vol.54-A no.08, February p.2969. 128

Bakan, P. (1959) Extroversion, introversion and improvement in an auditory vigilance task. British Journal of Psychology, vol.50 pp.387-9. 54

Baker, G., Baker, C. S. and Blount, H. P. (1974) Effects of taking notes on learning from a lecture. Paper presented at the American Educational Research Association, Chicago. Cited by Hartley J. and Davies I. K. 122, 123

Baker, L. and Lombardi, B. (1985) Students' lecture notes and their relation to test performance. Teaching of Psychology 12 no.1 pp.28-32. 122, 130

Baker, L. J. (1974) Comparison of a lecture course with a Keller course in introductory psychology for university freshmen. Irish Journal of Psychology, Winter vol.2 no.3 pp.183-201. 271

Bakhtar, M. and Brown G. (1988) Styles of lecturing: a study and its implications. Research Papers in Education, vol.3 no.2. pp.131-153. 149, 150

Bane, C. L. (1925) The lecture vs the class-discussion method of college teaching. School and Society, vol.21 pp.300-302. 225, 269, 271

Bane, C. L. (1931) The Lecture in College Teaching, Badger. 225, 269, 271

Barabasz, A. F. (1968) A study of recall and retention of accelerated lecture presentation. Journal of Communication, vol.18 no.3 pp.283-287. 202, 203

Bargainnier, S. S. (1996) A comparison in pedagogy of preventive health measures (condoms). Dissertation Abstracts International vol.56-A no.09, March p.3461. 281

Barnard, J. D. (1942) The lecture-demonstration versus the problem-solving method of teaching of a college science course, Science Education, vol.26 pp.121-32. 14, 275, 278, 280

Barnard, W. H. (1936) Note on the comparative efficacy of lecture and socialized recitation versus group study method. Journal of Educational Psychology, vol.27 pp.388-390. 272

Barnes, N. R., MacArthur, D. and Ballantine, P. R. (1983) A comparison of alternative techniques of instruction. South African Journal of Psychology, March vol.13 no.1 pp.6-9. 48, 68

Barnett, S. A. (1958) An experiment with free discussion groups. Universities Quarterly, vol.12 pp.175-80. 216

Barresi, C. M. and Gigliotti, R. J. (1975) Are drug education programs effective? Journal of Drug Education, vol.5 no.4 pp.301-316. 280

Barrett, J. E., Di Vesta, F. J. and Rogozinski, J. T. (1981) What is learned in note-taking? Journal of Educational Psychology vol.73 no.2 pp.181-192. 125

Barrington, H. (1965) A survey of instructional television researches. Educational Research, vol.8 no.1 pp.8-25. 53

Bassey, M. (1968) Learning methods in tertiary education, Nottingham Regional College of Technology, internal paper. 46, 47

Batson, C. D. and Johnson, A. (1976) Arousing intrinsic motivation as a goal for introductory classes: A case study.

Teaching of Psychology; vol.3 no.4 December pp.155-159. 46

Beach, L. R. (1960) Sociability and academic achievement in various types of learning situations, Journal of Educational Psychology, vol.51 pp.208-212. 269, 272, 273, 275

Bean, T. W., Searles, D., Singer, H. and Cowen, S. (1990) Learning concepts from biology text through pictorial analogies and ananological study guide. Journal of Educational Research, Mar-Apr vol.83 no.4 pp.233-237. 94

Beard, R. M., Levy, P. M., and Maddox, H. (1964) Academic performance at university. Educational Review, vol.16 no.3 pp.163-174. 63

Beard, R. M. (1967) On evaluating the success of teaching. British Journal of Medical Education, vol.1 no.4 pp.296-302. 156

Beard, R. M. (1970) Teaching and Learning in Higher Education, Penguin. 48, 170

Beard, R. M. and Pole, K. (1971) Content and purpose of biochemistry examinations. British Journal of Medical Education vol.15 pp.13-21. 25

Bechtel, L. P. (1963) Comparative Effects of Differentiated Teaching Methods on Certain Personality Characteristics of College Students, doctoral dissertation, New York University. 285

Becker, S. L. and Dallinger, C. A. (1960) The effect of instructional methods upon achievement and attitudes in communication skills. Speech Monographs, vol.27 pp.70-76. 271, 280

Behr A.L. (1988) Exploring the lecture method: an empirical study. Studies in Higher Education, vol.13 no.2 pp. 189-200. 154

Beighley, K. C. (1954) An experimental study of three speech variables on listener comprehension. Speech Monographs, vol.21 pp.248-253. 83

Beilin, R. and Rabow J. (1979) Effects of ethnicity and course structure on factual learning and critical ability. Annual Meeting of the American Sociological Association, Boston. August. 22pp. ERIC ED180902. 270, 273, 275

Bell, L. G. (1983) Effects of metaphorical communication on the acquisition, retention, and transfer of counselor goal-setting skills. Dissertation Abstracts International vol.44-A no.03 September p.670. 94

Belzer T.J. and Conti M.R. (1973) A comparison of grades achieved, attrition rates, and teacher evaluation in a traditional general biology course versus a non-traditional, audio-tutorial biology course. Nova University. ERIC ED094810. 274, 282

Bennett, E. B. (1955) Discussion, decision, commitment and consensus in "group decision". Human Relations, vol.8 pp.251-73. 18, 280, 287

Benson, S. B. (1996) A comparison of the effects of short-term small groups and lectures on the knowledge, attitudes and behavior of pharmacy students concerning alcohol / alcoholism. Dissertation Abstracts International vol.57-A no.06, December p.2353. 18, 271, 281, 288

Bentley, D. A. and Blount, H. P. (1980) Testing the spaced lecture for the college classroom. Paper to the Annual Meeting of the Georgia Psychological Association, Macon GA. 122, 124, 125

Benton, S. L., Kiewra, K. A., Whitfill, J. M. and Dennison, R. (1993) Encoding and external storage effects on writing processes. Journal of Educational Psychology, June vol.85 no.2 pp.267-280. 124, 129

Berliner, D. C. (1969) Effects of test-like events and notetaking on learning from lecture instruction. Paper to American Psychological Association, Washington D.C. 122,

Berliner, D. C. (1971) Aptitude-treatment interactions in two studies of learning from lecture instruction. Paper to American Educational Research Association. New York. 122

Berliner, D. C. (1972) The generalizability of aptitude-treatment interactions across subject matter. Paper to American Educational Research Association. Chicago. 122

Berlyne, D. E. (1960) Conflict, arousal and curiosity. McGraw-Hill. 67

Berry, R. (1965) Rapid reading reconsidered. Education, March, p.556. 146

Betts, D. S., and Walton, A. J. (1970) A lecture match, or "Anything you can do, I can do better". Physics Education, vol.5 no.6 pp.321-325. 52, 206, 254

Bhushan, A. and Sharma, R. D. (1975) Effect of three instructional strategies on the performance of B.Ed. student-teachers of different intelligence levels. Indian Educational Review, July vol.10 no.2 pp.24-29. 275

Biegert, L. E. and Withrow, M. J. (1978) A comparison of the effectiveness of individualized and traditional instruction methods for student nurses. ACT 24pp ERIC ED160140. 274

Bills, R. E. (1952) An investigation of student centred teaching, Journal of Educational Research, vol.46 pp.313-319. 272

Black, P. J. (1968) University examinations. Physics Education, vol.3 no.2. 25

Blackwood, H. and Trent, C. (1968) A comparison of the effectiveness of face-to-face and remote teaching in communicating educational information to adults. Extension Study 4. ERIC ED028324. 274

Bligh, D. A. (1970a) A pilot experiment to test the relative effectiveness of three kinds of teaching method. Research in Librarianship, vol.3 no.15 pp.88-93. 273, 278

Bligh, D. A. (1970b) Gropings for a design of objective tests of the effectiveness of teaching methods. University Teaching Methods Unit, University of London. 185

Bligh, D. A. (1970c) An experiment to compare the teaching effectiveness of a tape-recorded lecture at three speeds of delivery, unpublished ms. 201, 202

Bligh, D. A. (1974) Are varied teaching methods more effective? Doctoral Dissertation, University of London, 634pp. 41, 100, 184-190, 214, 273, 274, 278, 279, 285

Bligh, D. A. (1975) Improving teacher performance later in the day. In: Improving university teaching. Proceeedings of an International Conference held at the University of Maryland, Heidelberg. 59

Bligh, D. A. (1997) Explanatory Shifts, http://www.dcs.ex.ac.uk/~donald/explain. 112-119

Bloom, B. S. (1953) Thought-processes in lectures and discussions, Journal of General Education, vol.7 pp.160-169. 14, 16, 87, 275, 277, 278

Bloom, B. S. (ed.) (1956) Taxonomy of Educational Objectives: I. Cognitive Domain, Longman. 189

Bond, B. W. (1956) Group discussion-decision: An appraisal of its use in health education. Minnesota Department of Health. Reported in Ruth Eckert, Colleges and universities -

Programs, in Harris, C. W. (Ed) Encyclopedia of Educational Research, 3rd edn. 1960, College and University Programs. 269, 277

Bonwell, C.C. and Eison, J.A. (1991) Active learning: creating excitement in the classroom. Unpublished. ERIC no.ED340272. 225, 230

Bookman, A. B. and Iwanicki, E. F. (1983) The effects of method of test preparation on standardized mathematics achievement test performance. Journal of Research and Development in Education, Summer vol.16 no.4 pp.46-51. 279, 286

Boreham, N. C. (1984) Personality factors related to self-reported lapse of attention during lectures. Psychological Reports, August vol.55 no.1 pp.76-78. 50

Boreham, N. C. and Lilley, J. D. (1978) Scales to measure listening behavior during lectures. Perceptual and Motor Skills, October vol.47 no.2 pp.673-674. 50

Born, D. G. and Whelan, P. (1973) Some descriptive characteristics of student performance in PSI and lecture courses. Psychological Record, vol.23 no 2 Spring pp.145-152. 284

Boroffice, O. B. (1992) Fostering medical compliance in some Nigerian sickle cell disease patients. Journal of Applied Rehabilitation Counseling, Spring vol.23 no.1 pp.33-37. 280

Bourgeois, W. M. (1996) The impact of peer tutoring and lecture methods in urban college developmental mathematics courses on student academic performance. Dissertation Abstracts International vol.56-A no.10, April p.3868. 271

Bovard, E. W. (1951) The psychology of classroom interaction. Journal of Educational Research, vol.45 pp.215-24. 280

Bowles, C. R. (1982) Teaching practices of two-year college science and humanities instructors. Community/Junior College Quarterly of Research and Practice vol.6 (January - March) pp.129-144. 6

Bramki, D. and Williams R. (1984) Lexical familiarisation in economics text books, Reading in a Foreign Language vol.2 no.1 pp.169-181. 99

Brant, G., Hooper, E. and Sugrue, B. (1991) Which comes first the simulation or the lecture? Journal of Educational Computing Research; vol.7 no.4 pp.469-481 225

Brantley, W. T. (1974) A comparison of the audio-tutorial method with the lecture-demonstration method for producing student achievement in college level physical science survey classes covering physics and astronomy. Ed.D Dissertation University of Southern Mississippi, ERIC ED107322. 276, 282

Brinkley, S. G. (1952) Mental activity in college classes: student estimates of relative value of ten learning situations, Journal of Experimental Education, vol.20 pp.373-8. 277, 278

Brinson, S. A. T. B. (1989) A comparison of two teaching methods: a game and a lecture to review mandatory workplace safety in acute care hospitals. Dissertation Abstracts International vol.49-A no.07, January p.1680. 271

Broadbent, D. E. (1970) Review lecture, Proceedings of the Royal Society, vol.1, 175 B pp.333-50. 33, 41, 46

Brobst, K. E. (1996) The process of integrating information from two sources, lecture and text (reading, comprehension, memory). Dissertation Abstracts International vol.57-A no.05, November p.1957. 122

Brooks, V. S (1993) Alcohol education pedagogy: effects on knowledge and locus-of-control (health knowledge). Dissertation Abstracts International vol.53-A no.07, January p.2256. 275, 276, 285

Brown, D. E. and Clement, J. (1989) Overcoming misconceptions via analogical reasoning: Abstract transfer versus explanatory model construction. Instructional Science, December vol.18 no.4 pp.237-261. 93

Brown, F. L (1996) A comparison of two instructional methods aimed at modifying nutritional behaviors and attitudes of elderly African-Americans in Northeastern Ohio. Dissertation Abstracts International vol.56-A no.12, June p.4666. 286

Brown, G. A., Bakhtar, M. and Youngman, M. B. (1984) Toward a typology of lecturing styles. British Journal of Educational Psychology, vol.54 no.1 Feb. pp.93-100. 152

Brown, G.A. (1968) Lecturing and Explaining. Methuen, London. 134pp.

Browne, M. N., Hoag, J. H. and Berilla, B. (1995) Critical thinking in graduate programs: Faculty perceptions and classroom behavior. College Student Journal, March vol.29 no.1 pp.37-43. 225

Bryant, J., Comiski, P. W. Cime J. S. and Zillmann D. (1980) The relationship between college teachers' use of humor in the class room and students' evaluations of their teachers, Journal of Educational Psychology vol.72 no.4 pp.511-519. 96

Buck, L. (1963) Errors in the perception of railway signals, Ergonomics, vol.6 no.2 pp.181-92. 54

Buckley, K., Plaut, S. M. and Ruley, E. J. (1981) Teaching home monitoring of blood pressure to adolescents. Adolescence, Winter vol.16 no.64 pp.881-889. 287

Burke, H. R. (1955) An experimental Study of Teaching Methods in a College Freshman Orientation Course, doctoral dissertation, Boston University. Dissertation Abstracts, vol.16 pp.77-78. 68, 275

Burns, R. S. and Jones, R. C. (1967) Two experimental approaches to freshman composition - lecture-tutorial and team teaching. Central Missouri State College, Warrensburg. ERIC ED510214. 277, 283

Busan, T. (1974) Use your head. British Broadcasting Corporation. 126

Bussett G.M. (1965) A comparison of knowledge gained by adults when presentations are followed by discussion led by local volunteer and professional leaders with a positive or negative attitude toward the discussion task. PhD. Dissertation. Ann Arbor University. Michigan. 276

Byers W. S. and Hedrick R. E. (1976) A comparison of two teaching strategies: lecture vs. discussion in a small class environment at Florida Southern College, Report ERIC ED136741. 275, 282

Cabral-Pini, A. M. (1995) Cooperative learning: its effect on math education. Dissertation Abstracts International-A vol.55 no.12, June p.3772. 277, 285

Camorosano, J. R., and Santapolo, F. A. (1958) Teaching efficiency and class size, School and Society, September pp.338-41. 204

Camp, C. C. (1993) A comparison of the math anxiety and

math self-efficacy constructs. Dissertation Abstracts International-B vol.53 no.12, June p.6541. 276

Camp, D. L., Hollingsworth, M. A., Zaccaro, D. J., Cariaga L. L. D. et al (1994) Does a problem based learning curriculum affect depression in medical students? Academic Medicine, October vol.69 no.10, Suppl pp.S25-S27. 285

Campbell, J. O. and Lison, C. A. (1995) New technologies for assessment training. College Student Journal, March vol. 29 no.1 pp.26-29. 230, 249

Canelos, J. and Ozbeki, M. A. (1983) Application of the Keller instructional strategy of personalized instruction for the improvement of problem solving learning in technical education. Journal of Instructional Psychology, June vol.10 no.2 pp.61-69. 278

Cannon, S. B. (1985) The comparison of two instructional methods for mastery of eight selected communication constructs in a course for registered nurses. Dissertation Abstracts International-A vol.46 no.04, October p.881. 27

Carlsen, W. S. (1993) Teacher knowledge and discourse control: Quantitative evidence from novice biology teachers' classrooms. Journal of Research in Science Teaching, May vol.30 no.5 pp.471-481. 153

Carlson, C. R. (1953) A study of the relative effectiveness of lecture and directed discussion methods of teaching tests and measurements to prospective Air Force Instructors, Dissertation Abstracts, vol.13 pp.112-13. 271

Caro, P. W. Jnr (1962) The effect of class attendance and "time structured" content on achievement in general psychology, Journal of Educational Psychology, vol.53 pp.76-80.

Carpenter, F. (1956) Educational significance of studies on the relation between rigidity and problem solving, Science Education, vol.40 pp.296-311. 278

Carrç C. G. (1969) Audio-tutorials as adjuncts to formal lecturing in biology teaching at the tertiary level, Journal of Biological Education, vol.3 no.1 pp.57-64. 248

Carrier, C.A. and Titus A. (1981) Effects of note-taking pretraining and test mode expectations on learning from lectures. American Educational Research Journal, vol.18 no.4 pp.385-397. 121, 137

Carter, J. F. and Van Matre, N. H. (1975) Note taking versus note having. Journal of Educational Psychology, vol.67 no.6 December pp.900-904. 123, 124, 125

Carter, L. D. (1995) Effectiveness of case-based method versus traditional lecture in the retention of athletic training knowledge. Dissertation Abstracts International-A vol.56 no.06, December p.2164. 270, 272

Cartmell, A. E. (1971) The use of CCTV in the assessment of teacher effectiveness, Programmed Learning and Educational Technology, vol.8 no.3 pp.173-85. 169

Casey, J. E., and Weaver, B.E. (1956) An evaluation of lecture method and small group method of teaching in terms of knowledge of content, teacher attitude, and social status, Journal of Colorado-Wyoming Academy of Science, vol. 4, p.54. 272, 280

Caston, J. J. (1996) The relationship between community college instructor use of a teaching repertoire and successful course completion. Dissertation Abstracts International-A vol.56 no.09, March p.3424. 283, 285

Catts, D.C. (1987) The effects of teaching listening versus note-taking strategies on lecture performance and note-taking strategy awareness of underprepared college students,

Dissertation Abstracts International vol.48-A No.11 p.2816. 122, 123,

Cavanagh, S. J., Hogan, K. and Ramgopal, T. (1995) The assessment of student-nurse learning styles using the Kolb Learning Styles Inventory. Nurse Education Today, vol.15 no.3 pp.177-183. 150

Chaudron, C. and Richards, J. C. (1986) The effect of discourse markers on the comprehension of lectures. Applied Linguistics vol.7 no.2 Summer pp.113-127. 84

Chen, F-S. (1996) A computer tutorial and simulation system for teaching digital function minimization. Dissertation Abstracts International-A vol.56 no.07, January p.2541. 271, 279

Chmielewska, E. (1976) The effects of a lecture as a function of plan presentation. Polish Psychological Bulletin, vol.7 no.2 pp.105-114. 139, 140

Chu, G. C. and Schramm, W. (1967) Learning from television: what the research says, Stanford University Institute for Communication Research. 12

Churchill, R., and John, P. (1958) Conservation of teaching time through the use of lecture classes and student assistants, Journal of Education Psychology, vol.49 pp.324-327. 272

Churchill, R. D. (1960) Evaluation of independent study in college courses, doctoral dissertation, University of Minnesota. 272

Cicirelli, V. G. (1969) University supervisors' creative ability and their appraisal of student teachers' classroom performance: an exploratory study, Journal of Educational Research, vol.62 no.8, 375-81. 169

Clark, G. K., and Clark, E. B. (1957) The Art of Lecturing, Heffers. 88

Coats, W. D., and Smidchens, U. (1966) Audience recall as a function of speaker dynamism, Journal of Educational Psychology, vol.57 no.4, 189-191. 64, 67, 107, 261, 265

Cohen, A. R. (1964) Attitude change and social influence, Basic Books. 18, 218-221

Cohen, P. A. (1981) Student ratings of instruction and student achievement: a meta-analysis of multisection validity studies. Review of Educational Research vol.51 pp.281-309. 182, 184

Coldeway, D. O. et al (1974) Comparison of small-group contingency management with the personalized system of instruction and the lecture system. Conference on Research and Technology in College Teaching. Chicago, Illinois. ERIC ED096978. 269, 282

Collard, G. L. (1987) Lecture versus modified personalized system of instruction: differences in student achievement, attrition, and other selected variables. Dissertation Abstracts International, vol.49-A no.07 p.1681. 271, 280, 284

Collard, T. Y. (1994) "Hello ... Hello? Is anybody listening?": teacher as listener in the classroom. Paper presented to the International Listening Association, Boston. ED371413. 225, 230

Collier, K. G. (1966) An experiment in university teaching, Universities Quarterly, vol.20 no.3, pp.336-348. 69

Collingwood, V. and Hughes, D. C. (1978) Effects of three types of university lecture notes on student achievement. Journal of Educational Psychology, vol 70 no.2 pp.175-179. 138, 140

Conlin, B. J. et al (1971) The comparison of telelecture and

regular lecture in the trans fer of knowledge to adults, Minnesota ERIC ED070946. 274, 279

Connolly, J. (1992) Participatory versus lecture/discussion preretirement education: a comparison. Educational Gerontology, vol.18 no.4 pp.365-379. 272, 275, 280, 287

Cook, S. A. (1987) A comparison of two instructional formats for orienting new student clinicians to a psychology training clinic. Dissertation Abstracts International-B vol.48 no.01, July p.293. 284, 287

Cooper, S. M. (1995) Content decision making through two teaching methods: Simulations/traditional lectures and their effectiveness on students' achievement in social studies classes, Masters' Abstracts International vol.33 no.04 August p.1042. 274

Corey, G. F. (1967) An investigation of the Outcomes of an Introductory Psychology Course in a Junior College, doctoral dissertation, University of Southern California, School of Education. 280

Corey, S. M. (1934) Learning from lectures versus learning from reading, Journal of Educational Psychology, vol. 25 pp.459-70. 64, 276

Corman, B. R. (1957) The effect of varying amounts and kinds of information as guidance in problem solving, Psychological Monographs, vol.71 no.2, (whole no.431). 13, 209

Cormier, W. H., Cormier, L. S., Zerega, W. D. and Wagamann, G. L. (1976) Effects of learning modules on the acquisition of counseling strategies. Journal of Counseling Psychology, March vol.23 no.2 pp.136-141. 270, 278, 279

Correa, H. (1994) Optimal allocation of time between lectures and examinations for student motivation. Scientia Paedagogica Experimentalis, vol.31,no.1 pp.87-100. 67

Costanzo, M. (1992) Training students to decode verbal and nonverbal cues: Effects on confidence and performance. Journal of Educational Psychology, September vol.84 no.3 pp.308-313. 281, 286

Costin, F. (1972) Lecturing versus other methods of teaching: a review of research, British Journal of Educational Technology, vol.3 no.1, January pp.4-31 6

Costin, F. Greenough W. T. and Menges R. J. (1971) Student ratings of college teaching: reliability, validity and usefulness. Review of Educational Research, vol.41 pp.511-536. 180

Couch, R.W. (1983) Individualized instruction: a review of audio-tutorial instruction, guided design, the personalized system of instruction, and individualized lecture classes. Ph.D. Dissertation, University of Kansas. ERIC no.ED252178. 230

Courtney, D. P., Courtney, M. and Nicholson, C. (1994) The effect of cooperative learning as an instructional practice at the college level. College Student Journal, December vol.28 no.4 pp.471-477. 272, 280, 282, 285, 287

Craik, F. I. M. and Lockhart, R. S. (1972) Levels of processing: a framework for memory research, Journal of Verbal Learning and Verbal Behavior, vol.11 pp.671-684. 39

Cranton, P. and Smith R. A. (1990) Reconsidering the unit of analysis: A model of student ratings of instruction. Journal of Educational Psychology, vol.82 no.2 pp.207-212. 177

Crawford, C. C. (1925a) The correlation between college lecture notes and quiz papers, Journal of Educational Research vol.12 pp.282-291. 122, 123, 124, 130

Crawford, C. C. (1925b) Some experimental studies of the results of college note-taking, Journal of Educational Research vol.12 pp.379-386. 122, 123, 131

Creswell, K.W. and Lin C.A. (1989) Effects of televised lecture presentation styles on student learning. Journal of Educational Television, vol.15 no.1 pp.37-52. 67

Cross, M. Z. and Semb, G. (1976) An analysis of the effects of personalized instruction on students at different initial performance levels in an introductory college nutrition course. Journal of Personalized Instruction, March vol.1 no.1 pp.47-50. 269, 271

Cryer P. (1988) Video feedback sessions for improving lecturing: participants' reactions to this method of academic staff development. Programmed Learning and Educational Technology, vol.25 no.2 207

Culbertson, F. M. (1957) Modification of an emotionally held attitude through role playing, Journal of Abnormal and Social Psychology, vol.54 pp.230-33. 18

Curry, W. J. (1984) A comparison of the achievement and course attitudes of low-ability students taught by two methods of instruction in personal finance classes (Georgia; consumer competencies). Dissertation Abstracts International vol.45-A no.05, November p.1274. 271, 284

Daines, J. M. and Brown, G. A. (1983) Evaluating a training programme on lecturing. In: Aspects of Educational Technology, vol 15, Improving Efficiency in Education and Training, ed. Trott A., Strongman H. and Giddens L. Proceedings of 15th annual conference of AETT. 206

Damsteegt, D. C. (1982) Self-management and instruction in behavioral analysis. Psychological Reports, August vol.51 no.1 p.288. 271, 284

Dansereau, D.F., McDonald, B. A., Collins, K. W., Garland, J., Holley, C. D., Diekoff, G. M. and Evans, S. H. (1979) Evaluation of a learning strategy system, in O'Neil, H. F. and Spielberger, C. D. (Eds) Cognitive and affective learning strategies. Academic Press, New York. 126

Davies, B. (1976) Physics lectures and student notes. Physics Education, vol.11 no.1 pp.33-36. 130

Davis, W. K., Oh, M. S., Anderson, R. M., Gruppen, L. and Nairn, R. (1994) Influence of a highly focused case on the the effect of small-group facilitators' content expertise on students' learning and satisfaction. Academic Medicine, vol.69 no.8 pp.663-669. 246

Davy, S. and Dunkel, P. (1989) The heuristic of lecture note-taking: perceptions of American and international students regarding the value and practice of note-taking. English for Specific Purposes, vol 8 no.1 pp.33-50. 120, 124, 131

Dawson, M. D. (1956) Lecture vs problem-solving in teaching elementary social sciences. Science Education, vol. 40 pp.395-404. 14, 270, 275, 278

De Cecco, J. P. (1964) Class size and co-ordinated instruction, British Journal of Education Psychology, vol.34 pp.65-74. 204

DeCarrico, J. and Nattinger J. R. (1988) Lexical phrases for the comprehension of academic lectures. English for Specific Purposes, vol.7 no.2 pp.91-102. 104, 107

Deignan, F. J. (1956) A comparison of the effectiveness of two group discussion methods, Dissertation Abstracts, vol. 16 pp.1110-11. 272

Denton, J. J. et al. (1982) Assessing instructional strategies and resulting student attitudes regarding two-way television instruction. Unpublished. ERIC no.ED259709. 283, 285

Deutsch, M. (1949) Experimental study of effects of co-operation and competition upon group process, Human Relations, vol.3 pp.199-231. 68

Di Vesta, F. J. (1954) Instructor-centred and student-centred approaches in teaching human relations courses, Journal of Applied Psychology, vol.38 pp.329-335. 272, 280

Di Vesta, F. J. and Gray, G. S. (1972) Listening and note-taking. Journal of Educational Psychology vol.63 pp.8-14. 38, 122, 124,

Di Vesta, F. J. and Gray, G. S. (1973) Listening and note-taking II. Journal of Educational Psychology vol.64 pp.278-287. 122

Di Vesta, F. J. and Smith, D. A. (1979) The pausing principle: Increasing the efficiency of memory for on going events. Contemporary Educational Psychology, July vol.4 no.3 pp.288-296. 235

Diemer R. M. and Mazzocco D. M. (1974) A comparison between lecture and independent study methods of instruction in dental radiology with provision for individual differences. ERIC ED101130. 273

Dieterle, D. A. (1985) A comparative study: simulation method and lecture reading method effects on economic knowledge and attitude in teacher economic education, Dissertation Abstracts International, vol.47/02A page 387. 274

Diflorio, I. A. S. (1996) Cooperative learning: a study of nursing students' achievement and perceptions. Dissertation Abstracts International-A vol.56 no.09, March p.3431. 271, 280, 285, 287

Dixon, P. N. and Judd, A. (1977) A comparison of computer managed instruction and lecture mode for teaching basic statistics. Journal of Computer Based Instruction, August vol.4 no.1 pp.22-25. 279, 282

Dobson, B. E. (1987) Medical student opinion of methods used to teach child and adolescent psychiatry. Medical Education, March vol.21 no.2 pp.143-150. 284, 285

Dorsel, T. N. (1976) The effect of preference for method and type of method of comprehension of verbal material. Journal of Experimental Education, Fall vol.45 no.1 pp.30-33. 270

Dorward, N. and Wiedemann P. (1977) An evaluation of the mass lecture as a teaching technique in first-year economics. Economics, vol.13, pt.4 pp.110-111. 204

Dowell, D. A. and Neal, J. A. (1982) a selective review of the validity of student ratings of teaching, Journal of Higher Education vol.53 pp.51-62. 182

Dowell, D. A. and Neal, J. A. (1983) The validity and accuracy of student ratings of instruction: a reply to Peter Cohen. Journal of Higher Education vol.54 pp.459-463. 182

Downes, L. A. (1995) The effects of multimedia presentation on cognitive learning and psychomotor performance of intramuscular injection technique and nursing students' attitudes toward learning. Dissertation Abstracts International vol.56-A no.05, November p.1673. 271, 284, 287

Downs, V. C., Javidi, M. M. and Nussbaum, J. F. (1988) An analysis of teachers' verbal communication within the college classroom: Use of humor, self-disclosure, and narratives. Communication Education, vol. 37 no.2 April pp.127-141 96

Drake, M. A. (1987) The effects of the traditional lecture method of instruction and the personalized system of instruction on acquisition and retention of knowledge in a nutrition class, Dissertation Abstracts International, vol.48-A no.10 p.2524. 269

Dresner, M. (1989-90) Changing energy end use patterns as a means of reducing global warming trends. Journal of Environmental Education, vol.21 no.2 Winter pp.41-46. 280, 285

Drew, C. P. (1990) Are you spoon-feeding your students? A paper on facilitating a collaborative learning experience. Unpublished. ERIC no.ED324046. 225, 230

Dubes, M. J. (1987) Comparison of lecture, discussion and poster modes of instruction of adults ages 59 to 90 attending nutrition sites, Dissertation Abstracts International, vol.49-A no.06 page 1344. 271, 272

Dubin, R., and Taveggia, T. C. (1968) The teaching-learning paradox, Center for the Advanced Study of Educational Administration, Monograph no.18, University of Oregon. 11, 13, 142

Dubin, R. and Hedley, R. A. (1969) The medium may be related to the message: college instruction by TV. Eugene Oregon. Center for the study of Advanced Study of Educational Administration. 12

Dudley-Evans, A. and Johns, T. F. (1981) A team teaching approach to lecture comprehension for overseas students. The teaching of listening comprehension pp.30-46. The British Council, London. 149

Dunn, W. R. (1969) Programmed learning news, feedback devices in university lectures, New University, vol. 3 no. 4 pp.21-22. 15, 161

Dutt, K. M (1994) The cognitive and affective outcomes of cooperative learning in four college education courses (cognitive outcomes). Dissertation Abstracts International-A vol.54 no.08, February p.2986. 272

Dziadosz, T. H., Curran, J. P. and Santogrossi, D. A. (1977) Personalized instruction and the attenuation of test anxiety. Journal of Personalized Instruction, December vol.2 no.4 pp.194-198. 285

Earl, G. B. (1993) A comparison of accelerative learning and lecture methods on managerial retention and training transfer. Dissertation Abstracts International vol.54-B no.04, October p.2254. 275, 285, 287

Eglash, A. (1954), A group discussion method of teaching psychology, Journal of Educational Psychology, vol.45 pp.257-267. 272, 280

Ehlers, S. B. (1986) The influence of age and learning style on achievement: modified mastery learning teaching techniques vs. traditional lecture method in college algebra classes on a community college campus. Dissertation Abstracts International, vol.47-A no.08 page 2862. 269

Einstein, G. O., Morris, J. and Smith, S. (1985) Note-taking, individual differences, and memory for lecture information. Journal of Educational Psychology; October vol.77 no.5 pp.522-532. 122, 130

Eisner, S. and Rohde, K. (1959) Note-taking during and after the lecture, Journal of Educational Psychology vol.50 pp.301-304. 123, 132

Ekman, P. and Friesen, W. V. (1969) Categories, origins, usage and coding: the basis for five categories of non-verbal behavior, Semiotica vol.1 pp.49-98. 108

Elliott, G. E. (1986) A comparison of two instructional methods for teaching microcomputer competencies to extension personnel in Mississippi. Dissertation Abstracts International-A vol.46 no.10, April p.2894. 274, 285

Ellis, A. W. and Young, A. W. (1988) Human cognitive neuropsychology, Lawrence Erlbaum Associates, London. 36, 39

Ellis, L. and Mathis, D. (1985) College student learning from televised versus conventional classroom lectures: A controlled experiment. Higher Education; vol.14 pp.165-173. 274

Elsberry, J. B. (1995) A comparison of selected variables of instructional choice and achievement between group lecture method and facilitated self-paced method in college health science physics. Dissertation Abstracts International-A vol.55 no.07, January p.1790. 273

Elton, L. R. B. (1970), The use of duplicated notes and self-tests in university teaching, paper read at the 1970 National Conference of the Association for Programmed Learning and Educational Technology. 15, 142, 163, 210

Emese, G. L. (1993) The effects of guided discovery style teaching and graphing calculator use in differential calculus (discovery learning, calculus). Dissertation Abstracts International-A vol.54 no.02, August p.450. 273, 278

English S. L. (1985) Kinetics in academic lectures. ESP Journal; Vol.4 no.2. pp.161-170. 108

Entwistle, N. J., and Wilson, J. D. (1970), Personality study methods and academic performance, Universities Quarterly, vol.24 no.2 pp.147-56. 63

Entwistle, N. J. and Entwistle, D. (1970), The relationships between personality study methods and academic performance, British Journal of Educational Psychology, vol.40 no.2 pp.132-43. 63

Entwistle, N. J. and Marton, F. (1994) Knowledge objects: understandings constituted through intensive academic study. British Journal of Educational Psychology. vol.64 no.1 pp.161-178. 128

Erlich, R. (1979) Anxiety reduction in small groups learning and in frontal instruction classroom. Israeli Journal of Psychology and Counseling in Education; February No 1038-44. 22, 286

Erskine, C. A. and Tomkin, A. (1963), Evaluation of the effect of group-discussion method in a complex teaching programme, Journal of Medical Education, vol.38, December pp.1036-42. 269, 272, 278

Erskine, C. A. and O'Morchoe, C. C. C. (1961), Research on teaching methods: its significance for the curriculum, Lancet, vol.23 pp.709-711. 198

Ertwine, D. R. (1984) The Thayer concept versus traditional lecture instruction: a comparison of two teaching methods at the United States military academy (chemistry). Dissertation Abstracts International vol.44-B no.09, March p.2729. 271

Evans, B. J., Stanley, R. O., Burrows, G. D. and Sweet, B. (1989) Lectures and skills workshops as teaching formats in a history-taking skills course for medical students. Medical Education, July vol.23 no.4 pp.364-370. 93

Evans, G. E. (1988) Metaphors as learning aids in university lectures. Journal of Experimental Education; Winter vol.56 no.2 pp.91-99. 93

Evans, K. M. (1967), Teacher-training courses and students' personal qualities, Educational Research, vol.10 no. 1 pp.72-77. 63

Evans, R. D. and Evans, G. E. (1989) Cognitive mechanisms in learning from metaphors. Journal of Experimental Education, vol.58 no.1 Fall pp.5-19. 93

Facinelli, J. (1982) Music students and bibliography instruction: a study. University of Akron, Ohio ERIC ED242322. 139, 140, 142

Falchikov, N. (1993) Attitudes and values of lecturing staff: tradition, innovation and change. Higher Education; vol.25 no.4 pp.487-510. 155

Falk, B. (1967), The use of student evaluation, Australian University, vol.5 no.2 pp.109-21. 1

Falvo, D. R., Smaga, S., Brenner, J. S. and Tippy, P. K. (1991) Lecture versus role modeling: A comparison of educational programs to enhance residents' ability to communicate with patients about HIV. Teaching and Learning in Medicine; vol.3 no.4 pp.227-231. 274, 286

Farquhar, L. J . et al. (1986) Effect of two pre-clinical curricula on NMBE Part 1 examination performance. Journal of Medical Education; vol.61 no.5 pp.368-373. 273

Feather, N. T. (1969) Preference for information in relation to consistency, novelty, intolerance of ambiguity and dogmatism, Australian Journal of Psychology, vol.21 no. 3 pp.235-50. 67

Feldman, K. A. (1976) The superior college teacher from the student's point of view. Research in Higher Education vol.5 pp.243-288. 177

Feldman, K. A. (1977) Consistency and variability among college students in rating their teachers and courses. Research in Higher Education vol.6 pp.223-274. 180

Feldman, K. A. (1978) Course characteristics and college students' ratings of their teachers and courses: what we know and what we don't know. Research in Higher Education vol.9 pp.199-242. 180

Feldman, K. A. (1979) The significance of circumstances for college students' ratings of their teachers and courses. Research in Higher Education vol.10 pp.149-172. 180

Feldman, K. A. (1989) Instructional effectiveness of college teachers as judged by teachers themselves, current and former students, colleagues, administrators, and external (neutral) observers. Research in Higher Education vol.30 pp.137-194. 180

Feldman, K. A. and Newcomb T. M. (1973) The impact of college on students vol.2 pp.49-56. Jossey Bass. 180

Festinger, L. (1957) A Theory of Cognitive Dissonance, Harper & Row. 219

Fielding, G. D., Kameenui, E., Gersten, R. M. (1983) A comparison of an inquiry and a direct instruction approach to teaching legal concepts and applications to secondary school students. Journal of Educational Research; May-June vol.76 no.5 pp.287-293. 278, 279

Firstman, A. (1983) A comparison of traditional and television lectures as a means of instruction in biology at a community college. Unpublished. ERIC no.ED230264. 248, 274, 276, 282, 283, 285

Fisher, J. L. and Harris M. B. (1973) The effect of note-taking

and review on recall. Journal of Educational Psychology vol.65 pp.321-325. 122, 124, 140, 141

Fisher, J. L. and Harris M. B. (1974a) Note-taking and recall. Journal of Educational Research vol.67 pp.291-292. 122, 123, 125

Fisher, J. L. and Harris M. B. (1974b) The effect of note-taking preferences and type of notes taken on memory. Psychological Reports vol.35 pp.384-386. 123, 125

Fitch, M. L., Drucker, A. J., and Norton, J. A. Jnr. (1951) Frequent testing as a motivating factor in large lecture classes, Journal of Educational Psychology, vol.42 pp.1-20. 66

Fitzgerald, A. I. (1960). A Study of the Relative Effectiveness of Selected Instructional Procedures in a College Course in Children's Literature, doctoral dissertation, University of Missouri. 272, 273

Flanagan, S., Adams, H. E. and Forehand, R. (1979) A comparison of four instructional techniques for teaching parents to use time out. Behavior Therapy; January vol.10 no.1 pp.94-102. 286, 287

Fleschsig, A. J. and Seamans D. A. (1987) Determining the value of PLATO computer based education for a freshman engineering course, Engineering Education vol.77 no.4 Jan. pp.240-242. 274

Flexer, R. J. (1978) Comparison of lecture and laboratory strategies in a mathematics course for prospective elementary teachers, Journal for research in mathematics education vol.9 no.2 March pp.103-117. 274, 282, 284, 287

Flood Page, C. (1970), Students' reactions to teaching methods'. Universities Quarterly, July pp.266-72. 21, 283, 284, 285

Flowerdew, J. (1991) Pragmatic modifications on the "representative" speech act of defining. Journal of Pragmatics, March vol.15 no.3 pp.253-264. 99

Flowerdew, J. (1992) Definitions in Science Lectures Applied Linguistics, vol.13 no.2 pp.202-221. 99

Fodor, J. T. (1963), A comparative study of two approaches to health instruction at the college level, Doctoral Dissertation, University of California. 276

Fontenot, D. W. (1996) The effects of cooperative learning methods in conjunction with traditional lectures in seventh-grade earth science classes. Dissertation Abstracts International-A vol.57 no.01 July p.86. 270

Fortune, J. C., Gage, N. L., and Shutes, R. E. (1968), The generality of the ability to explain, paper presented to the American Educational Research Association, University of Massachusetts College of Education. 111

Fox, D. (1980) What are the principal concerns of new lecturers? in Higher Education at the Crossroad. Ed. R.Oxtoby SRHE. 207

Fox, J. A. (1986) A comparison of lecture based instruction and computer based individualized instruction. Dissertation Abstracts International, vol.47-A no.06 p.2132. 275

Foy, J. M. (1969), A note on lecturer evaluation by students, Universities Quarterly, vol.23 no.3 pp.345-8. 181

Frank, B. M. (1984) Effect of field independence-dependence and study technique on learning from a lecture. American Educational Research Journal, vol.21 no.3 Fall pp.669-678. 138

Frank, R. E., and Lesher, R. E. (1971), An evaluation of the effectiveness of taped lectures in a community college setting, Scientia Paedagogica Experimentalis, vol.8 no. 1 pp.16-21. 248, 283

Freyberg, P. D. (1956), The effectiveness of note-taking, Education for Teaching, February pp.17-24. 123, 124, 141

Friedman, C. P. et al. (1979) A comparison of personalized instruction and lecture/discussion courses in electrical engineering with self-selection of treatment. Unpublished. ERIC no.ED174131. 275, 284

Friedman, H. L. and Johnson, R. L. (1968), Compressed speech: correlates of listening ability, Journal of Communication, vol.18, 3 September pp.207-18. 91, 202

Furneaux, W. D. (1962), The psychologist and the university, Universities Quarterly, vol.17 pp.33-47. 63

Gadzella, B. M. (1977) Performance on objective and essay tests by individualized study, lecture, and group discussions in educational psychology. Perceptual and Motor Skills; vol.44 no.3, Pt 1 June pp.753-754. 272, 273, 275, 276

Gage, N. L., and Unruh, W. R. (1967), Theoretical formulations for research on teaching, Review of Educational Research, vol.37 pp.358-70. 111

Gage, N. L., Belgard M., Dell D., Hiller J., Rosenshine B. and Unruh W. (1968) Explorations of the teacher's effectiveness in explaining. Technical Report no.4 of the Stanford Center for Research and Development in Teaching, School of Education, Stanford University. 111

Gage, N. L. (1963), Handbook of Research on Teaching, American Educational Research Association, Rand McNally. 8

Gage, N. L. (1968), An analytical approach in research on instructional methods, Phi Delta Kappan, June pp.601-606. 84, 111

Gagne, R. M. (1965), The Conditions of Learning, Holt, Rinehart & Winston. 15

Galotti, K. M. (1995) Reasoning about reasoning: A course project. Special Issue: Psychologists teach critical thinking. Teaching of Psychology; February vol.22 no.1 66-68. 227

Gane, C. (1969), Educational technology vs the technology of education, Royal Television Society Journal, vol.12 no. 5 pp.101-104. 198

Garren, D. R. and Gathmann D. A. (1974) Audio-tutorial instruction and student-selected curricula. National Conference on Behavior Research and Technology in Higher Education. Lake Land College, Mattoon, Illinois. 274, 283

Gauger, P. W. (1951) The effect of gesture and the presence or absence of the speaker on the listening comprehension of 11th and 12th grade high school pupils. PhD Dissertation University of Wisconsin. 108

Gauvain, S. (1968), The use of student opinion in the quality control of teaching, British Journal of Medical Education, vol.2 no.1 pp.55-62. 21, 272, 284, 285

Geiger, W. M. (1996) The comparison of student engagement rates during classroom discourse, cooperative learning, and lecture methods of instruction in secondary schools. Dissertation Abstracts International vol.57-A no.03 September p.1086. 282

Geller, E. S., Chaffee, J. L. and Farris, J. C. (1975) Research in modifying lecturer behavior with continuous student feedback. Educational Technology; vol.15 no.12 pp.31-35. 200

Gerardo A. (1986) Computer-based learning in the engineering

technology curriculum: how effective is it? Engineering Education; vol.76 no.8 pp.759-761. 274, 279

Gerberich, J. R., and Warner, K. O. (1936), Relative instructional efficiencies of the lecture and discussion methods in a university course in American National Government, Journal of Education Research, vol.29 pp.574-9. 18, 269, 272, 275, 281

Gibb, L. M., and Gibb, J. R. (1952), The effects of the use of "participative action" groups in a course in general psychology, American Psychologist, vol.7. p.247 (abstract). 277, 280

Gibb, S. A. (1993) Evaluating first-year education students for retention and application of knowledge through a comparison of two teaching strategies: the lecture method and teaching-for-learning (knowledge retention). Dissertation Abstracts International-A vol.53 no.10, April p.3500. 270, 277

Gibbs, G. (1992) Improving the quality of student learning. Technical and Educational Services Ltd, Bristol, UK. 66, 232, 252, 253, 266

Gibbs, G., Lucas, L. and Simonite, V. (1996) Class size and student performance: 1984-94, Studies in Higher Education, vol.21 no.3 pp.261-273. 203

Giles, R. M., Johnson, M. R., Knight, K. E., Zammett, S. and Weinman, J. (1982) Recall of lecture information: a question of what, when and where. Med. Educ.; vol.16 no.5 pp.264-268. 55

Gist, M. E. (1989) The influence of training method on self efficacy and idea generation among managers. Personnel Psychology, vol.42 no.4 Winter pp.787-805. 278

Glanzer, M., and Cunitz, A. R. (1966), Two storage mechanisms in free recall, Journal of Verbal Learning and Verbal Behaviour, vol.5 pp.351-60. 40

Glass, G. V. (1976) Primary, secondary and meta-analysis of research, Educational Researcher, American Educational Research Association, vol.5 pp.3-8. 28

Glass, G. V. (1987) Class size, in The international encyclopedia of teaching and teacher education, Dunkin, M. J. (Editor) pp.540-545. 204

Glogovsky, R. J. (1970) A comparison of graphic arts processes practiced by contemporary industry with those taught in industrial arts teacher education. Ed.D. Dissertation University of Northern Colorado. 6

Gonzalez-Menendez, R. et al (1985) Dramatization and the lecture: Their comparative utility in the teaching of personality disturbances. Revista del Hospital Psiquiatrico de La Habana; vol.26 no.3 Jul-Sep pp.329-338. 270, 274

Goodhue, D. (1969), Tape-recorded lectures with slide synchronization. A description of the method, Journal of Biological Education, vol.3 no.4 pp.311-19. 248

Gore, A. E. (1962), Individualized Instruction Through Team Learning in a College Course in General Psychology, doctoral dissertation, Boston University. Reprinted in Dissertation Abstracts vol.23 no.04 p.1273. 241, 269

Gotke, E. (1931), cited in C. L. Bane, The Lecture in College Teaching, Badger. 272

Grant, J. M. (1983) The study of an individualized mode of learning: a comparison of contrasting methods in the teaching of freshman college biology. Dissertation Abstracts International vol.44-A no.03 September p.682. 271

Gray, P. L., Buerkel Rothfuss, N. L. and Yerby, J. (1986) A comparison between PSI based and lecture-recitation formats of instruction in the introductory speech communication course. Communication Education; April vol.35 no.2 pp.111-125.   269, 282, 285, 286

Greenberg, L. W. and Jewett, L. S. (1985) The impact of two teaching techniques on physicians' knowledge and performance. Journal of Medical Education; May vol.60 no.5 pp.390-396.   270, 278

Greene, E. B. (1928), The relative effectiveness of lecture and individual reading as methods of college teaching, Genetic Psychology Monographs, vol.4 pp.463-563.   276

Greene, E. B. (1934), Certain aspects of lecture, reading and guided reading, School and Society, vol.39 pp.619-24.   248

Grobe, R. P. and Pettibone, T. J. (1975) Effect of instructional pace on student attentiveness, Journal of Educational Research; vol.69 no.4 December pp.131-134.   201

Gross, R. W. (1985) A comparison of active experience and lecture-discussion methodology as means for developing musical knowledge, musical discrimination, and musical preference within an electronic music course at the high school level (synthesizer, composition, computer music). Dissertation Abstracts International vol.45-A no.10, April p.3088.   275, 284

Gruber, A. (1964), Sensory alternation and performance in a vigilance task, Human Factors, vol.6 pp.3-12.   52

Guetzkow, H., Kelly, L. E., and McKeachie, W. J. (1954), An experimental comparison of recitation, discussion and tutorial methods in college teaching, Journal of Educational Psychology, vol.45 pp.193-207.   64, 272, 273, 275, 277

Guilford, J. P. (1959), Three faces of intellect, American Psychologist, vol.14 pp.469-479.   64

Gulo, E. V., and Baron, A. (1965), Classroom learning of meaningful prose by college students as a function of sensory mode of stimulus presentation, Perceptual and Motor Skills, vol.21 pp.183-186.   276

Gulo, E. V., and Nigro, M. R. (1966), Classroom learning as a function of method of presenting instructional materials, Psychological Reports, vol.19 pp.971-977.   276

Gunter, B. Berry, C. and Clifford, B. R. (1981) Proactive interference effects with television news items: Further evidence. Journal of Experimental Psychology: Human Learning and Memory, vol.7 pp.480-487.   41

Gunzburger, L. K. (1993) U.S. medical schools' valuing of curriculum time: Self directed learning versus lectures. Academic Medicine; vol.68 no.9 September pp.700-702.   6

Gunzenhauser, G. W. (1989) The effects of an experiential learning strategy and a conventional lecture-laboratory strategy on teaching the mole concept, Dissertation Abstracts International, vol.50-A no.05 page 1227.   278

Guthrie, E. R. (1954) The evaluation of teaching: a progress report. Seattle. University of Washington.   180

Haigh, B. V., and Schmidt, W. H. (1956), Learning of subject matter in teacher-centred and group-centred classes, Journal of Educational Psychology, vol.47 pp.295-301.   272

Hale, E. (1964) Report of the Commitee on University Teaching Methods: Chairman Sir E. Hale. University Grants Committee.   6, 7, 20, 142, 283

Hale, R. E. and Camplese, D. A. (1974) Assessing the effectiveness of a mastery teacher education program.

Western Carolina University Journal of Education, Winter vol.5 no.3 pp.26-32.   286

Halpin, F. B. (1968), A predictive failure of veterinary students: a method of selection for counselling, British Journal of Medical Education, vol.2 no.3 pp.200-203.   264

Hamp-Lyons, E. (1982) Survey review of materials for teaching advanced listening and note-taking. Unpublished. ERIC no.ED225359.   134

Hancock, B. W., Coscarelli, W. C., and White, G. P. (1983) Critical thinking and content acquisition using a modified guided design process for large course sections. Educational and Psychological Research, Summer vol.3 no.3 pp.139-149.   276, 279

Hancock, D. R. (1994) Motivating adults to learn academic course content, Journal of Educational Research, Nov-Dec vol.88 no.2 pp.102-108.   65

Harden, R. McG., Wayne, Sir E., and Donald, G. (1968), An audio-visual technique for medical teaching, Journal of Medical and Biological Illustration, vol.18 no.1 pp.29-32.   161

Harding, C. M., Riley, I. S. and Bligh, D. A. (1981) A comparison of two teaching methods in Mathematical Statistics. Studies in Higher Education, vol.6 no.2 pp.139-146.   274, 279, 284

Harlow, H. F. (1949) The formation of learning sets, Psychological Review, vol.56 pp.51-56.   15

Harrington, K. V., McElroy, J. C., Morrow, P. C. (1990) Computer anxiety and computer based training: A laboratory experiment. Journal of Educational Computing Research, vol.6 no.3 pp.343-358.   281

Harris, R. E. (1984) An experimental study to determine the effectiveness of computer-assisted instruction in industrial arts wood laboratory safety. Dissertation Abstracts International vol.44-A no.08, February p.2390.   271

Harris, W. G., Jr. (1971) A comparison of student performance in a college engineering course between two lecture methods: a taped recording and a printed transcription. Ed.D. Dissertation. ERIC no.ED076322.   248

Hartley, J. (1976) Lecture handouts and student note-taking. Programmed Learning and Educational Technology, vol.13 no.2 pp.58-64.   138

Hartley, J., and Cameron, A. (1967), Some observations on the efficiency of lecturing, Educational Review, vol.20 no.1 pp.30-37.   19, 87, 130, 139

Hartley, J. and Davies I.K. (1978) Note-taking, a critical review. Programmed Learning and Educational Technology 15 pp.207-224.   120, 124, 131, 132

Hartley, J. and Marshall S. (1974) On notes and note-taking. Universities Quarterly, vol.28 no.2 pp.225-235.   124, 130

Harvey, J. N. and Barker D. G. (1970) Student evaluation of teaching effectiveness. Improving College and University Teaching. vol.18 pp.275-278.   180

Hedges, L. V. (1975) Personalized introductory courses: a longitudinal study. OASIS Research Report No 1. California University, San Diego, 19pp.   29, 269

Hedges, L. V. (1982) Estimation of effect size from a series of independent experiments, Psychological Bulletin vol.92 pp.490-499.   28

Heilman, J. D., and Armentrout, W. D. (1936), The rating of college teachers on ten traits by their students, Journal of Educational Psychology, vol.27 pp.197-216.   180

Heller, B. and Dale, M. (1976) Traditional teaching and learning modules: A comparative study. Exceptional Children, January vol.42 no.4 pp.231-232. 271

Henderson, N. K. (1970) University Teaching, Oxford University Press. 88, 247

Hendrix, V. L. (1968) Comparison of audio tape and lecture procedures in social science 131. Dallas County Junior College District, Texas. ERIC ED029636. 274, 282

Henk, W. A., Stahl, N. A. (1985) A meta-analysis of the effect of note-taking on learning from lecture. National Reading Conference Yearbook, no.34 pp.70-75. 123, 141

Hertz-Lazarowitz, R. et al, (1981) Student-student intraction in the classroom: a naturalistic study. Paper presented to the Summer workshop of the Association of Teacher Educators, Institute for research on teaching, East Lansing, MI. 227

Heverin, J. P. (1993) Marital preparation: a comparison of skill training and lecture on factors related to marital success (communication skills training, premarital intervention). Dissertation Abstracts International vol.53-A no.12, June p.4254. 285, 286, 287

Hicks, B. J. (1996) Student mastery of basic mathematics skills: a comparison of two instructional approaches (computer-assisted instruction, lecture, drill-and-practice), Masters' Abstracts International 34 no.06, December p.2139. 271

Higgins, K. and Boone, R. (1990) Hypertext computer study guides and the social studies achievement of students with learning disabilities, remedial students, and regular education students. Journal of Learning Disabilities, November vol.23 (9) 529-540. 270, 274

Hildum, D. C., and Brown, R. W. (1956), Verbal reinforcement and interviewer bias, Journal of Abnormal and Social Psychology, vol.53 pp.108-11. 221

Hill, R. J. (1960), A Comparative Study of Lecture and Discussion, New York Fund for Adult Education. 272, 280

Hiller, J. H., Fisher, G. A. and Kaess, W. (1969) A computer investigation of verbal characteristics of effective classroom lecturing, American Educational Research Journal vol.6 pp.661-675. 153

Hiller, J. H. (1971) Verbal response indicators of conceptual vagueness, American Educational Research Journal vol.8 pp.151-161. 153, 154

Himmelweit, H. T., and Swift, E. (1971), The class as a reference group, report to the British Psychological Society Annual Conference. 63

Hingorani, K. K. (1996) Information technology supported case studies for teaching higher level cognitive skills: a comparative evaluation of methodologies (professional development). Dissertation Abstracts International vol.56-A no.12, June p.4852. 277

Hinkle S. and Hinkle A. (1990) An experimental comparison of the effects of focused freewriting and other study strategies on lecture comprehension. Teaching of Psychology, vol.17, no.1 pp.31-35. 240

Hinrichsen, K. A. (1975) Evaluative comparison of programmed system of instruction and traditional lecture approaches in basic administration of justice class at Cerritos College. Nova University. ERIC ED114143. 269, 284

Hodgson, V. and McConnell, D. (1985) The development of student constructed lecture feedback questionnaires, Assessment and Evaluation in Higher Education, vol.10 no.1 Spring pp.2-27. 177

Hoffman, E. (1974) A comparison of team teaching and audiotaped lectures with traditional lecture method. Alvin Junior College, Texas. Ed.D Nova University. ERIC ED112963. 271, 283

Hohn, R. L., Gallagher, T. and Byrne, M. (1990) Instructor supplied notes and higher order thinking. Journal of Instructional Psychology, vol.17 no.2 June pp.71-74. 137, 138

Holen, M. C. and Oaster, T. R. (1976) Serial position and isolation effects in a classroom lecture simulation. Journal of Educational Psychology; vol.68 no.3 pp.293-296. 41

Hollingsworth, P. M. (1995) Enhancing listening retention: The two minute discussion. College Student Journal, vol.29 no.1 March pp.116-117. 227

Holloway, P. J. (1966), The effect of lecture time on learning, British Journal of Educational Psychology, vol.31 no.3 pp.255-258. 59

Holmes, S. H. (1988) A comparative assessment of computer based training (CBT) and the traditional industry lecture methodology upon job performance in application software training, Dissertation Abstracts International, vol.50-A no.05 p.1283. 285

Holt, J. D. (1973) Comparison of lecture-demonstration with self-instruction as they affect cognitive information when developing psychomotor skills in a competency-based module. Nove University. ERIC ED096277. 270

Hood, K. R. (1987) Effects of a lecturer's use of synchronous whole-body locomotion on student attitudes towards instruction. Ed.D dissertaion Texas Tech University. See also Dissertation Abstracts International (1988) vol.49 03-A p.441 No 098758. 107

Horak, V. M. and Horak, W.J. (1982) The influence of student locus of control and teaching method on mathematics achievement. Journal of Experimental Education vol. 51 (Fall) pp.18-21. 90

Houghton, H. V. et al (1994) Effectiveness of correspondence instruction in an extension vegetable gardening program. Journal of Agricultural Education, vol.35 no.1 pp.21-25. 276, 283, 285

Houtman, I. L. and Bakker, F. C. (1987) Stress in student teachers during real and simulated standardized lectures. Journal of Human Stress; vol.13 no.4 Winter pp.180-187. 199

Houtman, I. L. and Bakker, F. C. (1991a) Individual differences in reactivity to and coping with the stress of lecturing. Journal of Psychosomatic Research; vol.35 no.1 pp.11-24. 199

Houtman, I. L. and Bakker, F. C. (1991b) Stress and coping in lecturing, and the stability of responses across practice. Journal of Psychosomatic Research; vol.35 nos.2-3 pp.323-333. 199

Hovland, C. I., and Janis, I. L. (eds.) (1959), Personality and Persuasibility, Yale University Press. 220

Hovland, C. I., and Mandell, W. (1952), An experimental comparison of conclusion-drawing by the communicator and by the audience, Journal of Abnormal and Social Psychology, vol.47 pp.581-8. 14, 217

Hovland, C. I., Janis, I. L. and Kelley, H. H. (1953),

Communication and Persuasion, Yale University Press. 18, 219

Hovland, C. I., Lumsdaine, A. A. and Sheffield, F. D. (1949) Experiments on mass communication, Princeton University Press. 216,217

Howard, J. M. (1986) Effectiveness of two instructional modes for teaching vocational agriculture students of differing learning styles (Microcomputer-assisted lecture-discussion field dependent/independent). Dissertation Abstracts International, vol.47/07A page 2423. 274

Howe, M. J. A. (1970a) Notetaking strategy, review and long-term retention of verbal information. Journal of Educational Research, vol.63 p.285. 123, 124

Howe, M. J. A. (1970b) Using students' notes to examine the role of the individual learner in acquiring meaningful subject matter, Journal of Educational Research, vol.64 pp.61-63. 122

Howe, M. J. A. (1977) Learning and the acquisition of knowledge by students: some experimental investigations. In Howe M. J. A. (Ed) (1977) Adult learning: psychological research and applications. Wiley, London. 125, 132

Howe, M. J. A., Ormond, V. and Singer, L. (1974) Recording activities and recall of information. Perceptual and Motor Skills, vol.39 pp.309-310. 126

Howe, M. J. A. and Godfrey, J. (1977) Student note-taking as an aid to learning. Exeter University Teaching Services. 125, 130, 131, 147

Howerton, C. P. (1987) A comparative analysis of the guided-discovery method versus the traditional lecture-laboratory method in teaching introductory computer science (Fortran, Colorado). Dissertation Abstracts International, vol.48/05A page 1103. 273, 287

Hubbard, R. (1990) Tertiary mathematics without lectures. International Journal of Mathematical Education in Science and Technology, vol.21 no.4 pp.567-571. 230

Hudelson, E. (1928), Class Size at the College Level, University of Minnesota Press. 64, 203, 272

Huffaker, A. (1931), cited in C. L. Bane, The Lecture in College Teaching, Badger. 270

Hughes, C. A. and Suritsky, S. K. (1993) Notetaking skills and strategies for students with learning disabilities. Preventing School Failure, vol.38 no.1 pp.7-11 130, 134

Hull, W. L. and McClay D.R. (1965) A comparison of programed and lecture-discussion methods of teaching farm credit to high school youth and adults. ERIC ED013872. 275

Hult, R. E. et al. (1984) Differential effects of note taking ability and lecture encoding structure on student learning. Paper to the Annual Meeting of the Eastern Educational Research Association, West Palm Beach. 122

Hunkins, A. (1967 and 1968), papers read to American Educational Research Association. 209

Husband, R. W. (1951), A statistical comparison of the efficiency of large lecture versus smaller recitation sections upon achievement in general psychology, Journal of Psychology, vol.31 pp.297-300. 273

Huthaifi, K. F. (1989) Using instruction to change attitudes towards computers: a comparison of two instructional methods. Dissertation Abstracts International vol.49-A no.07, January p.1685. 280

Hyde, R. M. and Flournoy, D. J. (1986) A case against

mandatory lecture attendance. Journal of Medical Education, March vol.61 no.3 pp.175-176. 132

Isaacs, M. (1973) Precision teaching of the deaf. American Annals of the Deaf, December vol.118 vol.6 no.686-690. 271

Isaacs G. (1989) Lecture note-taking, learning and recall. Medical Teacher, vol.11 no.3/4 pp.295-302. 139

Isaacs G. (1994) Lecturing practices and note-taking purposes. Studies in Higher Education, vol.19 no.2 pp.203-216. 7, 120, 124

Jackson, J. and Bilton L. (1990) Lecture comprehension and note-taking for L2 students. Unpublished. ERIC no.ED323785. 130

Jackson, J. and Bilton L. (1990) Listening and note-taking in higher education. Unpublished. ERIC no.ED366189. 130

Jackson, J. and Bilton, L. (1994) Stylistic variations in science lectures: teaching vocabulary. English for Specific Purposes, vol.13 no.1 pp. 61-80. 99

James, D. W., Johnson, M. L., and Venning, P. (1956), Testing for learnt skill in observation and evaluation of evidence, Lancet, vol.2 pp.379-83. 14

Jamieson, G. H., James, P. E., and Leytham, G. W. H. (1969), Comparisons between teaching methods at the post-graduate level, Programmed Learning, October pp.243-9. 64

Janis, I. L. (1957), Motivational effects of different sequential arrangements of conflicting argument: a theoretical analysis, in C. I. Hovland (ed.), The Order of Presentation in Persuasion, Yale University Press pp.170-86. 218

Janis, I. L. and Feshbach, S. (1953), Effects of fear-arousing communications, Journal of Abnormal and Social Psychology, vol.48 pp.78-92. 67

Janis, I. L. and Field (1959), in C. I. Hovland and I. L. Janis, Personality and Persuasibility, Yale University Press, Reprinted in A. R. Cohen, Attitude Change and Social Influence, 1963, Basic Books. 220

Javidi, M. N. and Long, L. W. (1989) Teachers' use of humor, self-disclosure, and narrative activity as a function of experience. Communication Research Reports, vol.6 no.1 June pp.47-52 96

Jenkins, A. See Gibbs, G. (1992) Chapter 6, Encouraging active learning in structured lectures, in Improving the quality of student learning, Technical and Education Services. 232, 252, 253, 266

Jenkins, A. and Gibbs, G. (1984) Break up your lectures: or Christaller sliced up. Journal of Geographical Higher Education, vol.8 no.1 pp.27-39. 232, 252, 253, 266

Jenkins, R. L. (1952) The relative effectiveness of two methods of teaching written and spoken English, unpublished Doctoral Dissertation, Michigan State University, Reprinted in Dissertation Abstracts, vol.12, p.268. 272

Jensen, P. H. (1996) The application of Kolb's experiential learning theory in a first semester college accounting course. Dissertation Abstracts International vol.56-A no.08, February p.3201. 277

Jernstedt, G. C. (1976) The relative effectiveness of individualized and traditional instruction methods. Journal of Educational Research, February vol.69 no.6 pp.211-218. 269, 271, 275, 283

Jha, P. N. and Baral, J. R. (1973) Relative effectiveness of some group methods in agricultural information communication in Nepal. Indian Journal of Psychology, September vol.48 no.3 pp.65-74. 273, 275

Johnson, D. M., and Smith, H. C. (1953), Democratic leadership in the college classroom, Psychological Monographs, vol.67 pp.1-20, (whole no.361). 272, 277, 280

Johnson, J. A. (1967) Instruction: from the consumer's point of view. In Lee, C. B. T. Improving college teaching, American Council on Education, Washington D.C. 174

Johnson, K. A. et al. (1967) Comparison of conventional and programmed instruction in teaching communications procedures. Naval Personnel Research Activity. San Diego, California. 271, 282

Johnson, P. E. (1967), Some psychological aspects of subject matter structure, Journal of Educational Psychology, vol.58 no.2 pp.75-83. 112

Johnson, W. G., Zlotlow, S., Berger, J. L. and Croft, R. G. (1975) A traditional lecture versus a PSI course in personality: some comparisons, Teaching of Psychology, December vol.2 no.4 pp.156-158. 282

Johnston, J. O., and Calhoun, T. A. P. (1969), The serial position effect in lecture material, Journal of Educational Research, vol.62 no.6 pp.255-8. 41

Johnstone, A. H. and Percival, F. (1976) Attention breaks in lectures, Education in Chemistry, vol.13 no.2 pp.49-50. 58

Jone, N. W. (1980) A comparison between lecture and self-paced general geology. Journal of Geological Education, vol.28 no.5 pp.235-237. 273, 284, 285

Jones, H. E. (1923) Experimental studies of college teaching, Archives of Psychology No 68. 46, 122, 123

Joyce, C. R. B., and Weatherall, M. (1957) Controlled experiments in teaching, Lancet, vol.2 pp.402-407. 248, 272

Jumpeter, J. (1985) Personalized System of Instruction versus the lecture demonstration method in a specific area of a college music appreciation course, Journal of Research in Music Education, Summer vol.33 no.2 pp.113-122. 271, 282

Kaplan, R. M. and Pascoe, G. C. (1977) Humorous lectures and humorous examples: Some effects upon comprehension and retention, Journal of Educational Psychology February vol.69 no.1 pp.61-65 96

Karp, H. J. (1983) The use of Keller's Personalized System of Instruction, College Student Personnel Abstracts 0298-19 vol.19 no.1 Fall p.146. 6

Katona, G. (1940) Organizing and Memorizing, Columbia University Press. 67

Katz, D. (1950) Gestalt Psychology, Ronald Press. 43

Katz, N. (1990) Problem solving and time: Functions of learning style and teaching methods, Occupational Therapy Journal of Research, Jul-Aug vol.10 no.4 pp.221-236. 150, 277, 279

Kaul, P. N. (1976) Teaching styles and attitudes towards extension education. Asian Journal of Psychology and Education, March vol.1 no.1 pp.24-28. 140

Kazanas H.C. and Frazier E.L. (1982) A comparison of instructional approaches. Journal of Studies in Technical Careers, vol.4 no.4 pp.312-320. 275, 282

Keeble, M. and Weinman, J. (1986) Immediate and delayed recall of information presented in a live and a televised lecture, Medical Education, July vol.20 no.4 pp.281-285. 274, 276, 282

Kelley, H. H. and Pepitone, C. (1952) An evaluation of a college course in Human Relations, Journal of Educational Psychology, vol.43 pp.193-209. 280

Kelly, A. E. and O'Donnell, A. (1994) Hypertext and the study strategies of preservice teachers: Issues in instructional hypertext design, Journal of Educational Computing Research; vol.10 no.4 pp.373-387 125, 224

Kelly, N. and Kelly B. (1982) Backgrounds, education and teaching styles of teaching award winning professors. Unpublished. ERIC no.ED230080. 150

Khan, A. A. (1983) A comparison of the conventional lecture method of instruction with programmed instruction and the lecture-laboratory approach in teaching introductory physical geography at the university level. Dissertation Abstracts International vol.44-A no.02, August p.454. 275

Khoiny, F. E. (1996) The effectiveness of problem-based learning in nurse practitioner education. Dissertation Abstracts International vol.57-A no.01, July p.88. 277

Kiewra, K. A. (1985) Learning from a lecture: an investigation of notetaking, review and attendance at a lecture. Human Learning Journal of Practical Research and Applications, Jan-March vol.4 no.1 pp.73-77. 140

Kiewra, K. A., DuBois, N. F., Christensen, M., Kim, S., et al (1989) A more equitable account of the note taking functions in learning from lecture and from text. Instructional Science, September vol.18 no.3 pp.217-232. 124

Kiewra, K. A., DuBois, N. F., Christian, D., McShane, A. et al (1991) Note taking functions and techniques. Journal of Educational Psychology, vol.83 no.2 June pp.240-245. 47, 124

Kiewra, K. A. and Frank, B. M. (1988) Encoding and external storage effects of personal lecture notes, skeletal notes, and detailed notes for field-independent and field-dependent learners. Journal of Educational Research, Jan-Feb vol.81 no.3 pp.143-148. 138

Kiewra, K. A. et al. (1988) Providing study notes: comparison of three types of notes for review. Journal of Educational Psychology, vol.80 no.4 pp.595-597. 129, 138

King, A. (1989) Effects of self questioning training on college students' comprehension of lectures. Contemporary Educational Psychology, October vol.14 no.4 pp.366-381. 135, 211

King, A. (1990) Enhancing peer interaction and learning in the classroom through reciprocal questioning. American Educational Research Journal, vol.27 no.4 Winter pp.664-687. 135, 212

King, A. (1991) Improving lecture comprehension: Effects of a metacognitive strategy. Applied Cognitive Psychology, July-August vol.5 no.4 pp.331-346. 129, 210, 211

King, A. (1992) Facilitating elaborative learning through guided student generated questioning. Educational Psychologist, vol.27 no.1 Winter pp.111-126. 129, 135, 142

King, A. (1994) Autonomy and question asking: The role of personal control in guided student generated questioning. Special Issue: Individual differences in question asking and strategic listening processes. Learning and Individual Differences, vol.6 no.2 Summer pp.163-185. 17, 135, 212

King, B. T., and Janis, I. L. (1956) Comparison of the effectiveness of improvised versus non-improvised role-playing in producing opinion changes, Human Relations, vol.9 pp.177-186. 18

King, K. (1980) Modeling vs lecture/discussion in training undergraduates as teachers. Perceptual and Motor Skills, vol.51 no.2 October pp.527-531. 286

King, M. (1973) The anxieties of university teachers. Universities Quarterly, vol.28 pp.69-83. 207

Kintisch, W. and Bates E. (1977) Recognition memory for statements from a classroom lecture. Journal of Experimental Psychology: Human Learning and Memory vol.3 no.2 March pp.150-159. 41

Kipper, D. A. and Ben Ely., Z. (1979) The effectiveness of the psychodramatic double method, the reflection method, and lecturing in the training of empathy. Journal of Clinical Psychology, vol.35 no.2 April pp.370-375. 280, 281

Kirby, D. (1931) cited in C. L. Bane, The Lecture in College Teaching, Badger. 270

Klein, J. (1961) Working with Groups, Hutchinson. 238

Klein, M. A. (1983) An experiential versus a didactic approach to training counselors in interpersonal conflict management: a comparative study. Dissertation Abstracts International vol.43-A no.10, April p.3218. 285

Klentz, B. and Beaman, A. L. (1981) The effects of type of information and method of dissemination on the reporting of a shoplifter. Journal of Applied Social Psychology, vol.11 no.1 Jan-Feb pp.64-82. 288

Kletz, T. A. (1970) Putting knowledge to use, Education in Chemistry, vol.7 no.6 p.229. 246

Klinzing, H. G. (1988) Skill acquisition and reflection-based decision making in a teaching laboratory: an evaluative study. European Journal of Teacher Education, vol.11, nos.2-3 pp.167-175. 206

Koniak, D. W. (1982) A comparison of two teaching strategies using a performance-based evaluation to measure learning of a selected clinical nursing skill. Dissertation Abstracts International vol.42-B no.10, April p.4016. 287

Koo, A., Wong Leung, R. and Tam, M. (1993) Improving lectures by using interactive handouts. British Journal of Educational Technology, vol.24 no.2 pp.139-145. 162

Kowalski, R. (1987) Teaching less and learning more?: a personal experience. Programmed Learning and Educational Technology, vol.24 no.3 pp.174-186. 7

Kozoil, E. M. (1986) Kinetic structural analysis of selected college mathematics lectures (remedial). Dissertation Abstracts International vol.46-A no.09, March p.2606. 112

Kriner, R. E. and Vaughan, M. R. (1975) The effects of group size and presentation method on the impact of a drug presentation. HumRRO Technical Report, June No 75 p11. 280

Kubany, E. S. and Sloggett, B. B. (1991) Attentional factors in observational learning: effects on acquisition of behavior management skills. Behavior Therapy, Summer vol.22 no.3 pp.435-448. 286, 288

Kulik, J. A., Kulik, C-L.C . and Smith, B. B. (1976) Research on the personalized system of instruction. Programmed Learning and Educational Technology, vol.13 pp.23-30. 29

Kuna, D. J. (1975) Lecturing, reading, and modeling in counselor restatement training. Journal of Counseling Psychology, November vol.22 no.6 pp.542-546. 287, 288

Kuz'mina, L. S. (1976) Mental work capacity of students in listening to text materials and lectures. Voprosy Psikhologii, No.5 128-133. 67

Lacroix, P. S. (1987) The effects of cognitive style, notetaking and instructor-prepared handout materials on learning from lecture instruction. Dissertation Abstracts International, vol.48-A no.05 p.1104. 122

Ladas, H. (1980) Summarizing research: A case study. Review of Educational Research, Winter vol.50 no.4 pp.597-624. 121

Lam, Y. J. (1984-5) Longitudinal relationships of selected course structure, cognitive and affective factors and classroom behaviors of adult learners. Educational Research Quarterly, vol.9 no.3 pp.28-36. 277, 283

Lambiotte, J. G., Skaggs, L. P. and Dansereau, D. F. (1993) Learning from lectures: Effects of knowledge maps and cooperative review strategies. Applied Cognitive Psychology; vol.7 no.6 Nov. pp.483-497. 126, 138

Lambiotte, J. G. and Dansereau, D. F. (1992) Effects of knowledge maps and prior knowledge on recall of science lecture content. Journal of Experimental Education, Spring vol.60 no.3 pp.189-201. 138

Land, M. L. (1981) Combined effect of two teacher clarity variables on student achievement. Journal of Experimental Education, vol 50, Fall pp.14-17. 152

Land, M. L. and Combs, N. (1982) Teacher behavior and student ratings. Educational and Psychological Research vol.2 Winter pp.63-66. 152

Laurie, D. R. (1976) Live lecture versus slide-tape method of instruction for a health unit of physical fitness, Research Quarterly vol.46 no.4 December pp.683-686. 274

Lazarus B.D. (1988) Using guided notes to aid learning-disabled adolescents in secondary mainstream settings. 137

Leblanc, P. A. (1996) Attitudes of nursing students toward the elderly as influenced by lecture-discussion with and without simulation. Dissertation Abstracts International vol.56-A no.11, May p.4247. 280, 281

Lee, M. M. and McLean J. E. (1978) A comparison of achievement and attitudes among three methods of teaching educational psychology. Journal of Educational Research vol 72 no.2 Nov-Dec pp.86-90. 282

Lesniak, S. L. (1996) Active learning and other teaching activities as perceived by part-time faculty and students in a professional degree program designed for adult learners. Dissertation Abstracts International vol.57-A no.01, July p.127. 6

Leton, D. A. (1961) An evaluation of course methods in teaching child development, Journal of Educational Research, vol.55 pp.118-22. 272, 280

Levine, J., and Butler, J. (1952) Lecture versus group decision in changing behaviour, Journal of Applied Psychology, vol.36 pp.29-33. 280

Lewin, K. (1943) Forces behind food habits and methods of change, Bulletin of the National Research Council no.108 pp.36-65. Reprinted in A. R. Cohen, (1964) Attitude Change and Social Influence, Basic Books. 17, 280

Lifson, N., Rempel, P., and Johnson, J. A. (1956) A comparison between lecture and conference methods of teaching physiology, Journal of Medical Education, vol.31, 376-382. 273

Linn, M. D. (1973) Urban Black speech as the sixth clock. Paper presented at the Annual Meeting of the National Council of Teachers of English (63rd Philadelphia. Novemeber) ERIC ED094376. 152

Little, C. E. (1964) An Experimental Study of Programmed Instruction in College Algebra at Colorado State College, doctoral dissertation, Colorado State College. 227

Lloyd, D. H. (1968) A concept of improvement of learning response in the taught lesson, Visual Education, October pp.23-25. 54, 131, 227

Locke, E. A. (1977) An empirical study of lecture note-taking among college students, Journal of Educational Research vol.71 pp.93-99. 122, 130, 131,

Long, C. P. (1987) A comparative evaluation of lecture and clinical simulation for teaching nursing students about immediate care of the rape victim. Dissertation Abstracts International, vol.48-A no.11 p.2798. 276, 278, 279, 285

Loomis, S. D., and Greene, A. W. (1947) The pattern of mental conflict in a typical state university, Journal of Abnormal and Social Psychology, vol.42 pp.342-355. 68

Lovell, G. D. and Haner C. F. (1955) Forced choice applied to college faculty rating. Educational and Psychological Measurement, vol.15 pp.291-304. 180

Lowery, B. A. H. (1988) A comparison of computer assisted instruction and traditional lecture-discussion and their relationship to student cognitive style, faculty and student time involvement and cost. Dissertation Abstracts International, vol.49-A no.10 p.2914. 270

Lowery, B. A. H. (1989) A comparison of computer-assisted instruction and traditional lecture no.discussion and their relationship to student cognitive style, faculty and student time involvement and cost. Dissertation Abstracts International vol.49-A no.10, April p.2914. 270, 274

Lumsdaine, A. A., and Janis, I. L. (1953) Resistance to "counter propaganda" produced by one-sided and two-sided "propaganda" presentations, Public Opinion Quarterly, vol.17 pp.311-318. 217

MacDonald M. and Romano S. (1983) An investigation into student and teacher attitudes towards the value of handouts. British Journal of In-Service Education, vol.9 no.3 pp.149-158. 145, 146

Mackie, J. B. (1973) Comparison of student satisfaction with educational experiences in two teaching process models. Nursing Research, vol. 22 no.3 pp.262-266. 283

Mackworth, J. (1970) Vigilance and Habituation, Penguin. 59, 60

Mackworth, N. H. (1950) Researches in the Measurement of Human Performance, HMSO. 56

MacManaway, L. A. (1968) Using lecture scripts, Universities Quarterly, June pp.327-36. 123, 137

MacManaway, L. A. (1970) Teaching methods in higher education - innovation and research, Universities Quarterly, vol.24 no.3 pp.321-9. 53, 137, 163

MacMillan, M. (1965) Efficiency in Reading, English-Teaching Information Centre, occasional paper no.6. 146

Macomber, F. G., and Seigel, L. (1960) Final Report of the Experimental Study in Instructional Procedures, Miami University. 204

Maddox H. and Hoole E. (1975) Performance decrement in the lecture. Educational Review 28 pp.17-30. 55, 130

Magnusson, J. L. and Perry, R. P. (1989) Stable and transient determinants of students' perceived control: Implications for instruction in the college classroom. Canada Journal of Educational Psychology, September vol.81 no.3 pp.362-370. 65

Magoulis, B. (1986) Achievement in accounting I: a comparison of traditional instruction with a combined programmed and lecture participation approach. Dissertation Abstracts International vol.46-A no.07, January p.1816. 271

Maier, R. O. (1957) A comparison of two methods of teaching an engineering slide rule course. Masters Dissertation. ERIC ED023369. 270

Malleson, N. (1967) Medical students' study: time and place, British Journal of Medical Education, vol. 1 no. 3 pp.169-177. 63

Maqsud M. (1980) Effects of personal lecture notes and teacher-notes on recall of university students. British Journal of Educational Psychology, vol.50 no.3 pp.289-294. 122, 123, 125

Marks, L. E., and Miller, G. A. (1964) The role of semantic and syntactic constraints in the memorisation of English sentences, Journal of Verbal Learning and Verbal Behaviour, vol.3 pp.1-5. 44

Marr, J. N., Plath, D. W., Wakeley, J. H., and Wilkins, M. (1960) The contribution of the lecture to college teaching, Journal of Educational Psychology, vol.51 pp.277-284. 276

Marris, P. (1964) The Experience of Higher Education, Routledge and Kegan Paul. 6, 66, 160, 199, 200

Marsh, H. W. (1984) Students' evaluations of university teaching: dimensionality, reliabiltiy, validity, potential biases, and utility. Journal of Educational Psychology, vol.76 no.5 pp.707-754. 180, 181

Marsh, H. W. (1987) Students' evaluations of university teaching: research findings, methodological issues and directions of future research. International Journal of Educational Research vol.11 no.3 pp.253-388. 180, 181

Marsh, H. W., Overall, J. U. and Kesler, S. P. (1979) Class size, student evaluations and instructor effectivesness, American Educational Research Journal, vol.16 pp.57-69. 204

Marton, F., Hounsell, D. and Entwistle N. J., (Eds.) (1984) The experience of learning. Scottish Academic Press, 242pp. 180

Mason, C. A. (1996) An examination of two instructional delivery formats in community college developmental studies. Dissertation Abstracts International vol.57-A no.03, September p.953. 287

Mastin, V. E. (1963) Teacher enthusiasm, Journal of Educational Research, vol.56 pp.385-386. 64

Masuhara, J. T. (1984) The effects of a guided design problem-solving strategy and a concrete referent on achievement and attitude. Dissertation Abstracts International vol.44-A no.09, March p.2696. 273

McCarthy, P. R. and Schmeck, R.R. (1982) Effects of teacher self-disclosure on student learning and perceptions of teacher, College Student Journal vol.16 Spring pp.45-49. 96

McCarthy, W. H. (1970) Improving large audience teaching: the "programmed" lecture, British Journal of Medical Education, vol.4 no.1 pp.29-31. 163

McClain A. (1986) Improving lectures: challenge both sides of the brain. Unpublished. ERIC no.ED274954. 126

McClendon, P. I. (1958) An experimental study of the relationship between notetaking practices and listening comprehension of college freshman during expository lectures. Speech Monographs, vol.25 pp.222-228. 123

McCord, W. B. (1944) Speech factors relating to teaching efficiency. Speech Monographs, vol.11 pp.53-64. 64

McDonald, R. J. and Taylor, E. G. (1980) Student note-taking and lecture handouts in veterinary medical education. Journal of Veterinary Medical Education vol.7 no.3 Fall pp.157-161. 130

McDougall I.R., Gray, H. W. and McNichol, S. P. (1972) The effect of timing and distribution of handouts on improvement of student performance. British Journal of Medical Education vol.6 pp.155-157. 145

McFarland, R. E. (1982) Comparison of three safety 145training programs for physical plant supervisors at the University of Cincinnati. Dissertation Abstracts International vol.43-A no.05, November p.1390. 288

McGuire, C. H. (1963) A process approach to the construction and analysis of medical examinations, Journal of Medical Education, vol.38, p.556. 25, 218

Mcguire, M. S. (1984) A comparison of three methods to teach medical students sex history taking. Dissertation Abstracts International vol.44-A no.09, March p.2623. 286, 287

McHenry, D. E. (1969) The effect of notetaking activity on listening comprehension in an immediate recall situation. USAFA Educational Research Report 69-2, Directorate of Educational Research, USAF Academy. 122

McKeachie, W. J. (1990) Research on college teaching: The historical background. Journal of Educational Psychology, June vol.82 no.2 pp.189-200. 8

McKeachie, W. J., and Hiler, W. (1954) The problem oriented approach to teaching psychology, Journal of Educational Psychology, vol.45 pp.224-232. 277

McKeachie, W. J. (1963) Research on teaching at the college and university level, in N. Gage (ed) Handbook of Research on Teaching, Rand McNally pp.1118-1172. 198

McKeachie, W. J. (1965) Teaching Tips, 5th edn, D. C. Heath & Co. 67

McKibben M.L. (1982) Listening, study skills and reading: measuring and meeting college freshman needs in the 1980's. Unpublished. ERIC no.ED214111. 134

McLeish, J. (1968) The Lecture Method, Cambridge Monographs on Teaching Methods no. 1, Cambridge Institute of Education. 46, 54, 197, 283

McLeish, J. (1970) Students' Attitudes and College Environments, Cambridge Monographs on Teaching Methods no. 3, Cambridge Institute of Education. 20, 283

McLeish, J. (1976) The Lecture Method, Chapter VIII in The Psychology of Teaching Methods, the 75th Yearbook of the National Society for the Study of Education, Ed Gage, N. L. pp.252-301. 8

McMinn, M. R., Troyer, P. K., Hannum, L. E. and Foster, J. D. (1991) Teaching nonsexist language to college students. Journal of Experimental Education, Winter vol.59 no.2 pp.153-161. 287, 288

McQueen, W., Meschino, R., Pike, P. and Poelstra, P. (1994) Improving graduate student performance in cognitive assessment: The saga continues. Professional Psychology Research and Practice, August vol.25 no.3 pp.283-287. 47

Mears, M. J. (1996) The effects of cooperative learning strategies on mathematics achievement and attitude in college algebra classes. Dissertation Abstracts International vol.56-A no.12, June p.4690. 280, 281, 282

Meredith, G. M. and Ogasawara, T. H. (1982a) Instructional format and impact of graduate level teaching assistants. Psychological Reports, June vol.50 no.3, Pt 2 pp.1085-1086. 204

Meredith, G. M. and Ogasawara, T. H. (1982b) Preference for class size in lecture format courses among college students. Psychological Reports, December vol.51 no.3, Pt 1 pp.961-962. 204

Merrill, P. A (1995) A comparison of two teaching methods in basic cardiac life support training and education, Masters' Abstracts International 33 no.06, December p.1843. 273, 287

Metz, P. A. (1987) The effect of interactive instruction and lectures on the achievements and attitudes of chemistry students. Dissertation Abstracts International, vol.49-A no.03 p.0474. 275, 276, 280, 283

Miller, G. A. (1967) The magical number seven, plus or minus two: some limits on our capacity for processing information, in The Psychology of Communication, Penguin. 43, 71

Miller, K. A. J. (1996) Computer-assisted instruction to change attitudes and beliefs about violence against women in relationships: development and initial efficacy study. Dissertation Abstracts International vol.56-A no.09, March p.3458. 280

Miller, N. and Campbell, D. T. (1959) Recency and primacy in persuasion as a function of the timing of speeches and measurements, Journal of Abnormal and Social Psychology, vol.59 pp.1-9. 218

Miller, N. P. (1996) The effect of working memory, an advance organizer and modeled notetaking on listening comprehension of inner-city fifth graders. Dissertation Abstracts International vol.57-A no.06, December p.2344. 280

Miller, S. W. and Jackson, R. A. (1985) A comparison of a multi-media instructional module with a traditional lecture format for geriatric pharmacy training. American Journal of Pharmaceutical Education, vol.49 no.2 pp.173-176. 274

Millett, G. B. (1969) Comparison of four teacher training procedures in achieving teacher and pupil "translation" behaviours in secondary school social studies. American Educational Research Association. ERIC ED027256. 278, 279, 286, 288

Mills, D. G. (1966) The use of closed-circuit television in teaching geography and in training teachers of geography, Geography, vol.51 no.3 pp.218-223. 53

Milton, O. (1962) Two year follow-up: Objective data after learning without class attendance. Psychological Reports 11 pp.833-836. 123, 282

Miron, M. S., and Brown, E. R. (1968) Stimulus parameters in speech compression, Journal of Communication, September, vol.18 no.3 pp.319-325. 203

Mitnick, L. L. and McGinnies, E. (1958) Influencing ethnocentrism in small discussion groups through a film communication. Journal of Abnormal and Social Psychology, vol.56 pp.82-90. 18

Mohr, P. H. (1996) Cognitive development in college men and women as measured on the Perry scheme when learning and teaching styles are addressed in a chemical engineering curriculum. Dissertation Abstracts International vol.56-A no.08, February p.3020. 277

Moore, J. R (1994) A comparison of individualized self-study and classroom lecture in propane gas industry training. Dissertation Abstracts International vol.54-A no.08, February p.2921. 273

Morgan, C. H., Lilley, J. D. and Boreham, N. C. (1988) Learning from lectures: the effect of varying the detail in lecture handouts on note-taking and recall. Applied Cognitive Psychology, vol.2 no.2 April-June pp.115-122. 137, 138

Morgan, S. V. and Puglisi, J.T. (1982) Enhancing memory for lecture sentences: a depth perspective. Psychological Reports vol.51 no.2 October pp.675-678. 92

Morris, V. (1930) Quantitative measurements in institutions of higher learning, Yearbook no.18 of the National Society of College Teachers of Education, University of Chicago Press, p.114. 276

Mueller, D. J. (1974) Evaluation of instructional materials and prediction of student success in a self-instructional section of an educational measurement course. Journal of Experimental Education, vol. 42 no.3 Spring pp.53-56. 173

Murdock, B. B. (1961) The retention of individual items, Journal of Experimental Psychology, vol.62 pp.618-25. 42

Murray, H. G., Rushton, J. P. and Paunonen, S. V. (1990) Teacher personality traits and student instructional ratings in six types of university courses. Journal of Educational Psychology, June vol.82 no.2 pp.250-261. 180

Mussnug, K. J. (1984) A comparison of student achievement in competency based vocational education and traditionally instructed vocational drafting programs (individualized, personalized, modularized). Dissertation Abstracts International vol.45-A no.04, October p.1105. 286

Nager, N. R. (1983) How to create one-on-one feedback system for students and, at same time, organize notes for books, lectures with interactive electronic index card software. Classroom teaching guide; Speech/conference paper; Position paper. 249

Nance, J. L. and Nance, C. E. (1990) Does learning occur in the classroom? College Student Journal, December vol.24 no.4 pp.338-340. 6

Natfulin, D. H., Ware J. E. and Donnelly F. A. (1973) The Dr Fox lecture: a paradigm of educational seduction. Journal of Medical Education, vol.48 pp.630-635. 181

Nay, W. R. (1975) A systematic comparison of instructional techniques for parents. Behavior Therapy, January vol.6 no.1 pp.14-21. 274, 278

Nelson, G. L. (1989) The relationship between the use of personal examples in foreign teaching assistants' lectures and uncertainty reduction, student attitude, student recall, and ethnocentrism. PhD dissertation University of Minnesota (0130). See also, Dissertation Abstracts International vol.50A No.11 p.3414. 96

Nelson, G. L. (1992) The relationship between the use of personal, cultural examples in international teaching assistants' lectures and uncertainty reduction, student attitude, student recall, and ethnocentrism. International Journal of Intercultural Relations, Winter vol.16 no.1 pp.33-52. 96

Nelson, W. B. (1959) An experiment with class size in the teaching of elementary economics, Educational Record, vol.4 pp.330-341. 204

Newman, M. G (1996) A comparison of nursing students in problem-based learning and the lecture method, Masters' Abstracts International 34 no.02, April p.702. 273, 276, 279

Newsome, G. G. (1989) A comparison of the effects of guided design and lecture teaching strategies on the ability of student nurses to solve problems in the clinical setting, Dissertation Abstracts International, vol.50-A no.10 p.3144. 278, 285

Nisbet, J. (1966) Papers for a short course on university teaching methods - mimeographed papers, Department of Education, University of Aberdeen. 1

Nisbet, J. and Welsh, J. (1966) Predicting student performance, Universities Quarterly, vol.20 no.4 pp.468-80. 64

Northcraft, G. B. and Jernstedt G.C. (1975) A comparison of four teaching method styles for large lecture classes. Psychological Reports vol.36 pp.599-606. 137, 273

Nye, P. A. (1978) Student variables in relation to note taking during a lecture. Programmed Learning and Educational Technology; vol.15 no.3 pp.196-200. 125

O'Donnell, A. (1993) Searching for information in knowledge maps and texts. Contemporary Educational Psychology; April vol.18 no.2 pp.222-239. 128

O'Donnell, A. and Dansereau, D. F. (1993) Learning from lectures: Effects of cooperative review. Journal of Experimental Education; Winter vol.61 no.2 pp.116-125. 125

O'Neill, P. N. (1990) A comparison of student achievement and attitude between instruction via interactive videodisc instruction and classroom lecture. Dissertation Abstracts International vol.50-A no.12, June p.3839. 287

Oaks, T. D. (1996) Storytelling: a natural mnemonic. A study of a storytelling teaching method to positively influence student recall of instruction (memory). Dissertation Abstracts International vol.57-A no.02, August p.579. 76

Odubunmi, O. and Balogun, T. A. (1991) The effect of laboratory and lecture teaching methods on cognitive achievement in integrated science. Journal of Research in Science Teaching; March vol.28 no.3 pp.213-224. 271, 274

Oines, R. K. (1971) The comparitive effectiveness of individually prescribed instruction and the lecture demonstration method to achieve behavioral objectives for a descriptive astronomy course. Ed.D. Dissertation. Oklahoma State University. 273, 282

Onyejiaku, F. O. (1982) Cognitive styles, instructional strategies, and academic performance. Journal of Experimental Education; Fall vol.51 no.1 pp.31-37. 273, 276

Orr, D. B. (1968) Time compressed speech - a perspective, Journal of Communication, vol.18 no.3, September pp.288-292. 201, 202

Osterman, D. et al. (1985) The feedback lecture. Idea Paper no.13. Unpublished. ERIC no.ED302562. 230

Ostrow, C. L. (1984) Comparison of interactive effects of cognitive style, GPA and teaching methodology in nursing content area (learning style, PSI, lecture). Dissertation

Abstracts International vol.45-A no.05, November p.1311. 269

Oswald, I. (1966) Sleep, Penguin. 60, 87

Ott, B. A. (1996) The effect of expert-led, reflective discussion on academic achievement among health science students. Dissertation Abstracts International vol.56-A no.08, February p.2971. 273

Ovaiza, S. (1985) Listening comprehension: a lecture-based approach. ELT Journal; vol.39 no.3 pp.187-192. 109

Palkovitz, R. J. and Lore, R. K. (1980) Note taking and note review: why students fail questions based on lecture material. Teaching of Psychology vol.7 no.3 October pp.159-161. 125

Palmer, R. C. and Verner, C. (1959) A comparison of three instructional techniques, Adult Education, vol.19 pp.232-238. 273

Parlett, M. R. (1970) The syllabus bound student, in Hudson L. (Editor) The ecology of human intelligence pp.272-283. Penguin modern sociology readings. 180

Parnes, S. J. and Meadow, A. (1959) Effects of "brainstorming" instructions on creative problem solving by trained and untrained subjects, Journal of Educational Psychology, vol.50 pp.171-176. 251

Parsons, T. S. (1957) A comparison of instruction by kinescope, correspondence study and customary classroom procedures, Journal of Educational Psychology, vol.48 pp.27-40. 270, 273, 274

Patton, J. A. (1955) A study of the effects of student acceptance of responsibility and motivation on course behaviour, Dissertation Abstracts, vol.15 pp.637-638. 69, 273

Pauk, W. (1963) Does note-taking interfere with listening comprehension? Journal of Developmental Reading vol.6 pp.276-278. 123

Paul, J. B. (1932) The length of class periods, Educational Research, vol.13 pp.120-123. 276

Pederson, C. (1993) Promoting nursing students' positive attitudes toward providing care for suicidal patients. Issues in Mental Health Nursing; Jan-March vol.14 no.pp.67-84. 18

Pelz, E. B. (1958) Some factors in group decision, in Maccoby, E. E., Newcomb, T. M. and Hartley. E. L. (Eds) Readings in Social Psychology, Holt New York. 280

Pennington, D. F. Jr, Haravey, F. and Bass, B. M. (1958) Some effects of decision and discussion on coalescence, change, and effectiveness, Journal of Applied Psychology, vol.42 pp.404-408. 18

Pennington, H. (1992) Excerpts from journal articles as teaching devices. Teaching of Psychology, October vol.19 no.3 pp.175-177. 225

Peper, R. J. and Mayer, R. E. (1978) Note Taking as a Generative Activity. Journal of Educational Psychology vol.70 no.4 pp.514-522. 122, 131

Peper, R. J. and Mayer R. E. (1986) Generative effects of note-taking during science lectures, Journal of Educational Psychology, vol.78 no.1 pp.34-38. 122, 123, 126

Pepler, R. D. (1959) Warmth and lack of sleep: accuracy or activity reduced, Journal of Comparative and Physiological Psychology, vol.52 pp.446-50. 60

Perkins, H. V. (1950) The effects of climate and curriculum on group learning, Journal of Educational Research, vol.41 pp.269-86. 277

Perry, R. P., Abrami, P. C. and Leventhal, L. (1979) Educational seduction: The effect of instructor expressiveness and lecture content on student ratings and achievement. Journal of Educational Psychology; February vol.71 no.1 pp.107-116. 181

Perry, W. G. (1970) Forms of intellectual and ethical development in the college years: a scheme. Holt, Rinehart and Winston. 155, 180

Peters, D. L. (1972) Note-taking and rate of presentation on short-term objective test performance, Journal of Educational Psychology vol.63 no.3 pp.276-280. 123, 133

Peters, D. L. and Harris, C. (1970) Note-taking and review in recognition learning. In Di Vesta, F,. Peters, D., Saunders, N., Schultz, B. and Weener, P. (Eds) Instructional strategies: Multivariable studies in psychological processes related to instruction. ARPA Annual Report pp.107-124. 123, 125

Peterson, B. L. (1974) A comparison between achievement gains in multimedia instruction and conventional lecture method of instruction of nursing courses at Northern Virginia Community College. ERIC ED129282. 274

Peterson, L. R. (1966) Short-term memory, Scientific American, July, vol.215 no.1 pp.90-95. 41, 43

Peterson, L. R. and Peterson, M. J. (1959) Short-term retention of individual verbal items, Journal of Experimental Psychology, vol.58 pp.193-198. 41, 42

Pettibone, T. J. and Martin, D. W. (1973) Effects of lecturer pace on noise level in a university classroom, Journal of Educational Research, vol.67 no.2 pp.73-75. 201

Pigford, V. D. (1974) A comparison of an individual laboratory method with a group teacher demonstration method in teaching measurement and estimation in metric units to preservice elementary teachers. PhD Dissertation Florida State University. 274

Pohl, R., Lewis, R., Niccolini, R. and Rubenstein, R. (1982) Teaching the mental status examination: Comparison of three methods. Journal of Medical Education; August vol.57 no.8 pp.626-629 274, 284, 287

Poincare, H (1970) Mathematical creation, in P. E. Vernon (ed.) Creativity, Penguin pp.77-88. 73

Pollio, H. R. (1990) Remembrances of lectures past: notes and note-taking in the college classroom. Teaching/Learning Issues; Fall 134

Poppleton, P. K. and Austwick K. (1964) A comparison of programmed learning and note-making at two age levels. British Journal of Educational Psychology, vol 34 pp.43-50. 123

Poulton, E. C. (1961) British courses for adults on effective reading, British Journal of Educational Psychology, vol.31, (Part 2) pp.128-137. 146

Powell, C. L. (1987) A comparison of lecture versus discussion method in teaching assertiveness. Dissertation Abstracts International, vol.48-A no.12 p.3034. 287

Powell, C. L. (1988) A comparison of the lecture versus group discussion method in teaching assertiveness. Dissertation Abstracts International vol.48-A no.12, June p.3034. 284, 287

Rai, G. C. (1976) An experimental study of the effectiveness of lecture discussion, demonstration discussion and field trip discussion methods of training more intelligent and less intelligent farmers and farm women. Indian Journal of Applied Psychology, vol.13 no.2 July pp.57-69   270

Ramsden, P. (1992) Learning to teach in higher education, Routledge, London and New York 290pp.   6, 17, 154, 155

Randels, P. M., Kilpatrick, D. G., McCurdy, L. and Saunders, P. J. (1976) Comparison of the psychiatry learning system and traditional teaching of psychiatry. Journal of Medical Education; vol.51 no.9 September pp.751-757   269, 278, 286

Randolph, W. M. (1993) The effect of cooperative learning on academic achievement in introductory college biology. Dissertation Abstracts International vol.53-A no.08, February p.2756.   271

Rankowski, C. A. and Galey, M. (1979) Effectiveness of multimedia in teaching descriptive geometry. Educational Communication and Technology; vol.27 no.2 Summer pp.114-120.   271, 282

Ransdell, S. (1992) Incorporating educational software into large introductory psychology lectures and labs. 21st Annual Meeting of the Society for Computers in Psychology, San Francisco, California. Behavior Research Methods, Instruments and Computers; May vol.24 no.2 pp.172-173.   230

Rasor, R. A. (1980) Correlates of classroom retention. Research/technical report.   140

Razzell, P. and Weinman, J. (1977) The pre-clinical curriculum and information processing problem. Medical Education; vol.11 pp.257-261.   124, 125

Reddy, M. A. (1989) Search strategy skills: a two method comparison of teaching CD-ROM bibliographic searching techniques. Dissertation Abstracts International vol.49-A no.07 January p.1776.   274, 283

Reid, R. H. (1968) Grammatical complexity and comprehension of compressed speech, Journal of Communication, vol.18 no.3 pp.236-42.   201

Reid Smith, E. R. (1969) The measurement of level of student satisfaction by means of a course assessment questionnaire, Research in Librarianship, vol.10 no.2 January pp.100-107.   21, 283, 284

Remmers, H. H. (1934) Reliability and halo effect of high school and college students judgements of their teachers. Journal of Applied Psychology vol.18 pp.619-630.   180

Remmers, H. H. (1963) Rating methods in research on teaching, in N. L. Gage (ed.) Handbook of Research on Teaching, Rand McNally pp.329-378.   180

Rickard, P. B. (1946) An experimental study of the effectiveness of group discussion in the teaching of factual content, Summaries of Doctoral Dissertations, Northwestern University no.14 pp.72-77.   270, 272, 277

Rickards, J. P. and McCormick, C. B. (1988) Effect of interspersed conceptual prequestions on note-taking in listening comprehension. Journal of Educational Psychology, December vol.80 no.4 pp.592-594.   129, 139, 140, 141

Riedel, R. C., Harney, B. and LaFief, W. (1976) Unit test scores in PSI versus traditional classes in beginning psychology. Teaching of Psychology; vol.3 no.2 April pp.76-78   269

Riggio, R. E. and Throckmorton, B. (1987) Effects of prior training and verbal errors on students' performance in job interviews. Journal of Employment Counseling; March vol.24 no.1 pp.10-16   287

Ripple, R. E. (1963) Comparison of the effectiveness of a programmed text with three other methods of presentation, Psychological Reports, vol.12 pp.227-37.   276

Robbins, E. (1931) in C. L. Bane, The Lecture in College Training, Badger.   272

Roberts, M. R (1994) A comparison in the effectiveness of the delivery of an interactive computer-assisted instruction module to a traditional lecture-lab delivered module (CAI). Dissertation Abstracts International vol.54-A no.11, May p.4068.   271, 274

Robinson, P. (1995) A comparison of the effect on college students' academic achievement and course satisfaction by three teaching methods: cooperative learning, reciprocal peer tutoring and lecture only, Masters' Abstracts International 33 no.02, April p.677.   271, 272

Rock, I. (1957) The role of repetition in associative learning, American Journal of Psychology, vol.70 pp.186-193.   47

Rohrer, J. H. (1957) Large and small sections in college classes, Journal of Higher Education, vol.28 pp.275-279.   204, 272

Rooney, M. E. (1994) Comparison of traditional and non-traditional teaching methods and cognitive performance in nursing (nontraditional teaching methods. nursing education). Dissertation Abstracts International vol.54-A no.08, February p.3002.   273

Rosenshine, B. (1968) Objectively measured behavioural prediction of effectiveness in explaining, California Technical Report no. 4, Stanford Research and Development Centre in Reading.   111

Rosenshine, B. (1970) Enthusiastic teaching a research review. The School Review, vol.78 pp.499-514.   65

Rosenthal, R. (1984) Meta-analytic procedures for social science research. Sage, Beverly Hills, California.   28

Ross, J. M. (1989) Critical teaching behaviours as perceived by adult undergraduates. Paper presented at the American Educational Research Association Annual Meeting, March pp.27-31.   152

Ross, S. M. and Wasicsko, M. M. (1983) Teaching principles of learning and instruction through field experiences. Educational and Psychological Research; Winter vol.3 no.1 pp.1-10.   278, 279

Royer, P. N. (1977) Effects of specificity and position of written instructional objectives on learning from lecture. Journal of Educational Psychology; vol.69 no.1 February pp.40-45.   68

Rugg, H. (1921) Is the rating of human character possible? Journal of Educational Psychology, vol.12, pp.425-438 and pp.485-501.   176

Rugg, H. (1922) Is the rating of human character possible? Journal of Educational Psychology, vol.13, pp.30-42 and pp.81-93.   176

Ruhl, K. L., Hughes, C. A. and Gajar, A. H. (1990) Efficacy of the pause procedure for enhancing learning disabled and nondisabled college students' long and short term recall of facts presented through lecture. Learning Disability Quarterly, vol.13 no.1 Winter pp.55-64.   224

Ruhl, K. L. and Suritsky, S. (1995) The pause procedure and/ or an outline: Effect on immediate free recall andlecture notes taken by college students with learning disabilities.

Learning Disability Quarterly; vol.18 no.1 Winter pp.2-11. 58, 224, 235

Ruja, H. (1954) Outcomes of lecture and discussion procedures in three college courses, Journal of Experimental Education, vol.22 pp.385-94. 272, 275, 285

Ruskin R. S. and Hess, J. H. (1974) The personalized system of instruction: an annotated review of the literature, Georgetown University, Washington 43pp. 29

Russell, I. J., Hendricson, W. D. and Herbert, R. J. (1984) Effects of lecture information density on medical student achievement, Journal of Medical Education, vol.59 November no.1 pp.881-889. 43, 137

Russell, T. and Bryant, C. A. (1987) The effects of a lecture training program and independent study on the knowledge and attitudes of law students toward the mentally retarded offender. Journal of Offender Counseling, Services and Rehabilitation; vol.11 no.2 Spring-Summer pp.53-66 273, 280

Rysberg, J. A. (1986) Effects of modifying instruction in a college classroom. Psychological Reports; vol.58 no.3 June pp.965-966 269, 282

Sadatmand, K. D. (1995) The effect of computer-assisted instruction on algebraic problem-solving abilities of community college students. Dissertation Abstracts International vol.56-A no.03, September p.804. 279

Sage J.E. (1971) A comparison of the inquiry and lecture methods for the acquisition of knowledge relative to problem solving performance. Ph.D. Dissertation. University of Missouri, Columbia. 270, 278

Saunders, L. H. (1988) A comparison of the effects of lecture and combined lecture with clinical application on cognitive and psychomotor outcomes of experienced pediatric nurses following an intermediate physical assessment course, Masters' Abstracts International 26 no.03, Fall p.327. 275, 287

Saunders, M. et al. (1969) Report of the Commission on Teaching in Higher Education, National Union of Students. 6, 142, 200, 283

Saunders, W., Nielson, E., Gall, M. and Smith, G. (1975) The effects of variations in microteaching on prospective teachers' acquisition of questioning skills. Journal of Educational Research, vol.69 no.1 September pp.3-8 286

Sawyer, H. W. and Sawyer, S. H. (1981) A teacher-parent communication training approach. Exceptional Children; vol.47 no.4 January pp.305-306 278

Sazar, L. and Kassinove, H. (1991) Effects of counselor's profanity and subject's religiosity on content acquisition of a counseling lecture and behavioral compliance. Psychological Reports, December vol.69 no.3, Pt 2, Special Issue 1059-1070. 107

Scerbo, M. W., Warm, J. S., Dember, W. N. and Grasha, A. F. (1992) The role of time and cueing in a college lecture. Contemporary Educational Psychology, October vol.17 no.4 pp.312-328. 54, 131

Schachter, S., Christenfeld, N., Ravina, B. and Bilous, F. (1991) Speech disfluency and the structure of knowledge. Journal of Personality and Social Psychology, vol. 60 no.3 March pp.362-367. 154

Schachter, S., Rauscher, F., Christenfeld, N. and Crone, K. T.

(1994) The vocabularies of academia. Psychological Science, January vol.5 no.1 pp.37-41. 154

Schoenbaum, K. G. (1996) Using multimedia to promote cardiovascular health among adolescents, Masters' Abstracts International 34 no.04, August p.1349. 271, 280, 284

Schroeder, L. and Kent, P. (1982) Computer based instruction in dietetics education. Journal of Computer Based Instruction; vol.8 no.4 May pp.85-90 274, 283

Scott, W. A. (1957) Attitude change through reward of verbal behaviour, Journal of Abnormal and Social Psychology, vol.55 pp.72-75. 221

Seal, A. M. and Swerissen, H. (1993) Lectures, prompts and contracts to promote parental safety. Behaviour Change, vol.10 no.2 pp.103-107. 288

Self, D. J., Wolinsky, F. D. and Baldwin, De W. C. (1989) The effect of teaching medical ethics on medical students' moral reasoning. Special Issue: Teaching medical ethics. Academic Medicine, December vol.64 no.12 pp.755-759. 277

Selim, M. A. and Shrigley, R. L. (1983) The group dynamics approach: A sociopsychological approach for testing the effect of discovery and expository teaching on the science achievement and attitude of young Egyptian students. Journal of Research in Science Teaching; vol.20 no.3 March pp.213-224 270, 278, 280

Seymour W.D. (1937) An experiment showing the superiority of a light-colored "blackboard". British Journal of Educational Psychology vol.7 no.3 pp. 259-268. 88, 100

Shahabudin, S. H. (1987) Content coverage in problem based learning. Medical Education; vol.21 no.4 July pp.310-313 270, 275

Shaw, R. (1987) Determining register in sign-to-English interpreting, Sign Language studies vol.57 Winter pp.295-322. 152

Sheehy, M. B. (1989) The effectiveness of personalized system of instruction sections versus large lecture recitation classes on the achievement and attitudes of intermediate algebra students, Dissertation Abstracts International, vol.51-A no.04 p.1149. 269, 282

Sherif, M. A., and Sherif, C. W. (1956) An outline of social psychology, rev. edn., Harper & Row. 18

Sherman, L. W. (1975) Comparison of two instructional procedures in introductory educational psychology classes. 83rd Annual Meeting of the American Psychological Association, Chicago. Miami University, Oxford, Ohio. 283

Sherwood, J. J., (1965) A relation between arousal and performance, American Journal of Psychology, vol.78 pp.461-465. 48

Shine, S. S. (1983) A comparison of programmed instruction versus lecture-demonstration as a method for teaching digital computer arithmetic at the post-secondary school level. Dissertation Abstracts International vol.43-A no.11 May p.3529. 271

Siegel, H. B. (1973) McLuhan, mass media, and education. Journal of Experimental Education; vol. 41 no.3 Spring pp.68-70. 138, 270, 274, 276

Siegel, L., Adams, J. F., and Macomber, F. G. (1960) Retention of subject matter as a function of large group instructional procedures, Journal of Educational Psychology, vol.51 pp.9-13. 204

Siegel, L., Siegel, L. C., Capretta, P. J., Jones, R. L., and Berkovitz, H. (1963) Students' thoughts during class: a criterion for educational research, Journal of Educational Psychology, vol.54 no.1 pp.45-51. 14

Sime, M., and Boyce, G. (1969) Overt responses, knowledge of results and learning, Programmed Learning and Educational Technology, vol.6 no.1 pp.12-19. 209

Simpson, M. L. (1982) Oral language and written text presentations: a comparison of effectiveness. Dissertation Abstracts International vol.42-A no.10, April p.4210. 273, 274

Sinagra, M. D. and Lopez K. (1989) ARC: An alternative teaching strategy for developmental reading. Unpublished. 270

Singer, R. D. (1961) Verbal conditioning and generalization of pro-democratic responses, Journal of Abnormal and Social Psychology, vol.63 pp.43-46. 221

Smeltzer, L. R. and Watson, K. W. (1983) Improving listening skills used in business: An empirical comparison of discussion length, modeling and level of incentive. American Business Communication Association. ERIC ED229809. 244, 248, 278

Smith, C. W. (1996) The effect of class size on student achievement in the principles of economics courses. Dissertation Abstracts International vol.56-A no.10, April p.4063. 204

Smith, D. L. (1995) The effects of cooperative learning in a short-term, intensive, adult, religious education seminar. Dissertation Abstracts International vol.56-A no.07, January p.2549. 272, 275, 277, 282

Smith, G. A. (1987) The effects of various teaching strategies on the cognitive achievement of first year biology students. Dissertation Abstracts International vol.47-A no.08, February p.2984. 271, 279

Smith, G. and Wyllie, J. H. (1965) Use of closed-circuit television in teaching surgery to medical students, British Medical Journal, 10 July no.2 pp.99-101. 53

Smith, H. C. (1955) Team work in the college class, Journal of Educational Psychology, vol.46 pp.274-286. 270, 279

Smith, J. P. (1954) A study of outcomes on instruction in a psychology class with special reference to two teaching methods, Doctoral dissertation, Ohio State University. 272

Smith, L. R. (1984) Effect of teacher vagueness and use of lecture notes on student performance. Journal of Educational Research; vol.78 no.2 Nov-Dec pp.69-74. 140

Smithers, A. (1970a) Some factors in lecturing, Educational Review, vol.22 no.2 pp.141-150. 179, 200, 220

Smithers, A. (1970b) What do students expect of lectures? Universities Quarterly, vol.24 no.3 pp.330-336. 179, 200

Snowberg, R. L. (1973) Bases for selection of background colours for transparencies, Audio Visual Communication Review, vol.21 no.2. 100

Solomon, D., Rosenberg, L., and Bezdek, W. E. (1964) Teacher behaviour and student learning, Journal of Educational Psychology, vol.55 pp.23-30. 276

Sox H.C. et al. (1984) Tutored video-tape instruction in clinical decision-making. Journal of Medical Education, vol.59 no.3 pp.188-195. 248, 274, 283, 284

Specht, L. B. and Sandlin, P. K. (1991) The differential effects

of experiential learning activities and traditional lecture classes in accounting. Simulation and Gaming, June vol.22 no.2 pp.196-210. 270, 273

Spence, R. B. (1928) Lecture and class discussion in teaching educational psychology, Journal of Educational Psychology vol.19 pp.454-462. 272

Spence, R. B., and Watson, G. B. (1928) Lecture and class discussion in teaching Educational Psychology, Journal of Educational Psychology, vol.19 pp.454-462. 275

Spencer, R. E. and Aleamoni L. M. (1970) A student course evaluation questionnaire. Journal of Educational Measurement, vol.7 pp.209-210. 180

Spender, S. (1952) The making of a poem, in B. Ghiselin (ed) The creative process: A symposium, University of California Press pp.112-125. 73

Sperling, G. (1960) The information available in brief visual presentations, Psychological Monographs, (whole of no.498). 35

Spires, H. A. (1993) Learning from a lecture: Effects of comprehension monitoring. Reading Research and Instruction, vol.32 no.2 Winter pp.19-30. 135

Sprenkle, V. E. and Gillmore G. M. (1975) An evaluation of mastery instruction courses by use of student ratings. 284

Stanton, D. G. (1994) Utilizing hypercard for tutorial CAI in advanced professional training (Macintosh). Dissertation Abstracts International vol.54-A no.10, April p.3722. 270, 274, 282

Stanton, H. E. (1978) Confidence building in the university lecturer, Contemporary Educational Psychology. 200,

Stanton, H. E. (1979) Increasing lecturer self-confidence, Australian Psychologist, vol.14 no.3 November pp.329-335. 200

Startup R. (1977) Staff experience of lectures and tutorials. Studies in Higher Education, vol.2 no.2 pp. 191-201. 204

Stenehjem, K. A. (1986) A comparison of lecture-demonstration and augmented computer-assisted instruction methods for college students' laboratory learning experience (industrial technology, industrial arts education, photography). Dissertation Abstracts International vol.47-A no.04 October p.1219. 287

Stewart, R. A. (1989) Interaction effects of teacher enthusiasm and student notetaking on recall and recognition of lecture content. Communication Research Reports, vol.6 no.2 December pp.84-89. 64, 123

Sticht, T. G. (1968) Some relationships of mental aptitude, reading ability, and listening ability using normal and time-compressed speech, Journal of Communication, vol.18 no.3 Sept. 202

Stokley, M. D. (1990) Training direct care workers using audio-visual and lecture instruction, Dissertation Abstracts International, vol.51-A no.07 p.2242. 274, 276

Stolurow, L. M. (1960) Teaching machines and special education, Educational Psychology Measurement, vol.20 pp.429-48. 64

Stones, E. (1970) Students' attitudes to the size of teaching groups, Educational Review, vol.21 no.2 pp.98-108. 20, 93, 205, 283

Strasser S.E. and Ozgur C. (1995) Undergraduate business statistics - a survey of topics and teaching methods. Interfaces, vol.25 no.3 pp.95-103. 224,

Strodt-Lopez B. (1991) Tying it all in: asides in university lectures. Applied Linguistics, vol.12 no.2 pp.117-140. 94

Sullivan, A. M., et. al (1976-77) The relative effectiveness of instructional television. Interchange; vol.7 no.1 pp.46-51 276

Swartz, M. E. (1986) A comparative evaluation of programmed and lecture instruction in college business mathematics. Dissertation Abstracts International vol.46-A no.07 January p.1908. 269

Swezey, R. W., Perez, R. S. and Allen, J. A. (1988) Effects of instructional delivery system and training parameter manipulations on electromechanical maintenance performance. Human Factors; vol.30 no.6 December pp.751-762 287

Szczurek, M. (1982) Meta-analysis of simulation games effectiveness for cognitive learning. Dissertation Abstracts International vol.43-A no.04, October p.1031. 28

Tabar, C. R. (1990) Computer assisted interactive video instruction: An alternative to the lecture method for nutrition education in Baccalaureate Nursing (Video instruction), Dissertation Abstracts International, vol.51-A no.07 p.2258. 274

Taber, M. R. (1974) A comparison of using individualized instruction and conventional lecture techniques in the lecture section of electric circuits 540-126. Nova University. ERIC ED104512. 29, 269, 283

Tait, A. N. (1993) A comparison of didactic and modeling instruction in grief intervention skills training (didactic instruction, death education). Dissertation Abstracts International vol.53-B no.11, May p.6000. 287

Talbert, E. E., Wildemann, D. G., Erickson, M. T. (1975) Teaching nonprofessionals three techniques to modify children's behavior. Psychological Reports, vol.37 no.3 Pt 2 December pp.1243-1252. 287

Tannenbaum, P. H. (1953) Attitudes toward source and concept as factors in attitude change through communication, unpublished Doctoral dissertation, University of Illinois. 215

Tannenbaum, P. H. (1954) Effect of serial position on recall of radio news stories, Journalism Quarterly, vol.31 pp.319-323. 41

Tanner, D. (1968) Influencing student opinion in the college classroom, Journal of Educational Research, vol.62 no. 1 pp.30-33. 219

Taplin, G. (1969) The Cosford cube: a simplified form of student feedback, Industrial Training International, vol.4 no. 5 pp.218-219. 15, 161, 163, 198

Tatum, B. C. and Lenel, J. C. (1985) A comparison of self-paced and lecture/discussion teaching methods. Unpublished. ERIC no.ED267705. 271, 282

Taylor, D. W., Berry, P. C., and Block, C. H. (1958) Does group participation when using brainstorming, facilitate or inhibit creative thinking? Administrative Science Quarterly, vol.3 pp.23-47. 251

Taylor, M. (1987) The implementation and evaluation of a computer simulation game in a university course. Journal of Experimental Education; vol.55 no.2 Winter pp.108-115 278, 280, 282

Taylor, V. (1977) Individualized calculus for the lifelong learner: a two semester comparison of attitudes and effectiveness. ERIC ED146417. 282, 283

Teevan, K. G. and Gabel, H. (1978) Evaluation of modeling role playing and lecture-discussion training techniques for college student mental health professionals. Journal of Counseling Psychology; vol.25 no.2 March pp.169-171. 280, 286

Thoday, D. (1957) How undergraduates work, Universities Quarterly, vol.11 pp.172-181. 63

Thomas, E. J. (1972) The variation of memory with time for information appearing during a lecture. Studies in Adult Education, vol.4 pp.57-62. 123

Thomas, G. S., Aiken, E. G. and Shennum, W. A. (1975) Further investigations of coding/rehearsal strategies during a segmented lecture format. NPRDC TR 76-15 Navy Personnel Research and Development Center, San Diego. 122, 123

Thompson, L. A. (n.d.) A report on a note-taking experiment at Ohio University, Ohio College Association Bulletin no. 77, Ohio State University. 270

Thompson, S. (1994) Frameworks and contexts, a genre-based approach to analysing lecture introductions. English for Specific Purposes, vol.13 no.2 pp.171-186. 85

Thorson, E. and Lang, A. (1992) The effects of television videographics and lecture familiarity on adult cardiac orienting responses and memory. Communication Research, June vol.19 no.3 pp.346-369. 51

Thrasher, P. H. (1972) An evaluation of student team teaching in sophomore physics classes. Idaho University, Moscow. 276, 285

Tiffin (1974) PhD thesis of the University of London cited by Gimson, A. C. (1981) See Gimson. 109

Tillman, B. A. (1993) A study of the use of case methods in preservice teacher education. Dissertation Abstracts International vol.53-A no.11, May p.3877. 272, 277, 284

Timmel, G. B. (1954) A study of the relationship between methods of teaching a college course in mental hygiene and changes in student adjustment status, Doctoral dissertation, Cornell University. Reprinted in Dissertation Abstracts, vol.15 no.90. 285

Tomm, K. and Leahey, M. (1980) Training in family assessment: a comparison of three teaching methods. Journal of Marital and Family Therapy, vol.6 no.4 pp.453-458. 274, 275, 287

Treisman, A. (1966) Human attention, in B. Foss (ed.) New Horizons in Psychology, Penguin pp.97-117. 50

Trimble, L. (1985) English for science and technology: a discourse approach. Cambridge, Cambridge University Press. 99

Troisi, N. F. (1983) Effective teaching and student achievement, National Association of Secondary School Principals. ED231067. 225

Trown, A. (1970) Some evidence on the "interaction" between teaching strategy and personality, British Journal of Educational Psychology, vol.40 no.2 pp.209-11. 90

Trueman, M. and Hartley, J. (1978) Note-taking in lectures: a longitudinal study. Bulletin of the British Psychological Society, vol.31 pp. 37-39. 121, 123, 125

Tucker, B. N. (1989) A comparison of three note-taking strategies on immediate recall and retention. Dissertation Abstracts International vol.49-A no.10, April p.3003. 141

Tuohimaa, P., Tamminen, T. and Fabrin, V. (1993) Is it appropriate to speak of death during a dissection course?

Teaching and Learning in Medicine, vol.5 no.3 pp.169-173. 22, 286

Tuttle, H. S. (1930) Quantitative measurements in institutions of higher learning, Yearbook no.18 of the National Society for College Teachers of Education, p. 145.   270

Unruh W.R. (1968) The modality and validity of cues to lecture effectiveness. in Gage, N. L. et al, Explorations of the teacher's effectiveness in explaining. Technical Report no.4 Stanford Center for research and development in teaching. Stanford University. California.   64

Uren, O. (1968) The use of texts in language skill development - some problems, Innovations and experiments in university teaching methods, report of the 3rd conference organized by the University Teaching Methods Unit, University of London Institute of Education, April, pp.50-56.   210

Van Matre, N. H. et al. (1975) Learning from lecture: Investigations of study strategies involving note-taking. Navy Personnel Research and Development Center, San Diego. ED120684.   123

Van Metre, P., Yokoi, L., and Pressley, M. (1994) College students' theory of note-taking derived from their perceptions of note-taking. Journal of Educational Psychology vol.86 no.3 pp.323-338.   132, 133

Van Patten, J., Chao, C-I and Reigeluth, C. (1986) Knowledge Restructuring, Review of Educational Research, vol.56 no.4 pp.437-471.   112

Van Scoder, L. I. (1986) A comparison of the effectiveness of computer assisted instruction with traditional techniques for selected topics in respiratory therapy education (allied health, CAI). Dissertation Abstracts International vol.47-A no.01, July p.57.   274

Vincent, J. L. (1985) A comparison of learning outcomes of lecture, discussion and computer assisted instruction in a baccalaureate nursing program. Dissertation Abstracts International-B vol.46 no.05, November p.1514.   270

Vogel, M. R. (1996) Is humor a useful teaching tool in human sexuality education? Perspectives of sixth-grade students. Dissertation Abstracts International vol.56-A no.08, February p.3012.   96

Walbaum, S. D. (1989) Notetaking, verbal apptitude, and listening span: factors involved in learning from lectures. Paper to the Annual meeting of the American Educational Research Association, San Francisco.   124, 125

Walker, C. A. (1986) Effects of the lecture teaching method and discussion teaching method on the reading success and attitudes of bright learning disabled adolescents (secondary), Dissertation Abstracts International, vol.47-A no.04 p.1286.   270, 275

Walker, K. B. (1985) The comparison of three instructional techniques for teaching interaction management skills and rhetorical sensitivity (modeling, T-groups, lecture-discussion). Dissertation Abstracts International vol.45-A no.08, February p.2304.   287

Walton, D. J. A. (1986) A comparative study of computer assisted instruction, and lecture in the teaching of English conditional sentences to native speakers of Arabic. Dissertation Abstracts International, vol.47-A no.06 p.2012. 275, 280

Walton, H. J. (1968) An experimental study of different methods for teaching medical students, Proceedings of the Royal Society of Medicine, February, vol.61 no.2 pp.109-112.   280, 283

Walton, H. J. and Drewery, J. (1967) The objective examination in the evaluation of medical students, British Journal of Medical Education, vol.1 no.4 pp.255-264.   63

Wanlass, R. L. (1983) Sex education: a comparison of instruction formats. Dissertation Abstracts International vol.43-B no.07, January p.2363.   286

Wanlass, R. L., Kilmann, P. R., Bella, B. S. and Tarnowski, K. J. (1983) Effects of sex education on sexual guilt, anxiety, and attitudes: A comparison of instruction formats. Archives of Sexual Behavior; December vol.12 no.6 pp.487-502.   280, 281

Warburton, F. W., Butcher, H. J., and Forrest, G. M. (1963) Predicting student performance in a university department of education, British Journal of Educational Psychology, vol.33 pp.68-79.   64

Ward, J. M. (1956) Group-study versus lecture-demonstration method in physical science instruction for general education students, Journal of Experimental Education, vol. 24 pp.199-210.   270, 272, 275, 277

Watkins, G. L. (1996) Effects of CD-ROM instruction on achievement and attitudes (multimedia, computer assisted instruction). Dissertation Abstracts International vol.57-A no.04, October p.1446.   274, 276, 280

Watson, C. E. (1975) The case study method and learning effectiveness. College Student Journal; April-May vol.9 no.2 pp.109-116.   272, 278

Watson, J. M. (1983) Individualized mathematics instruction in an Australian university. Dissertation Abstracts International vol.43-A no.07, January p.2268.   269, 275

Watts, P. R. (1977) Comparison of three human sexuality teaching methods used in university health classes, Research Quarterly vol.48 no.1 pp.187-190.   272, 276, 280

Weaver, R. L. and Cotrell, H. W. (1985) Mental aerobics: the half-sheet response. Innovative Higher Education; vol.10 no.1 pp.23-31.   57, 200, 224

Weiland, A. and Kingsbury, S. J. (1979) Immediate and delayed recall of lecture material as a function of note taking. Journal of Educational Research, March-April vol.72 no.4 pp.228-230.   123

Wells, P. L. (1982) A comparison of the achievement of university students taught by an individualized instructional approach vs. the traditional instructional approach in a combined business math business machines course. Dissertation Abstracts International vol.42-A no.11, May p.4697.   270

Wertheimer, M. (1945) Productive Thinking, Harper & Row. 16

Whitaker, D. F. (1990) Comparison of computer retrieval text, computer assited instruction and programmed lecture in teaching statistics to physical education majors. Dissertation Abstracts International, vol.51-A no.11 p.3640.   274

White, L. D. and Chavigny, K. H. (1975) Direct tape access as an adjunct to learning. Nursing Research, vol.24 no.4 July-August pp.295-298.   141

Whitson, D. L. (1983) A comparison of microcomputer-assisted instruction, programmed instruction and the traditional lecture approach to bibliographic instruction in higher education. Dissertation Abstracts International vol.43-A no.12, June p.3743. 271, 274

Wieder, G. S. (1954) Group procedures modifying attitudes of prejudice in the college classroom, Journal of Educational Psychology, vol.45 pp.332-344. 272, 285

Wijasuriya, B. A. (1971) The occurence of discourse markers and intersentence connectives in university lectures and their place in testing and teaching of listening comprehension in English as a foreign language. MEd thesis, University of Manchester, England. 106

Wilding, J. M. and Hayes, S. (1992) Relations between approaches to studying and note-taking behaviour in lectures. Applied Cognitive Psychology, vol.6 no.3 May-June pp.233-246. 125

Wilkinson, R. T. (1959) Rest pauses in a task affected by lack of sleep. Ergonomics vol. 2 pp.373-380. 56

Wilkinson, R. T. (1961) Interaction of lack of sleep with knowledge of results, repeated testing and individual differences, Journal of Experimental Psychology, vol.62 pp.263-271. 60

Wilkinson, R. T. (1963a) After-effect of sleep deprivation, Journal of Experimental Psychology, vol.66 pp.439-442. 60

Wilkinson, R. T. (1963b) Interaction of noise with knowledge of results and sleep deprivation, Journal of Experimental Psychology, vol.66 pp.332-337. 60

Williams, D. C., Paul, J., and Oglivie, J. C. (1957) Mass media, learning and retention, Canadian Journal of Psychology, vol.11 pp.157-163. 270, 273

Williams, G. D. (1996) An examination of computer aided instruction, the self-concept and achievement levels of developmental mathematics community college students. Dissertation Abstracts International vol.57-A no.03, September p.992. 270, 282, 285

Williams, R.G. and Ware, J. E (1977) An extended visit with Dr. Fox: validity of student satisfaction with the instruction ratings after repeated exposures to a lecturer. American Educational Research Journal vol.14 no.4 pp.449-457. 181

Willis, J. and Gueldenpfenning, J. (1981) The relative effectiveness of lecturing, modeling, and role playing in training paraprofessional reading tutors. Psychology in the Schools; vol.18 no.3 July pp.323-329. 286, 287

Wilson, B. K. (1993) Comparison of two teaching strategies for teaching basic nursing skills to baccalaureate nursing students. Dissertation Abstracts International vol.53-A no.07, January p.2233. 270, 284, 285

Wilson, L. E (1993) A dynamic comparison between computer-based instruction and traditional methods of instruction as applied to teaching digital circuit analysis. Dissertation Abstracts International vol.54-A no.04, October p.1280. 274

Winocur, S. et al (1989) Perceptions of male and female academics within a teaching context, Research in Higher Education, vol.30 no.3 June pp.317-329. 150

Winteler, A. (1974) Factors in the effectiveness of the organization of academic learning. Psychologia Universalis; vol.30 pp.1-180. 282, 283

Wiseman, S., and Start, K. B. (1965) A follow-up of teachers five years after completing their training, British Journal of Educational Psychology, vol.35 pp.342-361. 169

Witkin, H. A. (ed.) (1962) Psychological Differentiation, Wiley. 220

Wood, C. C. and Hedley, R. L. (1968) Student reaction to VTR in simulated classroom conditions, Canadian Educational Research Digest, vol.8 no.1 pp.46-59. 53

Woodcock, R. W., and Clark, G. R. (1968) Comprehension of a narrative passage by elementary school children as a function of listening rate, retention period, and IQ. Journal of Communication, vol.18 no.3, September pp.259-271. 202

Woolford, G. A. (1969) Teacher influence in a College of Education, Educational Research, vol.11 no.2 pp.148-152. 21

Wyckoff, W. L. (1973) The effect of stimulus variation on learning from lecture. Journal of Experimental Education; vol.41 no.3 pp.85-90. 53

Yadav, R. S. (1982) An experimental study of effectiveness of demonstration method over lecture method in terms of learning objectives on VI grade students. Asian Journal of Psychology and Education, vol.9 no.3 pp.30-42 270

Yadav, R. S. (1984) An experimental study of contribution of learning objective to achievement scores through lecture and guided discovery methods. Asian Journal of Psychology and Education; vol.14 nos.1-4 pp.1-14 270

Yorde, B. S. and Witmer, J. M. (1988) An educational format for teaching stress management to groups with a wide range of stress symptoms. Biofeedback and Self Regulation; vol.5 no.1 March pp.75-90 22, 286

Yorke, D. M. (1977) Television in the education of teachers: a case study, British Journal of Educational Technology, vol.8 no.2 pp.131-141. 287

Young, L. and Fitzgerald, B. (1982) Listening and learning. Rowley Massachusetts Newbury House. 106

Young, M. E. (1986) A comparison of lecture-discussion and self-administered coping skills training for stress reduction (management, psycho-educational). Dissertation Abstracts International vol.46-A no.08, February p.2196. 285

Zacharakis-Jutz, J. (1983) Adult education guided design and student participation. Unpublished. ERIC no.ED244052. 230

Zimbardo, P. J. (1960) Involvement and communication discrepancy as determinants of opinion conformity, Journal of Abnormal and Social Psychology, vol.60 p.86. 18

Zsiray, S. W. (1984) A comparison of three instructional approaches in teaching the use of the abridged readers' guide to periodical literature. Journal of Educational Technology Systems 1983-4 vol.12 no.3 pp.241-247. 279

Index